SECOND EDITION

PUBLIC OPINION

SECOND EDITION

PUBLIC
OPINION

Carroll J. Glynn
THE OHIO STATE UNIVERSITY

Susan Herbst
TEMPLE UNIVERSITY

Garrett J. O'Keefe
COLORADO STATE UNIVERSITY

Robert Y. Shapiro
COLUMBIA UNIVERSITY

Mark Lindeman
BARD COLLEGE

A Member of the Perseus Books Group

All rights reserved. Printed in the United States of America. No part of this publication may be reproduced or transmitted in any form or by any means, electronic or mechanical, including photocopy, recording, or any information storage and retrieval system, without permission in writing from the publisher.

Copyright © 2004 by Westview Press, a Member of the Perseus Books Group

Published in the United States of America by Westview Press, A Member of the Perseus Books Group, 5500 Central Avenue, Boulder, Colorado 80301–2877, and in the United Kingdom by Westview Press, 12 Hid's Copse Road, Cumnor Hill, Oxford OX2 9JJ.

Find us on the world wide web at www.westviewpress.com.

Westview Press books are available at special discounts for bulk purchases in the United States by corporations, institutions, and other organizations. For more information, please contact the Special Markets Department at the Perseus Books Group, 11 Cambridge Center, Cambridge, MA 02142, or call (617) 252–5298. or (800) 255–1514, or email special.markets@perseusbooks.com.

Library of Congress Cataloging-in-Publication Data
ISBN 0-8133-4172-8

The paper used in this publication meets the requirements of the American National Standard for Permanence of Paper for Printed Library Materials Z39.48–1984.

CONTENTS

ILLUSTRATIONS

Figures

Boxes

PREFACE

This book began many years ago as a collaborative project among several scholars, all interested in the essential nature of public opinion. We all believe that public opinion is a vital component in the democratic process, and so we were drawn to the topic long ago as students ourselves. Now, as researchers and teachers, we still think that students of politics and communication should understand how people form opinions, how public opinion is measured, and how the data of public opinion are used in American policymaking and journalism. Without public opinion, we do not have much of a democracy at all, so the way public sentiments are expressed and evaluated is crucial for scholars, students, and citizens alike.

The authors of this volume come from the diverse fields of political science, communications, and journalism, and therefore we bring with us a large arsenal of ideas and perspectives. We take an open, interdisciplinary approach to the topic, unlike that seen in most public opinion textbooks. We look at public opinion from the macrohistorical level, the institutional level, the level of small group interaction, and the micropsychological level. We are interested in how Americans come to have opinions in the first place, how the media enable or prevent the formation of certain attitudes, and how our leaders acknowledge or fail to acknowledge the public mood with regard to various policies. There are a great many moments when public opinion matters, thus we study public opinion dynamics during campaigns and between them. It is the case that public opinion is most obvious during election campaigns or national crises, but here we try hard to study day-to-day attitude formation with regard to issues on the contemporary scene: affirmative action, unemployment, defense spending, and the like. You will find, in the course of reading through this comprehensive book, that Americans' attitudes are sometimes stable and at other times malleable, sometimes liberal and at other times conservative. We hope that you will enjoy reading about yourselves as members of the large and diverse American public, but we also hope that you will realize the challenges and complexities of public opinion.

This book was an enormous, although also very gratifying, undertaking. We have many people to thank, although a few stand out for their relentless and good-natured support. It is safe to say that the first edition of this book would still be a disorganized collection of smaller manuscripts and interesting ideas had it not been for Jill Edy, who is now at the University of Oklahoma. Bruce Williams was a contributor to the first edition, and many of his ideas appear in this one, particularly the section on methodology, which he helped write. We remain grateful to Bruce for his tremendous help. We were fortunate enough to receive suggestions from a variety of other scholars in the field of public opinion, and their comments are reflected in the much-revised pages that follow: Thanks go to Barbara Bardes, Charles Cameron, Jack Citrin, Rosalee Clawson, Sharon Dunwoody, Ted Jelen, Silvo Lenert, Franco Mattei, Maxwell McCombs, Greg Shaw, and Michael Traugott. A variety of students at Cornell University, Ohio State, and Northwestern University read parts of this manuscript, and we are indebted to them for their reactions to the text. For their excellent research and administrative assistance, we thank Serban Iorga, Martha Kayler, Grace Rees, Greg Shaw, David Park, Noah Kaplan, Dan Steinberg, and Oscar Torres-Reyna. We are also grateful to our editor, Steve Catalano, and to Jennifer Knerr (formerly of Westview), both of whom were loyal cheerleaders for this project. Special thanks to Steve for his incredible patience and to Joe Bonyata for guidance and support in preparation of the final manuscript.

Our families were vital in sustaining us during this multiyear project and generally enriched our lives. Many thanks to our significant others: James Turner, Doug Hughes, Nancy B. Rubenstein, the late Mary Lucy DeFlorio, Jane Viste, Lucy Miller, and Julie Schumacher. And to all of our children, whom we hope will be active and engaged democratic citizens someday: Patric, Ryan, Daniel, Becky, Margaret, Harriet, Emma, and Isabella.

PART ONE

INTRODUCING PUBLIC OPINION

1

The Meanings of Public Opinion

Were they alive today, our nation's founders might not be surprised that public opinion is still an important force in American politics. Yet, they would be astonished to learn just how pervasive discussions of public opinion have become. The president, members of Congress, candidates for public office, interest group leaders, journalists, and corporate executives, as well as ordinary citizens, constantly ask the same question: "What does the public think?" Our leaders need to know what sorts of policies and initiatives voters support, but a variety of other groups and individuals also need to have a working knowledge of public opinion at any given time. Interest group leaders must decide which battles to wage and how strongly their efforts will be supported by their constituents. Journalists, who are key players in the measurement and communication of public opinion, need to know what their readers and viewers want to hear about, but they also survey the political landscape for those of us who are curious about the attitudes of our fellow citizens. Even corporate executives must keep their "ears to the ground" to understand trends in American culture—what consumers think about, what they purchase, and, generally, how they choose to live.

Since so many parties need to understand the state of American public opinion, there are a variety of sources that interested groups and individuals can turn to for such information. One of the most obvious indicators of public opinion is the sample survey or opinion poll. These quantitative data can often give us a sense of how Americans feel about policy issues, social practices, or lifestyle issues. Another source of information about public opinion is vote tallies after elections or referenda.

These reports often reveal citizens' preferences in very dramatic ways. Yet students of American politics must go beyond these obvious techniques for assessing public opinion and think about all of the "places" that citizens' opinions can be found—in the scripts of television programming; at political rallies, town meetings, or city council hearings; in the rhetoric of journalism; in the dialogue among friends who frequent a coffeehouse or neighborhood bar; and in the political discussions one hears on talk radio or sees on the Internet. This book focuses on all the ways that public opinion is measured and expressed, taking a broad view of what the phrase "public opinion" really means. If one thinks of public opinion only as the result of opinion polls, one will not achieve a sophisticated understanding of our political culture.

There are three key terms that summarize the concerns of this text: politics, communication, and social process. What do we mean by these words? Politics, in the context of this book, refers to the ways we govern ourselves and divide national resources. Many of the chapters include discussions of how public opinion is translated into policy and how it shapes our institutions. Public opinion is certainly important during political campaigns, and journalists do—for better or worse— keep us abreast of the "horse race" as it unfolds. Yet public opinion plays an extremely important role in public and private policy debates—on both domestic and foreign affairs—among our legislators. A good example is President George W. Bush's decision to overthrow the regime of Saddam Hussein in 2003. On the basis of opinion polling, media reports, and other sources, Bush believed that Americans supported military action, so he pursued an aggressive foreign policy. It is doubtful that he would have engaged the Iraqi army had it not been for the supportive nature of public opinion. Bush, like his father before him and most late-twentieth-century American presidents, was extraordinarily dependent on public opinion.

The notion that public opinion and politics are connected is obvious, but communication issues have received far less scholarly attention than they deserve. How is public opinion expressed in America? Do the media influence the ways opinions are communicated, as well as the actual substance of those opinions? In the late twentieth century, we have come to assume that we are in an "information age," but what does that really mean with regard to public opinion? This book explores how both mass

FIGURE 1.1   Public opinion demonstration during the Vietnam War years. (Photo courtesy of the Library of Congress)

media and interpersonal forms of communication shape public sentiment. In the realm of interpersonal communication, for example, we draw upon social psychology to understand how a tendency toward conformity among citizens often guides the ways they behave and how they vote. And since the diffusion of film in the early years of this century, communication researchers have studied how mass media can construct the political world by reflecting our preferences and often dictating those preferences. In recent years, for example, talk radio has become an important forum for political discussion and has often had an immediate effect on politics. In one analysis, researchers have argued that talk radio almost single-handedly forced Zoë Baird, a nominee for U.S. attorney general, to withdraw from the confirmation process in 1992. This is a particularly interesting case of the importance of talk radio, as newspaper and broadcast journalists believed that Baird would be easily confirmed. Although national journalists predicted that Baird's nomination would receive a "rubber stamp" from the Senate, talk radio program hosts were inundated with calls from a public outraged by Baird's violation of the social security laws. In this case, as in many others, talk radio joined the conventional communication outlets of the moment (newspapers, nightly news broadcasts, and news magazines) as a powerful force in American politics.[1]

Finally, public opinion is the result of social processes, and social processes affect the nature of American attitudes. By this, we mean that public opinion is intertwined with a variety of societal forces and institutions, such as the changing American demographic profile, the problems of inner cities, and the state of family life. For example, in later chapters we spend some time discussing fads in fashion and language that reflect changing public attitudes, but we also consider how changes in material or linguistic culture might affect the ways we view our government, our leaders, and each other. The point is that public opinion is embedded in culture: It is not an entity that can be easily disentangled from social life, so we must always be aware of the conditions surrounding the communication of opinions and beliefs.

WHY STUDY PUBLIC OPINION?

Public opinion research is a very broad field, because scholars in many disciplines need to understand how attitudes about public affairs are formed, communicated, and measured. Public opinion study is as old as democracy itself: The ancient Greek philosophers knew that the analysis of popular sentiments was crucial to the design of government by the people. There are, however, some very specific reasons why so many scholars and public officials study and care about the state of public opinion.

1. Policy, in Democratic States, Should Rest on Public Opinion

Although democratic theorists have disagreed about how much of a role the public should play in the design of public policy, almost all believe that people should have some say in how they are governed. The role of public opinion in discussions of democracy takes two forms.

First, there are people's global opinions about institutions. For example, how much do members of the public trust their leaders? Do they believe that Congress is responsive to their needs? Do Americans think that political campaigns are instructive and efficient or simply "horse races" orchestrated by highly paid political consultants? The answers to these questions are complex and will be discussed in subsequent chapters of this book, but the point is that public opinion about the general state of politics is important and worthy of our attention. If trust in government is low or if a large segment of the population does not believe that their congressional representatives are responsive to their needs, a democratic state may deteriorate: Voting rates may decline dramatically, and demagogues might emerge with rather undemocratic ways of "fixing" the system. Over the last few decades, Americans have grown far more cynical about their institutions, but we have yet to witness the sort of severe decay in institutional loyalty that destroys many budding democracies.

Second, beyond the general attitudes people hold about political institutions and leadership are the opinions they have about specific policy matters. Chapter Nine explores the links between public opinion and public policy in depth, and that linkage is among the most important reasons why we study popular attitudes. Presidents, members of Congress, state legislators, and even local city council members must always be aware of public opinion as they design the sorts of regulations and programs that affect our daily lives. Sometimes, leaders promote a policy and the public quickly supports their ideas, as in the early days of a military conflict (the "rally round the flag" effect). Under other conditions, there is a groundswell of opinion, and leaders respond to expressions of public sentiment with legislative action (see Figure 1.1). In the vast majority of cases, however, the interaction between public opinion and the formation of public policy is far more complex because communication among involved parties is so imperfect. Journalists, for example, can often, either knowingly or unknowingly, distort public opinion through their reports, so policymakers find it difficult to figure out whose voices they are listening to—those of media professionals or average citizens. Alternately, journalists can misrepresent or fail to cover aspects of a policy debate, and that can affect the ways that the public responds to legislative endeavors.

2. Respect for Public Opinion Is a Safeguard Against Demagoguery

In all nations, and in all eras, there is a risk that a single demagogue or dictator may grab the reins of power. We have witnessed many such occurrences over the course of the twentieth century. Understanding and respecting public opinion is not an absolute safeguard against the rise of a dictator, yet public opinion is one of the few potentially effective checks on leadership available in a democracy.

In less dramatic cases, for instance, where leaders show bad judgment or are incompetent or corrupt, public opinion can force public officials out of office, either directly or indirectly. In the summer and fall of 1995, for example, U.S. senator Bob Packwood (R–Oregon) was pressured to resign from the Senate over allegations of sexual misconduct and financial improprieties. At the start of Packwood's troubles years earlier, his colleagues had mixed reactions to the charges, with some calling for his resignation and others arguing that the case against him was overblown. Yet public opinion, both in Oregon and around the nation, gradually turned against Packwood, and the Senate was forced to acknowledge popular sentiment. This acknowledgment most certainly played a role in the way the Senate Ethics Committee investigated the Packwood matter and in its eventual findings.

There are a variety of ways that public opinion serves as a check on leadership. In many instances, such as the Packwood case or the 2003 effort to recall Governor Gray Davis of California, a group or groups of citizens are upset about the actions of a public official and other leaders share those sentiments. Under these circumstances, there is an interaction between public officials and the electorate, with both reinforcing the other's opinions. In other cases, there is truly a "bottom-up" display of public annoyance or outrage with the actions of a leader, and government reacts or fails to react to that display. Finally, in some instances, political actors attempt to block the actions of other elites and try to persuade the public to join them in such maneuvering. In all three cases, public opinion serves as a powerful force that directs the actions of our elected and appointed leaders.

3. Public Opinion Provides Clues About Culture

Understanding public opinion on policy and social issues is crucial to students of American culture, because understanding popular sentiment toward specific issues gives us insight into larger currents in American life. Since it is difficult for social scientists to "measure" and report on the many dimensions of American culture, we need to make inferences about that larger culture from narrower studies of public attitudes.

An example of this approach—trying to understand cultural values and trends by studying particular issue attitudes—is research on public feeling toward welfare programs. Since the creation of a set of antipoverty programs in the 1960s, public opinion researchers have asked citizens how they feel about such initiatives. Although such questions present a variety of difficulties to survey researchers, as the way such programs are described can elicit very different answers from respondents, results of these studies tell us a lot about American norms and values. If survey researchers, over the course of several years, ask about whether welfare benefits should be tied to work on the part of aid recipients and respondents increasingly support this idea, we learn something about changing values: The trend may indicate a growing impatience with the poor, a renewal of the work ethic, or a general resurgence of conservative political ideology. All of these hypotheses need more rigorous study, but social scientists are often "tipped off" about larger cultural trends by survey results.

Although we will take up this issue in Chapter Three in our discussion of methodologies for understanding public opinion, one might argue that public opinion and culture are so intertwined as to be inseparable. In addition to being the source of aesthetic "products" (e.g., art, music, dance, and the like), culture is a sum of people's norms, values, and sentiments (see Box 1.1). Relatedly, the best public opinion research usually reveals norms, values, and sentiments. In this book, we try to take a broad approach to understanding public opinion, and although we do not use the phrase "public opinion" and the word "culture" interchangeably, we often draw parallels between the two concepts.

BOX 1.1   CULTURE, ART, AND PUBLIC OPINION

History often provides excellent examples of how culture and public opinion are interwoven. Let us take one interesting historical case of this relationship—the popularity of Shakespearean drama in nineteenth-century America—to illustrate that nexus. Our example comes from a book by historian Lawrence Levine, entitled *Highbrow, Lowbrow: The Emergence of Cultural Hierarchy in America*.

Levine argues that Shakespeare was incredibly popular in the nineteenth century, far more than today and across class lines, because his drama appealed to some basic beliefs among Americans at the time. In particular, Shakespearean drama emphasized the struggle of the individual: "His plays had meaning to a nation that placed the individual at the center of the universe and personalized the large questions of the day."[1] Levine gives an example of how popular political feeling of the period manifested itself in May 1849, when two leading Shakespearean actors (the American Edwin Forrest and the British star William Charles Macready) were giving competing performances in two different New York theaters:

> Forrest's vigorous acting style, his militant love of his country, his outspoken belief in its citizenry, and his frequent articulation of the possibilities of self-improvement and social mobility endeared him to the American people, while Macready's cerebral acting style, his aristocratic demeanor, and his identification with the wealthy gentry made him appear Forrest's diametric opposite. On May 7, Macready and Forrest appeared against one another in separate productions of *Macbeth.* Forrest's performance, at the Broadway Theater, was a triumph both dramatically and politically. When Forrest spoke Macbeth's lines, "What rhubarb, senna or what purgative drug will scour these English hence?" the entire audience, according to the actor Lester Wallack, "rose and cheered for many minutes." Macready's performance, at the Astor Place Opera House, was never heard—he was silenced by a storm of boos and cries of "Three groans for the codfish aristocracy," which drowned out appeals for order from those in the boxes, and by an avalanche of eggs, apples, potatoes, lemons, and ultimately, chairs hurled from the gallery, which forced him to leave the stage in the third act.[2]

The next evening, 1,800 people gathered at the Opera House to shout Macready down. A riot ensued, and when it was over, twenty-two people were dead and over 150 injured.

For our purposes, this colorful yet tragic incident in American theatrical history has a variety of implications. To begin with, it demonstrates how the performing arts rest upon ideology: Americans of the mid-nineteenth century, as well as those living in the late twentieth century, have often been hostile toward art and artists who somehow reflect unpopular beliefs. This example also underscores the fact that public opinion and culture are inextricably intertwined: Americans have never drawn a sharp dividing line between politics and art. Finally, the riot illustrates how political expression (violent expression, in this instance) manifests itself in a variety of forms. In this case, a dramatic performance served as a trigger for public discourse and action, but often speeches, telecasts, and actions of our leaders serve as catalysts for the display of pent-up ideological feeling.

NOTES

1. Lawrence W. Levine, *Highbrow, Lowbrow: The Emergence of Cultural Hierarchy in America* (Cambridge, MA: Harvard University Press, 1988), p. 63.
2. Ibid.

4. Public Opinion Must, at Times, be Mobilized

During national emergencies, and at times of war, presidents must urge citizens to act in prescribed ways. The most obvious circumstance is wartime, when Americans must make compromises—by sending sons and daughters off to war, by conserving scarce resources, and by volunteering where needed. During World War II, this sort of mobilization was not particularly difficult. That war was, to use Studs Terkel's phrase, a "good war," one in which our goals seemed just and there was consensus that we were engaged in a struggle for freedom. Other mobilizations for war have been more difficult or more complicated. A vocal and intelligent antiwar sentiment existed in the days before our entry into World War I, for example, as a variety of writers and artists attempted to persuade Americans that the United States should stay out of European affairs (see Figure 1.2). And much more recently, in the 1960s, President Lyndon B. Johnson attempted to convince an increasingly resistant public that U.S. military action in Vietnam was proper and morally sound.

Regardless of one's feelings about U.S. involvement in the two world wars or in Vietnam, it is clear that a president who needs to mobilize public opinion must first understand the nature of public opinion. The same holds true for students of politics, who try to make sense of government-inspired collective action. Under what circumstances do people support the president with patriotic fervor, and why? How should military leaders present the nature of a conflict to the public in order to make the cause a popular one? An understanding of public attitudes, beliefs, and values is important if leaders are to persuade us with their rhetoric, but they must also have a good grasp of public opinion dynamics—the interaction of

FIGURE 1.2   "Having their fling." This cartoon, drawn by artist Art Young in 1917, depicts a variety of parties who supported U.S. participation in World War I, which Young opposed. The drawing eventually was used in a landmark sedition case against Young and several other writers and artists who produced the antiwar, socialist magazine called the *Masses*. A jury found the group not guilty, although the *Masses* eventually folded due to a variety of other financial and political problems. Reprinted from the *Masses*, July 1917 issue.

media and public opinion, the notion that different channels of communication have different effects on audiences, and the like.

5. Public Opinion Dictates the Bounds of U.S. Foreign Policy

The relationship between foreign policy and public opinion is a complex one and will be discussed in greater detail in Chapter Nine. Yet this connection is so important that it should be mentioned here as one of the reasons that students of American politics need to be concerned with the nature of public opinion.

In general, making foreign policy is the domain of our leaders, who usually have both more expertise and more information than the average citizen. However, this does not mean that public officials design foreign policy without attention to popular sentiment: The president, Congress, and the State Department typically make foreign policy within ideological boundaries determined by American values and priorities. In other words, public opinion determines the broad framework within which foreign affairs are debated. How do our leaders discern this framework so they can act? Policymakers have a variety of tools for doing this. They can rely on opinion polls, which ask both general and specific questions about foreign affairs. A general question might concern citizens' notions about the purposes of foreign aid or whether the United States should tie trade agreements to human rights standards. Specific questions typically focus on contemporary events that demand some sort of response from American leadership.

Beyond polling, though, presidents and other policymakers can use history as a guide when trying to discern what policies or interventions Americans will accept or reject. Thus, for example, when the possibility of intervention in a foreign conflict arises, presidents and members of Congress often look for previous cases on which to base policy. In cases like the civil war in the former Yugoslavia, for instance, policymakers debated the suitability of intervention—particularly in the early days of the conflict. Many drew parallels between Nazi atrocities committed during World War II and the reports of torture inflicted upon Bosnian civilians by the Serbs. Many argued that the United States might have saved a large number of Jews had it intervened in the internal politics of Nazi Germany (e.g., bombing train lines to concentration camps) instead of just concerning itself with the threats to American interests and American soldiers. Whether such humanitarian actions were really possible or not, the analogy between Nazi Germany and the situation in Bosnia gave policymakers a framework for thinking about what sorts of foreign policy maneuvers Americans will or will not tolerate. Another example is the national debate over aid to the Nicaraguan contras in the 1980s (see Box 1.2). Many decision makers, both those who agreed with President Reagan's pleas for increased aid and those who disagreed, did worry about repeating American mistakes in Vietnam. Our policy toward Vietnam was a catalyst for a tremendous public outcry, although it took many years for this rebuff of administration policy to emerge.

At the time of this writing, in the middle of 2004, we are witnessing an extraordinary example of how public opinion can dictate the boundaries of action in foreign policy. In particular, the devastating events of September 11, 2001–the destruction of the World Trade Center towers, attack on the Pentagon, and hijacking of commercial airplanes–have made it possible for President George W. Bush to pursue a wide range of interventionist foreign policy endeavors. These range from the invasion and restructuring of Afghanistan to the overthrow of Saddam Hussein in Iraq. Public opinion, which rallied so strongly around Bush in the months and years after September 11, made it possible for him to undertake dramatic activity abroad, even when the United Nations and many allies disagreed with these ventures.

BOX 1.2   DID THE PUBLIC PLAY A ROLE IN THE CONTRA AID DEBATE?

In 1979, socialist rebels took over the government in the Central American nation of Nicaragua. They replaced a dictator, Anastasio Somoza, who had headed a largely corrupt government known for a horrific number of human rights abuses. President Reagan feared the changes a socialist government might make in Nicaragua and also argued that this left-wing regime would threaten U.S. interests in Latin America more generally. In 1982, a group of rebels who came to be known as the "contras" staged their first attack against the new Sandinista government in order to challenge its rule. Throughout the 1980s, Reagan asked Congress for funds to help the contras overthrow the Sandinistas. Much aid was approved. Fighting and bloodshed escalated until 1989, when President Daniel Ortega, representing the San-dinistas, agreed to hold open elections. In 1990, the UNO Party—a political faction supported by the first Bush administration—won the popular vote and the contras officially disbanded.

The case of U.S. military and nonmilitary aid to the Nicaraguan contras is an ironic one from the viewpoint of democratic theory. In this instance, the majority of Americans were solidly opposed to aiding the contras, even though President Reagan argued strongly for helping these rebels overthrow their government. Most surveys indicated that somewhere between 53 per-cent and 63 percent of Americans polled during 1986 and 1987 thought that we should not aid the contras.[1] Yet Congress regularly approved aid pack-ages, despite the wishes of the public as discerned through opinion polls. Why such a mismatch? Does this case demonstrate that democratic theory is flawed—that leaders do not listen to the public when making foreign pol-icy? William LeoGrande, a professor of political science and former staff member of the House Democratic Caucus on Central America, is in a good position to explain. He asks:

> Did the public matter? Not in the way that theories of democratic represen-tation would normally prescribe. Public opinion was consistently opposed to the Reagan administration's policy of aiding the Nicaraguan contras, yet the administration pursued it doggedly throughout the decade and the Congress supported it to one degree or another from 1982 to 1984 and again from 1985 to 1987. Both Congress and the executive could afford to be unrespon-sive to public opinion because the issue never achieved a high enough level of salience for the mass public to focus on it. When their opinions were elicited by pollsters, people expressed dissatisfaction with the direction in which the Reagan administration was headed, *but they had only the vaguest idea of what was going on in the region.* . . . Even though opposition to Rea-gan's Nicaragua policy remained uniformly high for almost a decade, De-mocrats never quite believed the polls. They worried that a crisis in the re-gion would allow Reagan to act decisively, the public would "rally 'round the flag," and the Democrats would be politically vulnerable. Thus the Democrats felt compelled to support some policy other than simply abandoning the con-tras, lest Nicaragua develop into "another Cuba.". . . The ghost of Joe Mc-Carthy and the hysteria over "Who lost China?" stalked the Democrats throughout the contra aid debates. (emphasis added)[2]

LeoGrande's remarks, which are the concluding section of his study, demonstrate just how complex the relationship between public opinion and foreign policy can be. In the case of Nicaragua, Reagan was not able to achieve his central goal—the immediate overthrow of the Sandinista government. But he was able to get aid to the contra rebels because it seemed less distasteful to Democratic congressmen than sending in U.S. troops and because public attitudes about Nicaragua were so vague and ill-formed. Thus, here is a case of a mismatch between public opinion and policy that was the result of weak expression of public opinion and also, one might argue, weak leadership skills on the part of Democratic congressional leaders. Conceivably, those leaders might have solidified public opinion further, in opposition to aid, and might have mobilized voters. But they did not.

Also interesting in LeoGrande's comments are the multiple references to history. We noted earlier how important collective memory is when it comes to making foreign policy. In the case of Nicaragua, policymakers had a variety of memories to contend with in their attempts to avoid upsetting Americans. Because Republicans feared "another Vietnam," they were cautious in their rhetoric about our involvement in the Central American nation, but Democrats were concerned that the traditional American fear of communism might persuade the public that Reagan's policy was the right one.

NOTES

1. Richard Sobel, ed., *Public Opinion in U.S. Foreign Policy: The Controversy over Contra Aid* (Lanham, MD: Rowman and Littlefield, 1993).

2. William M. LeoGrande, "Did the Public Matter? The Impact of Opinion on Congressional Support for Ronald Reagan's Nicaragua Policy," in Sobel, *Public Opinion in U.S. Foreign Policy,* pp. 185–186.

THE MEANING OF PUBLIC OPINION

Although "public opinion" is an essential concept in democratic theory, it has been very difficult to define. Given the importance of public opinion, it may seem odd that scholars do not agree on a definition. The reason for this lack of consensus is rooted in the fact that so many researchers and theorists from so many different disciplines have contributed to the field but have come to the study of public opinion with different assumptions and methodologies. Yet this is not the only reason that public opinion is hard to define. Some of the ambiguity in the term simply reflects the problematic nature of the concept, which is inherently vague and nebulous. In addition, the meaning of public opinion is also tied to historical circumstance—the sort of political culture that exists, the nature of communication technology, and the importance of public participation in the everyday workings of government.

A good place to begin our discussion of how to define "public opinion" is to consider what constitutes a "public." The concept of a public grew out of Enlightenment democratic ideals and the many important social transformations that took place in the late nineteenth and early twentieth centuries. A working definition of a public grew from its contrasts to other kinds of social formations, most prominently crowds and masses.

The Crowd

In the early twentieth century, the new science of "crowd psychology" (a forerunner of social psychology) developed to explain how individuals could be caught up in mass behavior and transformed. How was it that people were collectively enticed to do things they would never dream of doing alone? For example, how can cheerleaders at a football game get people in the stands to jump, shout, yell, and dance, behaviors in which these people would not normally engage? During the early twentieth century, societies were becoming more urban and the labor and socialist movements were beginning to assert themselves. There were strikes, riots, and other instances of collective behavior that many elites feared signaled future disaster.

The most prominent of the crowd psychology scholars was Gustave Le Bon, who wrote about public opinion in the early decades of the twentieth century. He believed that crowd behavior resulted from (1) the anonymity of crowd members resulting in a perception of "invincibility" and lack of personal responsibility, (2) the contagion of ideas and feelings in the crowd producing rapid shifts in behavior, and (3) the suggestibility of the crowd, enabling people to hold ideas and behave in ways they would not normally behave.[2] In fact, William Trotter likened crowds to animal herds—with the actions of the "lead" individuals transmitting to the others by "suggestion."[3]

The crowd is essentially defined by its "unity of emotional experience."[4] According to contemporary opinion researcher Vincent Price,

"The crowd develops in response to shared emotions."[5] However, the study of crowds has expanded to consider fads, crazes, and social movements, and some scholars believe that crowdlike phenomena could be central to the early formation and expression of public opinion.[6]

The Mass

Crowds are defined by their shared emotional experiences, but masses are defined by their interpersonal isolation. Sociologist Herbert Blumer notes that a mass is composed of anonymous individuals who engage in very little interaction or communication,[7] and Price notes that a mass is extremely heterogeneous, including people from all strata of society and all walks of life.[8] A mass "merely consists of an aggregation of individuals who are separate, detached, anonymous," reacting in response to their own needs, Blumer argues.[9]

This concept of mass also grew out of the social transformations occurring at the turn of the century. People became more mobile. They moved to the cities and became disconnected from their roots in family and village life. They worked long hours and returned home to anonymous neighborhoods. This kind of disconnection was troubling, because it removed the checks on antisocial behavior that are possible in families and villages where everyone knows everyone else. Blumer suggests that what binds a mass together is a common focus of interest or attention. Examples of a mass mentioned by Blumer include individuals "who are excited by some national event, those who share in a land boom, those who are interested in a murder trial which is reported in the press, or those who participate in some large migration."[10] People who are members of a mass share an experience or an idea in common, but they may be unaware of this fact because they are unaware of each other. Despite this lack of awareness, mass behavior can have social consequences, for example, when the individual buying decisions of millions of people turn an unknown recording artist into a star. Similarly, individual voting decisions can elect a new and largely unknown political candidate to office.

The Public

A public can be positively contrasted to a crowd and a mass. The crowd develops in response to shared emotions; the public organizes in response to an issue. Entering the crowd requires only "the ability to feel and empathize," whereas joining the public requires also "the ability to think and reason with others." The behavior of the public could be guided at least partially by a shared emotional drive, but "when the public ceases to be critical, it dissolves or is transformed into a crowd."[11]

Unlike a mass, a public is self-aware. Blumer defines a public as "a group of people (a) who are confronted by an issue, (b) who are divided in the ideas as to how to meet the issue, and (c) who engage in discussion over the issue."[12] Thus, the essence of a public's activity is discourse over a controversy. This process of discourse, according to Blumer, means that public opinion is always rational, though it is not always intelligent. When a public becomes a crowd, it creates "public sentiment" rather than public opinion.

Another important difference between a public and a mass was emphasized by the sociologist C. Wright Mills in the 1950s. In a public, individuals should be as capable of expressing opinions as they are of receiving them. Debate continues over whether a "true" public so defined actually exists in twentieth-century America. Some, like Mills, argue that American citizens are more like a mass of isolated individuals who receive opinions via the media. Others take a more positive view of public discourse, citing interpersonal discussions and phenomena like talk radio.

Despite a chronic definitional problem, public opinion research is still a field with boundaries. Not all studies of American culture are studies of public opinion, because the study of public opinion does concern the formation, communication, and measurement of citizens' attitudes toward public affairs. We believe that there are five reasonable definitions of public opinion that are distinct but that also overlap to some extent. It is best not to treat these categories as mutually exclusive, since the lines between them are not as clear as we might like.

Category 1: Public Opinion Is an Aggregation of Individual Opinions. Many researchers, journalists, policymakers, and citizens think of public opinion as the simple sum of many individual opinions. This is the most common definition of public opinion in contemporary American politics, and it serves as the justification for using surveys and polls to measure public opinion. By using the process of random selection, opinion polls enable an efficient aggregation of individual opinions. The fact that all professionally conducted polls randomly select individuals—across social groups—to be interviewed means that one can take the results of those interviews and make general claims about the entire population.

This definition is widely shared in public life today for several reasons. First, it gives one straightforward direction about how to measure the public mood: If public opinion is the aggregation of individual opinions, it is clear that we must interview individuals and add their opinions together to ascertain public opinion. Relatedly, the methodology of polling has become routinized over the last decade, so that any trained researcher with resources and computers can conduct a competent survey of the public. Second, this definition of public opinion resonates with the structure of the popular election, which serves as the basis for democratic process. Surveys are like elections in the way they tally "votes" (opinions), so they seem to fit our particular system of governance. Third, this sort of quantitative approach to understanding public opinion enables researchers, journalists, and others to engage in complex causal analyses of public opinion. If an analyst polls a sample of American citizens about welfare reform, for example, that makes it possible to test hypotheses about the relationship between support for reform and one's race, class, gender, political affiliation, or religion. Furthermore, the researcher can analyze how political attitudes and values are connected: Do those citizens who trust government officials tend to support reform? Or do those who have immense trust in government fear welfare reform proposals that reduce government's role in managing entitlement programs?

Polling is used by legislators, presidents, and journalists to get a sense of how people feel about various policy issues, but surveys also give us some insight into more general attitudes about social life. The mass media offer up an enormous number of surveys each day that describe public attitudes on race relations, gender roles, religious values, and the like. Sometimes these polls shed light on policy debates, but more often they are interesting notes on culture, in and of themselves.

Category 2: Public Opinion Is a Reflection of Majority Beliefs.   Several theorists argue that we need to think of public opinion as the equivalent of social norms—that the values and beliefs of the majority of citizens are the true basis of public opinion. Another way of saying this is that the only public opinion that really matters, when it comes to policymaking, is what most Americans think. Theorists who use this definition are not making a judgment about the majority being right or wrong on a particular subject: They are simply reporting that people do pay close attention to the opinions of friends, coworkers, and neighbors and tend to conform to majority opinion among their significant others.

One researcher who supports this definition of public opinion is Elisabeth Noelle-Neumann, whose work we discuss in subsequent chapters. She argues that public opinion is best defined as the "opinions on controversial issues that one can express in public without isolating oneself."[13] Noelle-Neumann believes that citizens do a surveillance of their environment, try to get a sense of what majority opinion is like on a particular topic, and then either express themselves or keep quiet on the subject. She calls this theory the "spiral of silence" because she thinks that people remain silent when they realize that they hold a minority opinion and, as a result, minority opinion appears to be even less pervasive than it really is. Noelle-Neumann bases her theory on the tracts of great philosophers (e.g., John Locke and Jean-Jacques Rousseau), as well as on the large number of conformity experiments in the field of social psychology.

There is considerable debate about Noelle-Neumann's hypothesis. First, there have been a variety of assaults on her methodology, that is, how she studies the problem of conformity in public opinion. Second, one wonders whether people really feel the need to conform to majority opinion on all policy and social issues. Finally, there is a bit of confusion about citizens' sources of information—where we learn about majority opinion. Do we learn about majority opinion from media reports and polls? Or are our significant others a more important source of information (and persuasion) than the mass media? These questions are complex, and Chapter Six explores them in greater depth.

If one believes that public opinion is simply the aggregation of individual opinions (the first definition above), it is easy to measure it through polls and surveys. Yet if someone believes that the opinions we express are not always honest, polling becomes much more problematic. When people say one thing to a pollster but in their hearts believe just the opposite, researchers need to develop much more sophisticated methods for understanding public opinions (those we are willing to articulate aloud) and private opinions (those opinions we keep to ourselves).

Category 3: Public Opinion Is Found in the Clash of Group Interests.   Some
scholars believe that public opinion is not so much a function of what
individuals think as a reflection of how their opinions are cultivated,
crystallized, and eventually communicated by interest groups. These may
be political parties, trade organizations, corporations, or activist groups
like the Sierra Club or the Christian Coalition. The strength of this definition is that it underscores power dynamics: In political reality, organized groups are the ones that lobby for legislation, have spokespeople
who influence journalists, and mobilize votes during election campaigns.
Under this definition, then, public opinion is the result of public debate
among groups.

   This definition of public opinion assumes that conflict is pervasive in
social and political life, that groups are constantly engaged in a struggle to
define social problems and provide solutions to them. People who ascribe
to this definition do not discount the opinions and attitudes of individuals but are most interested in how those opinions are translated into interest group opinion, since interest groups act in a more powerful fashion
than do individuals. Citizens can accomplish more when they join forces,
because policymakers and journalists are more likely to be interested in
group opinion than in single opinions.

   One theorist advocating this definition of public opinion is Herbert
Blumer, mentioned earlier in our discussion of masses and publics. In
1948, Blumer presented a now famous attack on survey research, in
which he argued that polls are an artificial means for describing public
opinion, since they do not tell us much about who the respondents are
and which interest groups they support (see Box 1.3). Opinion polls pur-
posefully treat all individual respondents equally: Each opinion is given
the same weight, and all opinions are seen as equally important. Blumer
believes that this is an unrealistic approach to understanding society,
since all citizens are not equal. Pollsters can find out the gender and race
of respondents and whether they are wealthy and educated or poor and
without much formal schooling. But it is much harder to discern
whether respondents are influential in their social circle or whether they
are active citizens who effectively lobby local public officials and journalists, give money to particular causes, and the like. Sophisticated survey research can, in theory, probe many aspects of respondents' behavior,

but this is both expensive and time-consuming for those respondents. Survey response rates have been declining in recent years and pollsters have been working to make participation in polls a positive (and brief) experience.

BOX 1.3   DO GROUPS MATTER MORE THAN INDIVIDUALS, WHEN IT COMES TO PUBLIC OPINION?

In his 1948 essay on opinion polling, sociologist Herbert Blumer tried to take the perspective of a legislator or executive. What kind of public opinion data is important to them: the results of surveys or the opinions communicated by interest groups?[1] He argued:

> [The administrator] has to view society in terms of groups of divergent influence; in terms of organizations with different degrees of power; in terms of individuals with followings; in terms of indifferent people—all, in other words, in terms of what and who counts in his part of the social world. This type of assessment which is called for in the instance of an organized society in operation is well-nigh impossible to make in the case of the findings of public opinion polls. We are unable to answer such questions as the following: how much power and influence is possessed by those who have the favorable opinion or the unfavorable opinion; who are these people who have the opinion; whom do they represent; how well organized are they; what groups do they belong to that are stirring around on the scene and that are likely to continue to do so; are those people who have the given opinion very much concerned about their opinion; are they going to get busy and do something about it; are they going to get vociferous, militant, and troublesome; are they in the position to influence powerful groups and individuals *who are known*; does the opinion represent a studied policy of significant organizations which will persist and who are likely to remember; is the opinion an ephemeral or momentary view which people will quickly forget? These sample questions show how markedly difficult it is to assess the results of opinion polling from the standpoint of the things that have to be taken into account in working in an organized society. (emphasis in original)

SOURCE: "Public Opinion and Public Opinion Polling," *American Sociological Review* 13 (1948):542–554, quoted passage at p. 547.

NOTES

1. On interest groups as public opinion, see also Susan Herbst, *Reading Public Opinion: How Political Actors View the Democratic Process* (Chicago: University of Chicago Press, 1998).

Category 4: Public Opinion Is Media and Elite Opinion. Twentieth-century students of politics have wondered whether public opinion is a reflection of citizens' opinions or simply the projection of what journalists, politicians, pollsters, and other "elites" believe. This notion—that public opinion is a creation of social leaders—may sound cynical, but it has a large number of adherents. The most famous is probably Walter Lippmann, a journalist and political philosopher who also served as a consultant to a variety of American legislators and presidents from World War I through the early years of the Vietnam War. He argued that the common citizen could not possibly stay informed on all affairs of state and, given this impossibility, could hardly be relied upon to produce intelligent opinions on all public affairs. As a result, "public opinion" is best conceptualized as a symbolic phrase used by orators to make their own arguments and fight their own battles with each other. Lippmann was not arguing that people are stupid or that they need to be guided by benevolent dictators. Yet he did believe that people lacked the time and the energy to focus on political matters in the ways called upon by high democratic theory.

One can find a large number of policy matters about which the American public knows very little. Our earlier discussion of the contra aid debate in Box 1.2 serves as a good example of Lippmann's point. Very few citizens even knew where Nicaragua was located! The public's confusion about the issue undoubtedly enabled the Reagan administration to construct public opinion in a manner most supportive of their policies. In general, the public knows far less about foreign affairs than it should if citizens are to form thoughtful opinions about America's overseas activities. Lippmann understood this, and as a result, he advocated that American government should be advised by bureaus of experts instead of by the average citizen. As his biographer Ronald Steele notes, Lippmann was so disillusioned with mass democracy that he could only turn to a government of "specialists" as a solution to the problem of an ignorant public.[14] Lippmann wrote in 1925:

> My sympathies are with [the private citizen], for I believe that he has been saddled with an impossible task and that he is asked to practice an unattainable ideal. I find it so myself for, although public business is my main interest and I give most of my time to watching it, I cannot find time to do what is expected of me in the theory of democracy, that is, to know what is going on and to have an opinion worth expressing on every question which confronts a self-governing community. And I have not happened to meet anybody, from a President of the United States to a professor of political science, who came anywhere near to embodying the accepted ideal of the sovereign and omnicompetent citizen.[15]

Thus, not only did Lippmann realize the problematic nature of an informed citizenry as described in democratic theory, but he also took issue with the possibility of public opinion being a useful entity and advocated that citizens be listened to less often in the construction of social policy.

Category 5: Public Opinion Is a Fiction. Whereas Lippmann and other scholars see public opinion as the expression of elite opinion, some theorists have gone even further in an attempt to question the meaning of the phrase "public opinion." They argue that public opinion is a phantom—a rhetorical construction used so freely in our newspapers and on television as to be meaningless. They posit, for example, that journalists and congressional representatives often talk about the state of public opinion on a particular issue when they have no evidence at all to back up such assertions about popular feeling. Critics in this category ask difficult questions. For example, if people use the phrase so indiscriminately, without qualitative or quantitative evidence to support their versions of how the public feels, does the phrase have any value at all? Even if a president or member of Congress has an opinion survey demonstrating support for the position he or she is taking, how solid are the opinions measured? Are they informed opinions? And equally important, would people act on those opinions?

Scholars who believe that public opinion is equivalent to media and elite opinion (category 4) may think that public officials and journalists construct images of public opinion to fit their own needs, but these elites are normally basing their arguments on some sort of empirical reality. Theorists in the present category are far more critical, believing that public opinion—in any form—really does not exist: It has no basis in the actual public sphere.

BOX 1.4   AN IGNORANT PUBLIC?

Civic knowledge levels among Americans, as measured by surveys, have always been lower than political scientists would like. Two researchers who have probed citizens about what they know are Michael X. Delli Carpini and Scott Keeter. In 1989, they conducted a study to measure knowledge about basic constitutional issues and contemporary events and people. Some of their results are recorded below. Do you think Americans should be able to answer these questions correctly?

Question	Percentage of Respondents Giving the Correct Answer
For how many years is a president of the United States elected—that is, how many years are there in one term of office?	96
Can you tell me the name of the current governor of your state?	74
Will you tell me who the vice president of the United States is?	74
What are the first ten amendments to the Constitution called?	46
Can you remember offhand the name of the U.S. congressman from your district?	29
Do you happen to know the names of the two U.S. senators from your state?	25

SOURCE: Michael X. Delli Carpini and Scott Keeter, *What Americans Know About Politics and Why It Matters* (New Haven: Yale University Press, 1996), questionnaire results throughout appendix, pp. 307–328.

Scholars in this category write at great length about rhetoric—about the fact that anyone can manufacture a public (and its opinions). For example, polls can be designed with questions asked in such a way that the results will be those desired. This sort of biasing of questions is often done unintentionally, but it might be done deliberately as well. Besides crafting quantitative data to support their claims, legislators or interest group spokespersons might simply use inclusive terminology when talking about a social problem, beginning their public statements with, "As Americans, we believe . . ." Public opinion can also be manufactured through sophisticated public relations efforts and the use of visual imagery, to make it seem as though there is majority opinion on a topic.

In addition to arguing that public opinion can be manufactured through rhetoric, critics in this category have other strong arguments based on linguistics and cognitive psychology. For example, scholars have noted that citizens think about politics using different terminology than do pollsters and policymakers. Some wonder whether average citizens and political elites (legislators, journalists, and pollsters, for example) even recognize the same problems as political in nature. Pierre Bourdieu, a French sociologist, put his objections to polling and the notion of public opinion this way:

> Journalists who want things to be simple, further simplify the already simplified [polling] data which they have been given, and when it reaches the public, it is likely to read as follows: "50 percent of the French are for the discontinuation of the railroads." A rigorous interpretation of the opinion polls would require an epistemological examination of each of the questions asked, plus, concerning the system of the questions, an analysis of the whole system of answers, which together would be *the only way to know what were the questions the people really thought they were answering.* (emphasis added)[16]

Bourdieu does believe that academics, with great care, can occasionally conduct useful surveys, but he does not think that these surveys necessarily measure a concrete entity called "public opinion." He and his colleagues have conducted surveys in which they ask questions like this one: "For you, is it political or not to go on strike, wear long hair, participate in a rock festival, etc." Yet even when such scholars try to figure out what

TABLE 1.1   Thinking About and Measuring Public Opinion: American Health Care

Definition of Public Opinion	In the Context of Health Care Reform
Category 1 (aggregation)	Researchers would argue that public opinion about health care delivery is the product of what most private citizens would say when questioned on the subject. These scholars would use sophisticated survey methods to probe American men and women about their visions of health care reform. Also, such researchers would question survey respondents about the various plans that have been introduced to reform the system, in order to get their opinions on the different plans. Focus groups might be used, also, in order to collect more data in a more conversational forum.
Category 2 (majoritarian)	Scholars would propose that public opinion is the most popular opinion—what people tend to say in public. Thus, if it is socially most acceptable to argue for a national system that guarantees low-cost coverage for all, that would be the "public opinion" worth paying attention to. Researchers in this category might use polls and surveys to discern this majority opinion, or they might conduct a content analysis of the mass media to get a sense of which opinion receives the most (and most favorable) news coverage.
Category 3 (clash of groups)	This approach would focus most rigorously on the "interests" and coalitions in the debate—the insurance industry, the American Association of Retired People (AARP), the administration, and a variety of other consumer and lobby groups. How do the leaders of these groups characterize the opinions of their constituents? Researchers taking this approach to understanding public opinion would study the public statements made by such groups but would also conduct interviews with group leaders and members. Most important, though, scholars in this category would attempt to understand the way groups clash—trying to discern points of contention, areas of common ground, and the evolution of groups' strategies and approaches.

(continues)

TABLE 1.1   *(continued)*

Definition of Public Opinion	*In the Context of Health Care Reform*
Category 4 (elite/media opinion)	Using this definition of public opinion, one would recognize that a variety of powerful players claim support among the public. All of them, however, may be exaggerating just how widely certain views are held. For example, the insurance industry representatives argued repeatedly in the 1993 debate about health care that choice among doctors was of utmost importance to the public. And there were some polls that indicated this was the case. Yet other polls indicated that people might be more flexible on the choice issue. The fact that the issue was complicated—in that citizens might trade off choice for some other benefits—was not part of industry rhetoric, however. One might argue that the insurance industry had a perspective, and set of interests, that drove it to construct public opinion in a way that suited its own agenda.
Category 5 (public opinion as fiction)	Scholars in this category would argue that people may have some feelings about health care reform and the kind of health care services they value but that the expression of these opinions is entirely constructed by interest groups, public officials, and media. These parties are exaggerating actual opinion at times, but often they are constructing "public opinion" out of nothing at all. The most worrisome aspect of this rhetorical construction of public opinion is that actual opinion—complex though it might be—gets overlooked.

it is people believe to be political activity or what they believe are political issues, they are troubled by the complexity of the results.

To further clarify how critics in this last category view public opinion, Table 1.1 takes up an example of an issue and discusses how each category of theorist might approach it. The restructuring of the health care system in America, an issue that will come up in subsequent chapters, is a good case for such an exercise.

All students of public opinion need to understand that the opinion expression and measurement process contains many dimensions. These dimensions are often evaluated using survey research instruments and give public opinion scholars an understanding of the nature of public opinion on various issues.

First, the direction of public opinion is important. That is, one must determine where people stand on issues. Often, direction is thought of as a simple "pro" or "con" answer for an issue, but more complex patterns are possible as well. For example, an individual may be in favor of a woman's right to decide whether to have an abortion but may be opposed to abortion after the first trimester of pregnancy or under certain conditions.

Second, the intensity of opinion can be critical. How strongly do people feel about an issue? Where an issue has intense advocates on either side, as the abortion issue does, the result can indicate deep social divisions. If an intense minority confronts a relatively apathetic majority, majority public opinion may be ignored by policymakers seeking to appease the vocal minority.

One of the unresolved problems of democracy is balancing majority and minority opinion. When a minority of people feels strongly on an issue, should its opinion outweigh that of the more apathetic majority? If neither majority nor minority is particularly intense, policymakers may view the public opinion environment as permissive and enact the policies they themselves favor. This situation occurred in the contra aid debate discussed earlier. Alternatively, if an issue draws an intense majority, policymakers may feel compelled to respond to the demands of public opinion.

Third, the stability of public opinion can affect scholars' and leaders' evaluation of the issue. Stability refers to the consistency of people's opinions over time. If public opinion on an issue is stable, leaders may be more likely to pay attention to it. If public opinion on an issue changes frequently, it is more likely to be dismissed. This tendency occurs because stable public opinion is believed to reflect true public desires, whereas unstable public opinion is perceived as capricious and uninformed. However, just because public opinion changes over time does not mean that those changes are not heeded by leaders. Political scientist Michael Corbett points out that "in 1953, 68 percent of Americans favored capital punishment for convicted murderers; then the proportion favoring capital punishment declined until it reached 42 percent in 1966; but then the proportion rose again until it reached 72 percent in 1985."[17] In this span of time, the death penalty was abolished, then reinstated.

The stability of public opinion can be affected by many things. One factor is intensity, which we have already discussed. But stability is also affected by the informational content of the opinion. Information content is the fourth quality of public opinion that scholars frequently explore. There is much evidence to suggest that people do not know very much about public issues. Some of this evidence you have already seen in Box 1.4, and a more complete discussion appears in Chapter Eight. For now, it may be enough to say that scholars are unsure about exactly how much information the public needs in order to form "rational" opinions about public issues. However, it seems unlikely that uninformed public opinion will have as much impact on political leaders as informed public opinion will.

WHICH MEANING OF PUBLIC OPINION IS BEST?

Which definition of public opinion is the correct one? That is difficult to say. In contemporary American life, all of the definitions are used, depending upon the circumstances in which the public mood is being discussed. Scholars certainly use all five categories in their work, as do journalists and public officials. Some might argue that because of the popularity of polling, the first category (public opinion as aggregation of individual opinions) is most common, but journalists and our leaders often gain knowledge of public opinion by speaking with interest group leaders. And almost all reporters and policymakers have, either knowingly or unknowingly, manufactured notions of public opinion through their spoken and written rhetoric.

The definition one chooses depends upon several factors, including the following:

1. The type of research one is conducting. For example, if one is exploring the ways that American women of the late nineteenth century viewed suffrage (the right to vote), they might look for evidence of public opinion in the letters of suffragettes or in the documents of women's rights organizations. This research assumes that public opinion is the product of interaction between individuals and organized interest groups. Since the question is a historical one, a researcher cannot define public opinion as the opinions of an

aggregation of individuals. That would demand a survey, and in this case the respondents died long ago!

2. Historical conditions often dictate the kind of definition of public opinion one uses. We will see in the next chapter, for example, how form of government can influence the ways leaders and citizens think about the public. In a dictatorship, public opinion is often used rhetorically (category 5) to manipulate the populace and make people think that leaders are acting in the interest of the citizenry. In a situation like this, public opinion really is a phantom, manufactured to make people feel as though they are listened to (even if that is not the case).

3. The kind of technology that exists in a particular society at a certain point in time may determine which meaning of public opinion is used. Take opinion polling as an example of technology. These days, computers are used extensively in the interviewing process and in analysis of survey data. Although opinion polling was developed to aggregate individual opinions (category 1), the technology for conducting a scientific poll has become so easy to use that people employ the aggregation approach because they can do surveys so quickly. This is not to say that the availability of technology always determines how we see the political and social world, but it is the case that we are attracted to techniques that enable us to understand the world in what seems an efficient manner.

As students of public opinion and political processes, we must live with ambiguity when it comes to defining public opinion. The fact that we cannot define the term with precision does not mean that the field has no boundaries, as we will see in subsequent chapters. The sorts of intellectual debates, political phenomena, and theories that are described in this book will give you a firm understanding of what the field of public opinion is about—what is included under the general heading of "public opinion studies" and what is not.

NOTES

1. See Benjamin I. Page and Jason Tannenbaum, "Populistic Deliberation: The Zoe Baird Uprising," paper presented at the Annual Meeting of the American Political Science Association, 1995, Chicago.

2. Gustave Le Bon, *The Crowd: A Study of the Popular Mind* (London: Unwin, 1948), pp. 27–38.

3. William Trotter, *Instincts of the Herd in Peace and War* (London: Oxford University Press, 1919).

4. Vincent Price, *Public Opinion* (Newbury Park, CA: Sage Publications, 1992).

5. Ibid., p. 26.

6. Nelson N. Foote and Clyde W. Hart, "Public Opinion and Collective Behavior," in Muzafir Sherif and Milbourne O. Wilson, eds., *Group Relations at the Crossroads* (New York: Harper and Bros., 1953), pp. 308–331.

7. Herbert Blumer, *Collective Behavior* (New York: Barnes and Noble, 1946).

8. Price, *Public Opinion.*

9. Blumer, *Collective Behavior.*

10. Ibid., p. 185.

11. Price, *Public Opinion,* p. 26; quotes from Robert E. Park, *The Crowd and the Public and Other Essays* (Chicago: University of Chicago Press, 1904), p. 80.

12. Blumer, *Collective Behavior,* p. 189.

13. Elisabeth Noelle-Neumann, *The Spiral of Silence: Public Opinion—Our Social Skin* (Chicago: University of Chicago Press, 1984).

14. Ronald Steele, *Walter Lippmann and the American Century* (New York: Vintage, 1980).

15. Walter Lippmann, *The Phantom Public* (New York: Harcourt, Brace and Company, 1925).

16. Pierre Bourdieu, "Public Opinion Does Not Exist," in Armand Mattelart and Seth Siegelaub, eds., *Communication and Class Struggle* (New York: International General, 1979), pp. 124–130.

17. Michael Corbett, *American Public Opinion Trends* (New York: Longman, 1991), p. 24.

2

The History of Public Opinion

In the previous chapter, we discussed the various possible routes to understanding and measuring public opinion in the context of contemporary life, but we only made brief reference to the historical development
of public opinion. This chapter is devoted to exploring the history of
public opinion—the ways that intellectuals, citizens, and leaders have
thought about that concept through the ages and the ways that these
same individuals communicated and evaluated the popular sentiment.

There are two approaches to investigating the history of public opinion. One can examine the intellectual history of the concept itself in an
attempt to follow the theoretical debates about the nature of public opinion. Intellectual history concentrates on how philosophers and theorists
have thought about public opinion in different epochs. Alternately, one
can pursue study of the sociocultural history of public opinion, paying
close attention to the techniques people have used to communicate their
opinions and the ways leaders have tried to assess those expressed beliefs.
Neither approach is "better." On the contrary, these two forms of historical analysis complement each other. In this chapter, we explore both
sorts of history so that you will understand the philosophical development of public opinion and the "nuts and bolts" of how public opinion
has been expressed and measured in different communities at different
points in history. We will begin with the intellectual history of the concept of public opinion and then move to social history.

Before we discuss philosophy, however, a few prefatory notes are in
order. First, since the history of public opinion—intellectual and social—
is so lengthy, we cannot explore all topics, debates, events, or theories in

35

great depth. We will, however, give you enough of an introduction to the history of public opinion so that you have a skeletal map of this narrative. Second, this chapter focuses on the ways that public opinion has been discussed, expressed, and assessed in the West—primarily in the United States, the United Kingdom, and European nations. This geographical exclusiveness is unfortunate, but contemporary notions of public opinion in America draw most heavily upon Western intellectual traditions. Through the ages, individuals in many South American, African, and Asian cultures have undoubtedly thought about the idea of public opinion, but not much of this thinking has been integrated into American political culture and institutions. Finally, just as different parties in contemporary American politics disagree on the meaning of public opinion, philosophers and citizens in different eras understood the phrase (or similar phrases) differently, depending on the political, technological, and cultural circumstances of the day (see Box 2.1). As a result, it may feel as though the meaning of the term is always shifting. This is exactly the point of the current chapter as well as this entire text: The meaning of public opinion is always in flux, depending upon the context in which the term is used.

BOX 2.1   ONE PHILOSOPHER'S VIEW

Jürgen Habermas is one of the most important and prolific philosophers of our time. Fortunately for us, he has focused his immense talents on the history and meaning of public opinion in a variety of books and journal articles. This chapter owes much to Habermas, a German scholar whose work has been enormously influential in almost all academic disciplines—political science, communications, sociology, philosophy, literature, anthropology, and history, among them. Habermas believes that the meaning of public opinion shifts in each era and that this meaning is always tied to the nature of the broader political and social arena that he calls the "public sphere."

The public sphere is the forum for discussion of politics outside of our homes but also outside of governmental circles. In other words, talk about family matters or discussion of politics within a household is not part of public sphere discourse, nor is talk among congressmen or between the president and his advisers. Public sphere talk is what one hears in a neighborhood bar or on talk radio. One can also find public sphere discussions in the editorial pages of newspapers, both regional and national, or in the large number of American current affairs magazines.

For Habermas, the meaning of public opinion and the ways we express it are always changing because the nature of public life itself is always shifting. In mid-nineteenth-century America, for example, women were typically not part of the public sphere. Middle-class women ruled the *domestic* sphere—caring for children and for their homes—but played only social roles in public (e.g., as hostesses, entertainers, or supporting players to husbands and fathers). Since women were largely absent from the *public sphere* in any serious sense, their voices were not considered part of *public opinion*. As a result, they could not vote and tended not to write letters to editors or vigorously campaign for political candidates. "Public opinion" in mid-nineteenth-century America meant the opinions of certain classes of men.

Habermas summarizes the connection between public opinion and public life in this way: "A concept of public opinion that is historically meaningful, that normatively meets the requirements of the constitution of a social-welfare state [such as our own], and that is theoretically clear and empirically identifiable can be grounded only in the structural transformation of the public sphere itself and in the dimension of its development."

SOURCES: Jürgen Habermas, *The Structural Transformation of the Public Sphere: An Inquiry into a Category of Bourgeois Society*, trans. Thomas Burger (Cambridge, MA: MIT Press, 1989), quoted passage at p. 244. An application of Habermas's ideas to the analysis of women in the nineteenth century is given in Mary Ryan's *Women in Public* (Baltimore: Johns Hopkins University Press, 1990).

WHY DOES HISTORY MATTER?

There are a great many important issues in the study of current public opinion: how Americans feel about U.S. intervention in foreign conflicts, whether we trust our president, differences in opinion among various social groups, among others. Given all the focus on contemporary attitudes, why should we be concerned about past notions of public opinion or the ways people expressed themselves centuries ago?

History matters for two major reasons. First, and most obvious, an understanding of history enables us to understand the present—how it is things got the way they are. Here is an analogy from social life: Suppose we want to understand a friend's behavior. If we are really interested in getting a full picture of why this friend acts the way she does, we need information about her life experiences—her family background, the region where she grew up, the sorts of schools she attended, and so on. Similarly, if we are to understand the political culture of contemporary America, we need to know about the past: how political parties evolved, how the Constitution has been amended, which social movements changed the practice of politics, and the like. In the narrower area of public opinion, we need to understand how opinions were communicated in the past in order to properly analyze the present. For example, one reason opinion polling became so popular in America is because George Gallup and others were so concerned with the way dictators—like Adolf Hitler—attempted to speak for the people instead of letting them express their own opinions. In the mid-twentieth century, after two bloody world wars and the rise of multiple totalitarian regimes, polling seemed like a very democratic way to communicate public opinion. The rise of surveys was, in part, a reaction to the menace of dictatorship.

Second, history gives us a sense of possibility. In the area of public opinion, we have become accustomed to polls and the statements of interest groups as indicators of public opinion, but history provides examples of the many innovative ways people have expressed themselves in the past. When we recognize, through our historical analyses, just how many options exist for communicating our beliefs, we can become more creative in expressing and evaluating public opinion. For example, later in this chapter we discuss the creative rituals of eighteenth-century Europeans and how those rituals expressed public sentiment about particular institutions. If we think about rituals in general as means for expressing public opinion, we begin to recognize that some of our own twentieth-century rituals are also expressions of public opinion. Rituals like Memorial Day parades or commemorations of the Hiroshima and Nagasaki bombings at the end of World War II enable citizens to express both love of country and critical attitudes toward government.

Let us begin our exploration of the intellectual history of public opinion. Much of the early theorizing of the concept is tied to broader inquiries philosophers have made about governance, representation, political participation, and even human nature. We begin our journey in ancient Greece, the setting for early experiments in democracy.

PRE-ENLIGHTENMENT PHILOSOPHIES
OF PUBLIC OPINION

The particular phrase "public opinion" was not used widely before the nineteenth century, but many of the great political philosophers of the ancient period used similar phrases to speak about the popular sentiment. Plato, a Greek philosopher of the fourth century B.C., was very much interested in public opinion. He was respectful of its powers and believed that the public will should be heeded, though he was somewhat skeptical of the common person's wisdom. An early twentieth-century scholar named Ernest Barker has noted that Plato and many of his contemporaries thought that members of the public needed to be educated in order to understand and appreciate their government and the laws they lived under. This view is contrary to the modern one that puts the public first: Public opinion should be the basis of all law, and laws should be altered as the public mood shifts. Barker puts it this way: "The Greeks believed in the need of education to tune and harmonise social opinion to the spirit and tone of a fixed and fundamental sovereign law. The modern belief is in the need of representation to adjust and harmonise a fluid and subordinate law to the movement of a sovereign public opinion or general will."[1]

Plato generally distrusted the masses: He was not sure that people could realize their own best interests or strive toward the creation of a morally sound state. As a result, he argued that the democratic state should be ruled by philosopher-kings. Above all, Plato valued reason and rationality as paths to the best sort of moral community. The people know what they want as far as immediate comforts (food, love, recreation) go, but they do not have the cognitive capacity to rule themselves in the most just and effective ways possible.

Plato represented an important strand of thought in ancient philosophy, but others writing in the same period disagreed sharply with his negative assessment of the public's capabilities. In particular, Aristotle argued most eloquently for the voice of the public, defending the wisdom of the common citizen. As scholar Robert Minar puts it, Aristotle believed in the power of community: "Aristotelian political theory seems to suggest that public opinion may be regarded as the vehicle of the spirit and continuity of the life of the organic community. It carries the enduring wisdom of the social organism and reflects that wisdom on the particular, immediate actions of government."[2]

Aristotle did not see public opinion as the sentiments people held toward particular issues of the day, although he saw those attitudes as important and worth articulating. Instead, he argued that public opinion is equivalent to the values, norms, and tastes of a civilization. This "climate of opinion," to borrow a phrase from sociologist Robert Merton, is then funneled through institutions (courts and schools, for example) that serve as moderating influences. In other words, institutions take "raw" opinion from communities, organize it, eliminate irrationalities, and make it coherent. Aristotle was undoubtedly more optimistic about the role and nature of public opinion than were many of his predecessors who advocated for democracy but still did not really trust the people (see Box 2.2).

BOX 2.2   ARISTOTLE VERSUS PLATO:
THE VALUE OF PUBLIC OPINION

Since Plato and Aristotle wrote about public opinion in the fourth century B.C., thousands of scholars of political theory have debated and reinterpreted their ideas. Even today, because those ancient texts were so immensely thoughtful and complex, a large number of thinkers scrutinize them, looking for cues about how democracy might work. Perhaps the best way to evaluate the argumentation of Plato and Aristotle is to turn to their original statements. These quotes are removed from their original contexts, but they will give you some idea of how these philosophers conceptualized the public will.

In *The Republic*, Plato explicates his famous analogy of "the cave" and writes on a variety of other topics from mathematics to child rearing. He argues that democracy produces a sort of chaos that makes its citizens lose sight of right and wrong, of beauty, and of all that is "good." Not all men have good character:

> In a democracy you must have seen how men condemned to death or exile stay on and go about in public, and no one takes any more notice than he would of a spirit that walked invisible. There is so much tolerance and supe-

riority to petty considerations; such a contempt for all those fine principles we laid down in founding our commonwealth, as when we said that only a very exceptional nature could turn out a good man, if he had not played as a child among things of beauty and given himself only to creditable pursuits. A democracy tramples all such notions under foot; with a magnificent indifference to the sort of life a man has led before he enters politics, it will promote to honour anyone who merely calls himself the people's friend. . . . These then, and such as these, are the features of democracy, an agreeable form of anarchy with plenty of variety and an equality of a peculiar kind for equals and unequals alike.

Thus, Plato is concerned about the "side effects" of democracy: neglect of social values, lack of enforcement of societal norms, and an undeserved sort of equality. Citizens are far from equal in their intelligence, education, aesthetic sense, or integrity. Democracy, Plato argues, demands more from the public than it is capable of.

In contrast, Aristotle sees wisdom in the ideas and expressions of citizens acting in public. He glories in the diversity and the very inequalities underscored by Plato. He notes in *The Politics:*

It is possible that the many, no one of whom taken singly is a good man, may yet taken all together be better than the few, not individually but collectively, in the same way that a feast to which all contribute is better than one given at one man's expense. For where there are many people, each has some share of goodness and intelligence, and when these are brought together, they become as it were one multiple man with many pairs of feet and hands and many minds. So too in regard to character and the powers of perception. That is why the general public is a better judge of works of music and poetry; some judge some parts, some others, but their joint pronouncement is a verdict upon the whole. And it is this assembling in one what was before separate that gives the good man his superiority over any individual many from the masses.

Interestingly, the arguments between Plato and Aristotle about the value of public opinion continue today, although in a somewhat different form. One need only think about the arena of foreign affairs, where policymakers wonder whether the public knows enough to be consulted on complex issues—whether the United States should commit to an international peacekeeping effort or whether it should tie its foreign aid to human rights considerations.

SOURCES: Plato, *The Republic,* ed. and trans. Francis MacDonald Cornford (New York: Oxford University Press, 1956), quoted passage at p. 283; Aristotle, *The Politics,* ed. and trans. T. A. Sinclair (Baltimore: Penguin Books, 1962), quoted passage at p. 132.

The next set of philosophers to consider public opinion were the Romans, who like Plato were skeptical of the common people and their desires. Cicero, the great statesman and orator, claimed, *"Sic est vulgus: ex veritate pauce, ex opinione multa aestimat,"* which can be translated as "This is the common crowd: Judging few matters according to truth, many according to opinion." It was not the case that Romans dismissed public opinion completely. They simply believed that public opinion mattered most in the case of leadership. Were statesmen honored by the people? Were they popular? Much discussion of public opinion in Roman times was oriented around this narrow dimension of politics.[3]

Although it seems odd to leap across centuries, no further significant theorizing about public opinion occurred until Niccolò Machiavelli, the Italian statesman and writer, began to write at the start of the sixteenth century (see Figure 2.1). He is best known for his book on political strategy, written as an advisory tract for potential rulers. In *The Prince,* which is undoubtedly one of the most eloquent and persuasive manuals on political maneuvering ever written, Machiavelli illuminates the various dilemmas of the prince, discussing how a prince should act in public ("bear himself"), whether he needs to build fortresses, and whether it is better to be feared or loved by the people. One issue he discusses at great length is the nature of the people and what occupies them:

For of men it may generally be affirmed that they are thankless, fickle, false, studious to avoid danger, greedy of gain, devoted to you while you are able to confer benefits upon them, and ready, as I said before, while danger is distant, to shed their blood, and sacrifice their property, their lives, and their children for you; but in the hour of need they turn against you. . . . Men are so simple, and governed so absolutely by their present needs, that he who wishes to deceive will never fail in finding willing dupes.[4]

FIGURE 2.1
Niccolò Machiavelli,
Political Adviser and Author
of *The Prince*. (Courtesy of
the Library of Congress)

Here we see how closely early theorizing about public opinion and governance was tied to observations about human nature. Before the twentieth century, it was conventional for philosophers to speculate about the essence of human nature so that they could provide a holistic picture of man as political animal: If one understands the inherent desires of people, their behavior in politics can be explored more fully. Machiavelli believed that humans are so obsessed with their immediate desires and comforts that they cannot rule themselves: They must be governed by a benevolent dictator.

Machiavelli was respectful of public opinion but only because it was a political force that could bring harm to the prince and to the state, not because public opinion has inherent value. He was not an advocate for the wisdom of public opinion as Aristotle had been two millennia earlier. Unlike Aristotle, Machiavelli was not concerned with the harmony of the community or the moral state of the polity. It might seem tangential to bring Machiavelli up at all, since he is not considered a democratic theorist. Yet many of his insights reflect contemporary thoughts about the citizenry that are held by journalists, policymakers, and citizens alike— whether they choose to make negative remarks aloud or not.

Machiavelli is best described as a conflict theorist, one who believes that underlying even the most peaceful society are conflicting values, unfulfilled needs, and animosities. For Machiavelli, there was a fundamental conflict in society between ruler and ruled. These two parties are always suspicious of each other, although the prince always has the upper hand. Machiavelli warns leaders to underscore this fact to the public, yet appear to be acting with kindness and grace in the best interest of the people. To summarize: For Machiavelli, public opinion was volatile, irrational, and potentially explosive. Leaders must be vigilant by keeping a cautious eye on the public, making sure the people hold their statesmen in high regard.

Following Machiavelli in the seventeenth century were Thomas Hobbes and John Locke, two English philosophers who also had a great interest in the relationship between the people and the state. Hobbes, like Machiavelli, also had a negative view of human nature, believing that people live in constant competition as they vie for property, reputation, and personal safety. And it was Hobbes who wrote in his book *The Leviathan* that life is "solitary, poor, nasty, brutish, and short." Hobbes' works are interesting from our perspective because he is an early "contract theorist," believing that public opinion is crucial to the formation of the state. Machiavelli does not discuss the public's role in the creation of government because statesmen design society in his philosophical world. Yet for Hobbes, people do participate in politics in that they devise the fundamental rules that establish government. After the state is established, Hobbes sees very little need for political participation by citizens and supports the notion of a benevolent dictator. Yet he does make it clear that the structure of the state is created through a "contract" between the public and its leadership. If the state were to crumble—due to internal or external pressure—it would be the citizenry that again creates a new governmental system.

John Locke, a contemporary of Hobbes, shared his belief in the contract—the agreement among people and leaders about how their community is to be governed. Yet Locke is far more optimistic about human nature and about the possibilities for genuine and regular participation in politics by citizens. His theory of government was so eloquent and democratic that it greatly influenced our own Founding Fathers, who drew upon Lockean political theory in their plans for uniting the American colonies. Locke spent considerable energy arguing for his theory of inalienable natural rights that should be protected by the state. He was, like many philosophers of his day, somewhat skeptical of popular opinion, though he believed fiercely in the articulation of public opinion as a critical part of politics.

It is strange that the idea of public opinion was valued by Aristotle but not picked up again until Locke wrote in the 1600s. Yet democracy itself, as we understand it, has had a fairly short history, given the length of human existence. Even the ancient Greeks, who are said to have "invented" the idea of democracy, were not quite democrats in the contemporary sense: In ancient Greece, women, foreigners, and slaves had no voice in politics whatsoever.

PUBLIC OPINION IN THE AGE OF REVOLUTION

The eighteenth century was a time of immense change: It is the century of the French and American revolutions, and both were grounded in political philosophy. The most important discussions of democracy and public opinion occurred in Europe, although it is important to note that American statesmen like Thomas Jefferson and Benjamin Franklin spent considerable time in France and Great Britain, often participating in the great debates about politics of the age. Many contemporary scholars believe that modern American politics really owes a debt to the thinkers of the eighteenth century—particularly the French philosophes. This loose network of French intellectuals produced some of the most original and compelling tracts on public opinion of all time during the eve of the French Revolution. This is a period often referred to as the Enlightenment, since there was so much emphasis on the development of the human mind and spirit through science, the arts, and participation in political discourse.

Perhaps the most important work on public opinion was produced by Jean-Jacques Rousseau, a brilliant and unruly Enlightenment thinker who challenged a variety of social norms and existing theoretical paradigms. The young Rousseau, who appeared on the Parisian philosophical scene from a rather humble background, developed an elegant theory of the state with public opinion occupying a central role. Again, like philosophers before him, he was somewhat suspicious of the commoner. But more than any thinker to date, Rousseau saw the necessity of placing a fair amount of power in the hands of the public.

Like John Locke, Rousseau was concerned with the rights of individuals. Yet he also placed an enormous value on community and the need for people to respect and listen to each other. The state, Rousseau believed, was based on the general will—what citizens want when they think about the whole of the community. In other words, the general will is our most empathetic set of attitudes, or what we believe is the best course of action to promote the general welfare of the populace. Although Rousseau's discussion of the general will is somewhat complex and even confusing at times, he makes the argument that public opinion is both an aggregation of individual opinions and a more organic force rooted in shared values and attitudes. For Rousseau, then, citizens think about themselves and their needs but are also capable of thinking about the general good of society (see Box 2.3).

BOX 2.3   ROUSSEAU ON THE GENERAL WILL

Jean-Jacques Rousseau.
(Courtesy of the Library of Congress)

In his book *The Social Contract*, Jean-Jacques Rousseau explicated the notion of a "general will," a broad form of public opinion. He believed, unlike so many philosophers before him, that people were difficult to manipulate. People, Rousseau argued, are basically honest and expect honesty from others—including their leaders. In the following passage he discusses human nature and its relationship to the general will in a chapter entitled "That the General Will Is Indestructible":

So long as a number of men in combination are considered as a single body, they have but one will, which relates to the common preservation and to the general well-being. In such a case all the forces of the State are vigorous and simple, and its principles are clear and luminous; it has no confused and conflicting interests; the common good is everywhere plainly manifest and only good sense is required to perceive it. Peace, union, and equality are foes to political subtleties. Upright and simpleminded men are hard to deceive because of their simplicity; allurements and refined pretexts do not impose upon them; they are not even cunning enough to be dupes. When, in the happiest nation in the world, we see troops of peasants regulating the affairs of the State under an oak and always acting wisely, can we refrain from despising the refinements of other nations, who make themselves illustrious and wretched with so much art and mystery?

Perhaps the most difficult line for us to understand is the one about how easy it is to discern the common good. Even with all of our modern techniques for measuring public attitudes, it is still tremendously difficult to state the public interest in any definitive fashion.

SOURCE: Jean-Jacques Rousseau, *The Social Contract and the Discourse on the Origin of Inequality,* ed. Lester G. Croker (New York: Washington Square Press, 1967), quoted passage at p. 109.

We should not leave the era of the French Revolution without mentioning the finance minister to Louis XVI, a man named Jacques Necker, believed by many to have popularized the phrase "public opinion." Necker recognized that political discourse and the nature of politics had shifted quite dramatically in the eighteenth century. For the first time, a bourgeoisie had emerged to gather and discuss politics through interpersonal dialogue and through the press. At the time, public opinion meant the opinion of the middle classes. Even in a monarchy, Necker recognized just how much of the institutional structure of the state rested on the benevolence of public opinion. He noted that most foreigners "have difficulty in forming a just idea of the authority exercised in France by public opinion; they have difficulty in understanding the nature of an invisible power which, without treasures, without a bodyguard, and without an army gives laws to the city, to the court, and even to the palaces of kings."[5]

In the nineteenth century, a variety of political philosophers tackled the difficult questions surrounding the nature of public opinion. Among that group were the English scholars known as the Utilitarians. Jeremy Bentham was the first of the Utilitarians to write extensively about public opinion, and he was most interested in how public opinion acts as a sanction. In other words, he believed that public opinion is a force that keeps society at equilibrium by preventing people from engaging in non-normative behavior. People are afraid of public opinion, so they dare not step outside the bounds of what is "acceptable" to most people. This may seem a dim view of human society, but Bentham and other Utilitarians were most concerned about maximizing happiness among the populace through the maintenance of social harmony. Bentham and John Stuart Mill, another in this British philosophical circle, were believers in democracy but emphasized the importance of majority opinion. In fact, they thought that laws are only needed where the "law of opinion" is not working effectively.

Similar views of public opinion as a force of social control were held by Alexis de Tocqueville, the French observer of nineteenth-century American politics. In his landmark study *Democracy in America*, still cited as one of the most important books in political theory, Tocqueville had this to say about the way that public opinion affects writers and artists:

> In America the majority has enclosed throughout within a formidable fence. A writer is free inside that area, but woe to the man who goes beyond it. Not that he stands in fear of an auto-da-fé [burning at the stake, a style of public sentencing from the Inquisition], but he must face all kinds of unpleasantness and everyday persecution. A career in politics is closed to him, for he has offended the only power that holds the keys. He is denied everything, including renown. Before he goes into print, he believes he has supporters; but he feels that he has them no more once he stands revealed to all, for those who condemn him express their views loudly, while those who think as he does, but without his courage, retreat into silence as if ashamed of having told the truth.[6]

It was also in *Democracy in America* that Tocqueville made his famous argument about political equality and its relationship to mass opinion. He noted that in societies where there is much inequality—in an aristocracy, for example—public opinion is not viewed as particularly important. This is because people of impoverished circumstances recognize that others are better educated and more worldly than they are and therefore have more informed opinions. Yet as citizens achieve greater and greater equality, they see that they are just as capable as their friends, coworkers, and neighbors. In these settings, people become interested in numbers:

> The nearer men are to a common level of uniformity, the less they are inclined to believe blindly in any man or any class. But they are readier to trust the mass, and public opinion becomes more and more mistress of the world. . . . In times of equality men, being so like each other, have no confidence in others, but this same likeness leads them to place almost unlimited confidence in the judgment of the public. For they think it not unreasonable that, all having the same means of knowledge, truth will be found on the side of the majority.[7]

This insight is particularly relevant in an age of mass communication where it is possible for all people to gather large amounts of information about the public affairs upon which they may base their opinions. Although not all Americans are equal in terms of education and income, it is the case that most have televisions and can watch the nightly network news. We have a sense that our opinions are just as valuable as anyone else's, so we have a tendency to value majorities.

It is interesting that while Tocqueville was writing about American politics, Karl Marx was also thinking and writing about political and social life from an entirely different standpoint (see Figure 2.2). In Tocqueville, on the one hand, we see a celebration of some aspects of democracy and deep concerns about others. In Marx, on the other hand, we see a man who was completely dissatisfied with the status quo and believed that democracy (like other forms of government) was subject to corruption by the forces of capitalism. This opinion is still very much alive in academic writing among scholars who note that democracy and capitalism are intricately intertwined but that democratic ideals have been crushed by consumer culture. The argument is complex, but simple examples of this conflation between democracy and capitalism abound. Neo-Marxists of the contemporary period cite examples of how Americans (and citizens of still-new Eastern European democracies) tend to think of freedom as consumer choice—the right to choose among a variety of products and lifestyles. Yet when it comes to serious engagement in freedom of speech—public debate about controversial issues—citizens

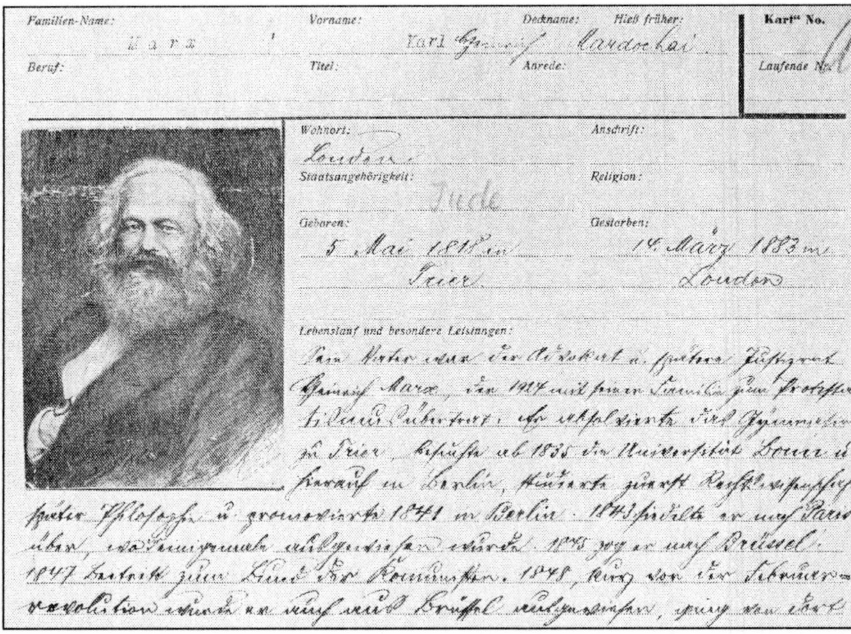

FIGURE 2.2   Karl Marx's Identity Card. Marx wrote about public opinion, although he used the language of class oppression to discuss formation of public attitudes. (Courtesy of the Library of Congress)

are less concerned. The fact that in 1995 Congress seriously debated a constitutional amendment to ban flag burning (a quintessential free speech right), without much public participation in this debate, might be used as an example of how little Americans value free speech.

This is not the proper place for a discussion of Marxian thought about politics, but it is important to mention at least one of Marx's basic insights about public opinion. Marx did not often use the phrase "public opinion," in part because the phrase was not commonly used in German philosophical thought until later in the century. Yet he and Friedrich Engels, his collaborator and patron, did argue strongly that organic, grassroots public opinion is hard to come by. In *The German Ideology,* for example, Marx and Engels noted that common citizens tend to mimic the opinions of those in the ruling class—people with great wealth and power. In fact, these philosophers believed that people accept as common wisdom the attitudes and values of the ruling elite—even though these attitudes are often not in their best self-interest. As a result, Marx and Engels argue, the working class does not wield much political power: It is unable to realize its interests because its members have come to believe that the ruling class knows what is best. This process, in which the ideas of an elite class become widely held, is often called hegemony in the academic literature. Marx and Engels made the initial statement about this phenomenon, although since 1846 much more has been written on the subject:

> The ideas of the ruling class are in every epoch the ruling ideas, i.e. the class which is the ruling material force in society, is at the same time its ruling intellectual force. . . . For each new class which puts itself in the place of one ruling before it, is compelled, merely in order to carry through its aim, to represent its interest as the common interest of all the members of society, that is, expressed in ideal form: it has to give its ideas the form of universality, and represent them as the only rational, universally valid ones.[8]

THEORY ABOUT PUBLIC OPINION: THE LATE NINETEENTH AND EARLY TWENTIETH CENTURIES

Late in the nineteenth century a British statesman named James Bryce visited the United States, traveling widely and observing the political scene. Bryce devoted large chapters in his two-volume masterwork *The American Commonwealth* to examining public opinion, in an attempt to understand how the concept fit into the constellation of American institutions. Bryce was interested in how the expression and measurement of public opinion were related to party activity, to legislatures, and to the mass media (newspapers, during this period). He is often cited as the first "modern" theorist of public opinion because his work was so sociological and empirical: Instead of speculating on the grand nature of public opinion, he looked for its manifestations in political culture. In fact, a criticism of Bryce is that he was far too empirical and that he might have spent more time developing a philosophical or social-psychological basis for his observations.

Regardless of the academic debate about Bryce's emphasis, one thing is clear: Bryce understood—as no one before him really did—the very critical role of newspapers in the communication of public opinion. Tocqueville certainly recognized the value of newspapers, but Bryce explicated their role in far more detail. Bryce believed that the mass media were incredibly powerful in fin de siècle America and should hold a place among our other institutions (Congress, the courts) as a molder of public opinion. He noted in 1891, during an age when newspapers were far more obviously partisan than they are today: "It is chiefly in its . . . capacity as an index and mirror of public opinion that the press is looked to. This is the function it chiefly aims at discharging; and public men feel that in showing deference to it they are propitiating, and inviting the commands of, public opinion itself. In worshipping the deity you learn to conciliate the priest."[9]

For Bryce, newspapers both reflect and direct public opinion, so the place of this medium in the political process is crucial. Bryce's work has a contemporary ring to it, and his belief in the importance of media is now commonplace. The fact that journalists now value objectivity as a goal far more than they did in the late nineteenth century means that the role of newspapers as advocates has changed slightly, but they are still powerful movers of public opinion. Newspapers endorse candidates at election time and, more important, value investigative reporting that can greatly change the course of public policy.[10]

Bryce also recognized that the American newspaper contained multiple forms of public opinion, not only news stories and editorials but letters from citizens as well. Letters to the editor had long been overlooked by theorists as a source of public opinion data, but Bryce underscored their role in the communication of popular sentiment. Near the end of his discussion of newspapers, however, Bryce makes it clear that no one— politicians included—can depend entirely on newspapers to gain a comprehensive view of public opinion. As he noted:

> Every prudent man keeps a circle of [four or five discerning friends of different types of thought] . . . by whom he can test and correct his own impressions better than by the almost official utterances of the party journals [newspapers]. So in America there is much to be learnt—even a stranger can perceive it—from conversation with judicious observers outside politics and typical representatives of political sections and social classes, which the most diligent study of the press will not give.[11]

One theorist of public affairs who had even more to say on the relationship between newspapers and interpersonal discussion was a French sociologist named Gabriel Tarde, who wrote about public opinion in the early decades of the twentieth century. He noted in his essay "Opinion and Conversation" that "conversation at all times, and the press, which at present is the principal source of conversation, are the major factors in opinion."[12] In fact, Tarde presented a unidirectional model of opinion formation that can be depicted graphically (see Box 2.4).

BOX 2.4   GABRIEL TARDE'S MODEL OF PUBLIC OPINION

Media ⟶ Conversation ⟶ Opinion ⟶ Action

This is one model to use when thinking about the relationship of newspapers to political action. Gabriel Tarde firmly believed that newspapers are a national springboard for political discussion. Conversation about politics, in turn, enables people to clarify their opinions about various political and social policies so that they can act accordingly by voting, volunteering for a campaign, attending a demonstration, and the like.

One might take issue with both the order of elements in this illustration and the linear nature of the model. For example, is it possible that conversation and discussion cause journalists to write particular articles? If that is the case, we need to put some sort of conversational variable in this equation *before* the element "media." And in terms of directionality, we might question whether exposure to the media commonly leads to political action. Some researchers have argued that media are more likely to debilitate or dissuade us from political action than they are to prompt us toward political participation.[1]

NOTE

1. There is growing interest in Tarde, thanks in large part to Elihu Katz. See Elihu Katz, "Press–Conversation–Opinion–Action: Gabriel Tarde's Public Sphere," Annenberg School for Communication at the University of Pennsylvania, 1997. On the question of whether media dissuade or encourage political activity, the classic discussion can be found in Paul Lazarsfeld and Robert Merton's "Mass Communication, Popular Taste and Organized Social Action," in Lyman Bryson, ed., *The Communication of Ideas* (New York: Harper and Brothers, 1948). The diagram above is Katz's interpretation of Tarde.

   After Tarde wrote, a variety of other political theorists tackled the fundamental questions about public opinion—what its meaning is, how it operates, and what its relationship to political institutions and culture is. And more recent twentieth-century discussions of public opinion, particularly those based on empirical research, are covered in some of the other chapters to come. Yet it might be instructive to end this particular section on public opinion theory with discussion of an important (although largely overlooked) scholarly event that took place in 1924.

As you can see from the vast historical territory covered in this chapter, by the early twentieth century a wide range of intellectuals had focused on the nature of public opinion. In fact, there were so many diverse perspectives on the nature and content of public opinion that political scientists became overwhelmed by the larger philosophical issues. Therefore, in 1924, a group of prominent scholars met at their yearly convention to conduct a roundtable discussion on the measurement of public opinion. After much argument, the researcher who wrote up the results of the roundtable noted:

> After some discussion of these points [about the nature of public opinion], it was agreed that an exact definition of public opinion might not be needed until after the technical problem of measuring the opinions of the individual members of the public had been disposed of. It was decided therefore that the round table might well proceed to consider the problem of measuring opinion, especially that related to political matters, *and avoid the use of the term public opinion if possible.* (our emphasis)[13]

In this book, we take just the opposite approach to understanding public opinion: By bringing together the most fundamental insights about public opinion from our greatest philosophers and illuminating the complexity of the topic, we hope to underscore that public opinion is a contested concept but still a rich and valuable one. Students need not avoid the term "public opinion" but instead can use it as a gateway for understanding the challenges of democratic theory and practice.

THE SOCIAL HISTORY OF PUBLIC OPINION: EXPRESSION AND MEASUREMENT

Intellectual histories of public opinion such as the brief one provided here are crucial if you are to understand the philosophical development of the concept in political theory. Yet the social history of public opinion—how popular sentiment has been communicated and measured over time—is equally important and interesting. When we explore how public opinion has been expressed and assessed in previous eras, we gain much insight into the advantages and disadvantages of our own techniques for communicating popular attitudes.

In this section, we often refer to methods of public opinion communication as technologies of public opinion. By this, we mean that citizens and leaders alike use a variety of tools to both express opinions and evaluate them. In contemporary American politics, the public opinion poll or survey is one of the premier technologies for opinion expression and measurement. And one could argue that the newspaper is still an important organ for the communication of popular sentiment, just as it was during the years when Alexis de Tocqueville and Lord Bryce traveled America in hopes of understanding the nature of democracy.

Interestingly, the tools that we use to express public opinion can also be considered tools for measuring public opinion. Let us take demonstrations as an example. When thousands of people gather in Washington, D.C., to protest a government policy or to demonstrate that a large number of Americans share a particular cause, identity, or political agenda, the marchers are expressing their opinions. At the same time, however, others are measuring those opinions. Journalists and policymakers alike can assess the size of the crowd as well as the rhetoric of the speeches and the intensity of feeling among rally attendants. Thus, the political demonstration, as a technology of public opinion, enables both the expression and the evaluation of public feeling.

Here we discuss some of the more important technologies that humans throughout the centuries have employed to communicate their attitudes about public affairs. Before we take up this list of techniques, however, it might be instructive to underscore the grand trends in technological innovation over time. There are three forces that have altered the nature of public opinion technologies through the ages:

1. An increasing emphasis on order and routinization.
2. Movement toward private and anonymous means for communication opinion.
3. A shift from local to national and even global opinion expression and assessment.

We shall see as we advance through periods in the history of public expression that our techniques for communicating attitudes have become increasingly standardized and routinized. In other words, we have developed more rigorous schemes for quantifying and aggregating public opinion so that it can be more easily understood. Furthermore, in capitalist societies, public opinion data are a valuable commodity, so it is important to develop standard methods of opinion measurement that are valued by consumers, be they citizens, legislators, or newspapers. Random sampling techniques that enable a researcher to poll a small number of citizens and then generalize to all Americans are a relatively new set of tools developed in the mid-twentieth century. The representative public opinion poll uses a much more standardized methodology than other technologies (such as counting the crowd members at a demonstration). This is not to say that opinion polls are somehow better than other nonquantitative techniques of the past or present. All methods of communicating public opinion have their positive and negative aspects, as we shall see during this discussion.

That opinion expression has become increasingly private is closely connected with the development of two opinion technologies in the nineteenth and twentieth centuries. These periods saw the emergence of secret balloting during elections and the rise of the straw poll (which evolved into the sample survey of today). Before the widespread diffusion of the secret ballot and the confidential poll—methods where one's identity remains anonymous—technologies of public opinion demanded that citizens either sign their name or show their faces: One had to sign a petition, for example, or appear at a political demonstration. There is no protection of a citizen's identity in these cases.[14]

Another important trend in the history of techniques people have used to express and measure public opinion is the increasing emphasis on national—as opposed to local—opinion. The scholar to write most eloquently about this shift is historian Charles Tilly, who argues that expressions of opinion were largely local before the mid-nineteenth century. He notes:

> Broadly speaking, the repertoire [of opinion techniques] of the seventeenth to nineteenth centuries held to a *parochial* scope: It addressed local

actors or the local representatives of national actors. It also relied heavily on *patronage*—appealing to immediately available power holders to convey grievances or settle disputes. . . . The repertoire that crystallized in the nineteenth century and prevails today is, in general, more *national* in scope: Although available for local issues and enemies, it lends itself easily to co-ordination among many localities. As compared with the older repertoire, its actions are relatively *autonomous*: instead of staying in the shadow of ex-isting power holders and adapting routines sanctioned by those power holders, users of the new repertoire tend to initiate their own statements of grievances and demands. Strikes, demonstrations, electoral rallies, and similar actions build, in general, on much more deliberately constructed organization than used to be the case. (emphasis in original)[15]

This shift from local expression of opinion to national expression of opinion was made possible, in part, by the development of mass media—the newspaper in particular. Yet other factors played a role as well: the ac-celerated importance of the nation-state as global actor, improvements in transportation infrastructure (roads, trains, and so on), and the expansion of the size of the federal government.

PRE-NINETEENTH-CENTURY OPINION COMMUNICATION TECHNIQUES

The number and variety of methods people have used to communicate and assess public opinion over time are extraordinarily large. Here we dis-cuss some of the major techniques, those that scholars of public opinion history have focused on most closely. It is best to divide up the technolo-gies into two periods, those used before the nineteenth century and those employed beginning in the early 1800s. The reason is that the nineteenth century is something of a turning point in the history of public opinion: Before the nineteenth century, technologies were less systematic, more public, and more local. After 1800, strategies for communicating public opinion became far more routinized, tended to focus on private expres-sion of opinion, and were much more national in scope.

One of the earliest techniques for opinion communication was rhetoric, the art of public speaking and persuasion. Oratory and rhetoric were employed by a variety of citizens and leaders of the ancient Greek city-states of the fifth century B.C. in order to argue for policy in those young democracies. As Wilhelm Bauer, the great German historian of public opinion, put it, citizens assembled in the marketplaces of ancient Greece, where "oratory rapidly developed as the technique best suited to the manipulation of public opinion and continued throughout later Greek and Roman times as the most powerful instrument of political propaganda and agitation."[16] Obviously, rhetoric is still used extensively today, as presidents, members of Congress, interest group leaders, and ordinary citizens try to persuade each other about policy in a variety of areas—in health care, labor relations, education, and economics, among others. The ancient Greek philosophers, Aristotle and Plato included, spent an enormous amount of time thinking about the art of oratory, since democracy revolves around political communication and the expression of ideas and values. Citizens of ancient Greece and Rome were sophisticated consumers of oratory, as so many scholars have noted. Kathleen Hall Jamieson, a contemporary scholar of rhetoric, writes:

> Ancient oratory was considered a fine art, an art regarded by its cultivators, and by the public, as analogous to sculpture, to poetry, to painting, to music and to acting. This character is common to Greek and Roman oratory. So, for example, Isocrates [a Greek orator] notes that listeners broke into loud applause when antitheses, symmetrical clauses, or other striking rhetorical figures were skillfully presented. . . . When the world of entertainment, persuasion and politics was in the main an oral one, listeners were drawn together in large numbers to experience a piece of communication.[17]

In ancient times, rhetoric occurred in unmediated forums. Speakers addressed crowds in arenas and marketplaces, at festivals and public meetings of all sorts. Such direct address still occurs today, as when legislators speak from the floor or when political candidates give speeches to gathered supporters. Yet these days, much of the public speaking in political life is mediated by television, and that technology has changed the nature of rhetoric itself (see Box 2.5).

BOX 2.5   EFFEMINATE VERSUS MANLY RHETORIC

Margaret Thatcher. (Photo courtesy of the Margaret Thatcher Foundation, © Terence Donovan)

In her book on the history of speech-making, Kathleen Hall Jamieson includes a section on the problematics of women's speech. She notes first that "womanly discourse" has traditionally been described as "shrill" and without merit:

For centuries, their opponents argued that women's fundamental irrationality and congenital emotionalism should disqualify them from public speaking and public office. The high pitch of the woman's voice was seen as symptomatic not of physiological differences in the vocal mechanism but of excessive emotionalism. . . . Noting that shrillness characterized the voices of eunuchs, women, and invalids, [the Roman rhetorician] Quintilian recommended that men increase the robustness of their voices by abstaining from sexual intercourse. Later theorists were equally concerned that men not sound womanish. "Some have a womanish squeaking Tone," wrote John Mason in *An Essay on Elocution and Pronunciation* (1748), "which, Persons whose Voices are shrill and weak, and overtrained, are very apt to fall into." . . . Eager to mute the inference that their voices signaled irrational or emotional natures, female politicians, Margaret Thatcher [former prime minister of Great Britain] among them, have sought voice retraining. Under the supervision of a tutor from the National Theatre, Mrs. Thatcher lowered the natural pitch at which she spoke in public.

Yet Jamieson also points out that the "feminine" rhetorical style so thoroughly disdained throughout history can be very effective in the age of television. She argues that President Ronald Reagan's success (he was often called "the great communicator" in the press) was due in part to his employment of a traditionally female rhetorical style—one based on self-disclosure and emotional display. About oratory over the airwaves, Jamieson writes:

> Television invites a personal, self-disclosing style that draws public discourse out of a private self and comfortably reduces the complex world to dramatic narratives. Because it encompasses these characteristics, the once spurned womanly style is now the style of preference. The same characteristics comprise a mode of discourse well suited to television and much needed in times of social stress or in the aftermath of divisive events. By revivifying social values and ennobling the shared past, epideictic or ceremonial discourse helps sustain the state.

SOURCE: Kathleen Hall Jamieson, *Eloquence in an Electronic Age: The Transformation of Political Speechmaking* (New York: Oxford University Press, 1988), quoted passages from pp. 78–79, 84.

Rhetoric is by far the oldest of all public opinion communication technologies, and there is quite a large gap in the history of public opinion between the development of the art of public speaking and the next major technique: the invention of the printing press (see Figure 2.3). Introduced in the sixteenth century, the printing press enabled the formation of modern publics. In other words, the publication of newspapers, books, and pamphlets made it possible for large numbers of dispersed people to communicate with each other. Before printing, one could communicate only with neighbors and those one met during travel (which was uncommon among ordinary citizens). With the introduction of printed materials about public affairs, however, people could ally themselves with causes, ideas, and organizations. The invention of printing was revolutionary in many respects, but its importance to public opinion expression cannot be overestimated. Thomas Jefferson once said about newspapers in a letter to a friend, "Were it left to me to decide whether we should have a government without newspapers, or newspapers without a government, I should not hesitate a moment to prefer the latter."[18] Tocqueville

FIGURE 2.3   "A True Representation of a Printing House with the Men at Work." The printing press enabled the development of modern "publics"— geographically dispersed people who shared the same interests or points of view. Depicted in this engraving is a 1752 printing house. SOURCE: John M. Lewis, *Anatomy of Printing: The Influences of Art and History on Its Design* (New York: Watson Guptill Publications, 1970).

and Bryce noted the importance of newspapers in nineteenth-century America, but their influence began much earlier in the European monarchies of the seventeenth and eighteenth centuries.

Printing made possible the mass distribution of knowledge itself. Common citizens, especially those in rural areas, could get access to ideas about politics, religion, and the arts. And the fact that so many inexpensive pamphlets, newspapers, and books were in circulation boosted the literacy rates in European nations. The explosion of printed materials was not accompanied by freedom of the press, of course, since monarchs could and did shut down newspapers when such publications threatened their rule. Indeed, there are multiple historical cases of printers being tortured and executed for publishing newspapers that criticized the state.

FIGURE 2.4   Lloyd's Coffeehouse in London, 1798. Coffeehouses and taverns served
as forums for political debate in the seventeenth and eighteenth centuries. Such sites
exist today, although during this earlier period people went to coffeehouses for the
express purpose of learning about—and talking about—public affairs. SOURCE: Heinrich
Eduard Jacob, *Coffee: The Epic of a Commodity* (New York: Penguin Books, 1935).

Interestingly, printing enabled the mobilization of groups for political
causes, the suppression of others, and served as a catalyst for the development of other public opinion communication techniques. The newspapers themselves carried opinions and letters to the editor, but they also
served as a starting point for discussion among citizens. In the seventeenth and eighteenth centuries, for example, newspapers and books were
vital to the evolution of two important opinion technologies: the coffeehouse and the salon.

Coffeehouses were popular places in England during the centuries following the introduction of printing (see Figure 2.4). Admission to these
forums was cheap, and one could spend hours in coffeehouses reading
newspapers and political tracts and arguing about ideas with other pa-
trons. Eighteenth-century descriptions of coffeehouses noted that the mix
of individuals in attendance varied greatly, with judges, journalists, and
lawyers sharing tables with tradesmen, workers, and even the occasional

thief or pickpocket. Perhaps the sociologist Lewis Coser best describes the importance of the coffeehouses as a technology of public opinion:

> A common opinion cannot be developed before people have an occasion to discuss with one another, before they have been drawn from the isolation of lonely thought into a public world in which individual opinion can be sharpened and tested in discussion with others. The coffeehouse helped to crystallize a common opinion from a multitude of individual opinions and to give it form and stability. What the newspaper had not yet been able to accomplish was achieved to a large degree by the coffeehouse.[19]

During the period in which coffeehouses were established, another forum for discussion and debate about public affairs became popular in France. Salons—gatherings of intellectuals, statesmen, and artists—were extraordinarily important to the development of political discourse in seventeenth- and eighteenth-century France. Salons were in many ways less "democratic" than coffeehouses, which were open to all for a small entrance fee. The salons were run with an iron hand by bourgeois women who decided who should be invited and what topics should be discussed. Much has been written about the exclusivity of the salons, but the effects of the conversations within these gatherings were tremendous. It was in the salons of ancien régime Paris that Rousseau developed the ideas for his *Social Contract,* an essay often cited as laying the philosophical groundwork for the French Revolution. Many writers and artists fine-tuned their ideas in the salons before they wrote books for mass distribution. But salons, like all public opinion technologies, were also technologies for public opinion measurement. There is substantial evidence that kings and their courtiers visited the salons on a regular basis in order to gather "data" about public opinion. These data reflected only a small, elite sampling of French opinion, yet since the ideas generated in salons were destined for diffusion throughout France and the world, such information was extraordinarily valuable to those interested in public opinion.[20]

Perhaps this is a good moment to reflect on one of the troubling issues in the field of public opinion raised in Chapter One: Who is a member of the public is always shifting, depending upon historical context and the agendas of those measuring public opinion. In terms of developing economic policy in the eighteenth century, for example, it was not as impor-

tant to the king of France to gather public opinion from the French countryside as it was to monitor the way influential bankers and businessmen
talked in the salons. This may seem to be a very elitist way of thinking
about the public and public opinion (i.e., public opinion is the discourse
of rather exclusive salon meetings), yet it is the most accurate meaning of
public opinion for that particular period. We mentioned in Chapter One
that the meaning of public opinion is contested in contemporary American politics, and the same was true in Europe and England in the seventeenth and eighteenth centuries. Some believed public opinion to be the
exclusive banter of the salons, whereas others argued that the discourse of
the more egalitarian coffeehouse was more representative and therefore
more meaningful as an indicator of public opinion.

The seventeenth and eighteenth centuries also witnessed the evolution
of other interesting techniques for communication of public opinion.
Two closely related ones are the petition and the public rally. Beginning
as early as 1640, citizens of England petitioned Parliament about a number of public affairs, from taxes and monopolies to social issues and peace.
Petitions were a very effective means of focusing legislators' attentions on
topics of importance to common folk. Petitions were presented peaceably
at times, but very often an angry mob delivered its petition to Parliament
in person. In a colorful description of violent petitioning during the first
English civil war (1642–1646), a British writer noted how women—who
were often the leaders in petitioning for peace—presented their demands.
The women, he said,

> kepte knockinge and beatinge of the outwarde dore before the parliament
> house, and would have violently forced the same open, and required Mr
> Pym, Mr Strode, and some other members . . . and threatened to take the
> rounde heades of the parliament whome they saide they would caste into
> the Thames [River].. . . These women were not any whit scared or
> ashamed of their incivilities, but cryed out so much the more, even at the
> doore of the house of Commons, Give us these Traytors that are against
> peace, that we may teare them in pieces, Give us Pym.[21]

Not all petitioners were angry mobs, but so much violence accompanied
the presentation of petitions to Parliament that in 1648, legislators passed
a bill against unruly petitioning. This was ineffective, so Parliament then

limited the number of people who could present a petition to twenty. Even this did not deter violence in conjunction with petitioning, so in 1699, all petitioners were required to give their petition to their representative in advance of parliamentary debate so that he could present it for them.

This series of incidents in British history could be interpreted in several ways. One might argue that the petitioners were too unruly to engage in the sort of rational political dialogue necessary for the construction of public policy. Alternately, we can read this as an attempt by Parliament to squash the intensity of public opinion by erasing the emotion underpinning the demands of petitions. Historians' interpretations of these events, as well as other acts of citizens during the English civil wars, are interesting and varied.[22]

Why add rioting and demonstrations to our list of opinion technologies, since the process of people gathering together to express their desires might be seen as a fundamental human activity? Although crowds gathered in the ancient city-states of Greece and throughout the ages, rioting escalated as a form of public opinion expression in seventeenth-century England. Most of these "popular disturbances" (as they were called at the time) centered on economics: Rioters protested fiscal policies of the Parliament as well as the food shortages and food price hikes resulting from those policies. In a 1938 book, British scholar Max Beloff reports on his archival research concerning the food riots of the late seventeenth and early eighteenth centuries. In late-twentieth-century America, we are not accustomed to food rioting, but such demonstrations were common during this period. Beloff writes of 1708:

> The steepness of the rise in [grain] prices was indeed sharper in these years than at any other time in the period under discussion. . . . The populace was not slow to react. In May of 1709 it was reported from Essex that mobs of women amounting to hundreds were on the move and had threatened to 'fire divers houses, and shoot several persons, by reason they have been dealers in corn to London, on pretense they make the same dear.'[23]

Rioting is one of the most obviously public of public opinion technologies: Although one can often get "lost in a crowd," those involved in riots expect to be recognized and heard. In contemporary American politics, we often witness demonstrations, strikes, and marches. Yet the intensity of these gatherings pales in comparison to the series of violent protests over government economic policy in seventeenth- and eighteenth-century England.

The next important opinion technology worthy of mention in this brief historical overview is the general election. There is evidence that elections were used in the early Greek democracies, although participation was limited only to male citizens, so they are not considered "general" in any contemporary sense.

Elections are interesting from the standpoint of public opinion history because they represent a turning point in public expression itself. Until the emergence of the secret ballot—generally used in democratic elections—opinion expression was public and attributed. One could not cast a vote anonymously and therefore had to take a certain amount of responsibility in one's local community for holding a particular opinion. With the diffusion of the general election, the anonymous communication of beliefs became possible on a large scale. Although not all were allowed to vote (e.g., slaves and women), general elections for the presidency in America began in the early nineteenth century. It is not surprising that straw polling emerged shortly thereafter.

Straw polling is "nonscientific" polling conducted with pen and paper, over the telephone, or by less formal means (e.g., a "show of hands"). In the early nineteenth century, journalists, party operatives, and citizens would poll people in their communities about upcoming elections. Major newspapers, like the *New York Times* and the *Chicago Tribune,* would publish polls from their reporters who were often traveling around the country covering political rallies and speeches. Many journalists conducted straw polls on long train or boat rides in order to get a sense of public opinion in the local community. Although straw polls are still conducted today (e.g., "call-in polls" on radio or television stations), most serious polling after 1936 utilized the sample survey or scientific poll.

Were these straw polls accurate? Probably not, but it is difficult to tell from our vantage point in the early twenty-first century. Claude Robinson, a professor at Columbia University, conducted an analysis of straw polling in 1932 and found much variance. Straw polls conducted in person tended to be more accurate than the sort that asked readers to cut a ballot from the newspaper and mail it back. Yet even the in-person interview did not always yield accurate forecasts of upcoming elections.[24]

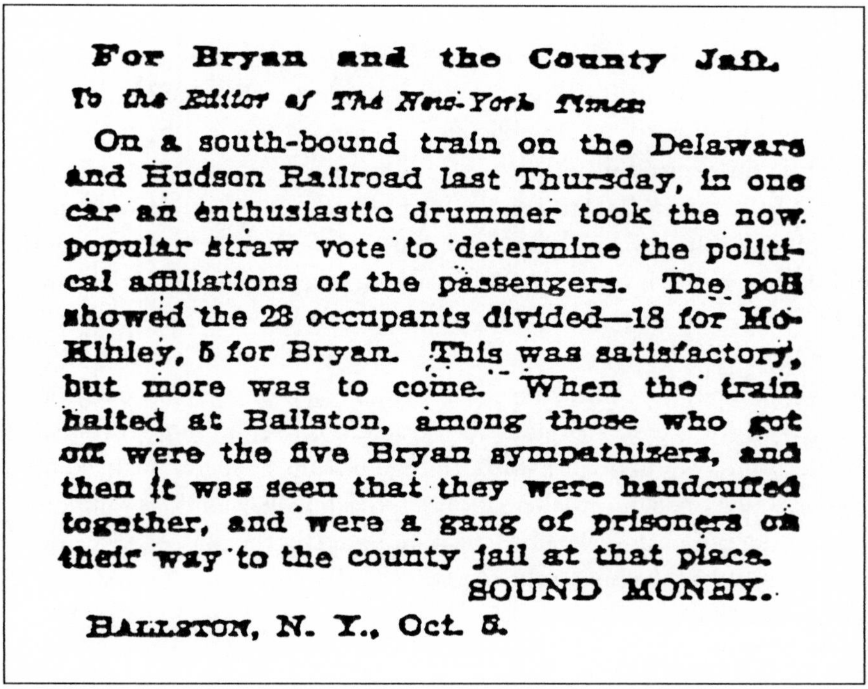

For Bryan and the County Jail.

To the Editor of The New-York Times:

On a south-bound train on the Delaware
and Hudson Railroad last Thursday, in one
car an enthusiastic drummer took the now
popular straw vote to determine the political affiliations of the passengers. The poll
showed the 23 occupants divided—18 for Mc-
Kinley, 5 for Bryan. This was satisfactory,
but more was to come. When the train
halted at Ballston, among those who got
off were the five Bryan sympathizers, and
then it was seen that they were handcuffed
together, and were a gang of prisoners on
their way to the county jail at that place.

SOUND MONEY.

BALLSTON, N. Y., Oct. 5.

FIGURE 2.5 In the nineteenth century, citizens would often poll their friends,
neighbors, and coworkers about upcoming presidential races. Often, businessmen who
were traveling around their own region would poll strangers in train cars and on
steamers. This humorous poll, sent to the *New York Times* in 1896 during the contest
between McKinley and Bryan, comes from a McKinley supporter who watched one of
his fellow passengers poll the riders on a New York train.

We believe that the accuracy of these straw polls is the least interesting
aspect of the phenomenon. Straw polls were important in the nineteenth
and early twentieth centuries because they were a vehicle for getting citizens involved in politics. First, straw polls made elections seem like
"horse races." On the surface this may sound like a negative assessment,
but it can be argued that news articles emphasizing the contest—who is
ahead and who trails—get voters excited about an upcoming election.
Second, people often conducted their own straw polls (see Figure 2.5) instead of waiting for journalists to poll them or their neighbors. This is another way that straw voting, as a formal political endeavor, increased citizen involvement. Finally, there is historical evidence that straw polling

was accompanied by political discussion: When people were polled, it usually followed or preceded a debate about the issues and the campaign. Thus, straw polling prompted people to engage their neighbors and coworkers in discussions of public affairs. Do today's scientific polls serve the same function of inspiring public discourse? It is a difficult question to answer but an important one for students of public opinion to ponder.

Opinion polling was so popular and useful throughout the nineteenth and early twentieth centuries that marketing researchers, political analysts, academics, and statisticians all worked intensely on developing a more accurate and rigorous way of assessing public opinion. In 1936, a year when a popular magazine called the *Literary Digest* mistakenly predicted that Alf Landon would defeat Franklin Roosevelt in the presidential election, a young man named George Gallup predicted just the opposite. Gallup, using a mathematical approach called random sampling, did not determine the election outcome perfectly (he was off by 7 percentage points), but his method was far better than the *Digest*'s or any other straw poll (see Box 2.6).

BOX 2.6   GEORGE GALLUP ON POLLING IN A DEMOCRACY

George Gallup, an early pollster who did much to popularize the opinion survey. (Photo courtesy of the Gallup Organization)

George Gallup's success as a pollster was primarily due to his early use of random sampling. His pioneering methodological spirit was only part of the reason for his success: He had an almost religious belief that polling could strengthen democracy in America and beyond. In 1940, he and Saul Rae wrote:

The kind of public opinion implied in the democratic ideal is tangible and dynamic. It springs from many sources deep in the day-to-day experience of individuals who constitute the political public, and who formulate these opinions as working guides for their political representatives. This public opinion listens to many propagandas, most of them contradictory. It tries in the clash and conflict of argument and debate to separate the true from the false. It needs criticism for its very existence, and through criticism it is constantly being modified and molded. It acts and learns by action. Its truths are relative and contingent upon the results which its action achieves. Its chief faith is a faith in experiment. It believes in the value of every individual's contribution to political life, and in the right of ordinary human beings to have a voice in deciding their fate. Public opinion, in this sense, is the pulse of democracy.

SOURCE: George Gallup and Saul Forbes Rae, *The Pulse of Democracy: The Public-Opinion Poll and How It Works* (New York: Simon and Schuster, 1940), quoted passage at p. 8.

The key to Gallup's success was sampling theory, which dictates that one use methods of random selection to choose respondents for a poll. If one carefully chooses members of a sample using this method and response rates are reasonably high, the sample should "simulate" the opinions of the population at large. The *Literary Digest* did not use sampling methods; it simply relied upon various lists of citizens (gathered from phone directories and auto registration records) and sent out millions of ballots, asking citizens to mark their preference for the upcoming election. From 1916 through 1936, the *Digest* used this method. After Gallup embarrassed the *Digest* by predicting the election more accurately than it had, the *Digest* issued a public apology and eventually shut down operations.

Our history of public opinion stops here because the introduction of representative sampling was the last revolutionary change in how we think about and measure public opinion. Petitions, rioting, and demonstrations are still influential means of expressing and assessing public opinion, but scientific polling is now the preeminent tool for communicating opinion. Since Gallup's earliest polls, a variety of technical improvements in the collection and analysis of survey data have made preelection polling much more accurate. Polling on issues—how people feel about health care reform, foreign policy, and other current affairs—is still extraordinarily difficult and complicated. Sampling and survey design will be addressed in Chapter Three, where you will be introduced to that method as well as to several other methods of assessing public opinion.

The story of public opinion is a long one, beginning with the ancient Greek philosophers who thought and wrote so much about popular sentiments and the meaning of those sentiments in a democracy. Some periods have seen more interest in public opinion than others owing to the predominance of certain forms of government: In autocratic regimes, public opinion is important only in that it must be tamed or controlled, whereas in democratic states, the nature of public opinion (in theory) determines the direction of public policy. In every era, new democracies emerge—the most recent set appearing in Eastern Europe—and the same enduring questions about public opinion arise: Who composes the public? And how might we know its desires? As we saw in Chapter One, these questions are difficult to answer. Yet no democratic state can evolve if its leaders and citizens fail to grapple with such monumental theoretical and practical issues.

NOTES

1. Ernest Barker, *Greek Political Theory: Plato and His Predecessors* (London: Methuen 1918), pp. 38–39, cited in Paul Palmer, "The Concept of Public Opinion in Political Theory," in C. Wittke, ed., *Essays in History and Political Theory in Honour of Charles Howard McIlwain* (New York: Russell and Russell, 1964).

2. Robert Minar, "Public Opinion in the Perspective of Political Theory," *Western Political Quarterly* 13 (1960):31–44.

3. Thanks to Professor Jean Goodwin for her translation and insights.

4. Niccolò Machiavelli, *The Prince,* trans. and ed. N. H. Thompson (Buffalo, NY: Prometheus Books, 1986), pp. 57–58.

5. Quoted in Palmer, "The Concept of Public Opinion in Political Theory," p. 239.

6. Alexis de Tocqueville, *Democracy in America,* ed. and trans. J. P. Mayer (New York: Anchor Books, 1969), p. 255.

7. Ibid., p. 435.

8. C. J. Arthur, ed., *The German Ideology* (New York: International Publishers, 1984), pp. 65–66.

9. James Bryce, *The American Commonwealth* (London: Macmillan and Co., 1891), p. 265.

10. See, for example, David Protess et al., *The Journalism of Outrage: Investigative Reporting and Agenda Building in America* (New York: Guilford Press, 1991).

11. Bryce, *The American Commonwealth,* p. 267.

12. Terry N. Clark, ed., *Gabriel Tarde: On Communication and Social Influence* (Chicago: University of Chicago Press, 1969), p. xx.

13. Arthur N. Holcombe, "Roundtable on Political Statistics," *American Political Science Review* 19 (February 1925):123–124.

14. For a more detailed discussion of these trends in the history of public expression, see Susan Herbst, *Numbered Voices: How Opinion Polling Has Shaped American Politics* (Chicago: University of Chicago Press, 1995).

15. Charles Tilly, "Speaking Your Mind Without Elections, Surveys, or Social Movements," *Public Opinion Quarterly* 47 (1983):465.

16. Wilhelm Bauer, "Public Opinion," in Edwin Seligman, ed., *Encyclopaedia of the Social Sciences* (New York: Macmillan, 1930), p. 671.

17. Kathleen Hall Jamieson, *Eloquence in an Electronic Age: The Transformation of Political Speechmaking* (New York: Oxford University Press, 1988), p. 5.

18. Quoted in Michael Emery and Edwin Emery, *The Press and America: An Interpretive History of the Mass Media* (Englewood Cliffs, NJ: Prentice Hall, 1988), p. 90.

19. Lewis Coser, *Men of Ideas: A Sociologist's View* (New York: Free Press, 1970), p. 20.

20. On salons and their place in political history, see Susan Herbst, *Politics at the Margin: Historical Perspectives on Public Expression Outside the Mainstream* (New York: Cambridge University Press, 1995).

21. Quoted in Patricia Higgins, "The Reaction of Women, with Special Reference to Women Petitioners," in Brian Manning, ed., *Politics, Religion, and the English Civil War* (London: Edward Arnold, 1973), pp. 190–191.

22. See Manning, *Politics, Religion, and the English Civil War,* or Maurice Ashley, *England in the Seventeenth Century* (Baltimore: Penguin Books, 1968). On petitioning and political meetings in British history, see Cecil Emden, *The People and the Constitution* (London: Oxford University Press, 1956).

23. Max Beloff, *Public Order and Popular Disturbances 1660–1714* (London: Oxford University Press, 1938), p. 68.

24. Claude Robinson, *Straw Votes* (New York: Columbia University Press, 1932).

3

Methods for Studying
Public Opinion

By now you might have guessed that public opinion is difficult to measure. Because it is a very complex force with so many psychological
and sociological dimensions, there are many ways to think about the concept. Researchers have puzzled over the best way to measure public opinion since the early decades of the twentieth century and have debated the
pros and cons of many techniques for evaluating this rather "slippery"
concept.

Despite continuing debates over how to measure public opinion, there
is some consensus among scholars, policymakers, interest group leaders,
and journalists. These parties use a variety of techniques to assess the
public mood: election returns, consumer behavior, stock market fluctuations, public meetings and demonstrations, and other such behavioral indicators. But when leaders or journalists want to understand the attitudes
that drive behavior, they often turn to four methods of opinion assessment: survey research or polling, focus groups, experimental research, and
the analysis of mass media content. In this chapter, we introduce each of
these methods in order to give you a general overview of them. Our introduction to these methods is not intended to make you an expert on
them, as this is not a methodology textbook. We do hope, however, that
you will refer to the many methodological texts on public opinion, including those referenced in this chapter.

SURVEY RESEARCH:
AGGREGATING INDIVIDUAL OPINIONS

Survey research has significantly shaped our view of publics and their opinions. We have seen in previous chapters how social theory in the early twentieth century grew more concerned with the concept of mass publics. A tool was needed that would empirically test notions of how large, dynamic groups of individuals thought and behaved. Sociologists had earlier been accustomed to carefully interviewing people in smaller group situations, such as the workplace or in discrete neighborhoods. Early social researchers analyzed their findings more from a qualitative than a quantitative perspective, not having accurate enough measures to reliably "count" public opinion trends across citizen populations. Informal preelection straw polls and "person-in-the-street" interviews by journalists were common, though notoriously unscientific and unreliable. In both cases, reporters simply asked people they knew or people they happened to run into whom they were going to vote for.

The main formal "counting" tool was the U.S. census, which every ten years tried to provide an actual head count and some raw demographics for the population as a whole. The most meaningful measures of public opinion were election results. Obviously, neither indicator provided the kinds of subtleties needed to show what people were thinking about public issues, let alone why they were thinking what they did.

The initial impetus to find ways of doing large-scale summations of people's attitudes and behaviors was heavily influenced by the growth of broadcast media in the 1920s and 1930s. Broadcasters needed ways of letting advertisers know how many people "out there" in the then poorly defined audience areas were listening. Concepts borrowed from probability sampling theory allowed measurement of smaller samples drawn from much larger populations, with the results representative of the whole. In effect, application of sampling theory allowed the findings of surveys of small samples picked from bigger populations to be generalized to those populations. We will explain how this works later.

In those early years, door-to-door interviewing was required to get close to a fair sampling of a population, and that process was—and remains—exorbitantly expensive and time-consuming. Polling by telephone tended mainly to reach the wealthier, who could afford telephones, and mail surveys suffered from lack of valid address lists. Nonetheless, early survey efforts yielded at least some representative indications of early radio audiences. Preelection polls also became more formal, although still primitive by today's standards.

By the late 1930s and into the 1940s, many elements came together to make large-scale opinion surveys the more reliable tool they are today. For one thing, people became easier to find, with increased telephone ownership and more sophisticated telecommunications networking, more accurate mailing lists, and population movement to urban areas. Equally important were advances in statistical theory and, later, the application of computers to statistical modeling. Computerizing both survey sampling and analytic techniques made surveys far more efficient and cost-effective.

Moreover, the birth of academic survey research centers at places such as the University of Chicago and the University of Michigan spawned many innovations in survey procedures and added greatly to their validity. Survey research today is a multibillion-dollar industry, with studies of nearly every type imaginable being conducted by academicians, market researchers, mass media, governmental agencies, and political pollsters. Without survey research, most of this book could not have been written.

It seems curious that after more than a half century of such experience, surveys are still assumed to be more complicated than they actually are by the people they study. Many people have misconceptions about what surveys can and cannot show and about how their results can be interpreted. We will outline some basic principles in the following, with particular attention to survey applications in public opinion research.

The Survey Process

Surveys consist of several entwined components, all strongly affecting one another. Key elements include:

1. The population of people that the survey is to provide data about.
2. The kind of sample of individuals that will be drawn from that population.
3. The method of data gathering to be used—usually involving personal, phone, or mail interviews.
4. The kind of questionnaire or interviewing instrument used.
5. The kinds of analyses done and inferences drawn.

The nature of the population is usually the one constant that the rest of the survey needs to be designed around. Sampling, data gathering, and other components will vary considerably depending on the composition of the population. Strategies will differ according to whether the population includes, for example, all U.S. adults, Democrats likely to vote in Ohio, chief executive officers of biotechnology companies, or freshmen students at a Midwestern state university.

The purpose of the survey obviously influences the kinds of analyses to be done and the inferences drawn. If our purpose is preliminary and exploratory—perhaps to get some broad ideas about how the Internet may affect political views of college students—we may begin with a rather small sample of students we know in one dormitory at a large university just to try out some questions. We might also use focus groups, described later in this chapter, to get a better fix on the situation. If, however, our goal is to predict a month ahead who is leading in a governor's race and why, our sampling needs to be larger and more representative of likely voters, and our items should be better formed and precise. Or if our purpose is to test the more formal hypothesis that television leads to less public social interaction, we had better have several well-validated indicators of television viewership, social interaction, and related variables. It may not be so important that our sample represents the U.S. population as a whole as that it adequately reflects types of people and situations that have bearing on the hypothesis.

Types of Surveys

Several types of surveys exist. We first define a survey as a research technique for measuring characteristics of a given population of individuals. Some surveys are done to count or describe characteristics of a population; others are more concerned with explaining why characteristics occur and how they relate to others. Simple descriptive surveys are sometimes called polls, when they are conducted more for political or election forecasting purposes. For instance, CNN might do a preelection poll to see who is ahead in a presidential contest, whereas during the same time period, the University of Michigan would be doing more extensive surveys to find out why people are choosing to vote as they are and what the consequences of those behaviors are for the body politic.

We can also distinguish among three broad types of surveys by looking at which people out of the population are actually counted or interviewed. Census surveys attempt to count every person in the population, as the federal government does every ten years. Sample surveys take a smaller sampling of people out of the population to measure. Probability sample surveys (also more loosely called "scientific" surveys) use statistical methods to select who is to be included in the sample. Using probability sampling methods lets us generalize our findings to the larger population, meaning that we can with some confidence assume that the findings will be approximately what we would have gotten had we interviewed the whole population. To be cost-effective, surveys attempt to choose the smallest, most accessible sample possible that will still allow meaningful generalizations to be made about the entire population.

Surveys are typically cross-sectional, meaning that they are done at one point in time to provide a "snapshot" of public views at that particular time. Panel surveys reinterview the same people over time to get a better picture of how opinions may change over months or even years. Surveys are often a main element in field experiments, in which samples may be divided into "experimental" or "control" conditions and are then subjected to different stimuli: One community, for example, may receive a particular public health information campaign, while another does not. Surveys may then be done to compare whether the recipient community gains in knowledge over the nonrecipient.

Sampling

Samples can be either probability or nonprobability based. Nonprobability samples cannot be viewed as representative of any larger population, but they can nonetheless be useful in certain instances. Intensive case studies of families or other small units, for example, can generate significant knowledge about specific social concepts or processes that may be overlooked in broader-scale survey efforts. That is, we can learn a lot in such case studies about how a particular family works, but we cannot be sure that family is typical of others. Nonprobability surveys may be useful in helping to develop concepts and measures to be tested later in larger samples.

"Person-in-the-street" or "mall-intercept" nonprobability interviews are favored by some marketing researchers. This method usually involves interviewers positioning themselves in a shopping mall or other well-traveled location and trying to interview as many people in desirable age or gender categories as possible. Although the information gained may be useful for some marketing purposes, the sampling is typically sloppy enough to avoid using the results for valid generalizations about any population. We simply have no way of knowing whether the people interviewed are typical of the larger community or even typical of other shoppers at a particular mall.

Probability sampling, by contrast, assumes that each person within a given population has a certain known chance of being included in a sample. In the most rigorous case of simple random sampling, each person in the population has the exact same chance as every other person of being sampled. Note that this is a far more demanding definition of "random" than we use in everyday talk, where the term usually implies doing things "by chance" or unsystematically. Rather, strict probability sampling methods carry systematic selection to an extreme. Sophisticated random number tables are often used to try to assure that the selection of each person for a sample is independent of the selection of every other person. The analogy often used is continuously shaking a bin of numbered balls, as in lottery drawings, between selections of the numbered balls. This effort to make each selection independent of every other selection helps assure that each unit chosen for the sample has the same chance of selection as any other unit in the sample.

The underlying assumption is straightforward: If you choose a sample from a population using probability techniques, you can generalize or make inferences from that sample back to the population by using the same probability techniques. Put another way, if you know the chances or odds that people in the population have of being included in the sample, you also know the chances or odds that whatever you measure in the sample also occurs in the population.

Suppose that you read a story in *USA Today* that a national probability sample survey of U.S. adults found that 66 percent support a balanced federal budget; another 24 percent do not, and 10 percent are undecided. The story also reports that the "error margin" for the findings is plus or minus 3 percent and that the sample size was 1,000. This means that because 66 percent of the sample supported a balanced budget, we can infer with 95 percent confidence that in the larger population somewhere between 66 percent plus 3 percent or 66 percent minus 3 percent (or between 63 percent and 69 percent) would have supported the balanced budget if they had been asked.

If we dissect this a bit, what we are saying first is that we can only generalize the 66 percent statistic to the larger population within a certain range of error. In this case, that range is plus or minus 3 percent. Thus, if the statistic is 66 percent, the true population percent (or parameter) is likely to be within plus or minus 3 percentage points of 66 percent. This error range is known as sampling error, or the error that results when we try to generalize or infer results from a sample to the larger population.

We can estimate sampling error because when probability sampling is used, we know the probability of each person being drawn into the sample in the first place. Using appropriate mathematical formulas, we can retrace those probabilities after the survey to estimate sampling error.*

Note that we have no way of absolutely knowing or proving what the true population value is. If we wanted to know "really" whether exactly 66 percent of the actual population supported a balanced budget, we would have to ask every one of the more than 200 million adults in the United States. Being unable or unwilling to do that, we hedge our bets. We specify what the odds are—or how confident we are—that the true population value is within that plus or minus 3 percent error range.

This confidence level is the final factor that concerns us in understanding probability sampling. The conventional confidence level associated with nearly all sample surveys is 95 percent: In the *USA Today* example, we estimate that there is a 95 percent chance that the true population value of balanced budget support lies within that plus or minus 3 percent error range. To put the notion behind confidence level another way, if we had drawn 100 random samples of 1,200 citizens each and interviewed all of them, we would expect that in 95 out of those 100 samples, somewhere between 63 and 69 percent would have supported the balanced budget. In sum, the larger the sample size, the lower the

---

*Strictly speaking, the sampling error is calculated from a value called the standard error, which is added to or subtracted from the population mean or percentage value. We do this theoretically, because we of course don't really know what the population mean or percentage truly is (if we did, we wouldn't have to draw the sample!). So in truth, we never know in the distribution of all possible samples we might have drawn exactly where our own sample lies.

sampling error, given the same confidence level. Population size for the most part has little effect on sampling error.

As a general rule of thumb, sample sizes of around 1,000 are often adequate to provide descriptive public opinion data for populations of around 100,000 or more—including the U.S. adult population of 200 million. Responses from samples of this size will usually yield a sampling error of roughly 3 to 4 percent. Sample sizes of 300 or so may often provide useful information about certain large populations-if a somewhat sloppy sampling error rate of 5 to 7 percent or more does not cause problems. (Consider that if a preelection poll has a sampling error of 5 percent and one candidate is found to have the support of 40 percent of the sample and the other has 45 percent, the race is statistically a dead heat.)

Several specific probability sampling methods may be used, depending on the nature of the population, the kind of sample needed, and whether respondents will be contacted in person or by phone or mail. In many cases, stratified sampling methods or oversampling are used, meaning that the sample is purposively weighted to better represent one population group or another. (For example, if the purpose of a study is to compare opinions of black versus white citizens on racial issues, a higher proportion of black respondents than would be drawn by chance alone may need to be included in the sample to have adequate numbers for statistical comparisons with whites.)

The Problem of Survey Participation

A key problem in survey research is that people statistically chosen to be included in a sample do not always choose to participate. Some individuals are more difficult to reach than others, and some are more willing to cooperate than others. Well-run professional general population telephone surveys often get response rates of 70 to 80 percent, meaning that 70 to 80 percent of the people included in the initial sample have been successfully interviewed.

The impact of low response rates on how well we can generalize findings to the population is a major concern. Many researchers argue that as long as it can be shown that those not participating in the survey are essentially the same as those who are, the problem is minimal. Most opinion surveys are able to compare the demographics of their respondents with U.S. census demographics (gender, age, race/ethnicity, and so on) of the populations of interest, and often they are highly similar; and even if they are not, weighting can be done before results are reported.

Other researchers argue, however, that even if demographics are similar, we can never really know how well the interviewed respondents stack up against the general population in terms of their public views, involvement, and behaviors. (If we knew in the first place, there would be no reason to do the survey!) There is the suspicion that people who agree to be interviewed may be somewhat more interested in public affairs, perhaps more knowledgeable, and more active; hence, such surveys may not represent the full range of public views. Thus, samples may be biased to over-represent some population characteristics at the expense of others.

However, it is clear that people are more willing to participate when they sense the study is legitimate (e.g., not a sales promotion), when they are interested in the subject area, and when they are given additional inducements, such as payment for their time. Paying respondents raises concerns about people who need money being more represented or about paid respondents wanting to provide answers they think will please the interviewer.

Methods of Gathering Survey Data

The three most common methods of getting survey data from respondents are in person, by telephone, and by mail. Each has advantages and disadvantages, and choosing a method again depends on how well it fits with other components of the survey.

In-Person Interviews. Most researchers would ideally prefer to do in-person, face-to-face interviews for nearly all surveys. One-on-one in-person interaction makes it easier for interviewers to build rapport with respondents. Better rapport can increase the quality of answers to questions in terms of both accuracy and completeness, especially in studies dealing with the more sensitive issues. Greater rapport can also promote longer, more detailed interviews. Interviewers are also able to note more emotive aspects of responses through facial expressions and body language. Another main advantage is that more complex and in-depth questions can be asked by using visual aids and other explanatory tools. Questions about campaign advertising, for example, can be asked by showing the actual ads, on portable VCRs, if appropriate.

A decided disadvantage of in-person interviews is their often excessive cost, and for this reason they are quite sparingly used. The cost per interview for, say, a twenty-minute in-person survey can average over $200 (versus one-fourth that amount or less for comparable telephone or mail interviews). Multiply this amount by the 300 to 1,200 respondents needed for most public opinion studies, and you quickly see that only the most well-endowed projects can afford personal interviews.

Much of the expense is due to interviewer time in tracking down, soliciting, and completing interviews in the respondents' home or workplace. Sampling costs are also higher, given the need to coordinate the actual physical location of respondents rather then relying only on lists of phone numbers or addresses. National population surveys cause special problems in this regard.

Telephone Interviews. Telephone interviewing is by far the most-used public opinion survey technique, and it has cost-effectiveness and interviewer convenience on its side. A twenty-minute telephone survey might run $50 or upward per interview, with most survey organizations having volume-discounted phone lines that minimize long-distance charges. As a result, a survey of 600 adults drawn from across the United States may not cost significantly more than the same survey carried out locally within a given city.

Most general population telephone samples are drawn by so-called random-digit dialing techniques. Telephone numbers to be called are probability-sampled from computerized lists of all possible telephone exchanges in the population area. As calls are made, nonworking numbers and business and other nonhousehold numbers are systematically excluded, leaving what is usually an excellent representation of all private household telephones within the specified geographic area. Software that automatically dials the selected numbers is now commonplace as well, easing tedious labor. Random-digit dialing methods are not only more cost-efficient but also avoid biases associated with the absence of unlisted numbers in telephone directories.

Telephone surveys are fast and flexible—hence the reliance on telephones for quick-reaction opinion polls on major news events, candidate debates, and the like. It is not unusual for an organization such as CNN to commission a national poll on reactions to a president's speech and to air the results within a few hours or less. Use of computer-assisted telephone interviewing (CATI) techniques has boomed, with interviewers posted at terminals that dial the numbers and allow interviewers to enter answers as respondents give them. Computation of results is in effect online, speeding up the process even more.

Although telephone surveys do not allow the rapport of personal interviews, they do a better job of it than the far more impersonal mail surveys to be discussed next. The telephone questionnaire format does need to be relatively simple, however, with easy-to-read and comprehend questions and response categories. The most effective maximum length for telephone surveys is about fifteen minutes, and anything over twenty minutes can be quite wearing on respondents, risking lower-quality data and the respondent hanging up before completion of the survey. Increased uses of answering machines and call screening devices by the public adds to the response rate problems of using telephone surveys.

Mail-Administered Surveys.   Collecting public opinion data by mail surveys has long been derided as a last resort, often not worth the trouble. Although this is typically the cheapest method—printing and postal costs are all that is needed—response rates can border on the horrific. General population mail surveys have been known to achieve response rates of less than 5 percent, usually nowhere near the minimal 50 percent or so needed for any statistical acceptability. Indeed, some mail "surveys" are often nothing more than promotional gimmicks, such as the questionnaires sent out by candidates, officeholders, or special interest groups to "gauge" public opinion, when the real reason is to build public awareness or to raise money.

Nonetheless, using the mails to assess opinion has its legitimate place. Mail surveys can be quite effective in collecting data from smaller, more specialized population groups. (One example of such a group is a college faculty, who routinely receive polls regarding their own areas of interest, academic policy, and student interests. Faculty typically respond in respectable numbers to these—whether this response is more a result of altruism, curiosity, compulsiveness, or self-interest is another issue.)

Physicians, civil servants, business executives, or just about any other occupational or interest segment can be successfully targeted—as long as the survey topic is of relevance and interest to members of that particular group.

Such surveys also require careful planning and administration. Advance notices that the questionnaire is en route, careful explanation of survey purposes, and repeated mailings to nonrespondents are needed to gain respectable response rates. The added costs of such inducements can approach those of telephone surveys, or even small-sample personal interviews.

Mail surveys have the added advantage of allowing more complex questions than telephone surveys, provided that appropriate visual aids are used. Desktop publishing techniques can provide highly attractive and readable formats that add to a questionnaire's appeal.

Alternative Techniques.   Multiple data collection techniques are now more in use. For example, mail questionnaires might be sent out first, with a telephone follow-up to nonrespondents. Conversely, a telephone interview might be used to gather basic data and to try to talk the respondent into allowing a more detailed mail survey to be sent or a personal interview to be scheduled. Workplace-related interviews now depend more on fax machines and E-mail. Internet web pages gather data by counting hits as acknowledgments of interest or opinion.

Questionnaire Design

Writing appropriate questionnaire items requires solid understanding both of the survey's subject matter and of the respondents' views of the world and their verbal skills. On average, the general U.S. adult population has had about a year of college beyond high school and is unlikely to know as much as researchers do about any given subject area. Survey designers need to explain topics and options clearly, in everyday, user-friendly terms.

As an example of a not-so-user-friendly item, take this question: "Do you agree or disagree that U.S. foreign policy should give more sympathetic consideration than it has in the past to Bosnian Serb appeals for greater autonomy?" We can simplify this question into the following: "Do you agree or disagree that the United States should side more with the Bosnian Serbs?" This puts it into the type of everyday language that most respondents will more readily understand. However, it also blunts the subtleties of the issue. This is a common trade-off for survey researchers: precision of meaning versus getting the general message across to a broad audience (see Box 3.1).

BOX 3.1   QUESTIONNAIRE WORDING AND THE HOLOCAUST DENIAL CONTROVERSY

In 1992, a well-respected survey research firm, the Roper Organization, fielded a national survey on attitudes of Americans toward the Holocaust and its impact on Jews and on the subject of intolerance more generally. To assess knowledge of the Holocaust, or more precisely, belief that the German government under the Nazis had purposively killed several million Jews in the 1940s, Roper asked the following question: "The term Holocaust usually refers to the killing of millions of Jews in Nazi death camps during World War II. Does it seem possible or does it seem impossible to you that the Nazi extermination of the Jews never happened?"

The findings appeared surprising, if not shocking, to many—because 22 percent of the respondents said it was "possible" the mass killings had not happened, 12 percent said they "didn't know," and 65 percent said it was "impossible" that the event had not happened. That nearly one-fourth of U.S. adults denied that the Holocaust had happened and that nearly one-third either denied it or did not know whether it had happened or not raised serious questions about the quality of knowledge about recent history. It also raised concerns of an anti-Semitic undercurrent involving rumors being spread at the time by some white supremacist and other extremist groups that the Holocaust had indeed been a hoax perpetrated by Jewish groups to gain sympathy and political favor.

Although news of the findings made headlines and focused on the denial and ignorance of much of the public, other survey researchers keyed in on the confusing, double-negative wording of the question and its possible impact on the responses. Criticisms included that the question was misleading and too hypothetical or that some people might have been led to respond that "anything's possible" and that technically, the Jews had not been fully "exterminated," as the question may have implied.[1]

The Roper Organization immediately admitted these possible problems and worked with a larger research team to do a more definitive study of the issue. (In fact, the question that was asked replaced an earlier version that was recognized as even more biased: "Does it seem possible to you that the Holocaust never happened?") The new study—and a number of others that followed up on the topic—demonstrated the way in which minor wording changes can influence responses to questionnaire items. The new items also restored some faith in the knowledge and values of the American public. A few examples follow, drawn from a detailed account of the controversy by Tom W. Smith.[2] In each case, the question is introduced by this sentence: "The Holocaust is a term used to describe the extermination of the Jews in World War Two."

> "Some people have said it is possible it never actually happened. In your own mind, are you certain that the Nazi extermination of the Jews happened, or does it seem possible to you that it never happened?" (93 percent "certain it happened"; 4 percent "possible it never happened"; 4 percent "don't know")[3]
>
> "Do you think the Nazi extermination of millions of Jews actually took place, or not?" (90 percent "yes, took place"; 4 percent mixed, maybe (volunteered); 3 percent "no, did not take place"; 5 percent "don't know")[4]
>
> "Do you doubt that the Holocaust actually happened, or not?" (9 percent "yes, doubt it"; 87 percent "no, don't doubt it"; 4 percent unsure, etc.)[5]

NOTES

1. Tom W. Smith, "Review: The Holocaust Denial Controversy," *Public Opinion Quarterly* 59 (1995):269–295.

2. Ibid.

3. May 1993 Bruskin polling organization telephone survey; see Smith, "Review: The Holocaust Denial Controversy."

4. January 1994 CBS telephone survey; see Smith, "Review: The Holocaust Denial Controversy."

5. January 1994 Gallup telephone survey; see Smith, "Review: The Holocaust Denial Controversy."

This question in either its complex or more simple form is also a "true" opinion or attitudinal question, as opposed to knowledge or behavior questions. Such opinion items are often the most difficult kind to ask and produce the least reliable assessment of responses—unless they are very carefully worded and placed in a proper context. Many people have a tendency to give their opinions about virtually anything, no matter how much they may know or not know about it. A respondent could easily answer "agree" to the Bosnia question, yet know next to nothing about what U.S. Bosnia policy actually is. One way around this problem is to first ask questions determining how much respondents know about the issue; another is to describe the issue more fully before asking opinion questions so that all respondents share similar information before answering. Questions asking people what they know about an issue or about how they behave or act—as in voting or other forms of political participation—are usually easier to write, as well as to answer, and tend to be more valid and reliable than opinion questions.

For similar reasons, surveys should try to avoid hypothetical questionnaire items. Asking questions on the order of "What would you think if the U.S. invaded Ireland tomorrow" or "What would you do if you lost your job" often leads to highly speculative answers with little grounding in reality.

Even clear, simple, and specific items can lead to biased answers. A leading question such as "Do you agree that the property tax should be raised by only 1 percent to fund a new high school" will most likely generate more agreement than if worded "Do you agree or disagree . . . ," with the "only" dropped. So-called double-barreled questions are another common problem: "The United States would be better off cutting welfare spending and using the money saved training more police." Some people might agree with welfare cuts but not to fund more police; others might want more police but more welfare as well. The result is that the survey results will indicate more "no opinion" answers, more confused responses, and less-valid, misleading data overall.

Questions also need to be worded to avoid respondents' wanting to give socially desirable responses or answers that they think are more socially acceptable to the interviewer. A common technique is to list for the respondent a range of statements that "other people have made" about an issue and ask respondents to choose the one closest to their own views. This opens the range of "acceptable" responses for interviewees, as does assuring the respondent that there are no "right" or "wrong" answers to opinion questions.

Question order effects can be a problem as well. For example, beginning an interview by asking respondents whom they will vote for in an upcoming election can force them into an attitudinal commitment for the rest of the questions: They may answer the remaining questions more in the way they think a supporter of that candidate should rather than as they would have ordinarily. Similarly, beginning an interview by asking respondents whether they had recently been victims of crime and then asking what they thought the most important problems facing the country were would likely bring the crime problem higher onto their issue agendas.

A key problem particular to opinion questions is to devise ones that adequately tap the range, depth, and complexity of public thinking about political issues. In many cases, we need to use more than single-item measures of public opinion: Groups of items, often analyzed by highly sophisticated statistical techniques, may be needed to more fully appreciate the complexity of public viewpoints. One example involves a controversy over how to measure "latent opinions" regarding broad political value concepts such as "postmaterialism." Latent opinions are assumed to be core values that underlie more obvious and observable opinions about issues like welfare, affirmative action, and so forth. Such latent opinions are difficult to tap using single survey opinion questions, so multiple indicators or varied groups of questions that may at first seem quite unrelated are asked. Responses to those are then analyzed using sophisticated response clustering techniques to try to tease out the underlying concept. This issue and related ones, and some of the controversies over them, will be discussed in more detail in later chapters.

Two key summary concepts in questionnaire design are validity and reliability. Validity generally refers to how well the questions measure what they are supposed to measure. For example, if we want to find out whether a person plans on voting for the Democratic or the Republican candidate for governor, simply asking the respondent about party membership would not be too valid an indicator of the person's planned vote, given what we know about party crossover voting. A more valid indicator would be to directly ask for whom the respondent planned to vote; that measure would also likely become more valid the closer it was asked to election day. Reliability, however, refers to how stable or consistent a measure is in getting the same result when asked again and again over time. More precise, unambiguous questions are usually more reliable: Asking a person's birth date is apt to be a more reliable item than asking, say, how much that person agrees or disagrees on a ten-point scale with current U.S. policy toward welfare reform.

Interviewer training is also a critical ingredient for in-person and telephone surveys. Most reputable survey organizations maintain permanent staffs of experienced interviewers who are expert at eliciting both cooperation and answers that are as honest and unbiased as possible from respondents. The best interviewers act as professional communicators, or information brokers, between researcher and respondent—and not as persuaders, helpers, teachers, or confidants in their calls. Good interviewers are alert, interested, and appreciative of the respondent's time but do not approve or disapprove of answers or prompt or imply what answers are expected.

Issues in Survey Research

Survey research over the years has generally proven its value as a tool for better understanding mass social processes and as a device for more accurately describing public moods and behaviors with respect to politics, mass media, marketing, and lifestyle. As with any technique, inappropriate uses of it, and overreliance on it, can cause problems.

A major complaint against political uses of surveys is that pollsters can ask questions in biased or distorted ways—or use inappropriate samples—to get the answers they want to prove their own points. Hardly a major election campaign goes by without such charges being leveled at one candidate or another, and often there is at least a grain of truth in the charges. Most responsible news media now refuse to report polls unless they can include the exact questions used and provide detail on how the survey was carried out. Many journalism organizations refuse to publish results of any polls except their own or those of other news media or of relatively unbiased public agencies. A recent extension of this problem has been the rise of so-called "push polls," or telephone surveys on behalf of one candidate in which views of opposing candidates are purposively misrepresented to respondents (see Box 3.2). Consumers of polls should carefully look for exact questionnaire wording—and the nature of the sampling, response rate, and survey sponsorship—before putting too much stock in the findings of any study.

BOX 3.2   PUSH POLLS

The 1992 and 1994 election campaigns saw an increased use of so-called push polls, or polls used by candidates or special interest groups to purposively promote their own agenda to respondents. More commonly, this takes the form of slamming the opposing candidate or viewpoint by asking questions that imply the opposition holds views that are generally unacceptable to voters.

An extreme example would be for Candidate A to conduct a phone survey that emphasized a question on the order of the following: "Candidate B (the opponent) has called for a federal law bringing back racial segregation in public schools. Do you agree with that position, disagree, or aren't you sure?" Obviously, the purpose is not to gather useful data but rather to use the phone poll format as a campaign technique to put out false and damaging information about the opposing candidate. Perhaps less offensive but equally disreputable from a professional polling perspective is using surveys that may ask some legitimate questions but that also promote the views of a given candidate. In either case, respondents are being misled as to the purpose of the survey.

Such uses of polls are difficult to track down, and candidates often deny any such doings. In truth, sometimes the line between data gathering and promotional efforts can be a fine one. Legitimate polls may provide some citizens with information about candidates they had not been aware of. The use of push polls may have declined in 1996 because of pressure from professional organizations such as the American Association for Public Opinion Research, which upholds strict standards against such practices by its members.

A broader issue is the reliance on survey data by policymakers in general—whether in government, private industry, or academia. Critics charge that too much dependence on surveys results in a leadership vacuum—with officeholders, for example, willing to recommend or do only what polls show that the public wants. Such dependence may reduce innovativeness in policy building or diminish leaders' willingness to recommend strategic but unpopular options.

In political campaigns, polls may well lead to candidates telling voters what they want to hear, as opposed to candidates revealing the truth of their own views. Still, policymakers and politicians at the least have access to a far broader spectrum of public views, far more than they would have listening only to their own advisers, lobbyists, and those few citizens who speak out at hearings and forums. Access to such information can enlighten judgment and lead to more effective communication with the public.

As a social research tool, surveys can also be faulted for turning too much attention to public opinion in the aggregate, with emphasis on mass social processes and without enough weight given to individual motivation and activity, and especially to the dynamics of smaller group interactions. As you will see, a central point of this book is that we need to take as holistic a view as possible of the public opinion environment. More studies now regard surveys as only one component of the research process and combine them with focus groups, content analyses, participant observation, and in some cases even intensive clinical psychological examinations. By taking this wider view, findings from surveys can be more validly interpreted in the full context of social behavior and interaction.

FOCUS GROUPS: USING GROUP DYNAMICS TO MEASURE PUBLIC OPINION

Although survey methods continue to dominate public opinion research, alternative methodologies are also gaining wide acceptance. One reason for this is that researchers have come to recognize that since public opinion is complex and multifaceted, it is necessary to explore it using multiple methods. One methodology that is being rediscovered is focus group interviewing.[1] Focus groups are "carefully planned discussion[s] designed to obtain perceptions on a defined area of interest in a permissive, non-threatening environment."[2] The roots of this method can be traced to sociologist Robert Merton's examination of propaganda during World War II, but it is a method of social inquiry that had been largely ignored in public opinion research. However, today focus groups are enjoying a modest resurgence, most notably in the areas of market research and campaign consulting but increasingly in journalism and academia as well.

Unlike survey methods that typically ask individual subjects to answer a series of closed-ended questions, focus groups involve open discussion among a group of subjects. The typical focus group discussion includes between six and ten participants, though as few as four and as many as twelve are not uncommon. Researchers vary considerably with respect to how many focus groups they conduct for particular projects. Participants are selected in a variety of ways, but unlike survey research, projects seldom strive for a true random sample of the target population. Most focus group projects include some form of standard paper-and-pencil questions, allowing, at a minimum, the collection of basic demographic and attitudinal information.

The discussions themselves follow a loosely structured protocol that a moderator uses as a guide, though this "script" is seldom stuck to completely. Conversations often take an unexpected but potentially valuable turn, and the moderator may decide to deviate from the protocol to pursue new terrain. Usually the protocol serves as a checklist to assure that by the discussion's end, all of the key points have been addressed. The typical focus group discussion lasts from one to two hours.

Individual groups are usually constructed so that participants share some specific demographic or attitudinal characteristic. This allows people to speak their mind without feeling intimidated or defensive. For example, in her analysis of attitudes toward gender roles, Roberta Sigel ran separate groups for men and women, also stratifying several groups further by age, class, and occupational status.[3] Participants in Pamela Conover, Ivor Crewe, and Donald Searing's study of perceptions of citizenship, discussed in more detail below, were stratified not only by citizenship (British or U.S.) but also by place of residence (rural or urban) and, in Britain, by social class.[4]

The structure of the focus group discussions has changed little from those conducted in earlier years by sociologist Robert Merton. Researchers attempt to put participants at ease by making the setting as natural and informal as possible. In the case of group meetings held in a public setting like a university, this usually means selecting a conference room that is comfortably appointed, providing refreshments, allowing people to move about with some freedom, and so forth. Sometimes, discussions are held in the home of a researcher or one of the participants.

Information generated by focus groups can be analyzed qualitatively (employing critical interpretation, as one might do with an in-depth interview) or quantitatively (through systematic content analysis, described in the next section). This information can stand alone as a way of providing insights into opinion formation and sometimes allows for cautious generalizations. Focus groups are also useful in conjunction with other methods such as participant observation, in-depth interviews, experiments, and surveys. These qualities make the focus group methodology well-suited to helping explore the complexities of public opinion by bridging the gap between more qualitative, interpretive methodologies and other more conventional social scientific methods. By offering some of the qualities of each, they are also ideal for studying the fluid and dialogic aspects of opinion formation.

It is also important to note that focus groups have certain limitations when compared to other methods of inquiry. The setting is less natural than participant observation. The researcher has less control than in an in-depth individual interview or an experiment. Results are less easily analyzed and generalized than in survey research. Nevertheless, focus groups have some significant advantages over these other methods. They allow one to examine the role of social interaction in opinion formation and expression. They combine the probing and flexibility of in-depth interviews with the ability to talk to a larger number of people. They help guard against research bias and shortsightedness by guaranteeing that interaction is not exclusively with the researcher alone and by allowing enough open-endedness for unanticipated views to emerge from the discussion. And they strike a compromise between the generalizability of quantitative analysis and the depth of qualitative analysis.

Focus groups are particularly well-suited to examine the fluidity and dynamics of attitude and opinion formation. They also allow one to examine politics in a communal setting and to focus on how citizens interact with each other in discussing public issues: "The hallmark of focus groups is the explicit use of the group interaction to produce data and insights that would be less accessible without the interaction found in the group."[5] As focus group research has become more common, the kinds of questions for which they are suitable has become clearer.

What Focus Groups Tell Us About Public Opinion

Focus groups have been used to address a wide range of substantive topics. Despite this diversity, however, focus group findings are quite similar in their conclusions about the general process of opinion formation and expression. These conclusions suggest that public opinion is exceptionally dynamic and complex, that opinions are constructed and reconstructed in ways that make them impossible to separate from the context from which they emerge, and that opinions emerge from a synthesis of personal, social, and mass-mediated information. Perhaps most important, in contrast to much survey research, focus group research paints a picture of a thoughtful citizenry. When it comes to the formation of public opinion, focus groups indicate that citizens can be—with some prompting—active, critical, and reasonably sophisticated. Focus group research does not always challenge the conclusions drawn from more traditional research methods, but it does illuminate and enrich them in valuable and unique ways. In fact, focus group methodologies have been used in at least two different ways in public opinion research: as a check on or supplement to traditional survey methods and as a method that can stand on its own and cast light on aspects of public opinion formation ignored by more traditional methods.

Supplementing Traditional Survey Methods.   Among the first researchers to reintroduce focus groups to the study of political psychology were Roberta Sigel and Cliff Zukin. They conducted six focus groups on the topic of gender relations. The groups were intended to serve two related purposes: to help in the construction of closed-ended survey questions measuring attitudes about gender relations and gender roles and to generate hypotheses to be tested with more quantitative techniques. The focus groups proved useful for these purposes, but Sigel also found them helpful in fleshing out the findings of subsequent quantitative analyses: "Notwithstanding their limitations, focus group observations . . . greatly enriched our understanding of men's and women's perceptions of gender relations. In fact, we found them to 'deliver' much more than we had anticipated. Originally conceived mainly as guides to questionnaire construction, it soon become obvious that they had an independent contribution to make."[6] There are other examples of using focus groups to supplement quantitative projects. For example, Conover, Crewe, and Searing, in their comparative study of citizenship, used focus groups as a "critical first step" in a larger survey research project.

Although they have their own potential for bias, focus groups do provide some checks on the danger, found in both depth interviews and survey questions, that the researcher's prior expectations will unduly influence the expression of public opinion. As Conover, Crewe, and Searing note, the focus group format assures that "participants talk to one another in their own language, rather than simply reacting to the questions and language of an interviewer in a one-to-one situation."[7] This, in turn, increases the likelihood of new, often unexpected conclusions emerging from focus group analyses.

The Unique Contributions of Focus Groups.   The uses described above are enough to recommend focus groups as a method of inquiry. However, their greatest utility lies less in what they have in common with other methods than in what is unique about them. Focus groups can illuminate aspects of public opinion that are less accessible through traditional methods. In particular, focus groups are valuable in revealing the process of opinion formation, in providing glimpses of usually latent aspects of this process, and in demonstrating the social nature of public opinion.

Opinions, from this perspective, are not fixed constructs that are "stored" and "retrieved" like data in a computer. Rather, they are continuously constructed through cognitive processes involving a myriad of complex schemata. Yet in spite of creative research designs and sophisticated data analyses, traditional methods of measuring opinions are not always able to capture this dynamism. For example, closed-ended survey items often reify opinions by forcing respondents to present them as self-contained and preexisting objects. The cross-sectional nature of most surveys adds to this static quality. Even panel studies and experimental designs encourage a mechanistic mode, in which opinions are measured, new information is introduced, and opinions are remeasured. Focus groups, by contrast, can be "catalyst[s] for the individual expression of latent opinion . . . for free-associating to life."[8] By essentially forcing people to "think out loud," they become windows through which to observe the process of opinion formation.

Researchers who use focus groups often do so because this method is suited to modeling these social processes. For example, Conover, Crewe, and Searing argue convincingly that given their interest in "discovering the commonplace meaning of political terms" such as citizenship, focus groups were an appropriate choice of method because they allow social scientists to study the actual language and categories people use in discussing political issues related to citizenship.[9] Tamar Liebes and Elihu Katz also consider the conversational and social nature of focus groups to be their greatest asset. In particular, they argue that focus groups are effective in illustrating "the processes of collective meaning-making" because they permit tentative interpretations to be floated by someone and shot down by someone else, because they permit bullies to try to impose themselves on the others, because expert opinion is sought out for guidance, and because interpretations are molded and twisted to fit the underground loves and hates that permeate interpersonal relations. This is what happens in life. They further argue that focus groups succeed because they replicate the kinds of exchanges that citizens actually have: "We were, in effect, operationalizing the assumption that the small-group discussion following the broadcast is a key to understanding the mediating process via which a program such as this enters into the culture."[10]

There are limits to the comparison of focus groups to "real life," however. As William Gamson correctly notes, "Most people do not spontaneously sit down with their friends and acquaintances and have a serious discussion for more than an hour on different issues in the news."[11] Gamson goes on to compare the exchanges that occur in focus groups with two other forms of discourse. Public discourse involves "speaking to the gallery," whereas sociable interaction is the informal, private conversation that occurs among friends, family members, and the like. Focus groups as usually constructed in academic research are a blend of these two types of communication. On the one hand, participants know that they are "speaking for the record" and that their views are being recorded, and thus they are being recorded and being expressed for an academic "gallery." On the other hand, the conversational format, the familiarity of participants with each other, and the relaxed setting in which they take place give the discussions elements of sociable interaction as well. Gamson labels this blend of public and private exchange "sociable public discourse."

This semipublic nature of focus group discussions may make them problematic for studying some kinds of discourse. However, though admittedly artificial, they are often less contrived than most experimental or survey-based research. Consider, for example, the dynamics of a telephone interview: At one moment, a person is sitting at dinner, watching TV, conversing with family members, and so forth and the next, engaged in a formal interview with a stranger answering questions about a variety of issues with no time to think about them. In addition, it is arguable that the way people talk about politics is closer to sociable public discourse than to either public discourse or sociable interaction. This is especially true when it occurs outside the home but holds to some degree regardless of where the conversation occurs or what the relationship of the people conversing. Rather, it is driven by the public nature of the topic. Viewed in this light, focus groups seem an especially appropriate method for studying how people talk—and therefore think—about politics (see Box 3.3).

BOX 3.3   AN ILLUSTRATION OF FOCUS GROUP RESEARCH

Like many other researchers, William Gamson uses groups as a method for studying the interplay of mass-mediated and interpersonal communications. Gamson argues that despite survey results documenting low levels of political knowledge, people are neither "passive" nor "dumb." Rather, they "read media messages in complicated and sometimes unpredictable ways, and draw heavily on other resources as well in constructing meaning."[1] To demonstrate this active negotiation process and explore implications, Gamson conducted thirty-seven "peer group conversations." He was interested in the way "working people"—a term that emerged from the participants' own self-references—talk about politics and how talk is translated into the potential for collective political action. The 188 individuals who participated in his peer group discussions were about equally split between men and women and between whites and blacks.

Drawing on social movement theory, Gamson argues that for citizens to turn "talk into action," they need "collective action frames."[2] These frames allow groups to see that an injustice has occurred, that they have the power—the agency—to address the injustice, and that they have a clear identity that distinguishes "us," the victims, from "them," the perpetrators. The mass media are obviously critical in determining how public issues are framed, and based on an extensive content analysis of several different news media, Gamson concludes that the extent to which the media use the frames of injustice, agency, and identity varies significantly from issue to issue. He also finds that the extent to which citizens use these frames in their own discourse is connected to the prevalence of these frames in the media.

More interesting, however, is his finding that this connection between media coverage and citizens' opinions is much looser and more complex than a simple persuasion or agenda-setting model would anticipate. Although often unable to construct their own injustice frames, citizens were able to resist some of those constructed by the media. For example, Gamson found that the media often presented the Japanese as the source of injustice regarding America's industrial problems. However, citizens seldom followed this cue, tending instead to discuss the Japanese with great admiration.

Gamson, like others, supports his conclusions through a combination of tables, verbal summaries, and direct quotes from transcripts. Through a careful reading of the transcripts, Gamson has discovered that in discussing public issues, citizens draw on a much wider range of media discourses than the news and therefore have a somewhat wider range of frames upon which to draw. For example, in discussing affirmative action, individuals in several groups referred to public service advertisements they had seen (e.g., to the United Negro Fund's slogan "A mind is a terrible thing to waste"). Similarly, in discussing nuclear power, the movies *Silkwood* and *The China Syndrome* were both referenced to make points.

Besides the media, citizens drew upon two additional "conversational resources" for construction-shared frames: "experiential knowledge" and "popular wisdom." Experiential knowledge was based on personal experiences or the experiences of relatives, friends, coworkers, and so forth. Popular wisdom transcended personal experience and was based on cultural "truisms" to be accepted at face value. They were often introduced or concluded with phases such as "As everyone knows" or "It's human nature." Establishing shared frames from discussing public issues allowed group members to find a common language, but it did not mean that the conversations were always consensual.

Gamson concludes that although the working people in his groups generally lacked political consciousness, they did have "the elements necessary to develop [it]." Further, the more participants could draw on integrated resources to frame their discussions, the better able they were to develop the collective action frames necessary for political consciousness. It is Gamson's reasonable suspicion that frames based on integrated strategies are also the most robust and are thus resistant to shifting media frames. And although the ability to draw on such an integrated strategy varies, Gamson argues that "media dependence . . . is only partial and is heavily influenced by the issue under discussion."[3]

NOTES
1. William Gamson, *Talking Politics* (Cambridge: Cambridge University Press, 1992), p. 6.
    2. Ibid., pp. 6–7.
    3. Ibid., p. 17.

Focus Groups and the Construction of Public Opinion

Our last example of focus group research draws on Michael Delli Carpini and Bruce Williams' exploration of the role of television in shaping discourse about public issues.[12] As a way of demonstrating the utility of focus groups for exploring the dynamics of public opinion formation, we focus here on two observations that emerged from their studies. The first is the fluid, often inconsistent nature of public opinion and the ways in which people construct rather than retrieve their views on complex issues. And the second is the role of the mass media, especially television, in this process of opinion formation.

Delli Carpini and Williams conclude from their close reading of the focus group transcripts that people regularly construct rather than retrieve their views on complex issues. The focus group methodology was central to this observation in several ways. Freed from the forced constraints of closed-ended surveys and from the self-consciousness of the one-on-one interviews, the contextual, fluid, and often inconsistent nature of opinions was presented in bold relief. And although this inconsistency partially reflects the participants' lack of information, interest, and so forth, the transcripts make clear that it also reflects the "inherent contestability" of most important public issues. Examining the complete set of comments made by a single participant regarding a particular topic demonstrated that even the most thoughtful citizens express views that are contradictory. Indeed, often the most consistent views were expressed by those who clearly were uninterested in and unreflective about the issues under discussion.

It was common for the same person to express opinions at different points in the conversation that, when placed back to back, appear incompatible. For example, consider the following two comments by one subject (Kara): "I think it definitely is [possible to protect the environment in today's world]. I mean, to think there's all these big rains and all this big money for making things, surely they can come up with some way to make them in a safe manner, or to protect the public, or the land or animals." Yet later in the conversation, she says: "There's just a lot of other stuff you have to deal with . . . I mean, you would just have to take over the world pretty much, it would have to be every person in the United

States, every company, every—I just don't think it would be possible [to protect the environment in today's world]. . . . I hate to be Miss Negative, but I just don't think so." What is Kara's view of the possibility of addressing the nation's problems? Delli Carpini and Williams argue that Kara's "true" opinions do not reside in one or the other of her statements. Rather, her opinions are to be found in the full set of statements made about a particular issue and can be understood only in the specific context in which they are made. More important, they argue that citizens play an active, if limited, role in the construction of these opinions and do so in part through ongoing conversations with other people and the mass media.[13]

At the same time that subjects recognized their dependence on the media, they often seemed troubled and ambivalent about the potential such dependence has for selectively shaping their perception of the importance of various political issues. Although the media may set the agenda, the public's concern over this process is often overlooked by researchers using more traditional methodologies, as is revealed in the following quote from the participant Mark:

> You know, I think that, in a way, most everybody says that we're definitely concerned, I mean, I think I'm concerned, but then on the other hand, I think I spend very little time thinking about it until I see something like this [gestures to the blank screen] or I see the oil wells burning out of control or something to bring it home. . . . I think we need to have more hard facts put before us. I think we need to be bombarded with more things to make us think about it and hopefully therefore to make us act.[14]

Some subjects moved beyond simple ambivalence to an understanding of the reasons for the shifting nature of media coverage. Such sophisticated understandings pen up the possibility of maintaining a critical distance between the media's definition of what is important and other hierarchies of importance. As the participant Paul said:

> One problem with the media is that . . . if they talk about some issue then two weeks later if it's not changed, they really don't want to do the story again. . . . They don't want to do the same thing over and over, they think the viewers are going to get bored and change to something else. I wonder

if the media's attention to environmental concerns is going to be fad like and then they're going to find something else to focus on six months from now. That can be a problem . . . when you involve the media.[15]

The Focus Group Alternative

The traditional survey methods are valuable tools for public opinion research. However, these methods, like any attempt to simplify something as complex as human thought and action, also miss a good deal of what is important in the formation and expression of public opinion. Focus groups offer an alternative method that, either in conjunction with more traditional methods or on their own, help avoid the oversimplification of these cognitive, social, and political processes.

Ultimately, this is more than an issue of methodology. One might argue that what survey research treats as "public opinion" might better be termed "private opinion." Citizens are viewed as isolated, individual decisionmakers consuming information and privately choosing at specific points in time among competing elites, parties, or ideas. In this "citizen as consumer" metaphor, politics is a marketplace (or more accurately, a mail order catalogue or home shopping network), and opinions are the currency with which public goods are purchased.

In contrast, focus group research emphasizes the inherently ambiguous nature of politics, leading to a significantly different conceptualization of public opinion than the one that emerges from mainstream research. Focus group studies assume that public opinion is about public issues that are discussed in public. It is through "conversations" that political opinions are continuously created and recreated. The need to consider seriously the position of others is what distinguishes private life from public life and private opinion from public opinion. Focus groups represent a methodology ideally suited to study these conversational aspects of public opinion.

EXPERIMENTAL METHODS AND OPINION RESEARCH

Since the 1940s, psychologists with an interest in public opinion have employed laboratory and field experiments in an attempt to understand political attitude change among citizens. Some of the earliest and most interesting work along these lines was conducted by a team of psychologists led by Carl I. Hovland and commissioned by the U.S. Army during World War II. Psychologists were asked to evaluate a series of films, produced by the American filmmaker Frank Capra to train American soldiers, to see whether these movies did influence enlistees. Capra had been asked to make the films, called the *Why We Fight* series, in order to boost the confidence of soldiers and educate them about the political importance of the war effort. Hovland and his associates took the opportunity to explore important issues in psychological theory and, at the same time, provide a "nuts and bolts" assessment of the films' effectiveness.

As in many experiments, the researchers divided the soldiers into two groups: an "experimental group" and a "control group." As those familiar with psychological experiments know, an experimental group receives the "treatment" or "stimulus" of interest to researchers—in this case, the Capra films under evaluation. The control group does not see the films. Both groups in this series of experiments were given questionnaires before and after the days the films were actually shown—although remember that only the experimental group watched them. Hovland and his colleagues found that the films did indeed have an effect on these men, who would be risking their lives in the Atlantic and Pacific theaters of battle. The films were most effective in teaching soldiers about the events leading up to the war. Yet the effects were disappointing on the whole: The films did not boost the motivation levels of the men who would fight. Why no effects on motivation were found is a complex issue, tied to both the experimental design and historical circumstance. Nonetheless, psychologists were inspired to try and figure out how mass media might change attitudes, and they focused on the laboratory as a site for such studies.[16]

These days, political psychologists still conduct experimental research in an attempt to understand how people form their opinions and how these opinions might be manipulated. For example, Shanto Iyengar and Donald Kinder have conducted laboratory experiments to see whether media can effectively "prime" or stimulate thought about issues in the minds of participants. They have also explored whether media can force people to think about certain issues as more important than others ("agenda-setting effects"). Their findings generally support the notion that media are highly effective in shaping the nature of individual cognition toward political leaders, events, and issues. The Iyengar and Kinder experiments are part of a long history in mass communication research, but they are far more sophisticated than the early wartime studies. Psychologists have become much more careful about controlling the experimental setting and designing the procedures of the experiments.[17] And perhaps it is valuable to quote Iyengar and Kinder about the value of experimentation. In the passage that follows, they emphasize issues of control and also of "random assignment"—the process of mixing up people across control and treatment groups so that these groups match each other in terms of demographic and attitudinal composition:

> For us, the essence of the true experiment is control. Experiments of the sort we have undertaken here are distinguished from other systematic empirical methods in the special measure of control they give to the investigator. In the first place, the experimenter creates the conditions under investigation, rather than waiting for them to occur naturally. In the second place, the experimenter randomly assigns individuals to those conditions, thereby superseding natural processes of selection. By creating the conditions of interest, the experimenter holds extraneous factors constant and ensures that individuals will encounter conditions that differ only in theoretically decisive ways. By assigning individuals to conditions randomly, the experimenter can be confident that any resulting differences between individuals assigned to varying conditions must be caused by differences in the conditions themselves.[18]

In Iyengar and Kinder's experiments, the researchers show their groups of participants a variety of news stories in order to manipulate the ideas and attitudes of citizens. Iyengar has also conducted further research on the nature of television news itself and how it frames political issues. In particular, he uses content analytic and experimental procedures to demonstrate that television news stories can be either "thematic" or "episodic." Thematic news frames highlight larger issues and general trends, using analysis to extend the viewer's understanding of a political issue. Many news stories, however, tend to be episodic, concentrating on particular life stories of individual citizens in order to illustrate a social problem or trend. Unfortunately, Iyengar argues, although episodic frames are entertaining, they often cause audiences of such stories to "blame the victim"—to hold individuals and not political leaders responsible for a social problem. Take the issue of unemployment, for example. Journalists have a choice of many news frames. They can do a very analytical segment on unemployment trends and data, emphasizing policy change. Or they might focus on the vivid story of one unemployed homeless man in New York City. The former news frame enables viewers to think about public policy on unemployment, whereas the latter news frame plays to viewers' emotions and focuses them on the plight of one individual. Which is more educational for citizens? And which sort of story enables them to assess political options more effectively? These are interesting questions, and Iyengar demonstrates how they can be explored through laboratory experimentation.[19]

Some experimental projects focus on the effects of particular sorts of media content (e.g., the frames of news stories), but others concentrate on the media technology itself. For example, W. Russell Neuman, Marion Just, and Ann Crigler have conducted experiments to find out whether citizens learn more about political issues from television, newsmagazines, or newspapers. They found that their experimental subjects gained more knowledge about issues from television and magazine news reports than from newspapers. This finding may be rooted in the different journalistic techniques used by reporters for different media, or it may have something to do with the way people actually use media—the way these various sources for news fit into peoples' lives and daily information-gathering patterns. Regardless, experiments can help researchers understand the ways that media formats influence political thinking, in addition to helping them study content itself.[20]

In all of the experiments mentioned, researchers were very cautious about maintaining both "internal" and "external" validity. These are scholarly terms, describing crucial criteria for good experiments. Experimental procedures must measure the concepts they are intended to measure (internal validity). Yet strong experiments must also simulate aspects of the world outside the laboratory by making stimulus materials that are professionally produced and by making sure that the experimental "protocol" (what the subjects must do) is a reasonable imitation of real life. For example, in Iyengar and Kinder's work, the researchers were sure to produce news programs (editing together existing news stories) that looked professional. And they made the laboratory more like a living room than a sterile experimental environment so that subjects felt comfortable. The arrangement is not quite like watching television at home, but at least some of the tension created by being in an experiment is reduced.

Yet there are other experiments in attitude formation and public opinion as well that are not necessarily keyed to media or how journalists present the world. One example is Kathleen M. McGraw and Clark Hubbard's work on persuasion. They were interested in how people process communications from public officials—particularly the way people accept or fail to accept politicians' accounts of their actions in the legislature. They found that citizens' predispositions and characteristics influence the ways they "read" persuasive accounts of their leaders. In these experiments, subjects were randomly assigned to various groups and given materials containing persuasive communications as well as a battery of tests about their own knowledge levels, sophistication, and personal characteristics. This sort of research is very important because it tests hypotheses that rhetoricians have generated for centuries. Since the time of the ancient Greek city-states, leaders and scholars have pondered the nature of political persuasion: Which messages persuade which segments of the population and why? Rhetoricians have done an excellent job in detailing the different forms political speeches can take, but we still need more research on the effects of political talk. The laboratory is one environment where researchers can control what people see or hear and then measure their responses to these stimulus materials. Hence, public opinion formation is studied in process: Experimentalists can observe effects very closely and very rigorously.[21]

There is one last sort of experiment in the area of public opinion that should be mentioned in this very brief look at some experimental designs. Some researchers have combined the idea of an experiment with survey research, creating multiple forms of a survey or survey question to see whether such manipulation changes the sorts of opinions citizens express. Some of the best work in this area has been conducted by Kinder and Lynn M. Sanders. In their work on race and racial prejudice, they demonstrate how the frame of a survey question affects people's answers to that question. Although the nature of the answers to any question is tied in part to a respondent's background and attitudes, the frame of the question still affects the kinds of opinions they give. Kinder and Sanders focus on affirmative action and on welfare, documenting how the rhetorical nature of a question—the words and phrases used—tends to stimulate people to think in particular ways about those issues.[22]

The advantages of experimentation are very clear. Experiments enable the researcher to have close control over the project and the subjects. It is the researcher who determines the subject pool, the sorts of procedures followed by subjects, and the exact timing of attitude measurement. And it is also important that because so much control is possible, researchers can draw inferences about "causal order" of variables. This is difficult to do. We always wonder, for example, whether conservative talk programming makes people more conservative, or whether conservatives are simply drawn to conservative programming. Media effects such as these may be easier to study in the controlled situation of the lab than they are outside the lab, where an enormous number of events cloud our vision of particular communication processes.

On the downside, experiments tend to have very narrow foci and can only take into account a limited number of variables at a time. Internal and external validity often present problems, and there are also challenges associated with what we call "demand characteristics." Were the experimental subjects somehow able to figure out the hypotheses of the researchers? If they do figure out the hypotheses, in either a specific manner or a more vague one, this is a dangerous occurrence: Experimental subjects tend to want to help and to please the researcher, so they may answer questions dishonestly just to be polite and cooperative. This sort of effect is to be avoided at all costs, of course, since experimental researchers are looking for people's honest opinions. The final problem with experiments is that they tend to document short-term effects only. Experimental subjects are queried either right after the experiment or (in rare cases) a few weeks later. But researchers rarely know whether a persuasive communication, news program, or political advertisement has long-term effects. Do the effects still hold long after the experimental subjects have left the lab? This is one of the central challenges of experimental work in the area of public opinion.

CONTENT ANALYSIS OF MASS MEDIA: "ARCHIVES" OF PUBLIC OPINION

When we think about measuring public opinion, we usually turn to research methods that ask citizens how they feel about a particular social or political issue. This seems a most direct and efficient way to evaluate the public mood. Yet as we have seen, both survey research and focus group testing—two popular methods for measuring public opinion—are problematic: How one asks a question, the mood state of respondents, whether the sample is a representative one, and a variety of other factors make such research challenging for students of public opinion. One way to measure public opinion that does not appear as often as polls or focus groups is content analysis, which is the systematic (and usually quantitative) assessment of media texts. Media researchers have performed such analyses on all sorts of mass-produced communications over the years— magazine and newspaper articles, advertisements, television programming, comic strips, radio talk shows, company newsletters, and even forms of dialogue on the Internet. Some scholars believe that content analysis simply demonstrates what the producer of that content (e.g., a journalist or a screenwriter) thinks. Yet we believe that media content represents much more than one individual's view of the world: The content of the mass media can reveal valuable evidence about public opinion.

Popular texts are popular because they somehow resonate with cultural norms, values, or sentiments. In a capitalist economy such as our own, it is crucial that mass media products resonate with public opinion: If they fail to appeal, they will not survive in a highly competitive world of images and discourse. Although we believe there are multiple ways to understand the public mood, it is often helpful to focus on the mass media texts that citizens "consume" during a typical day. If we can figure out what people like to read, listen to, and watch, we will have a good sense of their attitudes and opinions on public affairs.

It may seem obvious that you immediately learn something about citizens by knowing their public affairs media habits. If a friend reads the *National Review* and *Commentary,* for example, we know that he or she is probably politically conservative. Alternately, another friend might subscribe to the *Nation* or *The Atlantic.* Such media consumption indicates that person's leftist or possibly liberal approach to the world. Yet beyond media consumption that directly focuses on public affairs, it is also useful to study the more entertainment-oriented texts that citizens are drawn to. In the early 1990s, for example, a situation comedy called *Roseanne* focused on the problems of a working-class family in the Midwest. The program was extraordinarily popular, and audiences found it hilarious. There were many characters on the program who were created solely to elicit laughs from the audience. Yet the various episodes of *Roseanne* also touched upon some of the most controversial social and political issues of our time. Among these issues were the role of unions, economic worries faced by small businesses, abortion, and the rights of homosexuals.

Content analysis of texts—whether they are newspaper reports on a global conference or hilarious situation comedies—is complex and demands much subtlety and care. There are critics who believe that texts are "read" in so many different ways by so many different people that finding meaning about the public's mood in such texts is impossible. Yet the large majority of media and public opinion scholars feel that this sort of research is both possible and enormously revealing. Content analysis is very labor-intensive and often very costly. Yet it provides rich, textured public opinion data that students of politics and social life find useful and enlightening.

Content analysis is often called an "unobtrusive" or "nonreactive" way to measure public attitudes. It is a method that does not involve a conversation with citizens and therefore does not "intrude" on their time or space. Content analysis does not cause people to "react" in particular ways that may affect the research project. There are many advantages to unobtrusive measurement, since it avoids the inevitable problems that a researcher must face when interviewing members of the public. In other words, certain sorts of "errors" that are often unknowingly introduced into research by respondents and interviewers are avoided altogether.

How Is Content Analysis Done?

This section concentrates on systematic, quantitative content analysis. There are other forms of textual analysis that involve interpretive tools from the humanities—literary criticism and rhetorical analysis, in particular. Here, however, we focus on methods most commonly used by communication researchers, political scientists, and sociologists who study media content in hopes of learning about public opinion.

There are normally nine steps in the process of content analysis. At every stage in this process, the researcher must make crucial decisions. As long as those decisions can be justified through logical argumentation, they are acceptable.

Step 1: Select a Topic.   The first stage in a content analysis project is the selection of a topic. Topics are diverse and can represent all kinds of scholarly inquiry. Suppose we chose drug legalization as our topic, in an attempt to understand public opinion about this fascinating debate in American politics. The topic comes up on a regular basis, and a variety of intellectuals, policymakers, and citizens have debated it in many different forums.

Step 2: Develop a Hypothesis.   Before collecting data, one must have some distinct hypotheses that can be tested through content analysis. In the case of drug legalization, one might put forth the following two hypotheses: (1) "Advocates for drug legalization tend to receive negative coverage for their positions in the mass media," and, relatedly, (2) "Advocates for drug legalization get less coverage than those who advocate tougher antidrug laws and strict enforcement of present laws." By confirming or disproving these hypotheses, we learn about public opinion: If drug legalization is generally demeaned in the popular press as a policy option, it is likely that a large and influential segment of the population shares this negative stance toward the proposition.

Step 3: Operationalize Your Terms.   There are key terms in these two hypotheses that need to be operationalized or defined before content analysis can begin. How shall we define "negative," for example? One way would be to list negative adjectives that might be used to describe a legalization policy, such as "unworkable" or "dangerous." After creating such a list of negative terms, along with a list of positive ones, the researcher knows exactly what to look for when beginning the actual analysis of text. In terms of amount of attention received by advocates for drug legalization, one could count how much space (newspaper columns in inches or number of minutes during a television news broadcast) is actually devoted to one position versus the other.

Step 4: Decide on a Sample.   If we were interested in coverage of the drug legalization debate during a particular year, we could not look at every article published or every news broadcast aired that year. This would be far too time-consuming and is not necessary in order to test our hypotheses. Instead, we could choose a random sample of these texts that represents the discourse more generally. Just as 1,000 people are often polled in order to represent national public opinion, a small number of texts can be analyzed and used as a basis for broader generalization. In the case of drug legalization, we might want to randomly select 50 or 60 media texts, from a variety of sources: newsmagazines, news broadcasts, and large regional and national newspapers, as well as specialty public affairs magazines (e.g., the *New Republic, Harper's,* and so on).

Step 5: Construct a Coding Sheet.   A simple coding sheet is necessary if the analyst is to organize the data properly. In our example (Figure 3.1), the coding sheet filled out for each text (newspaper article, for example) is rather simple.

Coding Form

Name of coder _____

Text (publication/date/page) _____

Number of positive and negative statements made by journalist about drug legalization:

Positive _____

Negative _____

Number of paragraphs describing the prolegalization position vs. the antilegalization position:

Prolegalization _____

Antilegalization _____

FIGURE 3.1   Sample Content Analysis Coding Form

   This coding sheet is just one possible scheme for analyzing the articles. Before the research begins, the analyst should collect a small sample of texts and try the coding scheme first, to see whether it will be helpful in assessing the larger sample of articles. In the coding sheet in Figure 3.1, there may be a problem with "negative statements made by the journalist." It could be the case that an article contains a large number of negative statements about legalization, but they are not made by the journalist: The journalist's sources make the negative statements, which have simply been quoted in the article. If this is the case, one might need to develop two questions—one that assesses journalists' statements and one that assesses the statements of their sources.

Step 6: Train Coders.   It is best that a researcher get help in coding the articles in the sample. In the ideal case, the researcher who draws up the hypotheses does not in fact code the individual articles or news broadcasts. In any case, those who are evaluating each text must be trained: They must know what they are looking for. What is a negative statement and what is a positive one? Coders must be in agreement about these basic issues if they are to use the same tools and achieve consistency.

Step 7: Perform Coding.   Coding may sound simple, once the difficult work of developing hypotheses and coding sheets is finished. Yet there are many conflicts among coders that arise during the study, and those conflicts in analyzing texts must be discussed. Often, a coding scheme must be changed in the middle of analysis because there is too much conflict among different coders evaluating the same texts, and researchers must go back and recode the sample.

Step 8: Analyze Data and Calculate "Intercoder Reliability."   After the coding sheets are filled out, the analyst must see how much agreement or disagreement existed among the coders. There are a variety of ways to figure this out, and there are many books that contain useful discussions of this elementary statistical calculation. High intercoder reliability means that a researcher has tested the hypotheses with confidence. Low intercoder reliability means that there was so much disagreement about the coding scheme that the study was not a strong test of those hypotheses.

Step 9: Report Results.   This is by far the most enjoyable part of content analysis. The researcher can determine whether the hypotheses were confirmed and how strongly they were supported (see Box 3.4). If it is the case that those who advocate drug legalization get a tiny proportion of coverage and that the coverage is largely negative, this would reflect the general public bias against such a solution to our illegal drug consumption and trafficking problems.

BOX 3.4   AN EXAMPLE OF CONTENT ANALYSIS

One interesting study of media content took up the issue of environmental waste. In an attempt to build theory about the news media, scholars W. Lance Bennett and Regina Lawrence looked for evidence of concern about the environment in *The New York Times*. They produced the following chart, which demonstrates how dramatically the mentions of words like "recycling" and "environment" increased from the early 1980s through 1990. One might argue that the growing number of mentions of such environmentalism "keywords" is evidence that the public was becoming more concerned with environmental issues and that concern of the public is reflected in the pages of *The New York Times*.

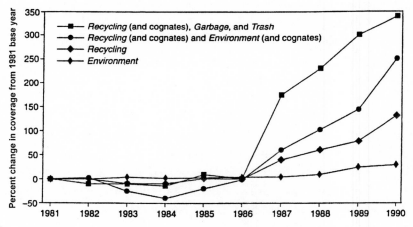

Creating a News I can: Changing Rates of Word Use
SOURCE: W. Lance Bennett and Regina G. Lawrence, "News Icons and the Mainstreaming of Social Change," *Journal of Communication* 45 (Summer 1995), figure 1, p. 32.

Problems Associated with Content Analysis

There are many benefits in performing content analysis of popular texts in order to understand public opinion. It is subtle, unobtrusive, and provides rich information about Americans' mood and values. Yet there are some problems associated with the method as well, and these problems (like the problems with survey research and focus group testing) must be acknowledged by the researcher, since they present limitations to a study conducted this way.

First, and most obvious, a researcher must be very cautious when putting together the sample of texts. If one "oversamples" from conservative or liberal magazines, the results of the content analysis will be suspect. Much thought should be given to the range of texts one collects, since a severely biased sample will yield useless results. The same problem is faced by survey researchers: The citizens who serve as respondents in their studies must represent the larger population on all relevant dimensions.

Second, the researcher must be sure to develop a coding scheme that is objective and fair. A coding scheme can reflect a researcher's biases, and this is dangerous. For example, a researcher who personally feels that drug legalization is a useful and necessary policy might slant the coding scheme in order to find more positive coverage than really exists. This biasing of coding schemes almost always happens without the researcher realizing it.

The third and most problematic limitation of content analysis is that it focuses on the manifest and not the latent content of media. Content analysis can only tell the researcher about surface-level meanings of media text—what can be readily counted, not the deep, often unconscious effects that a newspaper article or television program could have on a reader or viewer. In politics, it is reasonable to measure manifest content, since that is the content most often prompting policy debate, lobbying, and citizen participation. However, there is a feeling among many communication researchers that visual content of media may have subtle effects on the audience and that these effects are not readily noticed in the evaluation of manifest content of media. Research on how visual imagery represents and affects the public mood is only in its infancy, however, so media scholars have not as yet developed methods for coding latent meanings of visual content.

CONCLUSION

This chapter has explored four of the most common means for assessing public opinion, but there are others as well—analysis of election results or movement of the stock market, for example. The student of public opinion must decide upon the most effective means for understanding popular moods, and the tools chosen must fit the research question at hand.

Do keep in mind that all the methods discussed here assume certain conceptions or dimensions of public opinion. In conducting a poll, a researcher is arguing that public opinion can reasonably be defined as the aggregation of individual opinions, anonymously and scientifically collected. Yet if focus groups are used, the researcher wants to witness the processual nature of public opinion: how people develop opinions and change them, especially when they articulate their opinions in the presence of others. The survey researcher understands that a respondent's opinions have been influenced by others as well (in conversations before the survey), but the focus group researcher wants to watch how those opinions are formed. All of the approaches to understanding public opinion discussed in this chapter are valid, if used with care and rigor. And it is important to note that they are not mutually exclusive. In fact, the best research project would evaluate public opinion using multiple methods. But this is often unnecessary and also quite expensive, so researchers must make the best choices they can, based upon their theoretical concerns, the possibilities for collecting data, and budgetary constraints.

NOTES

1. Much of this section is based upon Michael X. Delli Carpini and Bruce A. Williams, "The Method Is the Message: Focus Groups as a Method of Social, Psychological, and Political Inquiry," in Michael X. Delli Carpini, Leonie Huddie, and Robert Shapiro, eds., *Research in Micropolitics* (Greenwich, CT: JAI Press, 1994), pp. 57–85.

2. Ronald Krueger, *Focus Groups: A Practical Guide for Applied Research* (Newbury Park, CA: Sage Publications, 1988), p. 18.

3. Roberta Sigel, *Caught Between Ambition and Accommodation: Ambivalence in the Perception of Gender Relations* (Chicago: University of Chicago Press, 1996).

4. Pamela Conover, Ivor Crewe, and Donald Searing, "The Nature of Citizenship in the United States and Great Britain: Empirical Comments on Theoretical Themes," *Journal of Politics* 53 (1991):800–832.

5. David Morgan, *Focus Groups as Qualitative Research* (Newbury Park, CA: Sage Publications, 1988), p. 12.

6. Sigel, *Caught Between Ambition and Accommodation,* p. 13.

7. Conover, Crew, and Saring, "Nature of Citizenship," p. 805.

8. Tamar Liebes and Elihu Katz, *The Export of Meaning* (Oxford: Oxford University Press, 1990), p. 28.

9. Conover, Crew, and Saring, "Nature of Citizenship," p. 805.

10. Liebes and Katz, *Export of Meaning,* p. 82.

11. William Gamson, *Talking Politics* (Cambridge: Cambridge University Press, 1992), p. 17.

12. Michael X. Delli Carpini and Bruce A. Williams, "Methods, Metaphors, and Media Research: The Uses of Television in Political Conversations," *Communication Research* 21 (1994):782–812.

13. Ibid., pp. 801–802.

14. Ibid., p. 804.

15. Ibid.

16. Some of the experiments are recounted in Carl I. Hovland, Arthur A. Lumsdaine, and Fred D. Sheffield, *Experiments in Mass Communication* (Princeton: Princeton University Press, 1949).

17. The Shanto Iyengar and Donald R. Kinder book is titled *News That Matters: Television and American Opinion* (Chicago: University of Chicago Press, 1987).

18. Ibid., p. 6.

19. Shanto Iyengar, *Is Anyone Responsible? How Television Frames Political Issues* (Chicago: University of Chicago Press, 1991).

20. W. Russell Neuman, Marion R. Just, and Ann N. Crigler, *Common Knowledge: News and the Construction of Political Meaning* (Chicago: University of Chicago Press, 1992).

21. Kathleen M. McGraw and Clark Hubbard, "Some of the People Some of the Time: Individual Differences in Acceptance of Political Accounts," in Diana C. Mutz, Paul M. Sniderman, and Richard A. Brody, eds., *Political Persuasion and Attitude Change* (Ann Arbor: University of Michigan Press, 1996), pp. 145–170.

22. Donald R. Kinder and Lynn M. Sanders, *Divided By Color: Racial Politics and Democratic Ideals* (Chicago: University of Chicago Press, 1996). For another important book on race, which involves experimentation with survey forms and also presents arguments in opposition to Kinder and Sanders, see Paul Sniderman and Thomas Piazza, *The Scar of Race* (Cambridge, MA: Harvard University Press, 1993).

PART TWO

THEORIES OF PUBLIC OPINION

4

Psychological Perspectives

Although many early democratic theorists contemplated the nature of public opinion, many of the earliest discoveries about public opinion in the social sciences came from the study of psychology. Psychologists and sociologists alike attempt to account for the variations in people's opinions. Why do some people favor prayer in schools while others do not? Why are some people convinced that George Bush stole the 2000 national election from Al Gore, while others believe he rightly assumed office as President of the United States? How do people decide which candidate to vote for? How do our internalized thoughts become public opinion? Psychologists consider how our individual mental states such as our moods, our attention span, or our thinking ability affect the opinions we express. Sociologists and social psychologists, whose work we will explore in the next chapter, examine how social factors like group membership and social norms affect the expression of public opinion.

We have to approach the study of public opinion from many different directions because public opinion expression is made up of so many different psychological factors and social experiences. The formation of public opinion can be seen as a merging of individual beliefs, values, and attitudes in a situational context. Ideally, a public opinion scholar should be familiar with ideas and techniques from several fields—psychology, sociology, political science, and communication. Here, we will introduce you to some of the most important contributions from the study of psychology.

WHAT PSYCHOLOGY CAN TELL US

Psychologists offer us insight into some of the most basic building blocks of public opinion. The concepts developed in this field help us to understand how elements of our psychological makeup can be altered by new information and yet affect the processing of new information. This research also suggests that psychological factors affect our behavior, although the links between what we think and what we do often are weak. Although this sort of research would seem to have a great deal of practical applicability, especially in designing persuasive messages (and resisting them!), public opinion researchers sometimes neglect these theories. Remember that here we are focusing on what goes on within the individual who is formulating an opinion. In Chapter Six, we will explore how social and psychological factors interact to influence our perceptions and produce expressions of public opinion.

SPEAKING THE LANGUAGE: BELIEFS, VALUES, ATTITUDES, AND OPINIONS

A traditional place to start when discussing attitude research is by defining the basic concepts. Definitions of the terms beliefs, values, attitudes, and opinions have been debated and discussed by scholars through the years. Regardless of the definitions, scholars agree that there are cognitive and social foundations for these concepts. In the sections that follow, we will offer brief descriptions of the terms that summarize this extensive debate.

Beliefs

Beliefs are the cognitive components that make up our understanding of the way things are, that is, the information that individuals have about objects or actions.[1] They are the building blocks of attitudes and opinions. Beliefs are often hard to identify, especially when they are widely shared. Such beliefs are the assumptions by which we live our lives, and we presume that others think of the world the same way that we do. Western Christian philosophies contain the belief that people are perfectible—that they can improve themselves or be improved. Given this assumption, it is difficult for Westerners to fathom the caste system, a structure that supports the belief that individuals do not rise above, or sink below, their origins.

Some beliefs are totally distinct, but many are grouped together as belief systems. These belief systems may be quite simple, consisting of only a few items, or they may be enormously complex, involving thousands of beliefs. A belief system, ideally, is internally and psychologically consistent. Clear examples of systems of this kind can be found in religion, in which large numbers of beliefs are interrelated to form a network guiding one's thought and action.

We often see conflicts between belief systems. In politics, for example, belief systems common to one party clash with belief systems typical of another party. In 2002, the Democratic belief system came into conflict with the beliefs of Republican judicial appointees. This conflict led to very few judges appointed to the bench while Democrats had control of the Senate, and Democrats announcing they would not allow appointees with strong conservative beliefs to be confirmed. Sometimes an individual's own belief systems clash, producing a state of psychological tension known as cognitive dissonance.

Values

Values are ideals. While beliefs represent our understanding of the way things are, values represent our understanding of the way things should be. According to Richard Perloff, values "are overarching goals that people strive to obtain." He says that values are "more global and general than attitudes."[2]

According to psychologist Milton Rokeach,[3] there are two kinds of values. Terminal values are the goals we want to reach. Instrumental values are the means we endorse to reach our goals. Terminal values might include end states like freedom, equality, or peace. Instrumental values might encompass honesty, responsibility, and loyalty.

Leaders of social movements often invoke values, sometimes incorporating them into a motto that describes the movement to others. Leaders of social movements often attempt to connect their activities to a desired goal. Mottoes like Patrick Henry's "Give me liberty or give me death" helped to frame the American Revolution in terms of the value of freedom. Individual liberties and personal accomplishment have been important characteristics of American culture. The French Revolution was built on a slightly different set of values: "Liberty, equality, fraternity." It is worthwhile to note that both revolutions were built on the more fundamental belief that people are perfectible, that they can improve themselves.

Because values, like beliefs, tend to be taken for granted or are treated as if they were universal characteristics, it is often difficult for us to comprehend that other cultures may have different values. As you travel to other cultures, especially those not rooted in Western European traditions, you may find that some of your values are not shared by the host culture.

One of the authors of this text once taught at a university in a foreign culture in which collective and societal attainment is an important value rather than the individual accomplishment valued in the United States. The professor confronted a student for cheating on an exam by getting answers from the person in front of her. The student said very little, except that she was "ashamed." The professor did not realize that this situation reflected a difference in values until she discussed the incident with another student. "Yes," the other student agreed. "I'd be ashamed as well. . . . Getting caught that easily is a very silly thing to do." The student explained, "It is not wrong to cheat, but it is very embarrassing not to cheat correctly."

Attitudes

Most scholars agree that attitudes are "general and enduring positive or negative feelings about some person, object or issue."[4] Psychologists describe attitudes as having three components: cognitions (or beliefs), affect (or feelings), and behavior.[5]

A major difference between attitudes and beliefs is that attitudes have a strong "affective," or emotional, component. Beliefs are primarily cognitive; they are the mental constructs by which we know the world. However, many beliefs are evaluative in nature. You may believe that a particular television program is funny, that your friend looks good with a nose ring, or that buying imported goods hurts the U.S. economy. If these are your beliefs, you perceive these evaluations as inherent characteristics of the objects of your beliefs. Attitudes, in contrast, reflect your personal likes and dislikes: that you enjoy the show *Friends*, that you admire your friend's tastes, that you dislike buying imports. These are attitudes because you recognize them as your own orientation toward objects rather than as characteristics that are somehow part of the objects themselves.

However, attitudes are only "predispositions to respond and/or react [and are] directive of behavior."[6] Changing people's attitudes does not always change their behavior. In fact, there is some evidence that under certain conditions, attitudes do not predict behavior at all!

In their simplest form, our attitudes are positive or negative feelings toward something. Nevertheless, attitudes can combine in complex patterns, and the outcome may be unpredictable. For example, I may like pizza and dislike anchovies, but my attitudes about each ingredient separately may be quite different from my attitude about both ingredients together. Perhaps I like anchovies only when they are on pizza, or I might just dislike pizza that has anchovies on it.

Let's consider a more complex example. I may have a friend whom I like very much. However, I may strenuously disapprove of people who live off welfare. If my friend goes on public assistance, I may decide that I no longer like him or that people on public assistance are not so bad. Or, I may live with the logical discontinuity.

Attitudes are built upon our beliefs and values. Our beliefs form the cognitive foundations for our attitudes (anchovies are too salty; people are basically good). Attitudes also are the manifestation of our values as they come into contact with the physical world and take specific form (people should be allowed to eat what they want; people should be responsible for their own lives).

Opinions

When an attitude is expressed, either verbally or through behavior, it is called an opinion. However, there is often confusion in the literature about the differences between attitudes and opinions. Although the terms often are used interchangeably, many researchers do see a difference. Opinions express attitudes, but not all attitudes are expressed. Attitudes are only predispositions to respond; opinions are the responses. Attitudes are seen as broader, more enduring, and less consciously held than opinions. They are "deeper" inside a person than opinions are.[7]

If you give it some thought, you will see that the same attitude can result in two different opinions, depending on the circumstance and the object being evaluated. For example, I may like small children enormously. However, after eight hours of caring for several rambunctious tots, I may opine, "I've had enough!" My attitude toward small children as

Opinions	I support equal rights for women. I wouldn't support a tax increase. I favor increased immigration.
Attitudes	I respect most people. I value public schools. I distrust censorship.
Values	We should respect diverse viewpoints. People should be free. Everyone should have the opportunity to succeed.
Beliefs	People are basically good. All people are created equal. Human beings can be perfected.

FIGURE 4.1   Beliefs, Values, Attitudes, and Opinions: A Cognitive Hierarchy. This figure shows how beliefs form the basis for values, values for attitudes, and attitudes for opinions.

essentially good, even wonderful people has not changed, but my opinion has, at least temporarily. Nonetheless, if I go for several weeks without seeing my little friends, I may miss them a great deal.

Opinions are usually, but not always, consistent with the attitudes to which they are related. I may believe that members of Congress in general are disreputable but have a lot of faith in the representative from my own district.

Figure 4.1 summarizes what we have been discussing in this section. Notice how attitudes are built upon beliefs and values and are finally expressed as opinions. Notice, too, that the same beliefs and values may produce divergent opinions that may even seem contradictory.

EARLY THEORIES OF
ATTITUDE FORMATION AND CHANGE:
THE LEGACIES OF BEHAVIORISM

When we study changes in attitudes, we are faced with an unusual problem. It is very difficult to determine whether beliefs or attitudes existed in a person prior to an experimental or survey-based research study. As researchers, we cannot be sure whether we are measuring existing attitudes or actually causing new ones to be formed. Thus, scholars often use the term "attitude change" quite broadly to mean either attitude formation or attitude change, or both. The distinction is not critical, since what really matters is the process. Psychologists who study "attitude change" are interested in how perception and other processes occurring in people's heads bring about the expression of an opinion.

Some of the earliest theories about how attitudes are formed and changed and about how they affect behavior were based on the assumption that people functioned like animals. Animals responded to stimuli without much thought. Researchers found that animals could be "conditioned" to respond in a certain way to a specific stimulus, and they believed people could be conditioned in much the same way.[8] This perspective is known as behaviorism, and the theories relevant to public opinion that derive from it are known as conditioning theories.

Early twentieth-century psychologist Ivan Pavlov's work with dogs provided researchers with the first clues that conditioning theories might explain the behavior of both animals and people.[9] Researchers such as Arthur and Carolyn Staats[10] thought that if the same stimulus were to produce more or less the same response in everybody, it might be possible to isolate the reasons people form certain attitudes and opinions. They felt that if stimuli received by the brain could be controlled, then presumably the attitude structure, the personality, and even the behavior of individuals could also be controlled.

Two variants of conditioning theories have been of special interest to public opinion scholars: classical conditioning and operant conditioning.

Classical Conditioning

Classical conditioning is a way to study attitude change from a stimulus–response perspective. Classical conditioning is said to occur when an initially neutral stimulus (the conditioned stimulus, or CS) is associated with another stimulus (the unconditioned stimulus, or UCS) that is connected inherently or by prior conditioning to some response (the unconditioned response, or UCR).

Pavlov's[11] classic study provides a good example. In that study, shown in Figure 4.2, a hungry dog is given a piece of meat (the UCS), which causes the dog to salivate (the UCR). When a bell is rung (the CS—an initial neutral stimulus) whenever the dog is given the meat, a CS–UCS pairing occurs. That is, by pairing the bell with the delivery

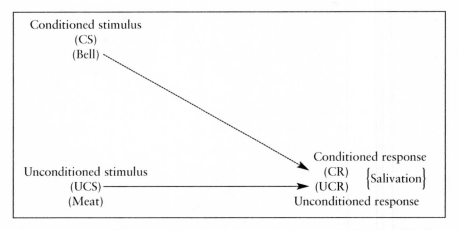

FIGURE 4.2   An Example of Classical Conditioning. SOURCE: R. E. Petty and J. T. Cacioppo, *Attitudes and Persuasion: Classic and Contemporary Approaches* (Dubuque, IA: William C. Brown Company, 1981), p. 41.

of the meat, Pavlov eventually created a situation in which the ringing of the bell alone caused the dog to salivate. By repeatedly ringing a bell when meat was presented to the dog, Pavlov created a conditioned response (CR). The salivation was the result of conditioning rather than the result of a link between the initial stimulus (the meat) and the response (salivation).

Attitude researchers believe that work by social psychologist Arthur Staats was paramount in stimulating research on conditioned responses as it pertains to attitudes.[12] Staats[13] was interested in whether animals (and by extension people) could be conditioned to develop a negative emotional response toward certain words, arguing that people may acquire attitudes in a manner similar to Pavlov's dogs. For example, as Alice Eagly and Shelly Chaiken[14] describe, a child eventually learns the evaluative meaning of the words "good" and "bad" if these conditioned stimuli are repeatedly paired with unconditioned stimuli such as food or physical punishment.

Theoretically, after an attitude has become associated with words such as "good" and "bad," the words can be used as unconditioned stimuli to establish attitudes toward other stimuli. Eagly and Chaiken describe how a child might acquire a negative attitude toward some minority group on the basis of these principles:

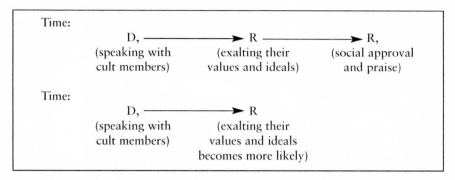

FIGURE 4.3 An Example of Operant Conditioning. SOURCE: R. E. Petty and J. T. Cacioppo, *Attitudes and Persuasion: Classic and Contemporary Approaches* (Dubuque, IA: William C. Brown Company, 1981), p. 48.

Imagine that the child hears a number of negative adjectives (e.g., bad, dirty, stupid) paired with the name of a particular minority group (e.g., blacks, Jews). In this application, the minority group name is the CS, and the negative adjectives are the UCSs. The UCSs are assumed to regularly evoke UCRs—in this case implicit negative evaluative responses. . . . With repeated pairings of the CS and the various UCSs, the minority group name comes to elicit a CR . . . the CR is an implicit negative evaluative response, or negative attitude toward the minority group.[15]

Prejudice is an important concept to understand in public opinion research, for it can lead to expressions of public opinion about other social groups, about candidates and leaders who represent those groups, and about social policies that affect them.

Operant Conditioning

Operant conditioning is based upon the supposition that people act to maximize the positive and minimize the negative consequences of their behavior.[16] We may come to adhere to attitudes that yield rewards and to reject attitudes that result in punishments.[17] Figure 4.3 illustrates how such operant conditioning might work for individuals who are being indoctrinated into a cult.

Numerous studies in the late 1950s and 1960s investigated the effects of such social reinforcement on the conditioning of attitude statements.

Typically in these studies, subjects might be asked to construct sentences, converse informally with the experimenter, or answer specific questions asked by an experimenter. The experimenter would reinforce certain verbal responses either positively or negatively.

A classic example of conditioned responses appears in a study conducted by Joel Greenspoon,[18] in which he used verbal rewards to change what people would say. Greenspoon was able to increase the frequency with which a subject used a plural noun by responding with "good," "mm-hmmm," or an approving head nod whenever the subject used a plural noun. Likewise, Greenspoon would react negatively with "bad," "humph," or a disapproving head movement or might not even react at all when the subject emitted an incorrect response (such as a singular noun). Many studies since have used this approach.[19]

A number of studies concerned with the verbal conditioning of attitudes suggest that people actually do change their attitudes as a result of rewards and that these attitudes persist.[20] However, no one has been able to explain why this works. Some studies suggest that attitudes change not as an automatic and unconscious consequence of reinforcement but because of "cognitively mediated social influence" (such as information or norms presented through one's culture). That is, people do not merely react to a stimulus. They actually think, and think strategically, about how to behave. Social factors as well as thought processes may interfere with the linkage between stimulus and response. For example, behavioral conditioning may result not in attitude change but in compliance. That is, subjects may not actually alter their opinions; they may merely "go along" with the experimenter.

Can this operant conditioning response be seen at work in more generalized public opinion situations? Operant conditioning might have been one of many complex factors at work in Nazi Germany during the 1930s, where German citizens were heavily rewarded for those activities one might think of as patriotic (e.g., saluting, joining a political party, attending a political rally; see Figure 4.4) and for feelings of historical greatness (costumes reflecting medieval customs, and so on). "Incorrect" responses in these situations (e.g., being against Hitler or the Nazi Party) were severely punished. Regardless of whether these public expressions of opinion represented compliance or genuine attitude change, the policies they supported had dramatic consequences for Germany and for the world.

FIGURE 4.4 A Mass Rally in Nazi Germany. Large rallies such as this one were common public opinion displays during the Nazi ascent to power. (Photo courtesy of the Library of Congress)

For many years, behavioral approaches to human psychology were prevalent. However, this perspective turned out to have important drawbacks, as you have probably already begun to see. Since behaviorism was predicated on the idea of acting without thinking, it was very difficult to explain why people did what they did. Much of the later psychological research into public opinion can be usefully categorized by the ways it addresses the failings of the behavioral perspective. Before we begin to elaborate on these shortcomings of the behavioral approach, you should recognize what is perhaps the most important contribution of behaviorism to understanding public opinion. Most people do not think very much about the opinions they express. Asked questions on a survey or in an exit poll, they are likely to answer without thinking.[21] These relatively automatic responses to a stimulus resemble in important ways the original vision of behaviorism.

Nevertheless, behavioral approaches have at least five significant drawbacks that later researchers have tried to remedy with other kinds of theories. First, although it is true that people often do not think very much before expressing an opinion, there are some cases where they think carefully and others where they do not. Information processing models try to diagram key elements of people's cognitive work before they respond to a stimulus. Other processing models try to describe some of the cognitive shortcuts people use to make sense of a complex, fast-moving world. Second, attitudes and opinions come in packages, and sometimes the way we respond to a stimulus is affected by a whole group of attitudes, beliefs, and values. Furthermore, different people package attitudes in different ways. It is clear that people actually engage in some cognitive work to produce an opinion rather than just to respond to a stimulus. Cognitive consistency theories try to explain how the elements in a package of attitudes interact when people are asked to express an opinion. Judgmental theories try to explain how people's current attitudes affect the processing of new information and the likelihood of attitude change.

A third problem behavioral approaches do not take into account is that two people may hold the same attitude for different reasons. Functional theories try to explain why people hold the attitudes they do. Fourth, behavioral theories cannot explain why people often do not behave in accordance with their attitudes. Social scientists believe there may be many reasons for this, and the theory of reasoned action attempts to explain the relationship between attitudes and behavior. Finally, emotions can play an important role in the formulation and expression of public opinion.

All of these later theories reject one of the central ideas of behaviorism: that people presented with the same stimulus will respond in the same way.[22] They also are informed by one of the most important recent findings about public opinion: People do not just remember their opinions and recite them when asked. They actually construct these opinions based on what they are thinking about at the time they are asked.[23] Let us consider some of these classic and contemporary theories in more detail.

COGNITIVE PROCESSING: WHAT HAPPENS WHEN PEOPLE THINK

Many scholars believe that if they can understand how a person cognitively processes a message, they can better understand the impact the message has on the individual's attitudes and behavior. Two main approaches have developed to explain how message processing occurs: cognitive processing models and cognitive response theories. Both of these approaches reject behaviorism's model of unthinking response to a stimulus, but both also recognize that the world is a complex place and people do not devote equal attention to all aspects of it. A third approach, the study of "heuristics," or mental shortcuts, also attempts to account for the fact that people can only make limited use of the information available to them.

Cognitive response theories assume that the brain is a "noisy" place. The basic idea behind these theories is that the brain is always active, trying to make sense of the information it is receiving, checking the accuracy of the information it is processing, and so forth. According to this model, the idiosyncratic thoughts—the cognitive responses that recipients generate, rehearse, and learn—interfere with various other mental activities. Therefore, ongoing cognitive activity interacts with incoming information in complex ways.

These responses are especially important in persuasion attempts.[24] According to the cognitive response model, people connect the information in persuasive messages to their existing feelings and beliefs about the message topic. The model suggests that message and information processing is a very active and interactive process; the complexity of the process suggests that cognitive responses mediate the effect of persuasive messages, determining both the direction and extent of attitude change.[25] One of the most important implications of this model for persuaders is that it suggests that people are easily distracted. Messages must often be repeated before they have any persuasive effect.

There are several cognitive processing models, but we have chosen to discuss the elaboration likelihood model (ELM)[26] as an example of models of this type. We have chosen this model in part because it has generated more research than other similar models but also because it was developed in response to the perceived shortcomings of the cognitive response approach.

In developing the model, Richard Petty and John Cacioppo felt that the cognitive response approach failed to consider the many ways in which people engage in thinking about issues relevant to the message. "Elaboration" thus refers to "the extent to which a person thinks about the issue-relevant arguments contained in a message."[27]

In the model, elaboration is described as falling on a continuum that ranges from complex thought processes to mainly superficial thoughts. People's reactions to a persuasive message can range from unthinking acceptance or rejection to active counterargumentation.

Petty and Cacioppo argue that a recipient of a persuasive message studies, analyzes, and evaluates issue-relevant information, comparing it to information already available in memory. Sometimes the recipient engages in a great deal of scrutiny about the central issues. In these situations, elaboration is high and the recipient will tend to ignore "peripheral matters" such as the credibility of the source. Other times, the recipient of the message does not (or cannot) engage in processing the message in any depth, and elaboration is low. The recipient may then rely on peripheral factors (such as source credibility) to form or change attitudes about the message and its content.

In their model, Petty and Cacioppo try to describe some of the conditions under which elaboration is likely to be high and situations where it is likely to be low. When people are motivated to think about a message—either because it seems directly relevant to them since they feel a sense of personal responsibility about the topic or simply because they like to think—then elaboration will be high. People will contemplate the message in issue-relevant ways. The same is true for messages that are repeated often to audiences that are relatively undistracted and have some knowledge of the issue. By contrast, when people are not motivated or able to process issue-relevant information, elaboration will be low, and the audience is likely to respond to simple cues in the message rather than giving it careful consideration.[28]

The diagram of Petty and Cacioppo's[29] elaboration likelihood model is presented in Figure 4.5. As the figure shows, the ELM process begins with a persuasive communication and ends with a negative or positive attitude change. For the most part, the central route, which depicts high elaboration, is presented on the left side of the figure. The peripheral route, representing low elaboration, appears on the right. Interconnections between the two routes are indicated in the figure. The final outcome is based on the individual's motivation and ability to process the message, which in turn influences the person's choice of processing strategy.

Consider the implications of this model for public opinion scholars and for those who design persuasive messages. The ELM suggests that there are two ways to produce attitude change: (1) by encouraging people

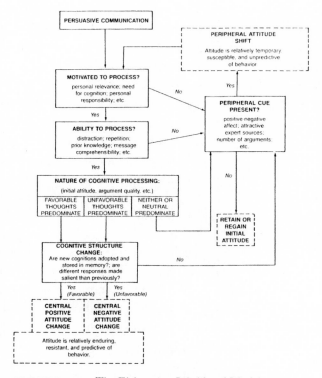

FIGURE 4.5   The Elaboration Likelihood Model.
SOURCE: R. E. Petty and J. T. Cacioppo, "The Elaboration
Likelihood Model of Persuasion," Figure 1, p. 126, in L.
Berkowitz, ed., *Advances in Experimental Social Psychology*
(San Diego: Academic Press, 1986).

to do a great deal of thinking about the message (the central route), or (2)
by encouraging people to focus on simple, compelling cues (the peripheral route). The effectiveness of the message will depend on people's ability and willingness to process it. Although Petty and Cacioppo's model
seems simple enough, applying it effectively to the real world can be
complex. Think of how people are likely to process messages about arms
control policy differently from messages about abortion. Campaign messages for a high-profile race such as the presidential campaign may succeed by encouraging high elaboration. The same kinds of messages may
fail miserably in a low-profile race for county supervisor, where voters
may follow a peripheral path. The same may be true for policy debates.
Alternatively, large national campaigns like the presidential race may

need messages that encourage low elaboration, since the voters who will go to the polls may not be very motivated to learn about the issues. Local races, where only the very dedicated turn out to vote, may do better by assuming that voters will follow the central route.

Notice that the ELM serves primarily as a descriptive rather than an explanatory model. That is, the model does not explain "why certain arguments are strong or weak, why certain variables serve as (peripheral) cues, or why certain variables affect information processing."[30] Nevertheless, as Eagly and Chaiken note, "the model represents a powerful and integrative empirical framework for studying persuasion processes."[31]

Theories about the use of mental heuristics also tend to describe rather than explain, but they have proved useful in exploring important aspects of public opinion and behavior. Samuel Popkin (see Chapter Eight) makes important use of this concept in his discussion of "low information rationality." The term heuristic is described from a Greek word meaning "to discover," and a heuristic is a device or an argument for letting someone personally discover the truth. The idea of the brain using heuristics is simply that even though certain procedures would appear to be the most logical ways of arriving at a solution to a problem, the brain may use fast, simple methods that are usually, but not always, the most clear-cut or the most likely to be correct.

Researchers find that when people process heuristically, they use a subset of available information so that they can employ fairly simple rules and decisionmaking procedures to formulate a reasonably accurate decision.[32] The most important thing to note about heuristics and their use in attitude change is that some relatively simple rules might be the best representations of people's attitude judgments.[33] Like most of the more recent theories about the psychological processes involved in attitude formation and change, theories involving mental heuristics assume people think about their opinions but that they do not think about them very much.

CONSISTENCY AND JUDGMENTAL THEORIES:
ATTITUDES COME IN PACKAGES

Attitudes are neither formed nor changed in a vacuum. The attitudes that we hold now affect the ways in which we process new information and assess persuasive messages. Existing attitudes form a frame of reference, a basis of comparison, for new ideas. Further, changing one attitude may result in changing a whole network of related attitudes. Although information processing models do not completely ignore this aspect of attitude change, the interconnectedness of attitudes is not something these models focus on.

Some theories about attitudes make the interconnections central in explaining why people's attitudes change and why people resist changing their attitudes. Consistency theories describe the ways in which attitudes are networked and how that networking is likely to affect opinion expression and attitude change. Judgment theories emphasize the ways that existing attitudes color the interpretation of new information. Let us consider each in turn.

Consistency Theories

All consistency theories share several concepts in common. They all describe cognitions (beliefs, values, attitudes, and so on) as being consistent, inconsistent, or irrelevant to one another. According to Leon Festinger,[34] two cognitions are consistent when one follows from the other (e.g., the cognition "I love ice cream" is consistent with plans to buy ice cream cones daily at the local dairy bar). Two cognitions are inconsistent (dissonant) when the opposite of one cognitive element follows from the other (e.g., the cognition "I eat lots of ice cream" is dissonant with the public health statement that too much ice cream results in high cholesterol levels). Finally, two cognitive elements can be irrelevant when knowledge of one tells you nothing about what you might expect regarding the other (e.g., the announcement that smoking can cause lung cancer has nothing to do with the expectation that five hurricanes will hit Florida in the year 2006). Relations among cognitions (elements) are determined by a person's subjective expectations regarding what will happen in these relationships rather than by the actual, logical interrelationships between the elements.

Balance Theory.   Many readers already may be familiar with balance theory, especially if they have taken a class in psychology. Balance theory, originally formulated by Fritz Heider,[35] provides a way to describe attitudes held by the individual and the relation of these attitudes to each other. This theory is often relevant to students because it deals with a triadic relationship and students often find themselves in this type of situation. Recently, a student advisee came to my office to discuss a problem she was having with her roommates. For simplicity's sake, let us say she had only two roommates, although she really had many more.

My student liked both roommates a great deal, and they, in turn, liked her. However, her two roommates disliked each other. Obviously, this would create a miserable situation for all concerned—it would create a state of imbalance.

According to Heider, a strain would arise because there is psychological pressure to restore balance. In this particular situation, there are several things that could be done. My student could: (1) play the role of peacemaker and work with the roommates on their relationship, hoping the roommates would change their attitudes and begin to like each other; (2) develop a dislike for one of the roommates and shift the imbalance; (3) move to a different apartment and leave the situation altogether (this is the solution my advisee decided upon).

Heider[36] presented these relationships as shown in Figure 4.6. Heider used the symbols P, X, and O to illustrate relationships of this kind, in which P is the perceiver, O is some other person, and X is either a third person or some attribute of O. The plus and minus signs in the figure indicate an attitude or sentiment. For example, P plus O indicates that P likes O. P minus O indicates that P dislikes O.

The general rule for determining whether a given situation is balanced or imbalanced is to multiply all the signs in the triad algebraically. Thus, a plus times a plus yields a product that is a plus; a minus times a minus yields a plus; a plus times a minus equals a minus. If the product of the three signs is a plus, the triad is balanced. If the product of the three signs is a minus, the triad is unbalanced.

It is clear that there are limits to the value of balance theory because it explains attitudes and relationships in relatively simple terms. However, it has been useful not only for understanding hypothetical situations in which people must react but also in field studies and experimental situations. Political scientists and public opinion scholars have applied the principles of balance theory when attempting to understand voters' perceptions of candidates' positions on issues and other public opinion phenomena. For example, Jon Krosnick[37] found that perceptions of political candidates' positions can be biased by perceiving that liked candidates

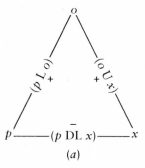

(a)

The given situation is unbalanced:
two positive relations and one
negative relation.

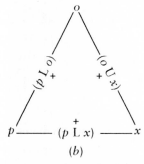

(b)

Change in sentiment relation
resulting in a balance of three
positive relations.

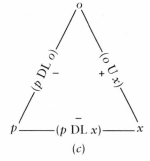

(c)

Change in sentiment relation resulting in a balance of two negative relations and one positive relation.

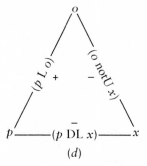

(d)

Change in unit relation resulting in
a balance of two negative relations
and one positive relation.

FIGURE 4.6 An Illustration of Balance Theory. SOURCE: F. Heider, *The Psychology of Interpersonal Relations* (New York: Wiley, 1958), Figure 1, p. 208.

agree with the voters' own positions on issues whereas disliked candidates disagree. In this case, individual voters seem to be trying to maintain a balanced triad between themselves, their candidates, and their issue positions by deliberately or unconsciously deceiving themselves.

It is clear that the principles of balance theory are enduring ones. Although interest in the theory waned in the late 1960s, it was revived in the late 1970s and 1980s[38] and research using the principles of balance theory continues to be of interest.

Congruity Theory.   One of the major criticisms of Heider's balance theory is that there are no provisions for degrees of liking or belonging between the elements. That is, a positive P and O sentiment is scored as plus 1, regardless of whether we are discussing friends, lovers, or virtual strangers. Congruity theory, as presented first by Charles Osgood and Percy Tannenbaum,[39] attempts to overcome this problem by quantifying gradations of liking. The theory is often considered a special case of balance theory.[40]

Congruity theory focuses on the manner in which we integrate a number of potentially conflicting communications concerning other people (or objects or issues). Rather than viewing problems as having simple yes or no solutions, congruity theory assumes there will be conflicting messages with shades of gray. Conflicting messages could result in "incongruity," which is a state of cognitive imbalance. This cognitive state causes us to change our attitudes in a way that D. W. Rajecki describes as a compromise between the initial polarities of our attitudes before we heard the communication: "A basic dictum of the model is that when a disliked person endorses a liked other, the resultant attitude will be the same toward both. By reason of association with each other, the person you initially disliked intensely will improve somewhat in your estimation."[41]

Balance theory lets us account for the fact that we sometimes disagree with our friends or our political leaders and yet continue to like and support them. However, over time, if our disagreements become more frequent or more important, we may decide to achieve balance by acquiring new friends or new political leaders whose views are more in tune with our own.

Much of the research on congruity theory has shown that people's attitudes on a particular issue can influence both their attitudes toward a person who expresses opinions on the issue and their attitudes toward other (unrelated) issues on which the person takes a stand. Eagly and Chaiken[42] discovered that the behavior of American politicians reflects their belief that they can enhance their image with voters by (1) associating themselves with popular causes, (2) disassociating themselves from unpopular causes, and (3) remaining mute on issues over which voter opinion is divided. We see an increasing trend in politicians who attempt to avoid all but the most basic issues and find both Republicans and Democrats speaking out primarily on issues on which both parties hold similar stands.

Cognitive Dissonance Theory. Cognitive dissonance theory takes the basic foundations of the consistency theories to new levels. First developed by Festinger in 1957, the theory has generated a tremendous amount of research and has become one of the most important attitude change theories of the last fifty years. As Perloff notes, since Festinger's book *A Theory of Cognitive Dissonance* was written, more than 1,000 studies of cognitive dissonance have been published! These studies have "tested different aspects of Festinger's theory, challenged hypotheses derived from the theory and applied it to contexts ranging from marketing to religion."[43]

Festinger[44] carries the examination of the interrelationships between the cognitive elements much further than these relationships are explored in balance theory or congruity theory. However, with balance and congruity theories, the interrelationships among a number of elements can be considered simultaneously to determine whether the structure of the elements is balanced or not. Dissonance theory considers only pairs of elements at a time.

One of Festinger's important statements is that an inconsistency between two cognitions (such that one cognitive element implies the opposite of the other) gives rise to the uncomfortable psychological state of "cognitive dissonance." For example, if I love ice cream yet I am aware of the dangers of high cholesterol, I would experience dissonance. Psychologically, it does not make sense to engage in a behavior that would endanger my health.

The magnitude of the dissonance depends on the importance of the cognitive elements to the person. If I value ice cream more than my health or if I am skeptical of the dangers of high cholesterol, it is doubtful that I will reduce my consumption of ice cream. Alternatively, if my health is the most important value for me (for instance, if I have a family history of heart trouble), I may give up ice cream all together. Dissonance is at its most powerful when the two cognitive elements are important and evenly valued—if I am really worried about my health but I really love ice cream.

Of course, if most of us had to live every day experiencing constant cognitive dissonance, it would not be long before we became stressed, mentally imbalanced, or worse! Obviously, something must be done to alleviate the stress associated with such dissonance. Festinger says that because dissonance is so very uncomfortable to us, we will do almost anything to reduce the dissonance in order to achieve consonance. As he notes, there are three ways in which dissonance can be reduced:

1. The individual can change one of the cognitions so that the relationship between the two becomes consonant (e.g., I could decide that eating ice cream is too dangerous so I actually give it up!).
2. The person might "add" consonant cognitions (e.g., I could think up all the reasons why I like ice cream and find these reasons are more important to me than any health concerns).
3. The person might alter the importance of the cognitions (e.g., I might rationalize that I need to eat ice cream every day because it has milk in it—I am getting older, after all, and ice cream might keep me from getting osteoporosis).

It is clear that cognitive dissonance is an important psychological state for researchers to study so they can determine how people react when they are faced with conflicting cognitive elements. In fact, researchers have examined the concept of cognitive dissonance from a number of perspectives, including (1) the requisite conditions needed for dissonance arousal,[45] (2) ways to determine when a person is experiencing cognitive dissonance,[46] or even (3) how cognitive dissonance "feels" to a person.[47]

How can students of public opinion apply dissonance theory to public opinion research? Clearly, studies of public opinion over a certain time period are needed to examine the nature of cognitive dissonance and public opinion. We might want to understand, for example, how important, or how dissonance arousing an issue is to a person before there is any commitment to a point of view. Another interesting question is whether dissonance could be a social-level phenomenon as well as an individual-level phenomenon. Can a group experience dissonance? It also seems possible that dissonance theories could help us explain some important public opinion phenomena, such as understanding political cynicism in America today. If individuals believe in their country but not in their leaders, could the cognitive dissonance created by these beliefs be expressed in the form of public cynicism?

It would also be interesting to study the formation of dissonance in association with the development of social issues so that we could understand the points at which people become committed to certain views. It is clear that when an issue is relatively new, it may have little direct importance to the public. Little cognitive dissonance would be aroused if the issue were examined or voted on; the public simply would not care enough about the outcome. In later stages, however, members of the public may have chosen sides on the issue and feel committed to those opinions.

Judgmental Theories

The underlying principle of most judgmental theories is that "all stimuli can be arranged in some meaningful order" on a psychological dimension. That is, attitudes toward an object can be arranged from the most negative (unfavorable) to the most positive (favorable) in the same way that people might be arranged in order from most attractive to least attractive, longest hair to shortest hair, and so forth. How positive or negative something feels or how it is rated on an attitude scale depends upon the frame of reference.[48] That is, our past experiences play an important role in the ways that we interpret new information.

Adaptation Level Theory. In adaptation level theory, a person's adaptation level is that point on the dimension of judgment that corresponds to the psychological neutral point. As Petty and Cacioppo explain, "If you were to put your hand in a bucket of very cold water, eventually your hand would adapt to the water temperature so that the cold water would feel neutral or normal. Subsequent judgments of how cold or warm another bucket of water felt would be made relative to the water temperature to which your hand had previously adapted."[49]

Adaptation level is important because other stimuli we experience are judged in relation to this level, which serves as an anchor or reference point. A contrast effect occurs when a new stimulus being judged is displaced, moved away from the adaptation level. For example, many Americans might be shocked at the tenor of debates in the British Houses of Parliament, where members cheer speeches given by others in their party and boo and hiss those given by the opposition. We are used to the more staid and "respectful" debates held in our own legislative chambers, so to us the British seem rowdy and undignified. Our judgment of their behavior is based on what we are used to rather than on the objective "propriety" of their actions. A number of studies have investigated contrast effects and have demonstrated that these effects do occur in the judgments of both social and physical stimuli.[50]

An interesting study of adaptation level theory was conducted by Philip Brickman, Dan Coates, and Ronnie Janoff-Bulman,[51] who tested the proposition that extremely positive events do not increase one's overall level of happiness. To use an example close to home: Recently, an accountant in a department in which one of us worked won the state lottery—$18 million. Brickman and associates suggest that this event should raise the accountant's adaptation level so that more common, mundane events become less pleasurable than they used to be.

When Brickman and associates tested this hypothesis, they asked people who had won from $50,000 to $1,000,000 in the Illinois state lottery how pleasant they found seven ordinary events like watching television and eating breakfast. People in a control group of nonwinners were asked the same questions. Lottery winners rated these events as less pleasant than the controls, even though earlier studies had found no differences in overall pleasure ratings between the two groups.

The researchers speculate that the extra pleasure of winning the money is offset by the decline in pleasure from ordinary events. Indeed, when the accountant-turned-millionaire, who is now able to enjoy the finer things of life, was asked if the pleasure of eating breakfast was reduced since winning the lottery, she answered, "Not on my [new] front porch!"

Social Judgment Theory.   Social judgment theory is similar to adaptation level theory in that it also assumes that people tend to arrange stimuli in a meaningful order on a psychological dimension (tall to short, fat to thin, and so forth). However, in social judgment theory, judgments about physical as well as social stimuli are thought to be subject not only to contrast effects but also to assimilation effects. In addition, in social judgment theory, one's own attitude is thought to serve as an internal anchor, and the opinions and attitudes expressed by others may be displaced and moved either toward or away from one's own position.[52] Attitudes that are relatively close to one's own are assimilated (seen as closer than they actually are), but attitudes that are quite discrepant from one's own are contrasted (seen as further away than they actually are).

How do we develop such misperceptions? According to social judgment theory, an attitudinal dimension is composed of three categories or latitudes. The latitude of acceptance includes the person's most preferred position but also includes the range of other opinions on an issue that the person finds acceptable. The latitude of rejection comprises the range of opinions that the person finds objectionable. Finally, the latitude of noncommitment comprises those positions that the person finds neither acceptable nor unacceptable.

Social judgment theory states that people's existing attitudes distort their perception of others' positions. These distortions influence how likely it is that a person's attitude will change. For example, say that you and a friend are discussing the issue of abortion. Assimilating your friend's attitude on abortion toward your own attitude would probably make you regard your friend's statements as "fair," "unbiased," and so forth, increasing the likelihood of attitude change.[53] However, contrast, which causes another's position to be seen as further from one's own point of view, would lead you to regard your friend's statements about abortion as "unfair" or "biased," reducing the likelihood that your attitude will change.

Whether the attitude or message being presented by someone falls within an individual's latitude of acceptance, rejection, or noncommitment determines whether the content is positively or negatively evaluated and also influences whether attitude change occurs. There are many more theories about how people process information in order to form opinions. We have discussed only a few to give you some idea of how the psychology of the individual can have a profound impact on the opinions of the whole, that is, on the formation of public opinion.

MOTIVATIONAL THEORIES:
SAME ATTITUDE, DIFFERENT REASON

When first considering public opinion, it may not be obvious that there are reasons for holding opinions. Perhaps the foregoing discussion of consistency theories helps to some extent, for these theories imply that we hold opinions not only because they seem logically "right" to us but because they seem consistent with other beliefs, values, and attitudes we find important. But there are many reasons for holding opinions. In the 1950s, two separate groups of investigators developed theories that argue that attitudes serve various psychological needs and have diverse motivational bases. These are known as functional theories. Other theories describe and explain how our concerns about our own self-image affects the attitudes we hold and the opinions we express. One of these theories, impression management theory, is discussed here because of its close links to cognitive dissonance theory. Several of the other theories that deal with this aspect of opinion formation are discussed in Chapters Five and Six.

Functional Theories

Obviously, there are a number of functions that attitudes can serve. Attitudes may be convenient summaries of our beliefs, they may help others to know what to expect from us, and they can express important aspects of our personality.[54] Central to functional theories, however, is the notion that there are specific personality functions that attitudes serve for the individual.

The key functional approach described here is Daniel Katz's[55] functional theory of attitudes. However, students should be aware that others, such as M. Brewster Smith, Jerome Bruner, and Robert White[56] and Herbert Kelman[57] also have described functional approaches to the study of attitudes.

Katz's Functional Theory of Attitudes

In his article entitled "The Functional Approach to the Study of Attitudes,"[58] Katz describes four functions that attitudes might serve for a person: the (1) ego-defensive function, (2) value-expressive function, (3) knowledge function, and (4) utilitarian function.

The ego-defensive function describes how attitudes are held to help people protect themselves from unflattering truths about themselves. These attitudes also may be held to protect individuals from unflattering truths about others who are important to them. A simplistic example of the ego-defensive function would be when a person with illegible handwriting states that "bad handwriting is the mark of a true genius." In the value-expressive function, a person holds an attitude in order to express an important value. For example, when people say that they try to vote in every election, they may be promoting the value of democracy.

The knowledge function helps people better understand events and people around them. For example, feeling revulsion and developing negative attitudes about the September 11th, 2001, attack on the World Trade Center twin towers may help a person to better understand terrorism. Finally, in the utilitarian function, attitudes help people gain rewards and avoid punishments. You may decide to take on the attitudes your professor expounds in class, hoping that this helps you to get an A on an exam.

Functional theories explore the notion that changing an attitude requires understanding of its motivational basis. That is, knowing what function an attitude serves dictates the form persuasion attempts should take.[59] For example, suppose you know that I approve of the way the president (say in this case George W. Bush) is handling his job and that this attitude serves a utilitarian function. All of my friends are Republican, and liking Bush is one part of fitting in with the social set to which I belong. You might persuade me to change my mind by telling me that my friends would not really mind if I did not approve of Bush, or you might convince me that it was more rewarding to belong to another group that favored Democrats. However, if my approval of George Bush is an attitude that serves an ego-defensive function, you may have to use a very different persuasive strategy. Suppose I approve of Bush because I think I know something about politics and I voted for Bush for president. If I were to disapprove of Bush, my image of myself as knowledgeable about politics would be threatened. Your persuasive tactics might include things like telling me that no one could be sure how Bush would handle the economy, that many people did not like the way he dealt with the war on Iraq, or that political experts are surprised at how poorly he is doing. In this way, you might make it possible for me to change my attitude without damaging my ego. In both cases, the attitude is the same, but the persuasive strategy is different because the same attitude may serve different functions.

RAS Model of Opinion Formation

In the early 1990s, political scientist John Zaller presented a model that outlined how people acquire information from the political environment by using persuasive arguments and cues, and transform that information into survey responses. The model is known as "RAS" (Receive–Accept–Sample Model). The RAS model of opinion formation explains how an individual develops an opinion before expressing it publicly.

In the model, Zaller describes four stages people go through when forming and changing their opinions. First, the message must be produced; second, the receiver must attend to and comprehend the message; third, the receiver must decide whether or not to yield to the suggestion in the message; and finally the receiver must act by accepting or rejecting the persuasive attempt.

The RAS model consists of four axioms. First, the Reception Axiom states that in order to receive the message, information must be diffused into society in a manner that allows the mass public to have access to it and to be able to understand it. Then, the mass public must attend to the message. Second, the Resistance Axiom describes the relationship between a receiver's political predispositions and whether or not he will receive a particular message. A person with liberal political predispositions is more likely to resist a politically conservative persuasive message.

The third axiom, the Accessibility Axiom, is central to Zaller's theory. The individual must draw from the considerations he has lodged in his memory, and recall those that are most accessible. Zaller argues that the collection of considerations that one can draw from depends upon the level of general prior knowledge the individual holds. He refers to this as "top of the head" thinking. The individual will not draw from all that he knows, but merely that which he has most recently been reminded of or thought about. It is here that the influence of mass media reports of events can play an important part in the considerations brought to mind. Finally, the fourth axiom is Response. The individual "averages" across all considerations brought to mind, and chooses from them how he will respond to the question posed to him by the researcher.

Zaller addresses attitudes in this model by explaining how an individual begins to form an opinion when asked. He does not support the notion that people walk around with fully formed attitudes and opinions in their heads, ready to share whenever asked. Instead, Zaller believes that people will sample from the information most accessible in their minds, and base their opinion on what thoughts occur to them. This, of course, can lead to a shift of opinion from one interview to another. This aspect of ambiguity, as Zaller calls it, has similarities to the mass communication theory of priming, discussed later in this text.

Impression Management Theory

A different approach to examining motivations for attitude change is found in studies that use impression management theory. Impression management theory deals with how people present an image to others in order to achieve a particular goal.[60] Most studies of impression management assume that the primary goal is attaining social approval.[61]

In this and other ways, impression management theory differs significantly from the cognitive consistency theories described earlier. In cognitive consistency theories, it is assumed that people are motivated to set their thoughts and actions in order and must decide how to achieve this consistency. Impression management theorists assume that people want to convey, given social constraints, as positive and consistent a public image as possible in order to obtain social rewards—regardless of whether that image is consistent with internalized attitudes.

In fact, James Tedeschi, Barry Schlenker, and Thomas Bonoma[62] proposed impression management theory as an alternative to dissonance theory. As Schlenker states: "Irrespective of whether or not people have psychological needs to be consistent . . . there is little doubt that the appearance of consistency usually leads to social reward, while the appearance of inconsistency leads to social punishment."[63]

Impression management theorists agree with Festinger that tension is produced when people act publicly in a manner contrary to their attitudes, but they do not agree that the tension is produced by dissonant cognitions. Rather, Tedeschi and colleagues,[64] among others, believe that this tension is produced by people's knowledge that they appear inconsistent to others. When people perceive that their attitudes appear inconsistent, they immediately begin to manage more carefully the impression they are making on others by restoring consistency to their actions or in their expression of attitudes.[65]

Because people are often motivated to impress other people and to create a desired effect upon others, they may change or report to have changed their beliefs and attitudes in an effort to create desirable impressions on others.[66] The result of this "false" reporting often leads to a difference between individuals' privately held and publicly held attitudes. I may say that I believe it is everyone's civic duty to report for jury duty, but I may reflect privately that it is an enormous waste of my time to do so. Impression management theory is of importance to the public opinion scholar because of this focus on potential differences between public and private attitudes. Public opinion researchers often investigate public opinion situations in which discrepancies between these attitudes and subsequent opinions occur.

Public opinion researchers are aware that people will sometimes provide misleading information on public opinion questionnaires in an attempt to appear more favorable in the eyes of the researcher. This phenomenon is called "social desirability bias." This bias occurs when respondents attempt to avoid admitting to certain behaviors or attitudes. Even during a survey that is being conducted anonymously, respondents will sometimes avoid admitting to an opinion or behavior that could be considered socially unacceptable. This becomes problematic when the survey is measuring opinions about sensitive matters such as racism, or attitudes concerning the poor or government entitlement programs. In these types of surveys, the respondent might see some benefit in answering according to her perception of a socially acceptable answer, rather that answering honestly.

LINKS BETWEEN ATTITUDES AND BEHAVIOR: WHAT PEOPLE THINK AND WHAT THEY DO

You probably assume that people say what they think and think what they say, act what they think and think what they act. This assumption has been a common one, made not only by researchers but by the general public. After all, how can we interact with those around us if we cannot make some predictions about how people will react in various circumstances?

Being able to predict how people will react is certainly important to public opinion scholars, who often view attitude–behavior linkages as key determinants of a public's opinion on any number of issues. The number of positions in polling firms would be dwindling dramatically and we would not be writing this book if it turned out that attitudes had no bearing on behavior.

Certainly, there are issues and situations that appear to result in clear (though not necessarily strong) relationships between attitudes and behavior. For example, numerous studies of voting behavior have shown that attitudes toward particular candidates predict voting for those candidates with considerable accuracy.[67] However, Howard Schuman and Michael Johnson state that although attitudes do predict behaviors in voting studies, the findings seem to "vary from small to moderate in size."[68]

In other words, the strength of the relationship between attitudes and behaviors is debatable. In fact, research over the years has shown that this linkage is more tenuous than intuition would have us believe. How many friends have you had who feel strongly about issues concerning the environment but could not care less about recycling, would gladly take a spin in a motorboat, or do not think twice about how much gas their car consumes? Or have you ever been involved in a relationship with someone who said you were special but treated you as if you were anything but?

Empirical studies suggesting weak relationships between attitudes and behaviors appeared in the 1930s, and such research continues to this day.[69] There may be many reasons for these discrepancies.

Measurement Issues

In addition to all of the other methodological concerns associated with experiments and surveys when they are used to measure public opinion (see Chapter Three for a discussion), studies that attempt to measure the links between attitudes and behavior have some special difficulties associated with them.

Different methods of data collection seem to produce contradictory evidence regarding the strength of the relationship between attitudes and behavior. For example, Kelman[70] and Schuman and Johnson[71] maintain that whereas weak and even negative relationships between attitudes and behaviors exist in experimental research, positive and moderately strong relationships are found using survey research. One reason for this may be that there is a tendency for survey research to examine "attitudes that are more important and involving and that therefore may be more influential in relation to behavior."[72]

Icek Ajzen[73] describes what he calls the "principle of correspondence." That is, attitude measures that do not correspond to behavioral measures will not predict behavior very well. High correspondence between measures will produce a higher consistency between the measures. For example, a general attitude about environmental protection may not predict the likelihood that someone will donate to the Sierra Club, but it might predict a respondent's overall "environmental concern" (e.g., attitudes about recycling, mass transit use, and so on), especially if that concern were measured over a period of time.

Obviously, you need to make sure that questions on a survey reflect clearly the behavior you want to measure. If you want to predict how much someone is likely to donate to a specific charity, for example, you are better off asking them about their opinion of that specific charity rather than about their general beliefs or values concerning donating, social responsibility, and so forth.

Individual Differences

Individual differences can account for some inconsistencies in attitude–behavior relationships. You probably have some friends who exhibit high consistency between their attitudes and behaviors. If they tell you they think something you can almost rest assured they will back up their purported attitudes with their behaviors. However, you can probably think of just as many or more friends who are known to exhibit inconsistencies between their attitudes and behaviors. They may say one thing and act in a completely different way.

As Perloff notes, your friends who fit the latter category may have a strong attitude about an issue, but "they will keep their opinion to themselves, or they may even argue for the opposite point of view."[74] You may have even known some people in group situations who will monitor the opinion "climate" before expressing an opinion—and then they make sure that the opinion they express is contrary to that being expressed by the majority of people in the group!

Perloff[75] describes two key individual differences that influence this consistency (or lack thereof) between attitudes and behaviors: (1) self-monitoring and (2) direct experience.

Mark Snyder developed the self-monitoring concept, which he describes as "the extent to which people monitor (observe, regulate, and control) the public appearances of self they display in social situations and interpersonal relationships."[76] Snyder developed a scale that classifies people as high self-monitors or low self-monitors.

As Perloff notes:

> High self-monitors are adept at controlling the images of self they present in interpersonal situations, and they are highly sensitive to the social cues that signify the appropriate behavior in a given situation. . . . Low self-monitors are less concerned with conveying an impression that is appropriate to the situation. Rather than relying on situational cues to help them decide how to act in a particular situation, low self-monitors consult their inner feelings and attitudes.[77]

Thus, high self-monitors are more likely to express public opinions that are different from their private opinions. Low self-monitors are likely to have private and public opinions that match.

In addition to self-monitoring, direct experience can influence the attitude–behavior relationship. Perloff[78] and Russell Fazio and Mark Zanna,[79] among others, contend that attitudes based on direct experience will predict behaviors better than attitudes based on indirect experiences.

Fazio and Zanna assert that attitudes based on direct experience are "more clearly defined, held with greater certainty, more stable over time, and more resistant to counter influence."[80] For example, if a five-year-old says he is "never gonna do drugs," he is probably basing this statement on television advertisements he has seen and on comments made by his teachers rather than on the fact that he has actually seen another kindergartner "do drugs." Based on the research by Fazio and Zanna, the statement would be more meaningful and would be more likely to predict his behavior if he had actually witnessed a friend have a bad physical reaction to a drug.

Social and Situational Factors

There are many social factors, including cultural differences and norms, that also may interfere with the linkages between attitudes and behavior. We will explore norms and other social factors that may influence the production and expression of public opinion in Chapters Five and Six. However, at this point, we want to describe a classic study, shown in Box 4.1, that demonstrates how social norms, such as politeness, can interfere with the expression of some opinions, such as prejudice.

BOX 4.1   TRAVELING AMERICA: WEAK LINKS BETWEEN PREJUDICED ATTITUDES AND PREJUDICED BEHAVIOR

A classic study by Richard LaPiere serves as an excellent example of the sometimes poor fit between behavior and attitudes. In this study, a number of surprising inconsistencies were found in the attitudes and behaviors of proprietors of hotels and restaurants toward Chinese people.

For the study, LaPiere was accompanied by "a personable Chinese student and his wife" on a trip across the United States. During their travels, the three would stop at restaurants, "auto camps," and hotels. The purpose of this study was to determine whether the proprietors would serve the couple in spite of any underlying prejudice. Notably, because the students were Chinese and because it was the 1930s, when a communist government had recently taken over in China, LaPiere assumed that many Americans would hold negative attitudes toward the couple.

Surprisingly, only one of the proprietors of a sample of 250 hotels and restaurants refused service to the visiting Chinese couple. Yet the proprietors presented quite a different attitudinal response in their answers to a mail questionnaire. As LaPiere notes:

> To provide a comparison of symbolic reaction to symbolic social situations with actual reaction to real social situations, I "questionnaired" the establishments which we patronized during the two year period. . . . To the hotel or restaurant a questionnaire was mailed with an accompanying letter purporting to be a special and personal plea for response. The questionnaires all asked the same question: "Will you accept members of the Chinese race as guests in your establishment?"

Although all but one of the hotel and restaurant employees served the Chinese couple, the survey results indicated that a vast majority of the proprietors (92 percent) would not be willing to "accept members of the Chinese race as guests."

Donald Campbell argues that in these situations, people who hold negative attitudes toward minorities may be reluctant to express their attitudes through public behavior because norms of tolerance and politeness are considered to be so important to Americans. More important, Campbell said that social norms may create different thresholds for expressing attitudes, producing apparent discrepancies between attitudes and behaviors, when, in fact, no real discrepancies exist.

There were several methodological problems in this study, including (1) not knowing whether the same person who waited on the Chinese couple was the one who filled out the questionnaire, and (2) the fact that the questionnaire did not evaluate whether the proprietors would accept a white man and a Chinese couple (who were known to be attractive and personable) into their establishment. However, it is also clear that social and situational factors weighed heavily in this case as well.

SOURCES: Richard T. LaPiere, "Attitudes vs. Actions," *Social Forces* 13 (1934):230–237, quoted portions from pp. 232–233; Donald T. Campbell, "Social Attitudes and Other Acquired Behavioral Dispositions," in S. Koch, ed., *Psychology: A Study of Science* (New York: McGraw-Hill, 1963), pp. 94–172.

When do attitudes predict behaviors? It is clear that there are a lot of cognitive and situational factors that must be considered in order to answer this question. A hot topic in psychology pertaining to the attitude–behavior relationship is the concept of "attitude accessibility."[81] That is, attitudes are thought to guide behavior partially through the perception process. Attitudes that are highly accessible (i.e., that come to mind quickly) are thought to be more likely to guide perception and therefore behavior. Studies indicate that more accessible attitudes predict behavior better than less accessible ones, independent of the direction and intensity of attitude expression.[82] Thus, knowing how quickly someone can express an attitude or opinion can provide useful information about how that person is likely to behave.

In addition to studying the attitude–behavior relationship from the perspective of attitude accessibility, researchers have also attempted to focus on this problem by developing more complex models. Martin Fishbein and Icek Ajzen attempted to explain the underlying psychological processes by which attitudes might predict behavior through a model called the theory of reasoned action. Later, Ajzen modified and enlarged the Fishbein–Ajzen model in an alternative theory of planned behavior. Both of these models will be described briefly.

Theory of Reasoned Action

Fishbein and Ajzen actually proposed the theory of reasoned action more than twenty years ago. Since then, the theory has generated a great deal of research in a variety of social science disciplines and has had important impacts in the area of attitude–behavior relations.

The theory of reasoned action specifies, in a mathematical way, the relationship among beliefs, attitudes, and behaviors. The theory is based on the assumption that humans are rational. Because they are rational, they calculate the costs and benefits of engaging in particular actions, taking into account the perceptions significant others might have concerning their actions. The theory specifically concerns voluntary behaviors—behaviors that people perform because they decide (or want) to perform them.

There are four basic components of the theory of reasoned action: (1) attitude toward the behavior (which includes behavioral beliefs and beliefs about the consequences of the behavior), (2) subjective norm (beliefs that specific individuals or groups think the behavior should or should not be performed), (3) behavioral intention (intention to perform a particular behavior), and (4) the actual behavior (see Figure 4.7).[83]

In general, the theory of reasoned action states that people intend to behave in ways that allow them to obtain favorable outcomes and that meet the expectations of others who are important to them. And this seems to make sense. Most of us want to get along with others in this world and would also like social, financial, or other rewards. We may find that some of our behaviors are determined by the likelihood of impressing others and achieving such rewards.

However, even though a number of studies have found that behavioral intentions can be predicted from the theory of reasoned action by measuring attitudes toward the behavior and subjective norms, there are some inherent problems. For example, the theory of reasoned action has been

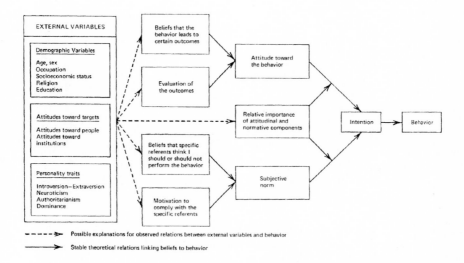

FIGURE 4.7   Theory of Reasoned Action. SOURCE: M. Fishbein and I. Ajzen, *Understanding Attitudes and Predicting Social Behavior* (Englewood Cliffs, NJ: Prentice-Hall, 1980), Figure 7.1, p. 84. Reprinted by permission of Prentice-Hall, Inc., Upper Saddle River, NJ.

criticized because it does not attempt to incorporate many of the more traditional factors that may affect behavioral outcomes such as characteristics of the environment or the situation (e.g., poverty or access to information) or characteristics of the person (e.g., mental or emotional illness). Many studies have found that such characteristics are directly relevant to the linkage between attitudes and behaviors.

In spite of these criticisms, many studies have found the premises of the theory of reasoned action to be useful. These studies have investigated a variety of different topics, including investigations of voting and presidential elections,[84] family planning,[85] and consumer product preferences.[86]

The relevance of the theory of reasoned action to public opinion studies is most clear in relation to public opinion perspectives that take account of individuals' perceptions of others (see Chapter Six). Looking at these perspectives, it is clear that a person has a concern about the expectations of others and sees certain opinions to be more acceptable than others. Thus, these perspectives are ripe for the inclusion of norms and motivations for opinion expression.

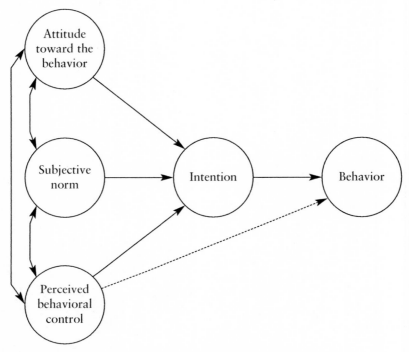

FIGURE 4.8   Theory of Planned Behavior. SOURCE: I. Ajzen, "The
Theory of Planned Behavior," *Organizational Behavior and Human Decision
Processes* 50 (1991):182.

Theory of Planned Behavior

Because of some of the criticisms of the theory of reasoned action, Ajzen
proposed an alternative theory of planned behavior that substantially en-
larges the original Fishbein–Ajzen model. Basically, Ajzen maintained
that the reasoned action model is most relevant when considering voluntary behaviors. He stated that the theory must be revised to account for
behaviors not wholly under voluntary control. The theory of planned behavior (see Figure 4.8) was developed to help account for these types of
behaviors—behaviors that may be mandated or that may result from situations outside of the person's control.

A major premise of the theory of planned behavior is that all behaviors
can be regarded as goals. For example, a behavior as voluntary as voting
in an election can be regarded as a goal. However, sometimes these goals
cannot be achieved because of experiences or events beyond a person's
control. The intention to vote may not result in actually voting if your car

breaks down on the way to vote and the tow truck does not arrive on the scene until after midnight.

According to the theory of planned behavior, the ability or inability to engage in the behavior is called perceived behavioral control, defined as one's perception of how easy or difficult it is to perform the behavior. This is a major difference between this theory and the theory of reasoned action. Thus, as shown in Figure 4.8, perceived behavioral control affects behavior in two ways: It influences intention to perform the behavior, and it may have a direct impact on the behavior.

In the area of public opinion research, the theory of planned behavior may help focus attention on the goal of the person giving the opinion. In some ways, then, it is similar to functional theories, except that it focuses on the goal of expressing the opinion rather than the motivation for holding the opinion. If, as we discussed with the theory of reasoned action, a person's goal is to be accepted among others, we may make very different predictions about the result of an opinion poll than we might make if we assume that most people's goals are to get the interview over with as quickly as possible. These issues have remained untouched by most current perspectives in public opinion.

EMOTIONS AND ATTITUDES

Your first reaction to the title of this section may be something like "What do emotions have to do with public opinion?" Previous texts on public opinion would probably answer, "Nothing." However, in recent years, researchers have been studying mood and emotions from many different perspectives and backgrounds. These scholars have been finding that emotions play a crucial role in how we act, what we think, and who we are. In short, emotions have a great deal to do with public opinion and the expression of our selves.

Early Conceptions of Emotion

Although much of our knowledge of emotions has been accrued during the past ten years, the founders of psychology and social psychology prescribed a crucial role for emotion in understanding psychological processes. William James' classic text *The Principles of Psychology*, which defined the field of psychology,[87] included a number of chapters describing the role of emotion in various psychological processes. However, with the rise of behaviorist theories and interpretations in the field of psychology during the 1920s and continuing through the 1950s and 1960s, very little research dealt with the concept of mood or emotions. Researchers concentrated on specific aspects of observable behavior, or, when it became necessary for them to describe aspects of mental operations, they relied on the notion of cognition as a kind of logical, almost mathematical operation.

When the influence of behaviorism began to wane during the 1950s, the computer analogy became the dominant model in psychology, and, as you might guess, there was little room for emotions in a computer model of the mind! The emphasis was on logic and logical consistency, as well as on the development of efficient algorithms to simulate decisionmaking and other processes.

By the 1970s, however, psychologists began to realize the need for incorporating emotions into psychology and the field has grown over the last twenty years to include many different ideas and perspectives. A number of these perspectives are important to help us understand emotions. However, we will limit this discussion to two major contemporary approaches to emotion and how our understanding of emotion may be applied to public opinion: the cognitive and the social approaches to emotion.

Cognitive Approaches

Cognitive approaches to emotion seek to determine how emotions develop and how they interact with what we typically think of as cognition, or logical, conscious thought processes. One of the most important of these approaches is developed in the work of Robert Zajonc, who is primarily interested in the relationship between thinking and feeling, or affect:

> There are practically no social phenomena that do not implicate affect in some important way. Affect dominates social interaction, and it is the major currency in which social intercourse is transacted. The vast majority of our daily conversations entail the exchange of information about our opinions, preferences, and evaluations. And affect in these conversations is transmitted not only by the verbal channel but by nonverbal clues as well—clues that may, in fact, carry the principal components of information about affect. It is much less important for us to know whether someone has just said "You are a friend" or "You are a fiend" than to know whether it was spoken in contempt or with affection.[88]

Public opinion research might profit from an examination of emotion as described by Zajonc.[89] For example, he notes that one often knows how one feels about something long before one has a thoughtful opinion about it. If Zajonc's conceptualization is correct, the implications for public opinion polling are staggering! Many polls about particular issues are taken in which people are asked their opinions, some of which may be in the early stages of development.

If affect and cognition are two different systems, these polls may in fact be tapping two different things—opinions, among those who have decided, and feelings, among those who have not thought enough about the issue to develop a cognitive appraisal leading to an opinion. It is interesting to note that the wording in many public opinion polls suggests that the researcher is inherently aware of the problem, as such polls often ask not for an opinion but instead ask how a person feels about an issue.

Researchers are also suggesting that emotions and cognition may not be separate systems but may work in tandem in motivating our attitudes and behavior. Lyn Ragsdale has studied people's emotional reactions to presidents. Ragsdale found that people seem to weigh the emotional aspects of evaluation at least as strongly as the presidents' stands on issues or their economic situation. In fact, statistical tests from Ragsdale's studies suggest that emotions are actually better predictors of presidential evaluation than more "rational" (less emotional) explanations.[90]

Social Approaches

A very different perspective on emotions is provided by social psychologists who examine what are called the "social emotions." These include embarrassment, pride, and shame. Charles Cooley[91] was among the first to describe the social role of emotions. Cooley centered on pride and shame as managing devices that helped maintain a social bond and even hold the social system together. Much more recently, Rowland Miller and Mark Leary[92] and Thomas Scheff[93] suggest that many emotions are in fact social emotions, as they usually arise from interactions with other people. In addition, Miller and Leary describe the social sources and functions of embarrassment.

These social emotions depend on the implied presence and attention of others: They depend on our concern for what others are thinking of us and would not occur if we were unaware of others' presence or did not care what others thought.[94] Undoubtedly, such current perspectives as the "looking-glass perception," "false consensus," pluralistic ignorance," and the "spiral of silence" (see Chapter Six for a discussion) could not be developed and the phenomena they describe could not occur except as social acts involving interactions with self and interactions with others.

As Miller and Leary[95] suggest, social emotions would not occur if we did not care what others thought. Similarly, the public opinion phenomena described above would not occur without the very same assumption. It is intriguing that these social emotions remain uninvestigated within these perspectives.

Whether one proceeds from a cognitive or a social perspective, there is clearly a need for describing the role of emotion in public opinion research and theory (see Figure 4.9). It is interesting to note that both social and cognitive perspectives suggest the important link between emotions and the separation of humans from other animals. It is no coincidence that one of the first scientists to describe the role of emotion in both cognitive and social perspectives was Charles Darwin,[96] who devoted an entire book to the interplay of biology, emotion, and communication. It is clear that emotion—always closely related but seldom, if ever, investigated in public opinion research—is destined to play a stronger and stronger role in future research efforts.

CONCLUSION

Beliefs and values most often affect the attitudes we hold, which are expressed as opinions. Much research has focused on how people form their attitudes. Early studies focused on the behaviorist views of classical and operant conditioning. More recent research has rejected conditioning's premise that all individuals will respond in the same way with the same stimulus and has developed several alternative explanations.

Cognitive response theories assume the brain is sorting through much information, ignoring or rejecting some, and using the rest to derive opinions. The Elaboration Likelihood Method and the theory of heuristics attempt to describe this cognitive process.

Attitudes are also studied in relationship to one another. Consistency and judgment theories focus on the interdependent relationship of attitudes. Cognitive dissonance and social judgment theories are among the

FIGURE 4.9   Emotion and public opinion. Cartoon by Jack Ohman, *The Oregonian*, 2000.

most well known in this category. Researchers are also interested in functional aspects of opinion expression—determining what motivations are involved when forming and expressing opinions. Some hold that the individual's goal is to achieve consistency in the attitudes held. Others argue that the individual goal is social approval, causing one to choose the position he considers most favored by an important (to him) social group.

Finally, emotions play a role in the development of public opinion. Zajonc's work in particular argues that affect has an influence on opinion, and can be a precursor to opinion. The study of emotion can have profound implications for the study of public opinion.

NOTES

1. Richard M. Perloff, *The Dynamics of Persuasion: Communication and Attitudes in the 21st Century*, 2nd edition (Mahwah, NJ: Lawrence Erlbaum, 1993), p. 29.

2. Ibid.

3. Milton Rokeach, *The Nature of Human Values* (New York: Free Press, 1973).

4. Robert B. Cialdini, Richard E. Petty, and John T. Cacioppo, "Attitude and Attitude Change," *Annual Review of Psychology* 32 (1981):357–404; Daryl J. Bem, *Beliefs, Attitudes, and Human Affairs* (Belmont, CA: Brooks/Cole, 1970); Stuart Oskamp, *Attitudes and Opinions* (Englewood Cliffs, NJ: Prentice-Hall, 1977).

5. Perloff, *Dynamics of Persuasion*; Milton J. Rosenberg and Robert P. Abelson, "An Analysis of Cognitive Balancing," in Milton J. Rosenberg et al., eds., *Attitude Organization and Change* (New Haven: Yale University Press, 1960), pp. 112–163.

6. Bernard C. Hennessey, *Public Opinion,* 5th ed. (Belmont, CA: Brooks/Cole, 1985).

7. Michael Corbett, *American Public Opinion: Trends, Processes, and Patterns* (New York: Longman, 1991).

8. Clark L. Hull, *Principles of Behavior: An Introduction to Behavior Theory* (New York: Appleton-Century-Crofts, 1943); Edward L. Thorndike, *The Fundamentals of Learning* (New York: Teacher's College Press, 1932).

9. Alice H. Eagly and Shelly Chaiken, *The Psychology of Attitudes* (Orlando, FL: Harcourt Brace Jovanovich, 1993).

10. Arthur W. Staats and Carolyn K. Staats, "Attitudes Established by Classical Conditioning," *Journal of Abnormal and Social Psychology* 57 (1958):37–40.

11. Ivan P. Pavlov, *Conditioned Reflexes* (London: Oxford University Press, 1927).

12. Arthur W. Staats, "Paradigmatic Behaviorism: Unified Theory for Social-Personality Psychology," in Leonard Berkowitz, ed., *Advances in Experimental Social Psychology* (San Diego: Academic Press, 1983), pp. 125–179; see also Eagly and Chaiken, *Psychology of Attitudes*; Chris T. Allen and Thomas J. Madden, "A Closer Look at Classical Conditioning," *Journal of Consumer Research* 12 (1985):301–315.

13. Staats, "Paradigmatic Behaviorism."

14. Eagly and Chaiken, *Psychology of Attitudes.*

15. Ibid., p. 400.

16. B. F. Skinner, *The Behavior of Organisms* (New York: Appleton-Century-Crofts, 1938).

17. Richard E. Petty and John T. Cacioppo, *Attitudes and Persuasion: Classic and Contemporary Approaches* (Dubuque, IA: William C. Brown Company, 1981).

18. Joel Greenspoon, "The Reinforcing Effect of Two Spoken Sounds on the Frequency of Two Responses," *American Journal of Psychology* 68 (1955):409–416.

19. For example, see Leonard Krasner, "Studies of the Conditioning of Verbal Behavior," *Psychological Bulletin* 55 (1958):148–170; Leonard Krasner, "The Therapist as a Social Reinforcement Machine," in Hans H. Strupp and Lester Luborsky, eds., *Research in Psychotherapy* (Washington, DC: American Psychological Association, 1962), pp. 61–94; Leon H. Levy, "Awareness, Learning, and the Beneficent Subject as Expert Witness," *Journal of Personality and Social Psychology* 6 (1967):365–370; Richard D. Singer, "Verbal Conditioning and Generalization of Prodemocratic Responses," *Journal of Abnormal and Social Psychology* 63 (1961):43–46.

20. See, for example, Petty and Cacioppo, *Attitudes and Persuasion.*

21. John Zaller, *The Nature and Origins of Mass Opinion* (New York: Cambridge University Press, 1992).

22. Staats and Staats, "Attitudes Established by Classical Conditioning."

23. Michael X. Delli Carpini and Bruce Williams, "The Method Is the Message: Focus Groups as a Method of Social, Psychological, and Political Inquiry," *Research in Micropolitics* 4 (1994):57–85.

24. Eagly and Chaiken, *Psychology of Attitudes*; Anthony G. Greenwald, "Cognitive Response Analysis: An Appraisal," in Richard E. Petty, Thomas M. Ostrom, and Timothy C.

Brock, eds., *Cognitive Responses in Persuasion* (Hillsdale, NJ: Lawrence Erlbaum, 1981), pp. 127–133.

25. Ibid.

26. Richard E. Petty and John T. Cacioppo, "The Elaboration Likelihood Model of Persuasion," in Berkowitz, ed., *Advances in Experimental Social Psychology,* pp. 123–205.

27. Ibid., p. 182.

28. Ibid.

29. Ibid., p. 126.

30. Ibid., p. 192.

31. Eagly and Chaiken, *Psychology of Attitudes,* p. 323.

32. Shelly Chaiken, "The Heuristic Model of Persuasion," in Mark P. Zanna, James M. Olson, and C. Peter Herman, eds., *Social Influence: The Ontario Symposium* (Hillsdale, NJ: Lawrence Erlbaum, 1987), pp. 3–39.

33. Eagly and Chaiken, *Psychology of Attitudes.*

34. Leon Festinger, *A Theory of Cognitive Dissonance* (Evanston, IL: Row, Peterson, 1957).

35. Fritz Heider, "Attitudes and Cognitive Organization," *Journal of Psychology* 21 (1946):107–112.

36. Fritz Heider, *The Psychology of Interpersonal Relations* (New York: Wiley, 1958).

37. Jon A. Krosnick, "Psychological Perspectives on Political Candidate Perception: A Review of Research on the Projection Hypothesis," paper presented at the meeting of the Midwest Political Science Association, Chicago, 1988.

38. Eagly and Chaiken, *Psychology of Attitudes.*

39. Charles E. Osgood and Percy H. Tannenbaum, "The Principle of Congruity in the Prediction of Attitude Change," *Psychological Review* 62 (1955):42–55.

40. Petty and Cacioppo, *Attitudes and Persuasion.*

41. D. W. Rajecki, *Attitudes,* 2nd ed. (Sunderland, MA: Sinauer, 1990), p. 64.

42. Eagly and Chaiken, *Psychology of Attitudes.*

43. Richard M. Perloff, *The Dynamics of Persuasion,* (Hillsdale, NJ: Lawrence Erlbaum, 1993).

44. Festinger, *Theory of Cognitive Dissonance.*

45. Philip E. Converse, "The Nature of Belief Systems in Mass Publics," in David Apter, ed., *Ideology and Discontent* (New York: Free Press, 1964), pp. 206–261; Anthony G. Greenwald and David L. Ronis, "Twenty Years of Cognitive Dissonance: Case Study of the Evolution of a Theory," *Psychological Review* 85 (1979):53–57.

46. Festinger, *Theory of Cognitive Dissonance.*

47. J. Zaller, *The Origin and Nature of Mass Opinion* (New York: Cambridge University Press, 1992).

48. Joel Cooper, Russell H. Fazio, and Frederick Rhodewalt, "Dissonance and Humor: Evidence for the Undifferentiated Nature of Dissonance Arousal," *Journal of Personality and Social Psychology* 36 (1978):280–285; Joel Cooper, Mark P Zanna, and Peter A. Taves, "Arousal as a Necessary Condition for Attitude Change Following Induced Compliance," *Journal of Personality and Social Psychology* 36 (1978):1101–1106.

49. Petty and Cacioppo, *Attitudes and Persuasion.*

50. Ibid., p. 96.

51. Albert Pepitone and Mark DiNubile, "Contrast Effects in Judgments of Crime Severity and the Punishment of Criminal Violators," *Journal of Personality and Social Psychology* 33 (1976):448–459; Marshall Dermer et al., "Evaluative Judgments of Aspects of Life as a Function of Vicarious Exposure to Hedonic Extremes," *Journal of Personality and Social Psychology* 37 (1979):247–260.

52. Philip Brickman, Dan Coates, and Ronnie Janoff-Bulman, "Lottery Winners and Accident Victims: Is Happiness Relative?" *Journal of Personality and Social Psychology* 36 (1978):917–927; Muzafer Sherif and Carl I. Hovland, *Social Judgment: Assimilation and Contrast Effects in Communication and Attitude Change* (New Haven: Yale University Press, 1961).

53. Eagly and Chaiken, *Psychology of Attitudes,* p. 368; Muzafer Sherif and Carolyn W. Sherif, "Attitude as the Individual's Own Categories: The Social Judgment-Involvement Approach to Attitude and Attitude Change," in Carolyn W. Sherif and Muzafer Sherif, eds., *Attitude, Ego-Involvement, and Change* (New York: Wiley, 1967), p. 130.

54. M. Brewster Smith, Jerome S. Bruner, and Robert W. White, *Opinions and Personality* (New York: Wiley, 1956); Daniel Katz, "The Functional Approach to the Study of Attitudes," *Public Opinion Quarterly* 24 (1960):163–176; Petty and Cacioppo, *Attitudes and Persuasion.*

55. Katz, "Functional Approach to the Study of Attitudes."

56. Smith, Bruner, and White, *Opinions and Personality.*

57. Herbert C. Kelman, "Compliance, Identification and Internalization: Three Processes of Attitude Change," *Journal of Conflict Resolution* 2 (1958):51–60.

58. Katz, "Functional Approach to the Study of Attitudes."

59. Ibid.; Eagly and Chaiken, *Psychology of Attitudes.*

60. Erving Goffman, *The Presentation of Self in Everyday Life* (New York: Anchor Books, 1959).

61. Robert M. Arkin, "Self-Presentation Styles," in James T. Tedeschi, ed., *Impression Management Theory and Social Psychological Theory* (London: Academic Press, 1981), pp. 311–333.

62. James T. Tedeschi, Barry R. Schlenker, and Thomas V. Bonoma, "Cognitive Dissonance: Private Ratiocination or Public Spectacle," *American Psychologist* 26 (1971):685–695.

63. Barry R. Schlenker, *Impression Management: The Self-Concept, Social Identity, and Interpersonal Relations* (Monterey, CA: Brooks/Cole, 1980), p. 204.

64. Tedeschi, Schlenker, and Bonoma, "Cognitive Dissonance."

65. Petty and Cacioppo, *Attitudes and Persuasion.*

66. Schlenker, *Impression Management.*

67. H. F. Weisberg, J. A. Krosnick, and B. D. Bowen, *An Introduction to Survey Research, Polling, and Data Analysis,* 3rd ed. (Thousand Oaks, CA: Sage, 1996).

68. Eagly and Chaiken, *Psychology of Attitudes*; Angus Campbell et al., *The American Voter* (New York: Wiley, 1960); Howard Schuman and Michael P. Johnson, "Attitudes and Behavior," *Annual Review of Sociology* 2 (1976):167.

69. For example, Bernard Kutner, Carol Wilkins, and Penny Rechtman Yarrow, "Verbal Attitudes and Overt Behavior Involving Racial Prejudice," *Journal of Abnormal and Social Psychology* 47 (1952):649–652; Richard T. LaPiere, "Attitudes vs. Actions," *Social Forces* 13 (1934):230–237; Irwin Deutscher, *What We Say/What We Do: Sentiments and Acts* (Glenview, IL: Scott, Foresman, 1973); Allan W. Wicker, "Attitudes Versus Actions: The Relationship of Verbal and Overt Behavioral Responses to Attitude Objects," *Journal of Social Issues* 25, 4 (1969):41–78.

70. Herbert C. Kelman, "Attitudes Are Alive and Well and Gainfully Employed in the Sphere of Action," *American Psychologist* 29 (1974):310–324.

71. Schuman and Johnson, "Attitudes and Behavior."

72. Eagly and Chaiken, *Psychology of Attitudes,* p. 157.

73. Icek Ajzen, "Attitudes, Traits and Actions: Dispositional Prediction of Behavior," in Julius Huhl and Jurgen Beckmann, eds., *Action Control: From Cognition to Behavior* (New York: Springer-Verlag, 1987), pp. 11–39.

74. Perloff, *Dynamics of Persuasion*, p. 85.

75. Ibid.

76. Mark Snyder, *Public Appearances/Private Realities: The Psychology of Self-Monitoring* (New York: Freeman, 1987).

77. Perloff, *Dynamics of Persuasion*, p. 85.

78. Ibid.

79. Russell H. Fazio and Mark P. Zanna, "Direct Experience and Attitude–Behavior Consistency," in Berkowitz, ed., *Advances in Experimental Social Psychology*, pp. 161–202.

80. Ibid., p. 185.

81. Jon A. Krosnick, "Attitude Importance and Attitude Accessibility," *Personality and Social Psychology Bulletin* 15 (1989):297–308.

82. Russell H. Fazio and Carol J. Williams, "Attitude Accessibility as a Moderator of the Attitude–Perception and Attitude–Behavior Relations: An Investigation of the 1984 Presidential Election," *Journal of Personality and Social Psychology* 51 (1986):505–514.

83. Icek Ajzen and Martin Fishbein, *Understanding Attitudes and Predicting Social Behavior* (Englewood Cliffs, NJ: Prentice-Hall, 1980), p. 6.

84. Martin Fishbein and Icek Ajzen, "Acceptance, Yielding and Impact: Cognitive Processes in Persuasion," in Petty, Ostrom, and Brock, eds., *Cognitive Responses in Persuasion*, pp. 339–359.

85. Martin Fishbein et al., "Predicting and Understanding Family Planning Behaviors: Beliefs, Attitudes, and Intentions," in Ajzen and Fishbein, eds., *Understanding Attitudes and Predicting Social Behavior*, pp. 130–147.

86. Martin Fishbein and Icek Ajzen, "Predicting and Understanding Consumer Behavior: Attitude–Behavior Correspondence," in Ajzen and Fishbein, eds., *Understanding Attitudes and Predicting Social Behavior*.

87. William James, *The Principles of Psychology* (New York: Holt, Rinehart and Winston, 1890).

88. Robert B. Zajonc, "Feeling and Thinking: Preferences Need No Inferences," *American Psychologist* 35 (1980):153.

89. Ibid.

90. Lyn Ragsdale, "Strong Feelings: Emotional Responses to Presidents," *Political Behavior* 13 (1991):33–65.

91. Charles H. Cooley, *Human Nature and the Social Order* (New York: Scribner, 1902).

92. Rowland S. Miller and Mark R. Leary, "Social Sources and Interactive Functions of Emotion: The Case of Embarrassment," in Margaret S. Clark, ed., *Review of Personality and Social Psychology* (Newbury Park, CA: Sage Publications, 1992), pp. 202–221.

93. Thomas J. Scheff, *Microsociology: Discourse, Emotion and Social Structure* (Chicago: University of Chicago Press, 1990).

94. Miller and Leary, "Social Sources and Interactive Functions of Emotion."

95. Ibid.

96. Charles R. Darwin, *The Expression of the Emotions in Man and Animals* (London: Murray, 1972).

5

Stereotyping, Social Norms, and Public Opinion

In Chapter Four, we considered the ways in which mental processes affect public opinion. In this chapter, we will examine the ways in which social forces affect public opinion formation and expression. It may seem strange to think of social factors influencing public opinion. American culture places a high value on individualism, and we tend to think in individualistic terms. The democratic ideal envisions an independent actor acquiring information, weighing choices, and rendering an evaluative judgment, all more or less without interference from the rest of the citizenry or from politicians.

This vision of the independent actor is further supported by the way that we most commonly measure public opinion. When we take a survey, we ask each individual, anonymously and privately, to express opinions on a variety of issues. Those individual responses are aggregated, and the result is called public opinion. However, opinion reality is often not like what we try to measure in survey research. People interact and acquire information from each other and influence each other; they are socialized into particular ways of thinking about social problems, and they often feel constrained by norms or standards of "correct" behavior in our society.

Unfortunately, much of what we know about public opinion is based upon the investigation of what goes on within the individual, because this individual perspective has guided most empirical public opinion research. In recent years, however, scholars have determined that public opinion is a phenomenon far more complex than the aggregation of individual opinions suggests. Once again, scholars have turned their attention to the social and group factors that influence the formation and expression of public opinion.

Literally dozens of social alliances can affect public opinion: culture, political affiliation, socialization, and group dynamics, for a start. Rather than attempt an encyclopedic approach to this area of research, we want to introduce you to some of the more important theories available to the public opinion scholar from the field of social psychology. To begin with, we will consider the ways in which our own beliefs about others affect public opinion by reviewing attribution theory and stereotyping. Then we will consider at length how social norms—the rules and values that govern our social behavior—can also affect the opinions we form and the ways in which we express them.

One of the most important ideas that runs through this chapter is the concept of groups and group identity. You probably belong to dozens of groups. You are a member of your family, of a racial or ethnic group, of a gender group, of a social class. You may also affiliate with sororities, fraternities, sports teams, or Star Trek fans. You may even be a member of groups you are not aware exist, such as demographic groups created by survey researchers. For example, in the late 1980s, survey research identified a group of people who came to be known as "DINKs," which stood for "double income, no kids." It is unlikely that people who fit this description realized that they were part of a group until the group was "discovered" by the researchers. However, if you do recognize yourself as having some important characteristic in common with others, you probably identify with that group, even if you have never met another member. The fact that we tend to think of ourselves as members of some groups and nonmembers of others has important implications for public opinion, as you will see.

ATTRIBUTION THEORY

Attribution theories emphasize how people's inferences about the reasons behind other people's behaviors or attitudes affect their own agreement with these behaviors or attitudes. Interest in attribution theory began in the 1960s with research conducted by Daryl Bem. Bem stated that people infer their own and others' attitudes by observing the behavior of others.[1] He also said that people infer underlying characteristics of others, including others' motivations and intentions, from the verbal and nonverbal behaviors they observe. Thus, "when there appears to be an obvious reason for some behavior, people confidently attribute that behavior to that cause."[2]

Attitudes toward an issue will change to the extent that people view a message being presented as conveying the "truth" about the issue. The change will not take place if the message is attributed "to factors that compromise truth value."[3] For example, information that appears in a news story is more likely to be believed than information that appears in an advertisement, even if it is the same information. We know that advertisers have an interest in selling a product or a candidate or an idea. Information that appears in the news is usually perceived as more objective than that which appears in ads, since news derives its value from being "true" information. For this reason, if the nightly news report says that aspirin may help prevent heart attacks, you are more likely to believe it than you would be if a company that made aspirin put the same information into one of its ads.

As Alice Eagly and Shelly Chaiken point out, the information people take into account in inferring the meaning behind messages will often include salient "contextual cues" such as the "communicator's personal circumstances and the audience the communicator is addressing."[4] In evaluating the truth value of a message, we may try to ascertain the reason the communicator is conveying the information and why we are the targets of the message. In the case of product advertising, a company is communicating with us in order to encourage us to buy its product, and we are targets of the message because we have resources (namely, money) that the company wants. No wonder we are often somewhat mistrustful of such messages.

Several researchers have found consistent biases in the ways we attribute our own and other people's statements and behavior. For one thing, we have a tendency to attribute our own negative behavior to aspects of the situation we are in. For example, if you fail to complete an assignment on time, you may attribute this to your busy schedule.

By contrast, we may attribute others' negative behavior to their personality. Your professor, receiving your late assignment, may attribute your lateness to your lack of commitment to that particular class. These biases often extend themselves to cover the groups to which we belong. That is, we tend to attribute negative behaviors of members of our own group to situational factors. We attribute negative behaviors of other groups to their personal characteristics.

Taxpaying citizens may see welfare mothers as lazy and undisciplined women who have children out of wedlock and leave others to pay the tab. The mothers may see themselves as poorly treated by men who abandoned them and by a society that does not provide them with adequate job training or child care. Attributions of this kind can clearly have an important impact on public opinion. People who believe that welfare mothers are lazy and undisciplined are unlikely to support social welfare programs to aid these women. People who see these women as victims of circumstance are more likely to favor such programs.

STEREOTYPING

Stereotypes are generalizations about people "based on category membership."[5] That is, stereotypes are beliefs that all members of a group have the same qualities or characteristics. Henry Tajfel argued it is because "stereotypes are shared by large numbers of people within social groups or entities" that they are truly social and are worth studying.[6] As social psychologists Michael Hogg and Dominic Abrams[7] note, a specific group member is assumed to be, and is often treated as, identical to other members of the group. The group, in turn, is perceived and treated by others as homogeneous.

Conceptually, most social psychologists define stereotypes as "socially shared sets of beliefs about traits that are characteristic of members of a social category."[8] Stereotypes tend to be shared by many members of a society, and it is not unusual for large portions of a society to agree on the stereotypes of particular groups—both in the language used to describe the group and in the way the group is treated by members of the larger society. These stereotypes are not always the product of direct experience. Many come to us indirectly from what we are told by other people or by the media.

The concept of social identity helps us understand stereotypes. Social identity is a "definition of the self in terms of group membership shared with other people."[9] These conceptualizations of the self are derived from membership in emotionally significant social categories or groups.[10] Individuals "fit" themselves into a particular category, affected in part by the comparison of one group to another. For example, S. A. Haslam et al. look at the way people from northern and southern states might categorize themselves when compared to one another, or when compared to non-Americans. When compared to non-Americans they are likely to describe themselves as Americans instead of as members of a region of the United States. The comparative context affects the way individuals categorize themselves into one group or another. Studies show that as people increasingly perceive themselves to be part of an in-group identity, the level of consensus among members increases along with perceptions of in-group homogeneity. Additionally, communication among in-group members has been shown to increase consensus concerning both in-group and out-group stereotypes, with the greater effect occurring for in-groups.[11]

In-group identity sometimes leads to group favoritism. However, rather than making comparisons based on an ethnocentric bias, in-group favoritism should instead be understood as a method to sometimes best understand the "fit" of traits that are being evaluated.[12]

If group membership is going to answer one's need for meaning and coherence, the clarity of the boundary that separates in-group membership from nonmembership becomes particularly important. Distinctiveness is an important aspect of social categories as a factor in group identification. Brewer's theory says that human beings have two powerful social motives: a need to be included, and the opposing need to be differentiated from others. One reason social identities are so powerful is that they satisfy the need both for inclusion (member of a group) and for differentiation (this group is different from other groups).[13]

Researchers have explored the issue of stereotypes from a number of perspectives and by investigating different stereotyped groups. Daniel Katz and Kenneth Braly[14] were among the first to study the stereotypes people hold concerning specific social groups. In these studies, respondents would select, from a long list, adjectives that they "believed to be typical of certain ethnic groups (in the United States)," groups such as Jews, Irish, and Turks.[15] The respondents would then indicate five adjectives that appeared to be most characteristic of each group. Often, more than 80 percent of responses indicated a general agreement between the respondents on what constitutes the stereotype of certain social groups.[16]

TABLE 5.1   Sample Lists for Generating Generalized and Individual Responses

List 1: Generalization	List 2: Individual
Jew	Albert Einstein
Californian	Richard Nixon
Professor	O. J. Simpson
Farmer	Janis Joplin
Texan	Jimmy Carter
Actor	

Linkages: Albert Einstein, Jew; Richard Nixon, Californian; O. J. Simpson, actor and Californian; Janis Joplin, Texan; Jimmy Carter, professor and farmer.
SOURCE: M. A. Hogg and D. Abrams, *Social Identifications: A Social Psychology of Intergroup Relations and Group Processes* (London: Routledge 1988), p. 76.

Think of the number of stereotypes you hold and how they affect your perceptions of others. It is clear that stereotypes often guide us in our attitudes toward and treatment of others. As an illustration, examine Table 5.1. Ask a friend, acquaintance, or parent to say whatever words or phrases come to mind when you say the words in the first list. Odds are very high that the response you get will be representative of stereotypes associated with each of these ethnic groups.

Now read the second list—the individual names—and jot down what is said about each of the people named. Compare the two results. How many descriptions of individuals matched a description of the general category to which they belong? The odds are that the phrases associated with the general category would not be very helpful in describing the individuals, even though each individual "fits" within one or more particular categories. It is clear that our notions of stereotypes require us to generalize certain characteristics so that it is often difficult to find an individual who matches the stereotype.

The early research of Katz and Braly[17] resulted in a number of descriptive studies on stereotyping. These studies ranged from explorations of gender and race stereotypes to studies on how we stereotype famous (as opposed to nonfamous) people, people in various professions, and people who live in certain parts of the United States. Descriptive studies on stereotyping are important because they aid us in establishing the stereotypes people hold of particular groups, understanding how strongly these stereotypes are held, and so forth. However, descriptive approaches do not help us understand underlying processes.

Stereotypes can profoundly influence people's lives and may influence decisions on personnel evaluations, job applications, and university admissions. These are decisions that can result in unintended discrimination against others.[18] The use of stereotypes in discrimination can result in very negative outcomes. Certainly you would not like to enter the workforce knowing that your skin or hair color, your gender, or even the part of the country in which you were born could affect hiring decisions. However, consciously or unconsciously, employers sometimes make decisions based on stereotypes.

Stereotypes also are a social force in the sense that they can have profound influence on how we deal with those around us. They can have a tremendous impact on public opinion, but they can also affect measurements of public opinion. We know from research on survey responses, for example, that people are more likely to give an opinion on an issue if they perceive that the interviewer is of their own race.[19] This, of course, is the result of the stereotypes we have of people of our own race and people of other races. A person who is white and of Anglo-Saxon descent in the United States has ideas about other white Anglo-Saxon Americans and other ideas about black African-Americans, and still other ideas about white Africans.

The very notion of stereotypes probably evokes a negative image in your mind. Typically, we think of stereotypes as bad, and we fear that if we stereotype, we are being narrow-minded or bigoted. But is this always the case? Stereotypes are quite cognitively complex, often containing both positive and negative elements. Although attitudes imply consistent evaluative responses, as Anthony Greenwald and Mahzarin Banaji note, a stereotype may "encompass beliefs with widely diverging evaluative implications." An example these researchers use is the stereotype of cheerleaders, which may "simultaneously include the traits of being physically attractive (positive) and unintelligent (negative)."[20]

Furthermore, in his classic discussion of stereotypes, Walter Lippmann argued that, in some sense, stereotyping is a necessary condition for functioning in this world. He notes:

> There is neither time nor opportunity for intimate acquaintance. Instead, we notice a trait which marks a well-known type, and fill in the rest of the picture by means of the stereotypes we carry about in our heads. He is an agitator. That much we notice, or are told. Well, an agitator is this sort of

person, and so he is this sort of person. He is an intellectual. He is a plu-
tocrat. He is a foreigner. He is a "South European." He is from Back Bay.
He is a Harvard Man. How different from the statement: he is a Yale Man.
He is a regular fellow. He is a West Pointer. He is an old army sergeant. He
is a Greenwich Villager: what don't we know about him then, and about
her? He is an international banker. He is from Main Street.[21]

One of the most fascinating and elaborate stereotypes ever developed
was the so-called criminal type. Many fiction writers, average people, and
even criminologists of the late nineteenth and early twentieth centuries believed you could tell a criminal by physical appearance alone (see Box 5.1).

BOX 5.1   LOMBROSO'S CRIMINAL TYPES

Modern criminology has its roots in the work of a nineteenth-century Italian doctor named Cesare Lombroso. Lombroso believed that there was in
fact a "criminal type." His theory was based on Charles Darwin's studies of
evolution, then a novel idea, and the beliefs in "higher" and "lower" races
that were also popular at the time. Lombroso argued that many criminals
were actually genetic throwbacks to earlier evolutionary stages of man:
These people were uncivilized and uncivilizable—born to a life of crime.[1]

Among Lombroso's most famous research efforts were his attempts to
define the physical characteristics of the born criminal. He argued that many
criminals had physical features reminiscent of those found in apes and other
animals:

Thus was explained the origin of the enormous jaws, strong canines . . . and
strongly developed orbital arches [brow line] which he had so frequently re-
marked in criminals, for these peculiarities are common to carnivores and
savages who tear and devour raw flesh. Thus also it was easy to understand
why the span of the arms in criminals so often exceeds the height, for this
is a characteristic of apes. . . . The other anomalies exhibited by criminals—
the scanty beard as opposed to the general hairiness of the body, prehensile
foot, diminished number of lines in the palm of the hand, cheek pouches,
enormous development of middle incisors and frequent absence of the lateral ones, flattened nose and angular or sugar-loaf form of the skull, common
to criminals and apes; the excessive size of the orbits [eye sockets], which,

combined with the hooked nose, so often imparts to criminals the aspect of a bird of prey, the . . . supernumerary teeth (amounting in some cases to a double row as in snakes) . . . all these characteristics pointed to one conclusion, the . . . criminal . . . reproduces physical, psychic, and functional qualities of remote ancestors.[2]

Criminals supposedly had sharp teeth, like rats, and, Lombroso claimed, some had the vestiges of a tail. They were more likely to be left-handed than "normal" people. It is from Lombroso's work that we derive the old saying that criminals have "shifty" eyes, "difficult to describe but . . . nevertheless apparent to all observers."[3]

Lombroso even argued that one could tell which sorts of crimes a born criminal might commit by looking at his or her physical characteristics:

The lips of violators of women and murderers are fleshy, swollen, and protruding. . . . Swindlers have thin, straight lips. . . . Dark hair prevails especially in murderers, and curly or woolen hair in swindlers. . . . Those guilty of crimes against the person have short, clumsy fingers and especially short thumbs. Long fingers are common to swindlers, thieves, sexual offenders, and pickpockets.[4]

These images probably seem quite familiar to you. Writers of both fiction and nonfiction became fascinated with this vision of the born criminal, and echoes of Lombroso's work appear in many popular texts of that era, including Sherlock Holmes stories. Even today, fictional villains often have many of the characteristics of the "born criminal."

Lombroso's descriptions confirmed and expanded existing stereotypes people had about what criminals looked like. His daughter explained why: "Like the little cage-bird which instinctively crouches and trembles at the sight of the hawk, although ignorant of its ferocity, an honest man feels instinctive repugnance at the sight of a miscreant and thus signalizes the abnormality of the criminal type."[5] Lombroso did modify his theory over time to take environmental factors into account, but consider the impact of these "scientific" stereotypes on the public! Would you offer a job to someone with thin lips and long fingers? Would you walk on the same side of the street at night with someone with dark hair and stubby hands?

Today, Lombroso's analysis of environmental contributions to criminal behavior still seem prescient, but his descriptions of the physical characteris-

According to Lombroso, these men display the typical physical characteristics of criminals. SOURCE: Gina Lombroso-Ferrero, *Criminal Man According to the Classification of Cesare Lombroso* (1911; Montclair, NJ: Patterson Smith, 1972).

tics of "criminal man" are actually offensive. Nevertheless, the concept of the born criminal has not completely died away. In 1997 the U.S. Supreme Court upheld the constitutionality of a Kansas law that permits the state to continue the incarceration of "sexual predators" after they have served their sentences. The law is based on the argument that "sexual predators" cannot be rehabilitated and remain a threat to society. In other words, sexual predators are born criminals. However, there is one important difference we should note. One possible reason that many Kansans would favor such a law is that they believe sexual predators look just like the rest of us.

NOTES

1. Leonard D. Savitz, Introduction to Gina Lombroso-Ferrero, *Criminal Man According to the Classification of Cesare Lombroso* (1911; Montclair, NJ: Patterson Smith, 1972); Lombroso-Ferrero, *Criminal Man According to the Classification of Cesare Lombroso*.

2. Lombroso-Ferrero, *Criminal Man According to the Classification of Cesare Lombroso*, pp. 7–8.

3. Ibid., p. 14.

4. Ibid., pp. 14, 18, 20.

5. Ibid., p. 51.

Lippmann says the most pervasive of all influences are those that "create and maintain the repertory of stereotypes."[22] He states:

> We are told about the world before we see it. We imagine most things before we experience them. . . . Were there no practical uniformities in the environment, there would be no economy and only error in the human habit of accepting foresight for sight. But there are uniformities sufficiently accurate, and the need of economizing attention is so inevitable, that the abandonment of all stereotypes for a whole innocent approach to experience would impoverish human life.[23]

Stereotypes are a "cognitive consolidation" of how the world works. They are so fundamental to the way that we make sense of the world that we often do not realize we are using them at all. Just think: Every time you observe, "People would rather die than ask directions" or "Politicians are all crooked," you are stereotyping.

The alternative to using stereotypes is to treat each individual as a unique person, having nothing in common with anyone else. In other words, stereotypes are necessary if we are going to generalize about others. Without stereotypes, we cannot even begin to discuss culture, which is a reflection of all the characteristics a group of people has in common. For example, we can talk about an "American" culture, which may include "African-American" culture, "Hispanic-American" culture, and "Irish-American" culture. The cultures, in a sense, reflect certain real aspects of the stereotype, and the stereotypes reflect certain real aspects of the culture.

Therefore, if stereotypes are necessary in order for us to consolidate information about our world, why do we cringe with embarrassment if someone says we are stereotyping a person or group? Because, as Lippmann says, it is important to consider the character of the stereotypes and "the gullibility with which we employ them."[24] Stereotypes are not necessarily evil and need not be offensive if we understand that our stereotypes are ways of coding information. We must realize that our stereotypes are merely that, and we should be willing to change these viewpoints when we find out that they are inaccurate. We should also adjust our stereotypes when we find that by using them, we are hurting others or are misusing stereotypes to our benefit.

One of the most troubling aspects of stereotyping is that we tend to stereotype groups we are members of (in-groups) in ways that result in positive evaluations but stereotype groups that we do not identify with (out-groups) in ways that result in negative evaluations. For example, you might describe members of the sorority you belong to as "extremely intelligent" but describe the members of the sorority across the street as "serious party types."

Sometimes, these stereotypes seem to develop according to what Henry Tajfel calls an "accentuation principle."[25] Tajfel believed that people stereotype objects by bringing into sharper focus certain aspects of the environment that have special importance for those people. He hypothesized that people tend to engage in "perceptual accentuation," which makes them more aware of similarities within groups and differences between groups.

Take, for example, perceptions of height differences in men and women. Tajfel hypothesized that there would be an accentuation of differences in height between the two groups (men would be seen as taller, women as shorter than they really are) and an accentuation of similarities within each of these groups (differences in height between men and differences in height between women would seem less than they really are). An example of perceptual accentuation is illustrated in Figure 5.1.

Often, we not only perceive that others possess certain stereotypical traits but also act toward individuals or groups of people as if they possess these traits. You may, for example, find yourself treating the sorority members across the street with disdain and talking to them sarcastically. If you see one of them drinking a beer on the front porch you might turn to one of your own "sisters" and say, "See, that's all they do is party over there."

In fact, researchers have found that stereotypes can be "self-fulfilling prophecies" through a process called "behavioral confirmation." According to D. W. Rajecki, behavioral confirmation occurs "when a holder of a stereotype behaves consistently with that attitude and elicits the expected behavior from" the individual about whom the attitude is held, whether or not the individual being stereotyped "really has a personal disposition to act in that fashion."[26]

Mark Snyder, Elizabeth Tanke, and Ellen Berscheid[27] attempted to investigate whether behavioral confirmation occurs by looking at the social

REALITY

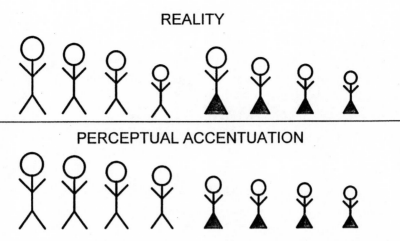

PERCEPTUAL ACCENTUATION

FIGURE 5.1   Perceptual Accentuation: Height Differences Between Men and Women. Stereotypes make us "see" larger differences than are actually there.

stereotype "What is beautiful is good" (described by Rajecki).[28] In their study, men and women were put in individual rooms and were told that the experimenter was "studying the acquaintance process."

The experimenter then explained to the men and women that they would be interacting socially with each other on the telephone. Prior to the telephone conversations, the researcher asked these men and women to write down general background information on a form, stating that the forms were to be exchanged as an aid to getting acquainted.

Each man received a woman's form with a photograph attached. The women, however, only received the form. Each man naturally assumed that the photograph was of the woman he would talk to on the telephone, but in reality it was not—it was the picture of a paid model. Of importance as well, half of the men taking part in this experiment were given photographs of women with low "attractiveness ratings," while half were given photographs of women with high "attractiveness ratings."

The researchers found that men with photographs of attractive women judged them to be "sociable, poised, humorous and socially adept."[29] Men who had photographs of unattractive women saw them as "unsociable, awkward, serious and socially inept." Behavioral confirmation occurred in that the men who subsequently talked to "attractive" women on the telephone treated them very differently during the telephone conversation

from the way "unattractive" women were treated by the men they talked
to on the telephone. This in turn affected the way in which the respective
women communicated with the men. The way the men talked to the
women "behaviorally confirmed" the stereotypes of attractive and unattractive women.

The findings of Snyder and his colleagues[30] have implications for
everyday interactions. For example, if you think that people with red hair
have bad tempers, you may treat a red-haired friend more gingerly than
you might a blonde friend. And, you might assume (because of stereotypes) that your blonde friend is not a math whiz and (perhaps equally incorrectly) that a Chinese friend is brilliant in math!

These perceptions, in turn, may affect whom you work with on projects or with whom you do homework. You may find that such stereotyping leads to disastrous results. But even if you end up flunking a math
exam because you trusted your Chinese friend and found out that your
blonde friend received an A on the math exam, would this cause you to
change your stereotypes of Chinese or blondes concerning brilliance in
math? Probably not.

Even animals are not immune from our stereotypes. You probably have
stereotypes for certain breeds of dogs or for how various species of animals will behave. Dobermans are vicious and aggressive; collies are loyal
and friendly. Grizzly bears have nasty tempers; dolphins are intelligent.
Even though it might cause you to stop and think, one interaction with a
friendly Doberman or a nasty dolphin would probably not change your
stereotypes of these creatures very much!

Tajfel[31] offers a list of the functions that stereotypes serve for the individual and for society as a whole that offers us insights into both how
stereotypes work and how they affect public opinion. They also serve as a
summary of some of the positive and negative aspects of stereotyping that
we have discussed here.

As indicated in Table 5.2,[32] individual functions of stereotyping include the cognitive function and the value function.

Cognitive Function
In this function, stereotyping serves an accentuation function, bringing
the world into "sharper focus" for the individual. As we said, this can help

TABLE 5.2   Individual and Social Functions of Stereotyping

Individual Functions	*Social Functions*
Cognitive (well-differentiated and sharply "focused" world)	Social causality (explanation of widespread and distressing social or physical events)
Value (relatively positive self-evaluation)	Social justification (rationalization or justification of treatment of social groups)
	Social differentiation (accentuation and clarification of differences between social groups)

people make sense of the complex world that they live in, but it can have negative effects if our stereotypes are inflexible.

Value Function

When stereotypes serve an evaluative function, they directly influence one's own value system and perception of oneself. They achieve this by contrasting the attributes of one's own group with the attributes of other groups. There is also an interest in preserving the "superiority" of the in-group and in retaining consistent exclusion of out-group members. Although we could think of examples of this type of exclusion occurring (girl scouts; men-only clubs), Tajfel[33] takes these examples one step further by citing a number of extreme historical events, such as the witch-hunts of Europe and the anti-Semitism of Nazi Germany. Such cases of out-group stereotyping resulted not only in exclusion but in mass murder and genocide. These cases were also known as powerful public opinion events! Unfortunately, the principle continues to surface periodically, with more recent events including insidious movements toward "ethnic cleansing" in Eastern Europe and the rise of neo-Nazis in Europe and the United States.

Tajfel describes some functions stereotypes serve for society, too. These are social causality, social justification, and social differentiation.

Social Causality

According to Tajfel, social causality is the search for an understanding of "complex and usually distressing large-scale social events" resulting in "scapegoating."[34] Out-groups are seen as the "cause" of the distress. Tajfel describes the use of Scots in Newcastle and Catholics in Oxford as scape-goats for the seventeenth-century plague in Britain as examples of social causality. Poor sanitation and a lack of quarantine practices had much more to do with spreading the disease.

Recently, public opinion about economic problems in the United States has been directed against the Japanese, for "causing" trade imbalances, and Mexicans, for "taking" American jobs (even though both countries are experiencing economic problems of their own). Politicians rely on scapegoating discrete sections of the American population as out-groups in order to increase the chances of political success. There may be some connection between our economic difficulties and the behavior of other nations, or the political behavior of various segments of our society and politicians' accusations. However, it is clear that social causality is at work to the extent that blame is placed on the others rather than on aspects of our own system that might explain the situation.

Social Justification

Tajfel uses the term social justification to refer to the use of specific stereotypes of a group in order to justify actions against that group. As an example, he describes "the way that colonialist powers of the last century constructed derogatory stereotypes (dim-witted, simple, lazy . . .) of exploited races (e.g., British stereotypes of the Irish)."[35] As Hogg and Abrams[36] note, such "dehumanization of a group makes its exploitation seem justified, natural and unproblematic" to individuals doing the stereotyping.

In the United States, a strong and very popular segment of the music industry at the end of the nineteenth and the beginning of the twentieth century took a decidedly racist turn, aimed at maintaining status differentials and segregation between whites and African-Americans, with heavy use of derogatory stereotypes in lyrics and titles in such chart-topping songs as "Stay in Your Own Backyard," "The Bully," and "All Coons Look Alike to Me."

Recordings of all three songs were major "hits" between 1900 and 1920. "Stay in Your Own Backyard" was a ballad in which a "mammy" directed her child (a "pickaninny") not to play with the white children; "The Bully" described a particularly "nasty nigger" who carried a razor for anyone who got in his way; and "All Coons Look Alike to Me" was a comic recording that depended on stereotyping for its humor. Songs like these helped reinforce existing laws and social rules that segregated African-Americans, kept them from voting, and prevented them from joining unions or obtaining many kinds of jobs.

More recently, the world has seen a rise in terrorist attacks around the world, and much of the violence has been said to be perpetrated by followers of Islam. This assumption has often been and continues to be caricatured in American films and television programs that focus on terrorist threats. Villains in these narratives are often portrayed as Muslim men who are thwarted by individuals of another religious and ethnic extraction. The films convey the message that the villains deserve the consequences that befall them because they are inherently evil. This stereotypical dramatization of a real world problem provides a degree of social justification to U.S. government attempts to contain terrorism, which has sometimes resulted in a limitation of civil liberties for Arab and Muslim men.

Social Differentiation

According to Tajfel,[37] social differentiation is the tendency for ethnocentrism (enhancing one's own social group) to occur through stereotyping. Social differentiation tends to be accentuated under conditions in which the uniqueness or distinctiveness of one's own group appears to be eroding or "when social conditions are such that low status is perceived to be illegitimate and changeable."[38] Clearly, one reason for the popularity of the racist recordings of the early twentieth century was the tremendous strides in civil rights that were being made at the time; because of the uncertainty of future status differentials, white people were feeling threatened, and social differentiation was used to attempt to maintain the status quo.

A similar tack was taken in the 1950s when rock and roll was beginning to develop, and black and white teenagers were beginning to socialize together. Educators and parents joined forces in denigrating the African influences on popular music, calling it the "devil's music" and referring to the "low" station from which it sprang. On national television, Steve Allen ridiculed Elvis Presley's performance of "Hound Dog" (a song first written for and recorded by African-American blues singer Big Mama Thornton) by having him perform the song in a tuxedo, singing to a real hound dog.

The implications of social differentiation for public opinion formation, though potentially vital, have not been researched in any consistent fashion. Part of the problem is that social change must be examined over a relatively long period of time, an expensive option for public opinion scholars. An outcome of social differentiation in the 1950s, for example, may have been a "boomerang" effect. That is, the differences between young and old (the so-called generation gap), which exhibited themselves in speech, dress, and lifestyle divergence between the generations, contributed to protests and other events a decade later, shaking the country's basic values and causing tremendous strife and turmoil in everyday life. However, this cause-and-effect relationship is difficult to prove because so little public opinion data have been collected in a consistent way over time.

In general, the effects of stereotyping on public opinion have been understudied by scholars, but our discussion should give you some idea of the major impact this human tendency may have on public opinion outcomes.

SOCIAL NORMS

A norm is "a principle of right action binding upon the members of a group and serving to guide, control and regulate proper and acceptable behavior."[39] Much like stereotypes and other group processes, social norms can profoundly influence public opinion formation and change. In fact, according to Hogg and Abrams norms have been defined as "the *stereotypic* perceptions, beliefs, and modes of conduct associated with a *group*" (emphasis ours)[40] Think of how norms influence the way you behave, dress, and even talk to those around you! If a student stood up in a large lecture class and began shrieking for no reason, you would probably be shocked. This behavior would be counter to the norms in our society—you have been taught that you should not shriek in class (unless it is an acting class). It is perfectly "normal," however, to stand up and shriek at a football or basketball game. The norms for the two situations are very different, and our public actions reflect that difference.

Similarly, when someone asks whom you plan to vote for in an upcoming presidential election, it is relatively "normal" to answer by naming either a Republican or a Democratic candidate. For certain elections, a third-party candidate (e.g., John Anderson in 1980, Ross Perot in 1992) is acceptable and considered a serious candidate by the public. Very rarely in the United States would someone even consider naming someone from the Communist Party, the Nazi Party, the Vegetarian Party, or any other political party. Part of the reason for this hesitation is that the norm in our society is for the U.S. political system to function as a two-party system, even though many viewpoints are omitted from consideration by both of those parties. The norm is so entrenched among most of us that most people do not take third-party candidates seriously.

Research on social norms has been around for a while. In fact, interest in norms dates back to the late nineteenth and early twentieth centuries, when scholars began attempting to measure the force of custom and tradition on society[41] or concerned themselves with mechanisms (such as norms) that lead to the influence of others and to compliance with the will of groups or individuals.[42] Often, scholars emphasized the usefulness of social norms for society.[43] Muzafer Sherif,[44] for example, says that norms "fulfill the function of ordering, simplifying, and regulating interaction"[45] and that once created, norms continue to influence group interaction even after the original members of the group are gone. In this section, we will discuss how norms develop, how they affect public opinion formation and expression, and how they are enforced.

Generating Norms

Many social norms are of such long standing that we rarely think about them at all. Violations of them seem quite strange. The social norm against public nudity is one we in the United States do not often consider. Other norms, however, develop and change frequently, such as norms about appropriate skirt lengths for women. We should also note that norms are created by groups, including cultures. Sunbathing topless in America violates a social norm. Sunbathing topless in Norway does not.

Some of the earliest studies of group norms explored the ways in which such norms develop. Sherif[46] conducted the first social psychological studies of norms. His classic experiments took advantage of what is called the "autokinetic phenomenon." Subjects shown a point of light in a darkened room, with no point of reference for it, will perceive the light to be moving even though it is stationary. Sherif showed such a light to groups of experimental subjects. He found that in this situation, people interacted socially to resolve the ambiguity of the light "movement."

Eventually, members of the group "converged upon a consensual group decision concerning the supposed movement of the light."[47]

There have been a number of autokinetic studies since the initial experiment conducted by Sherif. These studies consistently find that (1) a norm is a product of social interaction, (2) the reality of a norm is rooted in perceptions of the physical and social world, (3) a norm is a quality of the group rather than of individuals in the group, and (4) a norm "exacts" conformity from those who join the group.[48] The studies reveal that norms are negotiated among members of a group and that different groups develop different norms. Thus, the norms belong to the group. If you are a member of several groups, you are likely to obey different norms in each of them. By the same token, if you join a new group, you are subject to its norms, although they may be different from the norms of other groups you belong to.

Norms are often very persistent. We may obey the same rules for behavior and think with the same preconceptions for long periods of time. But norms can change, too. The historian Ken Cmiel, who has documented some of the changes in the norms for polite behavior that occurred during the 1960s, has found that African-Americans who staged sit-ins at lunch counters in the South both upheld the norms of politeness by behaving in the same way any other customer would and at the same time defied the norms of polite behavior by violating the norm that African-Americans and whites could not share the same public spaces. The hippie counterculture argued that a new norm of politeness based on authentic expressions of one's true feelings rather than social rules of etiquette should be established. The result of these and other struggles over the norms for politeness resulted in an informalization of American culture, Cmiel argues.[49] Norms about language, dress, sexual behavior, and other social activities became less rigid. New behaviors from growing sideburns to smoking pot became more acceptable in polite society.

When norms are in transition, people are often uncomfortable. Norms about social exchanges between men and women are currently changing, and both groups seem somewhat touchy on the subject. Should men hold doors open for women? Pick up the checks at restaurants? Some men feel that such behaviors represent courtesy and respect. Some women feel demeaned by them, arguing that to engage in such behaviors suggests that women are incapable of doing these things for themselves. Interpersonal encounters can have larger social ramifications as well, as women file claims of discrimination or even sexual harassment against men.

Social Norms and Public Opinion.   Several studies have found that social norms can play an important part in opinion formation and expression. For example, Theodore Newcomb[50] found that women from a conservative background who attended Bennington College were rapidly influenced by the liberal political norms of that college. Newcomb said that "conservative" juniors who were members of sororities with liberal seniors rapidly conformed to the more liberal norms. He also found that these effects persisted after graduation from Bennington and, in fact, were still present more than twenty years later.[51] Obviously, expressions of opinions on social issues and vote decisions are influenced and sustained by norms, and it is findings such as these that make the concept of norms fascinating for public opinion scholars.

However, despite a long history of research and extensive use of the concept, there is still no consensus about the explanatory and predictive value of social norms—nor is there a consensus on a common definition of social norms.[52] As Robert Cialdini, Carl Kallgren, and Raymond Reno[53] note, there are, on the one hand, "those who see the concept as crucial to a full understanding of human social behavior."[54] On the other hand, there are those who view the concept as vague, overly general, often contradictory, and ill-suited to empirical testing.[55]

Two Perspectives: Consensus and Conflict.   Two major perspectives we should discuss concern the roles norms play in our society: the "consensus" view of society and the "conflict" view of society. According to the consensus view, norms "embody the socially acceptable modes of action to achieve society's goals."[56] Thus, taking the consensus perspective, norms are responsible for uniformities of social behavior. Norms "arise to govern and ensure smooth and predictable social interaction and thus enable society to exist as a cohesive and stable entity. They suppress strife and conflict by furnishing consensus and agreement on an acceptable modus operandum for social life."[57]

Often, consensus norms are invisible in studies of public opinion. By definition, these norms are accepted by such a large proportion of the population that asking survey questions about them does not seem like a worthwhile activity. As Hogg and Abrams observe: "Norms can be concretized, through legislation, as the laws and rules of society, or more often they are so pervasive and so saturate society that they are 'taken for granted' and are invisible. They are the 'hidden agenda' of everyday interaction, the background to our behavior, the context within which things happen."[58]

Nevertheless, norms of this kind are very important. For example, as you will see in Chapter Seven, a basic consensus on democratic principles is necessary in order for our political system to function. In fact, in our society, the norm of democratic decisionmaking is a powerful consensus norm. We adopt the model of our national government in many of our private activities, and the norms of democratic decisionmaking are seen as the legitimate way to make decisions in these spheres. Unions, condominium associations, and many other private groups use democratic models to govern their interaction. Officers or leaders are elected, and frequently issues are voted on by the group as well. Majority rule is the rule of thumb. Yet there is no reason that makes it necessary for these groups to employ this model for organizing themselves. They are simply responding to an important social norm.

The conflict view of norms sees society as a "heterogenous collection of different groups of different sizes which stand in power and status relations to each other."[59] That is, different norms are seen as attached to different groups. Norms become the set of expectations concerning the attitudes, beliefs, and behaviors of particular groups. They also become the social uniformities that result in distinguishing characteristics among groups. According to the conflict view, norms describe and evaluate the typical behavior of a typical member of a particular group or social category. In addition, norms prescribe by pointing out to people or groups that they ought to behave in a particular "circumscribed" manner.

Deborah Tannen has explored the different norms that govern men's and women's conversational styles and has investigated what happens when people of opposite genders try to converse together.[60] One important difference is in the norms that govern what Tannen calls "troubles talk." Both men and women engage in talk about the difficulties they experience in life, but the norms governing appropriate responses to such talk are very different for each group. Women respond to troubles talk by confirming the feelings of the speaker. Such responses are interpreted as a way of building rapport between the conversants. Women's responses say, "I understand." Men respond to troubles talk by dismissing the troubles of the other and telling stories of their own troubles. Such responses are interpreted as a way of respecting the vulnerability of the teller by not usurping his status or being condescending. Men's responses say, "Hey, I'm no better than you are." When men and women converse together, their different conversational norms produce unsatisfying outcomes. Women who tell their troubles feel that men are unsympathetic.

Tannen's research into the differences between men's and women's conversational styles also has important implications for opinion expression. She argues that it is a difference in conversational style that may prevent women from being heard in male-dominant environments. Men may treat women as equals, as being as free to speak out in meetings or other public forums as the men are. Women, however, may not be comfortable with "competing for the floor." They are treated as equals, but the outcome is unequal. Tannen suggests that both genders have a responsibility to take the other's conversational norms into account.[61]

It is clear from both the consensual and conflict views that norms fulfill a critical function for the individual: "They simplify, render predictable, and regulate social interaction. Without them social life would be unbearably complex and stressful: the individual would collapse beneath the tremendous cognitive overload involved in interaction."[62]

It is useful at this point to consider how both consensual and conflictual views of norms can help us understand public opinion formation and expression. For one thing, norms can create a common perspective from which to view social problems. Emile Durkheim, who viewed society as consensual, called such common perspectives "collective representations." Serge Moscovici, who focused on the conflict view of society, called them "social representations."

Moscovici[63] notes that we derive only a small fraction of our knowledge and information from direct interactions between ourselves and the world. Instead, most of our knowledge is supplied to us by communication, which affects our way of thinking and creates new content via social representations.[64] According to Moscovici, then, social representations refer to the ideas, thoughts, images and knowledge that members of a collectivity share.[65]

Through these representations, members of a society are able to construct "social reality."[66] The concept of social representations subsumes stereotypes and normative beliefs, highlighting the function of norms for furnishing an explanation that accounts for events and experiences we have in our lives. As a society, for example, we must choose to act on certain social problems and to not act on others. To a large extent, our shared perceptions of these problems (our social representations) determine the amount of effort we put into their resolution. Thus, to the extent that our perceptions of certain issues and events are similar, we can talk about a specific social problem. These social problems become public issues that can be debated and discussed and that eventually may be slated for public action. To the extent that we all share these perceptions, our society can coordinate its efforts and set priorities. Communication scholars have explored the ways in which media guide us in building social representations, a concept they call "framing" (see Chapter Eleven).

Moscovici's research on conformity and group norms began with an influential study he and his colleagues conducted, testing majority pressure on minority perception of color.[67] They enlisted minority confederates to all agree in front of the rest of the group that blue was green. If the minority members were unanimous and consistent, they were successful in changing majority opinion. This study refuted the classic study by Solomon Asch that tested whether an individual in the minority would change his or her original answer (concerning which line was longest) that was correct, for an incorrect answer, in order to conform to the majority.

An additional insight later added to this finding is that when the majority changes to a minority opinion, the change in opinion does not revert back to the earlier position when surveyed at a later date. However, when the minority conforms to the majority for the sake of consensus, the minority typically changes back to its original position.

In a more recent work, Moscovici and Willem Doise[68] address conflict and consensus. When social conflict arises, the people involved (or groups involved) will seek communication in order to resolve the ambiguity. Again, the role of the minority is important in this time of consensus building. The group does not arrive at a consensus that represents the mean position of all the opinions expressed in the group. Rather, the position is "extreme," in the same direction as their original leaning. The position represents all positions considered, not the middle, or compromise, position. Moscovici and Doise describe this as part of the group polarization process, arrived at by each member of the group moving from an individualistic focus to an intragroup focus. Members of the group, upon being questioned later, will still hold the extreme position. Arrival at this consensus seems to last, and members continue to take a bolder position. It seems this new position becomes a part of the social norms of the group.

The theory of social representations has a certain amount of appeal for public opinion researchers, even though it is vague, imprecise, and difficult to understand. For example, Pierre Bourdieu[69] believes that public opinion is nearly impossible to measure because there is so much variety among social representations. He argues that unless the researchers and the respondents see an issue in more or less the same way, survey questions make no sense to the respondents and survey answers do not measure what researchers think they do. There appears to be much potential here for further study and refinement. We refer the interested student to works by Moscovici.[70]

Several other theories take a more explicitly conflictual view, as they describe the ways in which group norms affect the interaction among groups, social behavior, and public opinion. Tajfel's notion of social categorization attempts to explain how social norms aid in determining the ways people classify themselves and others as members of distinct categories and reference groups.[71] Social categorization research has shown that the simple act of classifying others into social categories is enough to provoke discrimination between in-group and out-group members.

This classification results in a variety of effects, including discriminatory group behavior, intragroup cohesion, and ethnocentric biases.[72] By simply defining a group, we appear to create a competition between "them" and "us," even when the distinction means nothing. After we have classified people as "them" or "us," we appear to look for (and find) differences, and the general weight of the differences is that "we" are better than "they" are.

One clear example of social categorization occurs in the abortion issue, where individuals have tended to align themselves as either "pro-life" or "pro-choice." As is clear from current headlines and news stories, both sides see their own group as "clearly in the right," as having morals somewhat superior to the opposing group. Another striking example was the result of an experiment on prison life conducted at Stanford University (see Box 5.2).

BOX 5.2   GROUP IDENTITY AND GROUP POLARIZATION: THE STANFORD PRISON STUDY

In the early 1970s, a group of researchers at Stanford University wanted to find out how prison conditions affected the people who lived and worked in them. Many people believed that prisons were harsh places because only the worst kinds of people were locked up there. Others believed that prisons were bad because those who chose to become guards often had a sadistic streak. Craig Haney, W. Curtis Banks, and Philip Zimbardo demonstrated that the group dynamics of the prison setting played a key role in making their mock prison an extremely uncomfortable place. This is what they did.

First, they prescreened a group of men for their psychological stability. Then, they selected the twenty-two who were the most psychologically "normal" for the study. These men were randomly assigned to be either a prisoner or a guard in a simulation that was to last two weeks. All subjects were told that "prisoners" would be guaranteed "a minimally adequate diet, clothing, housing and medical care"[1] for the duration of the study. Both "prisoners" and "guards" were paid $15 per day for their participation. Those who became prisoners were "arrested" at their homes by the Palo Alto police and taken to the "prison," which was built into the basement of a building on the Stanford campus. They remained in prison twenty-four hours a day until the experiment ended. The "guards" worked eight-hour shifts and spent the other sixteen hours each day doing what they normally did. Each group was given no real instructions about what its role was to be, though the experimenters did engage in several procedures that were designed to dehumanize the "prisoners," such as "delousing" them when they arrived at the "prison" and giving them uniforms with "prisoner numbers." The "guards," who were also issued uniforms to promote group differences, met with the experimenters the day before the "prisoners" arrived to create a set of rules for the prison. The experimenters imposed one cardinal rule: "Guards" were not to use violence against "prisoners." The researchers reported that all other "prison rules" were developed by "guards" and experimenters together.

The results of the experiment were stunning. "Prisoners" and "guards" became so involved in their roles that within days several prisoners had to be released because they were in so much emotional distress. The researchers decided to end the experiment early. Haney, Banks, and Zimbardo report:

> The most dramatic evidence of the impact of the mock prison upon the participants was seen in the gross reactions of five prisoners who had to be released from the study because of extreme emotional depression, crying, rage, or acute anxiety. The pattern of symptoms was quite similar in four of the subjects and began as early as the second day of imprisonment. The fifth subject was released after being treated for a psychosomatic rash which covered portions of his body. . . . When the experiment was terminated prematurely after only six days, all the remaining prisoners were delighted by their unexpected good fortune; in contrast, most of the guards seemed to be distressed by the decision to stop the experiment. It appeared to us that the guards had become sufficiently involved in their roles so that they now enjoyed the extreme control and power they exercised and were reluctant to give it up.[2]

Haney, Banks, and Zimbardo demonstrated that even "normal" people react in inhumane ways to the conditions of prison life. They also demonstrated that group norms are powerful and quick to develop. In only six days, "prisoners" and "guards" had adopted group norms and group identities that encouraged both polarization and inhumane treatment on the part of the "guards." Routine bodily functions like eating or going to the bathroom became privileges for the "prisoners," to be earned with good behavior. The "prisoners" began to lose self-esteem and respect for each other. The "guards" developed a group norm of never questioning another guard's treatment of a "prisoner," no matter how harsh.

The development of these norms at the Stanford prison both regulated behavior and maximized the differences between "prisoners" and "guards." The researchers report, "Not to be tough and arrogant was taken as a sign of weakness by the other guards." The "prisoners," by contrast, developed a norm of passivity as a means of coping with the arbitrary authority of the "guards." The results of the Stanford prison study tell a cautionary tale about the power of groups and group identity. As one "prisoner" in the study put it, "I learned that people can easily forget that others are human."[3]

SOURCE: Craig Haney, W. Curtis Banks, and Philip G. Zimbardo, "Interpersonal Dynamics in a Simulated Prison," in M. Patricia Golden, ed., *The Research Experience* (Itasca, IL: F. E. Peacock Publishers, 1976), pp. 157–177.

NOTES
1. Haney, Banks, and Zimbardo, "Interpersonal Dynamics in a Simulated Prison," p. 159.
2. Ibid., p. 164.
3. Ibid., pp. 173, 170.

When individuals classify themselves and others into categorical groups, there are perceptual effects: There is increased perception of differences among groups (polarization) and decreased perception of differences within groups (homogenization). These effects can result in standardization of public opinion within groups and an exaggeration of differences in public opinion among groups.

Group polarization is conformity to a polarized norm that defines one's own group in contrast to other groups within a specific social context.[73] Under conditions that render an in-group psychologically salient, people conform to the in-group norm, the position perceived as most "consensual."[74] In some circumstances, the group norm will be the position that is the average for the in-group distribution—the position that minimizes the differences between in-group members.

However, it is equally likely that the norm of the in-group will not be the group mean but some other point in the distribution. The resultant norm occurs because groups do not exist in isolation but in a wider social frame of reference that encompasses both in-groups and out-groups. The defining features of a group—its norms and stereotypes—not only characterize the in-group's qualities but also distinguish the in-group clearly from relevant other groups, thus maximizing differences between in-groups and out-groups.[75] As you can see, these norms can also have an impact on perceptions of public opinion, maximizing differences between the in-group and the out-group.

For example, we might expect to see group polarization effects when loggers and environmentalists interact, even though both groups ultimately wish to see the forest survive. Environmentalists, in the face of opposition from loggers, may come to argue that the forest must be pre-served in a pristine state and that no logging activity is acceptable. They may take this position even though many of their members once believed that some logging was compatible with saving the forest and they may even have worried about the loggers losing their jobs. The loggers, by comparison, may come to argue that jobs are more important than saving the forest and advocate clear-cutting and replanting, even though many of their members once believed that preserving old-growth trees was a worthy goal.

The actual position of the in-group norm is often a trade-off between minimizing intragroup differences and maximizing intergroup differ-ences. The homogenization of group members' opinions becomes a part of the polarization effect as members seek to differentiate themselves from the out-group.

Vincent Price[76] suggests that news stories cue their recipients to think about the reported issue in terms of their particular group perspective. This perspective leads to polarized or exaggerated perceptions of group opinions, finally leading to expression of personal opinion consistent with the exaggerated perception of the group norm. Price interprets his data as indicating that media reports emphasizing group conflicts may play a role in the formation of public opinion. Thus, groups may affect public opin-ion even when no interpersonal interaction occurs within them.

The influence of in-groups and out-groups upon public opinion has been manifested in another way.[77] For instance, the effect of a negative political campaign varies according to whether the political message orig-inated from an in-group or an out-group candidate. In a Budesheim, De-Paola, and Houston study, participants were sensitive to the content of a message from both sources, but surprisingly they used less stringent cri-teria when evaluating the message of an out-group source than an in-group source. The authors advance several reasons for this, the most likely being that members of the group judge unpleasant behavior (the negative ad) more harshly for another member of the group, because the behavior is seen as aberrant.

Two Functions: Descriptive and Injunctive Norms.   Cialdini, Kallgren, and Reno[78] distinguish two types of norms. Norms that characterize what is commonly done (the perception of what most people do) are descriptive norms; the norms that characterize the perception of what most people approve or disapprove (what ought to be done) are injunctive norms. Descriptive norms have an informational function, whereas injunctive norms have a sanctioning function.

Descriptive norms motivate people by providing evidence of effective or appropriate actions (e.g., "If everyone is doing or thinking or believing it, it must be a sensible thing to do or think or believe"). Descriptive norms are important to consider when studying public opinion as perceptions of what others might be doing or thinking. During the 1990s in the United States, many people began to invest in mutual funds. This behavior became, in some ways, normative. For some, investing in mutual funds might have been something they did rationally, because of low interest rates or because it will be many years before they retire. However, for others, these investments represent normative behavior. They invested in mutual funds because others do so and appeared to reap rewards. While there are additional norms that affect investor behavior, this simple example illustrates the role of normative behavior in society. Festinger's[79] social comparison theory (see Chapter Six for a more complete discussion) suggests an important role for descriptive norms in providing the comparison base by which individuals validate their opinions. Opinions that are normative for the group provide a validity check for individuals, because others (who were already judged to be similar to the individual) hold a particular opinion norm.[80] According to Festinger, the opinion norm thus provides the closest thing to an "objective" measure of what is real, true, or the "correct" opinion to hold. For instance, opinion norms about the future of the American economy are the closest we can come to "knowing" what will happen to the economy in the next few years. Thus, descriptive norms play an important role in opinion formation.

In contrast, injunctive norms specify what ought to be done, that is, they are the "moral rules of the group."[81] These norms can affect public opinion expression through a phenomenon known as "social desirability." Injunctive norms help people determine whether it would be "wrong" for them to reveal what they really think.[82] (For a further discussion of social desirability phenomena, see Chapter Six.)

People might be asked for their opinions on an issue related to racial unrest, for example, and a certain percentage of respondents might want to give a particular opinion but might perceive that such an opinion would probably be considered racist by others. The injunctive norm at work here—that racism is bad—would stifle opinion expression, though it might not stifle the opinion itself. An example of the role of injunctive norms in public opinion expression is provided by Barbara Anderson, Brian Silver, and Paul Abramson, who suggest that survey respondents often "exaggerate their conformity with socially approved norms": "However well theoretical concepts are defined, survey questions are formulated and data are analyzed, the data are the product of an interview. The interview involves an interaction between the interviewer and respondent in which the stimulus is not just the 'question' as it is written in the survey booklet, but also the social context in which the question is asked."[83]

One way to think about the relationship between these two types of norms and public opinion is to recognize that descriptive norms tend to influence opinion formation, whereas injunctive norms tend to influence opinion expression.

Enforcing Norms

Group conformity (and the enforcement of group norms) is of interest to public opinion scholars who examine how and why people conform to group pressure when forming and expressing their opinions. Conformity is the mechanism by which norms affect public opinion. Thus, understanding group conformity can be critical to understanding the relationship of norms to the public opinion process.

Solomon Asch conducted some of the first studies that attempted to look at the pressure that groups can exert on individuals to conform. In these studies, groups of seven to nine people would sit in a semicircle. The subjects were then shown lines of clearly varying lengths and were asked which lines were the longest and which were the shortest.

Only the last person to respond in the group was a true "naive" subject. All of the other members of this "group" were confederates (people who were "planted" in the group by the experimenter). When it was their turn to speak out loud, the confederates would give a unanimous incorrect judgment.[84]

Obviously, Asch was interested in how the subjects would respond to group pressure, since in reality there was only one clearly correct answer (the lines varied significantly in size) (see Figure 5.2). However, it is in-

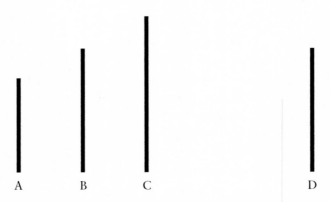

FIGURE 5.2   The Asch Lines. Which line is longer?

teresting to note that the subjects accepted the incorrect group position about one-third of the time.

The fact that some people conform more than others has led to a great deal of research on establishing whether there may be a "conformist syndrome" or a "conformist personality."[85] For example, conformists appear to have low self-esteem,[86] a high need for social approval,[87] low IQ, high anxiety, insecurity, and so forth.[88] Stanley Milgram's[89] experiments, however, showed that "average" people conform to authority when they are placed in situations where that authority seems relevant.

Actually, people may conform publicly without changing their attitudes. Eagly and Chaiken[90] suggest that when influence is of an injunctive nature (when it is socially desirable to conform), social pressures may produce public agreement with other group members but provide little or no private acceptance. For example, imagine that you and some friends are watching TV and a show you particularly enjoy comes on. One of your friends says that the show is "really stupid," and another person quickly agrees. Another chimes in, then asks you what you think. Faced with feeling different, many people in this kind of situation will verbally conform to the group norm—not liking the program—while not actually changing their attitude toward the program at all.

Paul Nail[91] has distinguished four possibilities in the compliance–acceptance situation. We will take each in turn:

1. Conforming privately and publicly (conversion). In this case, the individual becomes convinced that the group norm is the "correct" or

best opinion to have on the matter and changes his or her own attitude toward the subject (private acceptance) as well as agreeing with the group verbally (publicly).

2. Conforming publicly but not privately (compliance). This behavior is like the example above regarding the TV program. In this case, the individual is willing to alter personal opinion publicly but will not change his or her attitude about the topic (privately).

3. Conforming privately but not publicly (anticompliance). This is the odd situation in which the individual agrees with the group norm in private but will not say so in public. This situation may be found when a person is very committed to a position but does not want to admit the possibility of being wrong and therefore maintains the original position long after not believing in it anymore.

4. Nonconformity at both private and public levels (independence). In this case, the individual simply does not care what others think and will assert an opinion publicly even when it contradicts the group norm.

Thus, although many researchers use the term conformity to refer to public agreement, Nail suggests that conformity may not be an accurate label for what occurs.[92] The idea of private and public aspects of conformity should have considerable interest for researchers in public opinion and provides an important consideration for research on public opinion and norm conformity. Expression of an opinion that is in keeping with a social norm does not necessarily indicate that behavior or even an individual's belief on the subject is consistent with what was expressed.

Michael Hogg and John Turner argue that issues such as those of private and public aspects of conformity can be integrated and simplified in order to arrive at a distinction between two forms of social influence that "share the burden of explanation": normative influence and informational influence.[93] According to Morton Deutsch and Harold Gerard,[94] normative influence results from the individual's need for social approval and acceptance. It creates conformity that "is merely public compliance with, rather than private acceptance or internalization of, the group's attitudes, beliefs, opinions or behaviors."[95] Conformity in this case is not associated with true internal change. The individual will go along with the group, however, to be accepted by the group, to avoid punishment, and so forth.

Normative influence can arise under conditions in which the group (or individual) is perceived to have coercive power (e.g., the power to criticize, threaten, and so on) or the ability to reward (such as the power to give affection or praise). An important precondition for normative influence is the perception of surveillance by the group. Individuals are unlikely to comply with norms they have not internalized unless they believe they might get "caught."

Hogg and Turner also suggest that normative influence may be powerful if the reference group is very important to the individual.[96] Because reference groups are implicitly defined in terms of emotional attachment (such as liking and admiration),[97] pressures for uniformity within such groups will be powerful, based on a strong desire for approval or acceptance. Thus, we would expect that a person would be more likely to conform to the norms within a tight circle of friends than among strangers. We simply are more concerned about what the people we care about think than we are about what strangers think of our behavior.

Unlike normative influence, informational influence results from the individual's need to be correct.[98] It is "true influence" in that it results in private acceptance or internalization of beliefs, attitudes, and behaviors.

According to Hogg and Abrams, the power of informational influence "resides in the perceived expertise or expert power (i.e., possession of knowledge that others repeatedly need to draw upon), or the informational power (possession of a specific piece of information that is needed) of others. The precondition for informational influence is subjective uncertainty or lack of confidence in the validity of one's beliefs, or opinions."[99]

In most circumstances, normative and informational influence "operate together to create conformity." However, there are those individuals who will fight or resist these influence attempts, especially if they are perceived to threaten individual freedoms.

Public opinion scholars have begun to use conformity research as a basis for some of their theoretical work on public opinion formation. For example, Elisabeth Noelle-Neumann asserts that much of her research on the "spiral of silence" is based on conformity studies. Her "fear of isolation" concept is based in part on the experimental work of Asch[100] and Milgram.[101] Noelle-Neumann states that people often fear isolation because of their need to be associated with others; they have a strong need to conform in order to be accepted (for a more complete discussion, see Chapter Six).

A FURTHER LOOK AT
SOCIOLOGICAL EXPLANATIONS

In practice we can look to sociological approaches to explain a number of the most visible and identifiable findings from public opinion research. What, then, are some of these patterns and regularities in public attitudes and behavior that we find in sample survey data?

Many of these are not surprising and they are implicit if not explicit from earlier discussions. We will return to them in later chapters. A number of these variations and patterns follow logically from group polarization perspectives and discussions of processes of socialization in the next chapter.

Table 5.3 presents data of that sort that have long been standard in the analysis of patterns of differences in public opinion. Chapter Eight will consider related data in the context of research on voting and on debates about the implications of these kinds of subgroup differences for drawing conclusions about the "competence" of the American public. This voting research was a sociological analysis that came to be known as the "Columbia model" that stressed the influence of social groups and relationships on political attitudes and behavior.[102] This emphasis showed the extent to which people held opinions and behaved as "in-groups." That is, there is longstanding support in survey data on voting (see Chapter Eight) and on expressed attitudes, as we can see in Table 5.3 that the public's opinions and political behavior are associated with certain personal characteristics of individuals.

The key group-related differences are those associated with the socioeconomic stratification in the electorate and, by extension, the public more broadly. The early data suggested that the key stratifying variables that divided the Democratic and Republican parties and that related to social and economic matters were economic status (material possessions and education), occupation, religion, residence, and age.[103] Individuals lower in economic status, Catholic, urban, and young were associated with voting Democratic and taking "liberal" as opposed to "conservative" positions concerning government activism on economic matters.

TABLE 5.3   Average thermometer rating for "people on welfare" by group: 1980, 1986, 1994, 2000

	1980	1986	1994	2000
Democrats (including leaners)	57	52	50	55
Independents	49	50	44	49
Republicans (including leaners)	46	45	40	48
17–24 year olds	52	46	47	52
25–34 year olds	50	48	44	51
35–44 year olds	49	49	45	50
45–54 year olds	52	49	46	51
55–64 year olds	54	51	45	54
65–74 year olds	58	52	45	51
Whites	49	47	44	51
African Americans	71	59	58	59
Hispanics	58	54	50	51
Men	50	48	44	50
Women	54	50	47	53
Center cities	58	50	48	53
Suburbs	49	50	46	50
Rural / small towns	51	48	43	53
Income in 1st–16th percentile	62	57	54	56
Income in 17th–33rd percentile	55	51	48	53
Income in 34th–67th percentile	51	48	44	50
Income in 68th–95th percentile	46	44	40	50
Income in 96th–100th percentile	44	47	42	54

SOURCE: American National Election Studies surveys. Entries are average thermometer reading on a 0-100 "cold" to "warm" scale, in which high scores represent more positive feelings toward "people on welfare." Greg M. Shaw provided these tabulations to be included in Greg M. Shaw and Robert Y. Shapiro, "Welfare," in Benjamin Radcliff and Samuel Best, eds., *Polling America: An Encyclopedia of Public Opinion* (Westport, Conn: Greenwood Press, forthcoming).

These are not startling findings. The reason for this is that results such as these from social science research and early opinion polling by Gallup and others have long become a regular part of public discussion and common knowledge about American social and political life. Indeed, a lot that we take for granted about our society and politics has come from past social science research, and we should give credit where original credit is due. To understand more fully these survey results, we need to ask, what are the underlying bases or *causes* of these patterns of subgroup differences that were apparent in the 1940s and are still apparent today, as shown in Table 5.3.

On the face of it, according to Columbia University sociologist Paul F. Lazarsfeld and his colleagues, people of the same economic or social status, same religion or religious strength, and place of residence tended to think in somewhat similar ways compared to those who are different from them on these attributes. In the case of attitudes toward the poor, described using the term "welfare" in Table 5.3, it is easy to elaborate upon explanations. The differences associated with economic status (income) and race, given the racial divisions in economic status in the United States, might be attributable to self-interest: People who are rich do not want to be taxed heavily to support others, whereas those who are poor want government assistance available to them if they might need it. Or the differences might be explained by empathy and humanitarian attitudes. Or, as Lazarsfeld and his colleagues saw it, people tend to hold opinions like most people of their social class, religion, and place of residence (urban or rural) did, and these might be tied also to their political attitudes toward the Republican and Democratic parties and their candidates (see Chapter Eight).

While we can speculate on the sources or influences for different attitudes and opinions (as described earlier and in later chapters), Lazarsfeld and his colleagues emphasized sociological processes that they saw as more direct or proximate influences. Specifically, they argued that differences in opinions and behavior had much to do with how people's personal interactions with family and friends, coworkers, fellow churchgoers, and others influenced their political views. These interactions, which other sociologists later theorized further about in terms of "networks" that can involve close or distant—or "strong," "weak," or even very distant—connections or "ties," provide mechanisms for the direct influence or reinforcing of people's past opinions or predispositions. People may rely on particular family members or friends or others in their network for information. Lazarsfeld and his associates referred to some of these as "opinion leaders" who pay regular attention to issues and politics and who have well-formed opinions or partisan views that affected their reactions to events. Through interactions and discussion with these opinion leaders, *especially in the same social environment*, people will tend to adopt their opinions.

The emphasis on the social setting is important, since even aside from the influence of opinion leaders, people tend to live and work with people who are more likely to be similar to themselves rather than different. Attitudes and opinions that people develop that are related to their socioeconomic and other characteristics will be *reinforced* through interactions with others like themselves. The influences of the opinion leaders among these like others presumably would be the strongest (see further discussion in Chapter Eight). What really set the Columbia school apart was its interest in how social relationships—with family, friends, coworkers, and other acquaintances—influenced people's attitudes. Lazarsfeld's research explored social influences by asking many people, in a limited geographic area, detailed questions about their conversations with other people. This tradition is currently carried on, for instance, in the research of Robert Huckfeldt and John Sprague.[104]

The sociological approach to understanding public opinion is very appealing. It makes intuitive sense, and news reports and public discussions of issues very often cite subgroup reactions. For example, the debate in 2003 about affirmative action brought up racial differences in opinions on this issue. In the case of ongoing disagreements about same-sex marriages and other issues related to sexual orientation, opinion differences related to religion and religiousness come to the fore. It is easy to imagine that in these cases racial and religious subgroup opinions are related to shared values within subgroups and to people's interactions with others of the same race and religion or degree of religiousness.[105] This sociological explanation is useful in understanding persistent and especially large differences associated with demographic and social characteristics.

This approach seems less useful for explaining the *dynamics* of public opinion—how opinions and behavior change. Group interests and deeply held values are not likely to change. If opinion leaders in people's close or more distant networks are what matter most, then these leaders could be the catalysts for change. If so, then we are left with the question of explaining changes in the attitudes of the opinion leaders. We will consider further the strengths and limitations of sociological and psychological approaches in our discussion of another approach, one derived from another social science—economics—in Chapter Seven.

CONCLUSION

Public opinion scholars seldom attempt to understand the influence of social and institutional forces (such as laws, courts, and social value systems) on public opinion processes, and vice versa. Instead, much like research in collective behavior,[106] public opinion research is a field that presents a perfunctory image of the social process but relies heavily on individualistic explanations. Most public opinion scholars approach the study of public opinion as individual behavior while paying lip service to the collective or sociological aspects of public opinion.

Certainly, sociological factors are critical to the understanding of public opinion processes and functions, and it would be useful if more research were conducted that examined this phenomenon from a sociological perspective.

For example, one decidedly sociological public opinion phenomenon is what sociologists refer to as collective behavior. Collective behavior can include organized expressions of opinion such as strikes, sit-ins, or letter-writing campaigns. It also includes disorganized expressions of opinion such as riots, fads, and episodes of "mass hysteria." Although these phenomena are clearly social in nature, much of the research on collective behavior has focused on psychological aspects of it.

Most notably, scholars have worked for years to understand what motivates people to act on their opinions. For example, many acts of collective behavior are undertaken by groups agitating for civil rights. Such rights would be bestowed on all members of a social group regardless of their participation in the collective behavior. When the right to vote was extended to women, it was extended to all women, not just to the suffragettes. So why would a woman risk jail, public disgrace, or worse to obtain these rights if she would gain them anyway by letting others take such risks? In the case of an episode of mass hysteria, scholars have been interested in the psychological differences between those who were caught up in the panic and those who were not.

Other sociological aspects of collective behavior have often been neglected as well, especially as they relate to opinion expression. Few studies have explored such issues as the relationship of group organization to opinion expression.

One potentially fruitful area of research is what Thomas Scheff says is the most crucial human motive, the "maintenance of social bonds."[107]

Scheff suggests that secure social bonds are the force that holds a society together, for an intact social bond balances the needs of the individual with the needs of the group. Scheff suggests that social scientists need to study the social bond if they are ever to understand human behavior. A number of ideas related to public opinion are clearly relevant to this approach, including the study of social desirability effects in interviewers, Noelle-Neumann's idea of "fear of isolation," the "false consensus," and "pluralistic ignorance" phenomena (see Chapter Six), and many other concepts described in this book. We encourage students of public opinion to explore the potential of sociological theory in understanding public opinion processes.

NOTES

1. Daryl J. Bem, "Self-Perception Theory," in Leonard Berkowitz, ed., *Advances in Experimental Social Psychology* (San Diego: Academic Press, 1972), pp. 1–62.

2. Richard E. Petty and John T. Cacioppo, *Attitudes and Persuasion: Classic and Contemporary Approaches* (Dubuque, IA: William C. Brown Company, 1981), p. 163.

3. Alice H. Eagly and Shelly Chaiken, *The Psychology of Attitudes* (Orlando, FL: Harcourt Brace Jovanovich, 1993), p. 351.

4. Ibid.

5. Michael A. Hogg and Dominic Abrams, *Social Identifications: A Social Psychology of Intergroup Relations and Group Processes* (New York: Routledge, 1988).

6. Henry Tajfel, "Social Stereotypes and Social Groups," in J. C. Turner and H. Giles, eds., *Intergroup Behavior* (Oxford: Blackwell, 1981), p. 147.

7. Hogg and Abrams, *Social Identifications*.

8. Anthony G. Greenwald and Mahzarin R. Banaji, "Implicit Social Cognition: Attitudes, Self-Esteem, and Stereotypes," *Psychological Review* 102, 1 (1995):14.

9. S. A. Haslam, P. J. Oakes, K. J. Reynolds, and J. C. Turner, "Social Identity Salience and the Emergence of Stereotype Consensus," *Personality and Social Psychology Bulletin* 25, 7 (1999):809–818.

10. M. Brewer and R. Brown, "Intergroup Relations," in D. Gilbert, S. Fiske, and G. Lindzey, eds., *The Handbook of Social Psychology*, Vol. II, 4th ed. (Boston: McGraw-Hill, 1998).

11. Haslam et al., "Social Identity Salience," p. 811.

12. K. J. Reynolds, J. C. Turner, and S. A. Haslam, "When Are We Better Than Them and They Worse Than Us? A Closer Look at Social Discrimination in Positive and Negative Domains," *Journal of Personality and Social Psychology* 78, 1 (2000):64–80.

13. Brewer and Brown, "Intergroup Relations."

14. Daniel Katz and Kenneth W. Braly, "Social Stereotypes of One Hundred College Students," *Journal of Abnormal and Social Psychology* 28 (1933):280–290.

15. Hogg and Abrams, *Social Identifications*, p. 67.

16. Katz and Braly, "Social Stereotypes of One Hundred College Students."

17. Ibid.

18. Greenwald and Banaji, "Implicit Social Cognition."

19. K. R. Athey, J. E. Coleman, A. P. Reitman, and J. Tang, "Two Experiments Showing the Effect of the Interviewer's Racial Background on Responses to Questionnaires Concerning Racial Issues," *Journal of Applied Psychology* 44 (1960):244–246; S. Hatchett and H. Schuman, "White Respondents and Race of Interviewer Effects," *Public Opinion Quarterly* 39 (1975–1976):523–528.

20. Greenwald and Banaji, "Implicit Social Cognition," p. 14.

21. Walter Lippmann, *Public Opinion* (New York: Harcourt, Brace, 1922), p. 59.

22. Ibid.

23. Ibid., pp. 59–60.

24. Ibid., p. 60.

25. Henry Tajfel, "The Anchoring Effects of Value in a Scale of Judgments," *British Journal of Psychology* 50 (1959):294–304; Henry Tajfel, "Social and Cultural Factors in Perception," in Gardner Lindzey and Elliot Aronson, eds., *Handbook of Social Psychology* (Cambridge, MA: Addison-Wesley, 1969), pp. 30–45.

26. D. W. Rajecki, *Attitudes,* Vol. 2, 2nd ed. (Sunderland, MA: Sinauer, 1990), p. 282.

27. Mark Snyder, Elizabeth D. Tanke, and Ellen Berscheid, "Social Perception and Interpersonal Behaviour: On the Self-Fulfilling Nature of Social Stereotypes," *Journal of Experimental Social Psychology* 11 (1977):1–13.

28. Rajecki, *Attitudes.*

29. Ibid., pp. 282–285.

30. Snyder, Tanke, and Berscheid, "Social Perception and Interpersonal Behaviour."

31. Henry Tajfel, *Human Groups and Social Categories: Studies in Social Psychology* (Cambridge: Cambridge University Press, 1981).

32. Hogg and Abrams, *Social Identifications,* p. 76.

33. Tajfel, *Human Groups and Social Categories.*

34. Hogg and Abrams, *Social Identifications,* p. 77.

35. Ibid.

36. Ibid.

37. Tajfel, *Human Groups and Social Categories.*

38. Hogg and Abrams, *Social Identifications,* p. 77.

39. *Webster's New Collegiate Dictionary* (Springfield, MA: G. and C. Merriam Company, 1981), p. 776.

40. Hogg and Abrams, *Social Identifications.*

41. Walter Bagehot, *Physics and Politics* (1869; New York: Knopf, 1946); William G. Sumner, *Folkways* (Boston: Ginn, 1906).

42. Edward A. Ross, *Social Control: A Survey of the Foundations of Order* (New York: Macmillan, 1901).

43. Robert K. Merton and Alice S. Kitt, "Contributions to the Theory of Reference Group Behavior," in Robert K. Merton and Paul F. Lazarsfeld, eds., *Studies in the Scope and Method of "The American Soldier"* (New York: Free Press, 1950), pp. 40–105.

44. Muzafer Sherif, "A Study of Some Social Factors in Perception," *Archives of Psychology* 27 (1935):1–60; Muzafer Sherif, *The Psychology of Social Norms* (New York: Harper and Brothers, 1936).

45. Hogg and Abrams, *Social Identifications,* p. 160.

46. Sherif, "Study of Some Social Factors in Perception"; Sherif, *Psychology of Social Norms.*

47. Sherif, "Study of Some Social Factors in Perception"; Vincent Price and Hayg Osha-gan, "Social-Psychological Perspectives on Public Opinion," in Theodore L. Glaser and Charles T. Salmon, eds., *Public Opinion and the Communication of Consent* (New York: Guilford Publications, 1989), pp. 177–216; Muzafer Sherif, B. Jack White, and O. J. Harvey, "Status in Experimentally Produced Groups," *American Journal of Sociology* 60 (1955):370–379.

48. Hogg and Abrams, *Social Identifications*, p. 161.

49. Kenneth Cmiel, "The Politics of Incivility," in David Farber, ed., *The Sixties: From Memory to History* (Chapel Hill: University of North Carolina Press, 1994), pp. 263–290.

50. Theodore M. Newcomb, *Personality and Social Change: Attitude Formation in a Student Community* (New York: Holt, Rinehart and Winston, 1943).

51. Theodore M. Newcomb et al., *Persistence and Change: Bennington College and Its Students After Twenty-five Years* (New York: Wiley, 1967).

52. Carroll J. Glynn, "Public Opinion as a Normative Opinion Process," in Brant R. Burleson, ed., *Communication Yearbook 20* (Thousand Oaks, CA: Sage Publications, 1996), pp. 157–183.

53. Robert B. Cialdini, Carl A. Kallgren, and Raymond R. Reno, "A Focus Theory of Normative Conduct: A Theoretical Refinement and Reevaluation of the Role of Norms in Human Behavior," in Mark P. Zanna, ed., *Advances in Experimental Social Psychology* (San Diego: Academic Press, 1991), pp. 201–234.

54. Sherif, *Psychology of Social Norms*; David J. McKirnan, "The Conceptualization of Deviance: A Conceptualization and Initial Test of a Model of Social Norms," *European Journal of Social Psychology* 10 (1980):79–93.

55. Dennis L. Krebs and Dale T. Miller, "Altruism and Aggression," in Lindzey and Aronson, eds., *Handbook of Social Psychology*, Vol. 2, pp. 1–72; Margaret M. Marini, "Age and Sequencing Norms in the Transition to Adulthood," *Social Forces* 63 (1984):229–244.

56. Hogg and Abrams, *Social Identifications*, p. 159.

57. Ibid.

58. Ibid.

59. Ibid.

60. Deborah Tannen, *You Just Don't Understand: Women and Men in Conversation* (New York: Random House, 1990).

61. Ibid.

62. Hogg and Abrams, *Social Identifications*, p. 159.

63. Serge Moscovici, "On Some Aspects of Social Representations," paper presented at the symposium on "Representations" of the American Psychological Association, Anaheim, CA, 1983.

64. Glynn, "Public Opinion as a Normative Opinion Process."

65. Serge Moscovici, *La psychanalyse, son image et son publique* (Paris: Presses Universitaires de France, 1961); Serge Moscovici, "The Coming Era of Representations," in Jean-Paul Codol and Jacques-Philippe Leyens, eds., *Cognitive Analysis of Social Behavior* (The Hague: Martinus Nijhoff, 1982), pp. 115–119.

66. Glynn, "Public Opinion as a Normative Opinion Process."

67. Serge Moscovici, E. Lage, and M. Naffrechoux, "Influence of a Consistent Minority on the Responses of a Majority in a Color Perception Task," *Sociometry* 32 (1969):365–380. Reproduced in M. Hewstone, A. S. R. Manstead, and W. Stroebe, eds., *The Blackwell Reader in Social Psychology* (Malden, MA: Blackwell, 1997), pp. 527–542.

68. Serge Moscovici and Willem Doise, *Conflict and Consensus: A General Theory of Collective Decisions* (Thousand Oaks, CA: Sage Publications, 1994).

69. Pierre Bourdieu, "Public Opinion Does Not Exist," in Armand Mattelart and Seth Siegelaub, eds., *Communication and Class Struggle*, Vol. 1 (New York: International General, 1972), pp. 124–130.

70. Serge Moscovici, "On Some Aspects of Social Representations"; Moscovici, *La psychanalyse*; Moscovici, "Coming Era of Representations"; Serge Moscovici, "On Social Representations," in Joseph P. Forgas, ed., *Social Cognition* (London: Academic Press, 1981), pp. 80–95.

71. Price and Oshagan, "Social-Psychological Perspectives on Public Opinion"; Henry Tajfel, "The Social Psychology of Intergroup Relations," *Annual Review of Psychology* 33 (1982):1–39; John C. Turner and Penelope J. Oakes, "Self-Categorization Theory and Social Influence," in Paul B. Paulus, ed., *Psychology of Group Influence* (Hillsdale, NJ: Lawrence Erlbaum, 1989), pp. 233–278.

72. John C. Turner, "Towards a Cognitive Redefinition of the Social Group," in Henry Tajfel, ed., *Social Identity and Intergroup Relations* (Cambridge: Cambridge University Press, 1982), pp. 15–40; John C. Turner, "Some Comments on . . . 'the Measurement of Social Orientations in the Minimal Group Paradigm,'" *European Journal of Social Psychology* 13 (1983):351–367.

73. Michael A. Hogg, John C. Turner, and Barbara Davidson, "Polarized Norms and Social Frames of Reference: A Test of the Self-Categorization Theory of Group Polarization," *Basic and Applied Social Psychology* 11, 1 (1990):77–100.

74. John C. Turner et al., *Rediscovering the Social Group: A Self-Categorization Theory* (Oxford and New York: Blackwell, 1987).

75. Hogg, Turner, and Davidson, "Polarized Norms and Social Frames of Reference."

76. Vincent Price, "Social Identification and Public Opinion: Effects of Communicating Group Conflict," *Public Opinion Quarterly* 53 (1989):197–224.

77. T. Budesheim, S. DePaola, and D. Houston, "Persuasiveness of In-Group and Out-Group Political Messages: The Case of Negative Political Campaigning," *Journal of Personality and Social Psychology* 70, 3 (1996):523–534.

78. Cialdini, Kallgren, and Reno, "Focus Theory of Normative Conduct."

79. Leon Festinger, "A Theory of Social Comparison Processes," *Human Relations* 7 (1954):117–140.

80. Glynn, "Public Opinion as a Normative Opinion Process."

81. Cialdini, Kallgren, and Reno, "Focus Theory of Normative Conduct," p. 203.

82. Glynn, "Public Opinion as a Normative Opinion Process."

83. Barbara A. Anderson, Brian D. Silver, and Paul R. Abramson, "The Effects of the Race of the Interviewer on Race-Related Attitudes of Black Respondents in SRC/CPS National Election Studies," *Public Opinion Quarterly* 52, 3 (1988):290.

84. Solomon E. Asch, *Social Psychology* (Englewood Cliffs, NJ: Prentice-Hall, 1952).

85. Hogg and Abrams, *Social Identifications*.

86. Milton J. Rosenberg and Robert P. Abelson, "An Analysis of Cognitive Balancing," in Milton J. Rosenberg et al., eds., *Attitude Organization and Change* (New Haven: Yale University Press, 1960), pp. 112–163.

87. Philip R. Costanzo, "Conformity Development as a Function of Self-Blame," *Journal of Personality and Social Psychology* 14 (1970):366–374.

88. Richard S. Crutchfield, "Conformity and Character," *American Psychologist* 10 (1955):191–198.

89. Stanley Milgram, "Nationality and Conformity," *Scientific American* 205, 6 (1961):45–51.

THEORIES OF PUBLIC OPINION

90. Eagly and Chaiken, *Psychology of Attitudes.*

91. Paul R. Nail, "Toward an Integration of Some Models and Theories of Social Response," *Psychological Bulletin* 83 (1986):603–627.

92. Ibid.

93. Michael A. Hogg and John C. Turner, "Social Identity and Conformity: A Theory of Referent Information Influence," in Willem Doise and Serge Moscovici, eds., *Current Issues in European Social Psychology* (Cambridge: Cambridge University Press, 1987), pp. 139–182.

94. Morton Deutsch and Harold B. Gerard, "A Study of Normative and Information Social Influence upon Individual Judgment," *Journal of Abnormal and Social Psychology* 51 (1955):629–636.

95. Hogg and Abrams, *Social Identifications,* p. 166.

96. Hogg and Turner, "Social Identity and Conformity."

97. Hogg and Abrams, *Social Identifications*; Harold H. Kelley, "Two Functions of Reference Groups," in Guy E. Swanson, Theodore M. Newcomb, and Eugene L. Hartley, eds., *Readings in Social Psychology* (New York: Holt, 1952), pp. 410–414.

98. Deutsch and Gerard, "Study of Normative and Information Social Influence upon Individual Judgment"; Kelley, "Two Functions of Reference Groups."

99. Hogg and Abrams, *Social Identifications,* p. 167.

100. Solomon E. Asch, "Effects of Group Pressure upon the Modification and Distortion of Judgments," in H. Guetzkow, ed., *Groups, Leadership, and Men* (Pittsburgh: Carnegie Press, 1951), pp. 177–190.

101. Milgram, "Nationality and Conformity."

102. Paul F. Lazarsfeld, Bernard Berelson, and Hazel Gaudet, *The People's Choice: How the Voter Makes Up His Mind in a Presidential Campaign* (New York: Columbia University Press, 1968 [1944]); Bernard R. Berelson, Paul F. Lazarsfeld, and William N. McPhee, *Voting: A Study of Opinion Formation in a Presidential Campaign* (Chicago: University of Chicago Press, 1954); Elihu Katz and Paul Lazarsfeld, *Personal Influence: The Part Played by People in the Flow of Mass Communications* (Glencoe, IL: The Free Press, 1955).

103. Lazarsfeld, Berelson, and Gaudet, *Voting,* Chaps. 3 and 4.

104. Robert Huckfeldt and John Sprague, *Citizens, Politics, and Social Communication: Information and Influence in an Election Campaign* (New York: Cambridge University Press, 1995). On contemporary network analysis and theory in sociology, see Mark S. Granovetter, "The Strength of Weak Ties," *American Journal of Sociology* 78 (1973):1360–1380; Duncan J. Watts, *Six Degrees: The Science of a Connected Age* (New York: W. W. Norton & Company, 2003).

105. One of the most significant studies of race and racial attitudes is Howard Schuman, Charlotte Steeh, Lawrence Bobo, and Maria Krysan, *Racial Attitudes in America: Trends and Interpretations,* revised edition (Cambridge, MA: Harvard University Press, 1997).

106. H. Lee, "A Study of Spiral of Silence Theory," Master's thesis, University of Wisconsin–Madison, 1987.

107. Thomas J. Scheff, *Microsociology: Discourse, Emotion, and Social Structure* (Chicago: University of Chicago Press, 1990).

6

Perception and Opinion Formation

You have probably heard it before: It is not reality that matters but rather the perception of that reality. Nothing could be truer. A homeless man on the street corner may be perfectly harmless, but if you perceive him as a threat, that becomes the reality. You will cross the street to avoid passing him. As Perry Hinton[1] writes, we are more than "simply recorders of information . . . we are processors of information." That is, we do not simply take in information through our eyes and ears; we make inferences and derive meaning from that information.

We make judgments about other people all the time, and we base these judgments on our perceptions. Think of the many times you rely on your perceptions. If a recent acquaintance walks past you without saying hello, you may perceive the action as coming from either rudeness or preoccupation. You may perceive a fellow student who expounds loudly and extensively in class as being either obnoxious or extremely intelligent. You may perceive that people are angry or sad, that they are dishonest or sincere.

And these perceptions can be very important. In trials, perceptions of the accused as well as the victim can have important implications on the outcome. In a recent sensational trial concerning the murder of a woman and her unborn son, perceptions of her husband, Scott Peterson, and his character, as well as the character of others involved in the crime such as police officers, attorneys, or even other family members involved in the case, can influence jury members and potentially affect the outcome of the trial. When you apply for a job, the employer's perception of you can provide you with a job opportunity or keep you in the ranks of the unemployed.

Our perceptions help us understand the world around us. We try to predict what others will do or say and rationalize others' motives in order to provide explanations for their behaviors. We constantly perceive our world, and we rationalize what is going on in that world based on our perceptions. In many ways, these perceptions provide the foundation for a public's opinion.

As Walter Lippmann describes, there is a world outside and there are the pictures in our heads. He argues:

> Whatever we believe to be a true picture, we treat as if it were the environment itself . . . the real environment is altogether too big, too complex, and too fleeting for direct acquaintance . . . the analyst of public opinion must begin then, by recognizing the triangular relationship between the scene of action, the human picture of that scene and the human response to that picture working itself out upon the scene of action.[2]

This chapter concentrates on the theories and perspectives that deal with perceptions of others' opinions and the roles these perceptions play in the public opinion process. Nearly every psychology text deals with perception as the processing of information received through the five senses. This textbook on public opinion uses the term "perception" in a very different way, in a use closer to its conversational meaning. That is, "perception" here means a summary attitude that is based on all of our past and present sensory information.

There are a number of perspectives we will discuss, among them "pluralistic ignorance," "the spiral of silence," and "looking-glass perception." For each of the perspectives we discuss, perceptions of others' opinions are the principal focus; for some, communication plays a particularly important role.

It is at this point that we ask students of public opinion to turn their attention to the fascinating world of perception—a world that is both internal and external to ourselves, a world that not only influences what we think or say but how we act. In essence, the perceptual world is the world of public opinion (see Figure 6.1).

FIGURE 6.1   How Do People Perceive the Opinions of Those Around Them? SOURCE: © Tom Tomorrow. *Greetings from This Modern World* (New York: St. Martin's Press, 1992).

THE LIMITS OF PERCEPTION

As we discussed in previous chapters, early social-psychological theories of attitude and behavior change argued that human beings were not much different than animals. That is, responses were thought to be spontaneous. Instinct, heredity, and social evolution were thought to be the main factors influencing an individual's attitudes and behavior.

Obviously, humans are more complex creatures than researchers originally thought. Charles Cooley argued that humans are different from other animals because of their greater inherent potential for complex thought processes and capacity for "mental sharing."[3] However, humans, like other animals, face physical, spatial, and other limitations when attempting to perceive and interpret the actions of others.

For example, we obviously experience a variety of sense limitations. As George McCall and J. L. Simmons note, the "physical characteristics of our sense organs impose limitations on both the breadth and the acuity of our perceptions."[4] You can only see so far, and the clarity with which you can see things (say, for example, small objects that are far away) is quite limited. In addition, our perceptions are limited by the perspective or position from which we do the observing. If we are looking ahead of us we obviously cannot see behind us. If we look to our left we cannot see to our right.

McCall and Simmons also note that even more important than these sensory limitations and the limits imposed by the position of the perceiver are other cognitive limitations—the selective attention and inattention of the perceiver.[5] People tend to pay attention to social objects (people and events) that are most relevant to their lives.

If you look outside one of your classroom windows, you might notice a group of soldiers walking by. Their presence might barely register with you—because it is probably a group of ROTC students. If you were in Baghdad, the sight of soldiers might be of grave concern to you—perhaps signaling life-threatening danger.

McCall and Simmons note that the perceptions we have of others are always incomplete and are usually less than accurate.[6] In fact, Jerome Bruner comments:

> In the interest of economizing effort we do three things . . . we narrow the selectivity of attention more or less to those things that are somehow essential to the enterprises in which we are engaged. . . . Secondly, we "recode" into simpler form the diversity of events that we encounter. . . . Sometimes recoding information serves an economical function but leads to a serious loss of information. . . . Not only is information lost, but also misinformation is added. . . . Finally, we deal with the overload of information provided by the environment . . . by the use of technological aids.[7]

These processes are so basic to the way we live that it is difficult to provide an example in which these things do not occur. Suppose we were to have a discussion with a friend while attending a soccer game. If we wanted to talk during the game, we would have to narrow our focus so that we could alternate our attention to develop the conversation we were trying to have but also keep track of the main occurrences during the game—the things that Bruner describes as "essential to the enterprise."

According to Bruner, we then alter the information we receive from the game in order to make it simpler to keep track of both things at the same time. We might, for example, begin to clap at an almost subconscious level each time the people around us clapped and cheered. Most of the time, we would not even know what we were clapping about (because we were paying attention to the conversation, not the game). In accord with Bruner's suggestion that we then turn to technological aids, we might begin to watch the scoreboard more carefully to see who was ahead and how many minutes were left to play so that the scoreboard would become an aid in keeping track of the game for us. Perceptual limitations of this kind can also restrict, confine, and help define public opinion on any particular issue.

PERCEPTION AND OPINION: SOCIALIZATION AND SOCIAL COMPARISON

In spite of the limitations of our perceptual abilities, our perceptions play critical roles in the formation of our opinions—and in the formation of a public's opinion. In fact, many of the perspectives we will discuss in this chapter are based on the fundamental principle that comparison of ourselves to others and our perceptions of others' opinions are critical aspects of our lives.

It is obvious that human activity does not occur in isolation. It is true that we have our own unique personalities and the formation of our opinions will be limited in part by the individual intellectual and emotional characteristics of our personalities. Indeed, our perceptions of the world around us are influenced by these intellectual and emotional factors. However, our perceptions are not formed simply by the combination of our innate intelligence, our unique personalities, and our senses. Equally important to our opinion formation and our perceptions is the contact we have with others in our physical and social world through processes such as socialization and social comparison. Who these others are and their effect on our perceptions and opinions are obviously elements that change as we go through life.

Socialization

A great deal of attention has been spent in the political and social sciences on understanding how what we learn and what we perceive as we go through various life stages affect our beliefs, opinions, and even behaviors in later life. In some sense, this process, known as socialization, includes the transmission of culture from one generation to the next. One critical aspect of socialization is the way that perceptions of what important others think affect our lives.

There are many forms of socialization, for children learn about all sorts of things from their parents and other influential adults. However, in this book, one of the dimensions we are interested in is political socialization—how it is we develop particular ideological orientations and policy preferences. Political socialization is enormously difficult to study because it is very hard to track individuals over time, from their earliest political experiences (e.g., shaking a congressperson's hand at age eight) to their adult voting choices. In addition, political culture is always shifting, so even when children imitate or reject their parents' political orientations, it is challenging to sift out these reactions from reactions to political events or more general changes in the political environment.

Several scholars have tried to document the political socialization process.[8] For example, political scientist Paul Abramson has studied the ways that party identification, feelings of political efficacy, and trust in government change over the course of one's life span. He concludes that party loyalty is fairly stable over time: We tend to keep our ideological affiliations even as we grow older, find partners, and advance in our careers. Abramson finds, in his analysis of survey data, that there is little evidence to support the notion that people shift to the Republican Party or become more conservative as they age. Interestingly, he finds that young adults feel more efficacious (able to influence the course of government) than do older adults. These findings are tentative, however, and we do need more study of how political attitudes change over the course of one's life. But it is obvious that our parents or those who raised us play a major role in shaping our belief systems and the development of our values. Even when we live apart from these individuals—so vital in our socialization to the world—their ideas tend to stay with us, shaping our perceptions.

Social Comparison

Leon Festinger[9] provides us with an interesting discussion of the importance of social comparison and perception for opinion formation and public opinion. In fact, his discussion is so relevant and important for this chapter that we have provided a summary of his major points in Box 6.1.

BOX 6.1   FESTINGER'S SOCIAL COMPARISON THEORY

When he first outlined social comparison theory, Leon Festinger developed a number of hypotheses and derived their corollaries. These formed the essential basis of his theory and suggested many of its implications for public opinion. Here are some of his hypotheses and corollaries that have proved especially useful:

Hypothesis 1: There exists, in the human organism, a drive to evaluate his opinions and his abilities.

Hypothesis 2: To the extent that objective, non-social means are not available, people evaluate their opinions and abilities by comparison respectively with the opinions and abilities of others.

Hypothesis 3: The tendency to compare oneself with some other specific person decreases as the difference between his opinion or ability and one's own increases.

Hypothesis 6: The cessation of comparison with others is accompanied by hostility or derogation to the extent that continued comparison with those persons implies unpleasant consequences.

Hypothesis 7: Any factors which increase the importance of some particular group as a comparison group for some particular opinion or ability will increase the pressure toward uniformity concerning that ability or opinion within that group.

Corollary 7a: The stronger the attraction to the group the stronger will be the pressure toward uniformity concerning abilities and opinions within that group.

Corollary 7b: The greater the relevance of the opinion or ability to the group, the stronger will be the pressure toward uniformity concerning that opinion or ability.

Hypothesis 9: Where there is a range of opinion or ability in a group . . . those close to the mode of the group will have stronger tendencies to change the positions of others, relatively weaker tendencies to narrow the range of comparison and much weaker tendencies to change their own position compared to those who are distant from the mode of the group.

This last hypothesis has been modified by other researchers. Some studies have found that in order to maintain a distinctive group identity, groups sometimes adopt an opinion that is more extreme than that of the mode of the group. This more extreme opinion helps the group differentiate itself from other groups. However, many of Festinger's hypotheses have been tested with great success. These studies clearly show that social comparison is an important factor in opinion formation.

SOURCE: Leon A. Festinger, "A Theory of Social Comparison Processes," *Human Relations* 7 (1954):117–140.

According to Festinger, we like to use objects in the physical world to test the correctness or appropriateness of our opinions. However, there are many situations where the use of the physical world is not possible. As Festinger notes:

> One could . . . test the opinion that an object was fragile by hitting it with a hammer, but how is one to test the opinion that a certain political candidate is better than another or that war is inevitable? Even when there is a possible immediate physical referent for an opinion, it is frequently not likely to be employed. The belief, for example, that tomatoes are poisonous to humans (which was widely held at one time) is unlikely to be tested.[10]

When we are not able to evaluate or compare our opinions to concrete events in the physical world, we will resort to comparing ourselves, our opinions, and our beliefs with the opinions and beliefs of others around us. As you can see from Festinger's[11] hypotheses in Box 6.1, the importance, use, stability, and so forth of our opinions based on these comparisons depend upon a number of social factors. Festinger particularly underscores the important role that consensus plays as an information base for our perceptions and opinions. He argues that social communication results from this need for consensus.

A consequence of social communication is that either members of the group change their opinions to achieve the required conformity, or they change their relationships. The correctness or validity of an opinion is anchored in a group of people with similar beliefs, opinions, and attitudes. An important aspect of social comparison theory is that social influence occurs, not because of the existence of a social norm, but because people "seek out and are informed by comparative social appraisals."[12]

Researchers continue to study human behavior using social comparison theory. A. W. Kruglanski and O. Mayseless[13] conducted experiments in order to determine the motivational bases for people when comparing their opinions with agreeing or disagreeing others. The researchers present three motives for social comparison: avoiding invalid opinions, the desire to possess knowledge on a subject, as opposed to "confusion or ambiguity," and maintaining certain conclusions that are pleasing, even if not entirely accurate.[14] They find that people seek out particular others for comparison based upon the goal sought. An individual might seek out social comparison in order to learn about opposing positions on a controversial matter. Another might seek out comparison in order to hear agreeable opinions from those seen to be similar to them.

Many of the perspectives we will discuss in this chapter attempt to look at some of these important social underpinnings in order to explain how perceptions of others' opinions influence and affect our lives. That is, these perspectives attempt to discern the connections between the psychological, or the self, and the social, or the other. Such comparisons between self and other are the very essence of public opinion, for public opinion does not exist in the absence of a social system. Indeed, public opinion reflects the essence of our social system—the idea that people live with and accommodate others. However, please keep in mind that much work still needs to be done in these important areas.

PERCEIVING OTHERS' OPINIONS

Hinton describes five social factors that influence our perceptions: (1) the information from the actor, (2) the influence of the perceiver on this information, (3) the relationship between the perceiver and the actor, (4) the social context, and (5) the cultural setting.[15] The student of public opinion needs to consider each of these.

First, the information the actor presents to us can influence our perceptions in profound ways. This information can include unusual behaviors, style of dress, or formal information such as a résumé. Second, our own expectations can influence our perceptions about the actor. We might expect someone of Italian descent to act differently than someone of Irish descent.

In other words, these expectations can form the basis for stereotyping those around us. Third, the relationship we have with those we perceive can affect our perceptions. Our perceptions will differ if a friend, a stranger, or a colleague at work performs the action we observe. A hug by a friend we have not seen in a long time will be taken quite differently from a hug by a stranger. Fourth, the social context can influence our perceptions. We would perceive someone laughing loudly in church very differently than we would if the person laughed at a raucous sorority party. And finally, the cultural setting needs to be considered. For example, in the United States, people from states in the South are often thought to be warmer and more "touchy" than are people who were raised in the Northeast.

Our perceptions of the actions and opinions of others will depend upon factors such as these. Our reactions and formation of our own opinions will also be affected by these factors.

NEW APPROACHES TO
PUBLIC OPINION FORMATION

As Carroll Glynn, Ronald Ostman, and Daniel McDonald[16] note, the past two decades have seen the development of a number of new approaches that include the study of perception as it pertains to public opinion formation. Each of the perspectives described in this chapter is based on certain assumptions: that individuals care what others think about public issues, form perceptions of what others think, and, to an extent, modify their own opinions or behaviors, or both, on the basis of these perceptions. Each perspective we will discuss attempts to make some use of the factors spelled out by Hinton[17] in the previous discussion. Many of these perspectives make it clear that our everyday lives are rich tapestries of "interwoven roles, groupings and social norms to which the individual continually adapts, obtains information and provides information for others."[18]

This chapter examines seven public opinion perspectives: (1) looking-glass perception, (2) pluralistic ignorance, (3) disowning projection, (4) conservative/liberal/ideological biases, (5) false consensus effect, (6) impersonal impact and unrealistic optimism, and (7) the third-person effect.

These perspectives, or frameworks, all include perceptions of others' opinions in one form or another. As you read this chapter, notice how different perspectives on public opinion examine different parts of the process and, in fact, define public opinion in different ways. Some perspectives appear to present public opinion as the majority opinion; others present it as generated within individuals. Although many dimensions of the perspectives we will discuss are compatible, in some instances, they reveal differences that simply cannot be resolved or incorporated within a common framework. It is also important for you to note which of the many components of public opinion—a spoken opinion, a perception of the majority opinion, or the aggregation of spoken opinion—are considered to be most relevant for each perspective.

Because public opinion studies subsume a number of academic disciplines, including sociology, social psychology, political science, and communication, some of these perspectives result from the investigation of similar processes in different fields. Often, public opinion scientists from one field who are studying these processes are unaware of the similarities of their own approaches to those in other fields!

Where confusion is a possibility because different labels mean essentially the same thing, we have combined discussion of some of these processes or we use the most commonly used label. It is important for you to remember not to limit your literature explorations to one field when conducting your own investigations or writing papers dealing with public opinion. Much rich understanding can come from incorporating the ideas of scholars working in a variety of disciplines.

Many of the perspectives presented later in the chapter focus on individuals' comparisons of their own opinions with actual groups of others (although, typically, specific individuals within these groups remain unnamed). However, as Ruben Orive[19] notes, there is a more implicit type of comparison that can occur when individuals do not or cannot compare their opinions with actual others. That is, Orive says that in the absence of knowledge of others' actual opinions, consensus will in effect be "self-generated." Individuals will make educated guesses about what others' opinions might be, based upon such things as group characteristics and the individual's own opinion. The psychological mechanism through which the person fabricates this consensus is termed "social projection."

The typology developed by Glynn, Ostman, and McDonald,[20] shown in Figure 6.2, should help you understand the differences in these approaches, and you should refer to it frequently during the discussion of each approach.

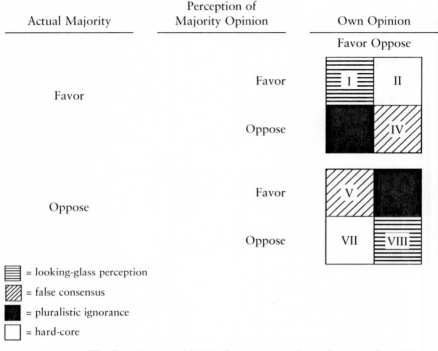

Actual Majority	Perception of Majority Opinion	Own Opinion

FIGURE 6.2   The Distribution of Public Opinion on an Issue. SOURCE: Carroll J. Glynn et al., "Opinion, Perception, and Social Reality," in Theodore L. Glasser and Charles T. Salmon, eds., *Public Opinion and the Communication of Consent* (New York: Guilford Press, 1995), Figure 10.1, p. 269.

One corner of this typology deals with people to whom Glynn and associates refer as "hard core." These are people who hold minority views and are aware of the fact that most people disagree with them. Because this chapter is primarily concerned with how others' opinions affect our own, we will not consider "hard-core" people here.

Looking-Glass Perception

Looking-glass perception is a phenomenon that is said to structure perceptions of the opinions of others on social issues.[21] Basically, the looking-glass perception occurs when people see significant others as holding the same opinions on issues that they themselves hold.[22] It appears from most research findings on looking-glass perception that in many situations and for many public or social issues, people will feel that most other people have opinions similar to their own.

When someone has a looking-glass perception on a particular issue or when a group of people are found to have engaged in looking-glass perception, this may, in fact, be the "correct" perception. That is, looking-glass perception tends to occur for issues that are noncontroversial or that people simply do not care much about and for which there seems to be (and actually is) almost universal agreement. If someone asks you your opinion about whether you think freedom of speech should be a basic right and then whether you think others believe there should be a right to free speech, you would probably find that both answers are essentially the same. This finding would not be surprising.

However, looking-glass perception can also occur when the "true" opinion is exactly the opposite of one's own, for instance, when (1) there is an issue or behavior that is divisive, and (2) one misperceives others as in "agreement with oneself," when in fact there may not be agreement.[23] Sometimes this occurrence results in "false consensus" (see the discussion later in this chapter).

Extensive research has not been conducted on the looking-glass hypothesis, and what research there is has tended to focus on whether or not the phenomenon occurs rather than on why it occurs, under what conditions, and so forth. If more research were conducted, we might understand some of the psychological and social factors leading to this outcome. As Glynn and associates note, there are no conditions detailed for when this phenomenon will or will not occur or when it will affect some people and not others.

Pluralistic Ignorance

According to Glynn, Ostman, and McDonald,[24] pluralistic ignorance is one of the more researched concepts in the perceptual influence literature.[25] Pluralistic ignorance occurs when the majority position on issues is incorrectly perceived to be the minority position[26] (see Figure 6.2). Richard Schanck[27] originally labeled this phenomenon "misperceived consensus" or "misperceived sharing."

In public opinion research, studies of pluralistic ignorance are most concerned with "perceptual accuracy," in which the researcher analyzes the role of social perception in public opinion and the accuracy of this perception. Pluralistic ignorance occurs when individuals underestimate the proportion of others who think, feel, or act as they themselves do.

Hubert O'Gorman and Stephen Garry describe pluralistic ignorance as the "false ideas held by individuals regarding the groups, social categories and collectivities to which they belong." They found that even members of "small and relatively cohesive groups frequently misjudge the values and attitudes of other members." They also note that this phenomenon is apt to occur in larger, more impersonal settings and that in times of "accelerated social change it tends to become extensive" (although why this is so is not articulated).[28] In general, pluralistic ignorance can be seen as a special case of inaccurate perceptions of majority opinion.[29]

For example, you may believe that abortion is wrong yet perceive that all your friends think abortion is appropriate in most situations. If, in fact, most of your friends "really" think abortion is wrong in most situations, this is a case of pluralistic ignorance. In this particular situation, you would be misperceiving the majority position of your friends on the abortion issue.

Often, pluralistic ignorance is tested by asking someone's opinion on a particular issue and then subsequently asking the same individual his or her perceptions of majority support. For example, in one study, O'Gorman and Garry[30] asked white respondents their opinions on segregation, followed by questions about their perceptions of majority support. As shown in Table 6.1, most white respondents did not personally support segregation. However, when respondents were classified by demographic characteristics, as is done in Table 6.1, perceptions of segregationist support were greatly overestimated. That is, regardless of sex, age, education, income, and so forth, there was a marked tendency among white respondents to overestimate support for segregation.

Glynn and associates note that in research on pluralistic ignorance, the major assumption is that people have an inherent perception of others' opinions that is often inaccurate. Little or no explanation is provided in research for why or how these perceptions are inaccurate. "Pluralistic ignorance merely describes the coincidence of an issue with inaccurate perceptions."[31]

Researchers such as Dale Miller and Cathy McFarland suggest that fear of embarrassment is one of the key motivating factors behind pluralistic ignorance.[32] This fear could inhibit individuals from expressing true opinions on issues, resulting in pluralistic ignorance. If you believe you have a socially unacceptable opinion about an issue, you may respond to a

TABLE 6.1 Whites in Favor of Racial Segregation and Whites' Perception of White Support for Racial Segregation, by Status Characteristics

Status Characteristics	(N)	North[a] (1)[c] (%)	(2)[d] (%)	(3)[e] (%)	(N)	South[b] (1)[c] (%)	(2)[d] (%)	(3)[e] (%)
Sex								
Male	(215)	13	47	24	(88)	36	86	55
Female	(251)	11	53	27	(133)	27	70	41
Age								
18-29	(119)	5	52	20	(67)	16	79	50
30-39	(78)	3	46	25	(40)	36	82	52
40-49	(83)	25	45	29	(40)	36	73	42
50-59	(71)	12	51	30	(24)	35	60	40
60 and older	(114)	16	56	26	(49)	37	79	45
Education								
Grammer school	(104)	23	65	32	(52)	49	84	54
High school	(223)	12	52	28	(115)	27	76	48
College	(138)	4	36	16	(53)	18	70	36
Income								
Less than $3,000	(54)	16	69	31	(30)	40	80	44
$3,000-$5,999	(60)	14	64	40	(41)	32	56	38
$6,000-$8,999	(127)	8	52	22	(74)	32	84	42
$9,000-$14,999	(125)	12	47	26	(42)	29	83	57
$15,000 and over	(84)	13	31	14	(23)	5	74	53
Occupation								
White-collar	(169)	8	40	19	(72)	25	75	47
Blue-collar	(146)	19	66	34	(56)	34	79	47
Religion								
Protestant	(272)	10	49	25	(196)	31	76	45
Catholic	(130)	15	56	28	(14)	17	75	58
Political party								
Democrates	(169)	15	54	26	(97)	37	74	43
Republicans	(138)	13	43	26	(46)	13	76	45
Independents	(150)	7	53	25	(78)	32	80	52

[a] All states except the Deep South and the Border South.
[b] Deep South and Border South.
[c] Favors racial segregation.
[d] Believes that half, most, or all of the whites in area favor racial segregation.
[e] Believes that most or all of the whites in area favor racial segregation.
SOURCE: Hubert O'Gorman and Stephen L. Garry, "Pluralistic Ignorance: A Replication and Extension," *Public Opinion Quarterly*, 40 (1976), table 2, p. 254.

question about that issue in the opposite direction from the way you feel. However, you may "project" your true opinion onto others. Pluralistic ignorance will be the outcome. This special case of pluralistic ignorance sometimes takes the form of a disowning projection.

Disowning Projection

In 1947, Cameron, discussed disowning projections in a book entitled *The Psychology of Behavior Disorders*.[33] This phenomenon has not been dealt with much in research since then, but its occurrence is probably quite common. Cameron notes that disowning projection occurs when an individual "tends to attribute selfish motives, evil intent and stupid attitudes to others and to disclaim them for oneself, *even though objectively* the reverse of this may seem true to an impartial observer" (emphasis ours).[34] In many ways, disowning projections are a special case of attribution theory, which we discussed in Chapter Five.

As Cameron describes:

> A child accused by a playmate of some act, attitude, motive or characteristic, which his peers condemn or ridicule, commonly denies it and immediately ascribes it to his accuser—"I am not! You are!"—or shifts the accusation at once to a scapegoat whom everyone dislikes. . . . The average adult still uses direct denial and counteraccusation when he is surprised into it, and when he is frightened or angry. When a person is normally on guard and neither angry nor frightened, his denials, counteraccusations and scapegoating are carried out by indirect techniques—by implication, by stressing opposite trends, by distracting others, etc.[35]

We have all known someone who engages in disowning projection at one time or another. You may, for example, have known a young man who complained constantly about how competitive other people in his classes were, when in fact he was the most competitive student of all! Although disowning projection can obviously be used by people without mental health problems, Cameron takes disowning projection a step further by noting that schizophrenic and paranoic individuals engage in this type of projection. Cameron states that schizophrenics engage in disowning projection by "reacting to their own behavior as if it were the behavior of others," such as when a schizophrenic says, "They say I am the Blessed Virgin."[36]

The O'Gorman and Garry study we described earlier[37] may have un-covered disowning projection on the part of its respondents as well, given that this study was conducted in the early 1970s. Attitudes toward segre-gation may not have been changing as rapidly as laws. In fact public opin-ion about segregation may have been perceived as changing faster than it actually was. Perhaps respondents felt safer reflecting their own points of view through their perceptions of what others were thinking!

Survey researchers refer to this sort of phenomenon as "social desirabil-ity." Respondents believe that there is a "right" answer to the question—for example, that they should be opposed to segregation. When asked about their own opinion, they give the socially desirable answer. If asked about others' opinions, they respond by telling the interviewer what they think the real distribution of opinion is, and if a disowning projection is occur-ring, what their own opinion is as well. The social desirability of some re-sponses to survey questions can make true opinion hard to measure.

Conservative, Liberal, and Ideological Biases

Instances of conservative and liberal (or ideological) bias could also be considered instances of pluralistic ignorance, if they involve mispercep-tions of others' opinions on issues. These biases occur when individuals see others' opinions as either more liberal or more conservative than their own, regardless of whether this is actually the case.

For example, James Fields and Howard Schuman[38] investigated the perceptions of racial opinions of Detroit, Michigan, residents. In this study, the researchers asked white respondents their perceptions of others' opinions on several interracial issues by asking them to consider hypo-thetical, but very feasible, situations. For example, in one question they outlined the following scenario:

> One day a six-year-old asks her mother if she can bring another girl home to play. The mother knows that the other girl is a Negro, and that her own daughter has only played with white children before. What should the mother do? Here are three possible responses:
> A. She should tell her daughter that she must never play with Negroes;
> B. The daughter should be told that she may play with Negro children in school, but not at home; or
> C. The Negro child should be permitted to come to the home.[39]

TABLE 6.2   Perceptions of Majority Opinion

	% Distribution of Actual Opinion	% Believing Alternative to Be Majority Opinion in Detroit Area	% Believing Alternative to Be Majority Opinion in Own Neighborhood
Never play with Negroes	2	11	12
Play only at school	22	56	50
OK to play at home	76	33	38
Total	100	100	100
N	(617)	(543)	(505)

SOURCE: James M. Fields and Howard Schuman, "Public Beliefs About the Beliefs of the Public," *Public Opinion Quarterly*, 40 (1976), p. 430.

This question was repeated when asking respondents' perceptions of what most people in "this neighborhood" and most people "in Detroit" thought about this particular issue. (You should note that in 1956, when this question was first asked, "Negro" was an approved racial term, and as the authors indicate, "even in 1971 the term was still probably the most suitable for interviews with whites.")

The authors also asked questions on other racial issues and on two civil liberties issues (including whether an atheist should be permitted to speak on a college campus and whether a child should be allowed to refuse the pledge of allegiance in school).

Most of these issues probably seem quite foreign to you now, and in fact, most of you would find it hard to believe that opinions and perceptions on these issues would vary much at all! However, at that time, Fields and Schuman found that for most of these issues, perceptions of others' opinions tended to "lean in a conservative direction," as respondents seemed to assume that others held more conservative opinions than their own.[40] That is, respondents would tend to answer "C" in the question above while they perceived that others would respond "A" to the same question. Some of their results are shown in Table 6.2.

If study respondents thought others would say it is not appropriate for a white child to play with an African-American child but, in fact, a majority of respondents feel that it is appropriate, pluralistic ignorance has occurred.

In a study of neighbor perceptions of others' opinions on local, state, and national issues, Glynn[41] found evidence of disowning projection and

TABLE 6.3   Perceived Ideological Differences

Issue	More Liberal (%)	Same (%)	More Conservative (%)
Wilderness			
Neighbors	21	42	37
City	27	47	26
National defense			
Neighbors	21	41	39
City	35	41	24
Nuclear power			
Neighbors	28	42	31
City	36	37	27
Death penalty			
Neighbors	30	40	30
City	43	35	22
Taxicab subsidy			
Neighbors	20	46	33
City	29	46	25
School closing			
Neighbors	29	49	22
City	34	39	27
Home for the retarded			
Neighbors	5	34	61
Solar enegry panel			
Neighbors	10	51	39

SOURCE: Carroll J. Glynn, "The Communication of Public Opinion," *Journalism Quarterly* 64 (1987), table 2, p. 695.

conservative bias. However, she also discovered that in some situations, there can be a "liberal bias" where respondents see others as having more liberal opinions than their own.

In Glynn's study, individuals in specific geographic neighborhoods within a city were asked their perceptions of what others thought about eight issues salient for that particular point in time: two each from the national level (national defense spending and wilderness development), the state level (nuclear power plant bans and death penalty approval or disapproval in the state in which the data were collected), the local level (providing a late-night cab fare subsidy for women and closing underused schools in the city), and the neighborhood (building a home for the mentally retarded in the neighborhood and petitioning against a neighbor's solar panel).[42] Her results are shown in Table 6.3.

Glynn notes that

> on every issue without exception, respondents viewed individuals living in
> the city as having more "liberal" opinions than their own, regardless of
> whether it was a national, state or local issue. On the other hand, with only
> one exception, respondents viewed their neighbors as having more "conser-
> vative" opinions on issues than their own . . . [providing] considerable ev-
> idence for . . . the existence of a "conservative bias" at least at the local level
> . . . [the findings also suggest] that respondents can, and do, have differ-
> ing perceptions about different groups of people.[43]

Glynn's findings are remarkable because the people she interviewed
were residents of both the neighborhoods and the city. They believed
opinion in their city was more liberal than their own and that opinion in
their neighborhood was more conservative than their own, even though
they themselves were the elements composing the "public" they were
speculating about.

Glynn notes that there is difficulty in using the labels "liberal" and
"conservative" bias because "such terms are subject to much change in interpretation over time." Instead, she recommends using the term "ideological bias" to indicate discrimination among groups based upon "perceived ideological differences."[44]

False Consensus Effect

As if things were not confusing enough, researchers also consider that
there are situations where individuals perceive their own opinions and behaviors as "normal" and all other opinions and behaviors as strange. That
is, individuals overestimate the number of other people who agree with
their views. Sometimes false consensus is nothing more than a special
case of looking-glass perception.[45] Conceptually, "false consensus" refers
to the tendency for individuals "to see their own behavioral choices and
judgments as relatively common and appropriate to existing circumstances *while viewing alternative* responses as uncommon, deviant and inappropriate" (emphasis ours).[46]

Typically, false consensus occurs when a person engaging in a given
behavior estimates that same behavior to be shared by a larger propor-

tion of others in a group than is estimated for that same reference group by a person engaging in the alternative behavior.[47] Lee Ross, David Greene, and Pamela House found that false consensus is a relatively common phenomenon.[48] These researchers studied a group of college students to determine the extent of false consensus on a variety of issues. For example, as you can see in Table 6.4, college students who thought about dying estimated that 44 percent of all college students also thought about dying. However, college students who reported that they did not think about dying estimated that only 25.6 percent thought about dying. This same false consensus occurred for a number of issues ranging from perceptions of shyness or optimism to preferences for brown versus white bread.

Steven Sherman, Clark Presson, and Laurie Chassin[49] suggest three motivations for false consensus: self-enhancement, motivation to view the other as oneself, and need for social support and validation. Basically, they argue that false consensus is the product of a need to feel confident in one's own views and behaviors.

Ross describes two possible explanations for false consensus: (1) False consensus could represent an unintentional perceptual distortion that results from a selective exposure to and recall of other people who agree with oneself, or (2) false consensus could represent a motivated and intentional strategy to appear normal, appropriate, and rational.[50] In other words, false consensus could be a product of the perceptual limitations discussed earlier in this chapter. Alternatively, false consensus could occur for people who, out of fear or embarrassment, want to believe that what they feel or do is most appropriate for the situation.

It is not easy to separate out these two explanations. For example, a student who took a test that seemed very difficult may perceive that most other students thought the test was very difficult, even though most students in the class may have thought the test was easy. Ross's first explanation for this false consensus phenomenon would be that the student associates with other students who studied in a similar fashion and who also probably thought the test was difficult.[51] Using the second explanation, however, we might suggest that the student is embarrassed by not having done well and so saves face by perceiving that others felt the test was difficult.

TABLE 6.4   Some Examples of False Consensus Effects Among College Students

Questionnaire Item: Category 1 (Category 2)	Raters' Estimates of Percentage of College Students in Category 1		Direction of Difference (+ Predicted; – Opposite to Predicted)	t
	Mean Estimates by Raters Placing Themselves in Category 1	Mean Estimates by Raters Placing Themselves in Category 2		
Personal traits and views				
Shy (not shy)	45.9	35.9	+	2.66‡
Optimistic (not)	61.9	50.4	+	2.58†
Competitive (not)	75.1	69.9	+	1.35
Politically left of center (not)	59.7	58.0	+	<1
Supporter of women's lib (not)	57.3	33.4	+	3.96§
Unweighted mean of five items	60.0	49.5		
Personal preferences				
Brown (white) bread	52.5	37.4	+	3.26‡
To be alone (with others)	36.0	30.7	+	1.18
Italian (French) movies	51.6	43.4	+	2.00†
City (country) life	51.4	49.8	+	<1
Basketball (football)	36.7	37.7	–	<1
Unweighted mean of five items	45.6	39.8		
Personal characteristics				
Male (female)	58.7	57.1	+	1.01
Brown (blue) eyes	58.3	54.5	+	1.63
Subscribe (don't) to magazines on list provided	56.9	42.7	+	2.76‡
First-born (laterborn) child	42.2	37.1	+	1.57
Hometown more (less) than 200,000	58.2	51.9	+	1.68*
Unweighted mean of five items	54.9	48.7		
Personal problems				
Think about dying? yes (no)	44.0	25.6	+	2.87‡
Hard to make friends? yes (no)	38.7	35.1	+	<1
Difficulty controlling temper? yes (no)	42.1	27.9	+	3.26‡
Frequently depressed? yes (no)	55.1	39.2	+	3.25‡
Emotional needs satisfied? yes (no)	52.9	42.2	+	2.29†
Unweighted mean of five items	46.6	34.0		

(continues)

TABLE 6.4   *(continued)*

Questionnaire Item: Category 1 (Category 2)	Raters' Estimates of Percentage of College Students in Category 1		Direction of Difference (+ Predicted; − Opposite to Predicted)	t
	Mean Estimates by Raters Placing Themselves in Category 1	*Mean Estimates by Raters Placing Themselves in Category 2*		
Personal activities				
Watch TV 30 hours/month? yes (no)	49.2	40.9	+	<1
Play tennis once a week? yes (no)	33.0	30.3	+	<1
Attend religious service once a month? yes (no)	26.5	27.5	−	<1
Donate blood once a year? yes (no)	22.6	21.2	+	<1
Long distance phone call once a week? yes (no)	50.7	45.0	+	1.06
Unweighted means of five items	36.4	33.0		
Personal expectations				
Marriage by age 30? yes (no)	74.5	71.9	+	<1
Better financial status than parent? yes (no)	68.3	61.8	+	1.86*
Live outside U.S. for one year in next 20? yes (no)	37.4	36.9	+	<1
Great satisfaction from job or career? yes (no)	53.5	43.3	+	<1
Death before 70th birthday? yes (no)	57.6	43.9	+	2.81‡
Unweighted mean of five items	58.3	51.6		
Political expectations				
Removal of Nixon from office? yes (no)	deleted			
Woman in Supreme Court within decade? yes (no)	63.3	34.6	+	6.19§

SOURCE: Lee Ross et al., "The 'False Consensus Effect': An Egocentric Bias in Social Perception and Attribution Processes," in the *Journal of Experimental and Social Psychology* 13 (1977), table 3, p. 287.

Although false consensus is a product of individuals' perceptions of the climate of opinion, it can have major impact on public opinion formation and on public debate. In the case of the abortion debate, public discourse was radically altered by a case of false consensus (see Box 6.2).

BOX 6.2   A CASE OF FALSE CONSENSUS: MOBILIZING THE PRO-LIFE MOVEMENT

One of the most remarkable examples of the effects of false consensus in contemporary times is the case of the pro-life movement. Prior to the Supreme Court's 1973 decision in *Roe v. Wade,* there were many activists involved in trying to make abortions easier to obtain legally, but there was almost no grassroots movement opposed to abortion. Kristin Luker argues that this is because most people who opposed abortion believed that theirs was the majority view:

> Perhaps the most important reason why pro-life activists were not well prepared to resist abortion reform was that they simply couldn't believe such a movement would get very far. They tacitly assumed that the unsavory connotation of abortion rested on a deep belief in the sacredness of embryonic life, and they found it hard to understand how such a belief could be changed so quickly. They counted on public opinion to be outraged and were stunned when most of the public was either unaware or unconcerned.

Luker's qualitative interviews with pro-life activists show that this case of false consensus stemmed from their selective exposure to the social world. Most pro-lifers had never had abortions themselves, nor did they know anyone who had experienced an abortion. Thus, they believed that it was an uncommon event. These people also misperceived the "unsavory connotation of abortion":

> In particular, they interpreted the relative invisibility of abortion prior to the 1960s as proof that their opinion was the common one. And in a way, their assumption was plausible. If people didn't talk about abortion very much (or talked about it only in hushed tones in back rooms), wasn't that because most people believed it was the taking of an innocent life, hence morally repugnant? What these early pro-life activists did not understand was that for many people abortion was "unspeakable" not because it represented the

death of a child but because it represented "getting caught" in the consequences of sexuality. Sex, not abortion, was what people didn't talk about.

Because of this false consensus effect, the pro-life movement did not become well-organized or prominent until after the *Roe v. Wade* decision was
handed down, and its early years were rocky ones. People who opposed
abortion were so surprised to find themselves in the minority that they had
difficulty formulating persuasive arguments to support their opinions:

> Their belief that everyone accepted a common definition of the meaning and
> moral nature of abortion left these pro-life people with few arguments to use
> against the abortion reformers. They tried to appeal to what they thought
> was the commonly shared value, but when it turned out to be not so com-
> mon after all, they were literally at a loss for words.

As you can see, false consensus can have both psychological and social
consequences. In this case, the shape of public debate was altered by people's perceptions of majority opinion.

SOURCE: Kristin Luker, *Abortion and the Politics of Motherhood* (Berkeley: University
of California Press, 1984), quoted passages from pp. 128–131.

It might be easiest to see the differences and similarities between the
looking-glass perception, ideological biases, false consensus, and pluralistic
ignorance through an example. Suppose that the campus paper at your
university reported that one of the most famous researchers there had a
very large grant to study cancer and was using dogs in his studies. Suppose
that the dogs underwent painful operations and were exposed to a number
of toxic chemicals before being killed. The issue of animal experimentation would probably become a major topic at your university. Now, if you
spend the weekend at your parents' home and a relative asks how most of
the students at your school feel about the issue, what would you reply?

According to the "looking-glass" perception, you would most likely respond that the students feel the same way you feel about the issue. However, if you are very conservative by nature and you see the students as
very liberal in comparison, the "ideological bias" might influence you to
suggest that most of the students feel exactly the opposite of the way you
do. If, in fact, the majority feel the same way you do but ideological bias

comes into play, we may find a state of pluralistic ignorance—the minority position will be perceived as the majority position. Alternatively, you may see your own opinion as being very typical of college students and think that your opinion is the "norm" for your college, even when it is, in fact, the minority view. In this case, we would have a situation in which there is false consensus about the issue.

Impersonal Impact and Unrealistic Optimism

The basic thesis underlying research on impersonal impact and unrealistic optimism is that individuals often see themselves as being somehow different from others in terms of the probability of good or bad things happening to them. That is, when people estimate the likelihood that they will be involved in certain life events (such as having car accidents, getting cancer, and so forth), they tend to be unrealistically optimistic.[52] People tend to think they are invulnerable (especially young people!). As Neil Weinstein says, people "expect others to be victims of misfortune, not themselves."[53]

According to the unrealistic optimism hypothesis, you will tend to believe that negative events are less likely to happen to you than to others and to perceive that positive events are more likely to happen to you than to those same others.[54] Researchers have found that this phenomenon occurs across a wide range of topic areas from perceptions of being murdered to perceptions of winning the lottery.[55]

Although impersonal impact and unrealistic optimism have been considered two different research areas, the differences between them are quite subtle. In order to avoid confusion, we will discuss the broad, underlying assumptions for both rather than confuse you by discussing the small differences.

Tom Tyler and Fay Cook[56] note that there is a major assumption to consider when investigating impersonal impact and unrealistic optimism: that people can and do distinguish between two possible levels of judgment—personal and societal.[57] Individuals' beliefs about their own degree of risk from life's hazards form the personal level of judgment. Individuals' beliefs about groups of others and their likelihood to experience these events form a "societal" level of judgment.

For example, Weinstein conducted a study that looked at college students' perceptions of future life events and the extent to which students expressed unrealistic optimism about these life events.[58] Table 6.5 presents some of his results.

TABLE 6.5 Unrealistic Optimism for Future Life Events

	Measures of Optimism	
Abbreviated Event Description	*Mean Comparative Judgment of Own Chances vs. Others' Chances (%)*[a, b]	*No. of Optimistic Responses Divided by No. of Pessimistic Responses*[b, c]
Positive events		
Like postgraduation job	50.2[f]	5.93[f]
Owning your own home	44.3[f]	6.22[f]
Starting salary > $10,000	41.5[f]	4.17[f]
Traveling to Europe	35.3[f]	2.25[f]
Starting salary > $15,000	21.2[e]	1.56[d]
Good job offer before graduation	15.3[e]	1.42
Graduating in top third of class	14.2	1.02
Home doubles in value in 5 years	13.3[d]	1.78[d]
Your work recognized with award	12.6[d]	1.72[d]
Living past 80	12.5[e]	2.00[e]
Your achievements in newspaper	11.3	1.66[d]
No night in hospital for 5 years	8.5	1.23
Having a mentally gifted child	6.2[d]	2.26[e]
Statewide recognition in your profession	2.1	1.00
Weight constant for 10 years	2.0	.82
In 10 years, earning > $40,000 a year	− .7	.64[d]
Not ill all winter	− .7	.89
Marrying someone wealthy	− 9.1	.36[d]
Negative events		
Having a drinking problem	−58.3[f]	7.23[f]
Attempting suicide	−55.9[f]	8.56[f]
Divorced a few years after married	−48.7[f]	9.50[f]
Heart attack before age 40	−38.4[f]	5.11[f]
Contracting venereal disease	−37.4[f]	7.56[f]
Being fired from a job	−31.6[f]	7.56[f]
Getting lung cancer	−31.5[f]	4.58[f]
Being sterile	−31.2[f]	5.94[f]
Dropping out of college	−30.8[f]	3.49[f]
Having a heart attack	−23.3[f]	3.18[f]
Not finding a job for 6 months	−14.4[f]	2.36[f]
Decayed tooth extracted	−12.8	2.22[f]
Having gum problems	−12.4[e]	1.39
Having to take unattractive job	−11.6[d]	1.84[e]
Car turns out to be a lemon	−10.0[d]	2.12[e]
Deciding you chose wrong career	− 8.8	1.43

(continues)

TABLE 6.5 *(continued)*

	Measures of Optimism	
Abbreviated Event Description	*Mean Comparative Judgment of Own Chances vs. Others' Chances (%)[a, b]*	*No. of Optimistic Responses Divided by No. of Pessimistic Responses[b, c]*
Tripping and breaking bone	− 8.3[d]	1.66[d]
Being sued by someone	− 7.9	2.38[f]
Having your car stolen	− 7.3	2.94[f]
Victim of mugging	− 5.8	3.17[f]
Developing cancer	− 4.4	1.28
In bed ill two or more days	− 3.2	1.75[d]
Victim of burglary	2.8	1.21
Injured in auto accident	12.9[d]	.80

[a] In making a comparative judgment, students estimated the difference in percent between the chances that an event would happen to them and the average chances for other same-sex students at their college. N = 123 to 130, depending on rating form and missing data. Student's t was used to test whether the mean is significantly different from zero.

[b] For positive events, the response that one's own chances are greater than average is considered optimistic, and the response that one's own chances are less than average is considered pessimistic. For negative events, the definitions of optimistic and pessimistic responses are reversed.

[c] Significance levels refer to a chi-square test of the hypothesis that frequencies of optimistic and pessimistic responses are equal.

[d] $p < .05$.

[e] $p < .01$.

[f] $p < .001$.

SOURCE: Neil D. Weinstein, "Unrealistic Optimism About Future Life Events," *Journal of Personality and Social Psychology* 39 (1980), table 1, p. 810. Copyright 1980 by the American Psychological Association. Reprinted with permission.

As you can see from this table, for college students, unrealistic optimism is alive and well. When you read the table, note that a positive value in the first column indicates that the students tended to believe their chances were greater than average that a good thing would happen to them; a negative value indicates that students believe their chances are less than average that a bad thing would happen to them.

The numbers in the second column indicate the ratio of optimistic to pessimistic responses. For example, students felt that their chances were greater than those of their classmates for liking their post graduation job—the ratio of optimistic to pessimistic responses was almost 6 to 1 (5.93).

Another important consideration for both the impersonal impact and unrealistic optimism hypotheses is the effect the media have on these perceptions. Tyler and Cook state that mass-mediated messages affect people's perceptions of how often certain problems or risks occur in general but do not affect people's perceptions of their own personal risks. For example, they found that people who had seen a television newsmagazine story about fraud in home health care services were more likely afterward to view the problem as serious. However, they were still equally confident in their own ability to secure good home health care for themselves or their relatives.

Third-Person Effect

The third-person effect essentially occurs when people think that the media will have greater impact on others than on themselves. Sociologist W. Phillips Davison was the first to coin the term "third-person effect" in an article he wrote in *Public Opinion Quarterly* in 1983.[59] Davison is a wonderful storyteller and writer, and he introduced his discussion of this effect by describing an incident that happened to a historian while "combing through cartons of U.S. Marine Corps documents from World War II."

Davison documents the following:

> There was a service unit consisting of Negro troops with white officers on Iwo Jima Island in the Pacific. The Japanese learned about the location of this unit and sent planes over with propaganda leaflets. These leaflets stressed the theme that this was a white man's war and that the Japanese had no quarrel with colored peoples. They said, more or less, "Don't risk your life for the white man. Give yourself up at the first opportunity, or just desert. Don't take chances." The next day that unit was withdrawn.[60]

This is a classic example of the third-person effect. There was no apparent evidence that the propaganda had an effect on the troops at all. Rather, the effect of the propaganda appeared to be on the white officers who withdrew their troops.

As Davison notes:

> in its broadest formulation, this hypothesis predicts that people will tend to overestimate the influence that mass communications have on the attitudes

and behaviors of others . . . more specifically . . . individuals who are members of an audience that is exposed to a persuasive communication . . . will expect the communication to have a greater effect on others than on themselves.[61]

The third-person effect is very similar to the idea of unrealistic optimism, only instead of a concern with good or bad things occurring, concern is about the perceived effects of the mass media. Davison's ideas have generated a good deal of research.

Jeremy Cohen, Diana Mutz, Vincent Price, and Albert Gunther studied the third-person effect by asking people to read defamatory newspaper articles. They found that readers who were exposed to these newspaper articles estimated that others would be significantly more affected by the messages than they themselves had been.[62]

James Tiedge, Arthur Silverblatt, Michael Havice, and Richard Rosenfeld conducted an interesting study that investigated the third-person effect in specific messages.[63] For example, they examined whether the third-person effect occurred when buyers saw advertising slogans such as "Buy Now While Supplies Last." In this clear-cut case of third-person effect, respondents expected others to run out and buy when they saw these ads. In fact, the others might have been running, but the respondents themselves were running right along with them.

Dominic Lasorsa studied the third-person effect as it pertained to the airing of a controversial miniseries called *Amerika*.[64] The program was controversial because it contained what George Kennan[65] noted were false suggestions—that the dangers of a Soviet takeover of the United States with the help of the United Nations were "quite real."[66]

Lasorsa notes that "despite rising expectations of blockbuster ratings, just before the show aired one of the program's primary sponsors pulled its multimillion-dollar advertising campaign, apparently worried that the juxtapositioning of the program's controversial message with its own 'Pride in America' advertising campaign might cause viewers to turn away from its products."[67]

In his detailing of the third-person effect, Lasorsa also discusses how the third-person effect seems to be

driven by a belief that others are unlike me in important ways that relate to their inability to evaluate "correctly" a mass medium message. I reason that others may not be as insightful, as experienced, as interested—as knowing, generally—as I am and, therefore, I believe they are more susceptible than I am to media influence. Ironically, however, it may be I who, in an indirect yet important way, am most susceptible to the influence of the message.[68]

Glynn and Ostman did not find evidence for the third-person effect until they investigated responses in specific subsets of the population under study. They note, "These two groups [those who perceive a third-person effect and those who do not] might be very different from each other in the way they view public opinion and public opinion processes."[69] They suggest that one important difference might be in the way people seek out and use information about others' opinions. Most people would seem to be somewhat susceptible to the third-person effect. How many times have you watched a television show, only to turn the set off at the end and say, "Boy, people are sure going to be upset about that!"

PUBLIC OPINION AS A SOCIAL PROCESS

As noted earlier in this book, there continues to be a tremendous amount of debate concerning the meaning of public opinion. As you will probably find in class, students of public opinion often spend a significant amount of time discussing the meaning of public opinion, or determining whether they think there is a public opinion at all. The definitions presented in this book and elsewhere point to a process of public opinion. Some definitions such as those proposed by Machiavelli state that public opinion is an opinion formed by the elite, while others such as Phil Davison[70] ask for researchers to consider the importance of social, political, and communication factors in the process. As Glynn[71] points out, some scholars have developed definitions that challenge public opinion scholars to look beyond the one point in time view of public opinion to its more dynamic nature: "These scholars look beyond a static perspective of public opinion, describing a more exciting process that considers the ebb and flow of issues, events, opinion presentation, debate and decision making."

At the beginning of this chapter we outlined a variety of perspectives of public opinion that focused on opinion outcomes. These perspectives can often look very similar and it is sometimes difficult to separate their differences and similarities. Part of the difficulty is that these perspectives view public opinion largely as an outcome, with little or no rationale as to why these outcomes may occur. A much more productive, though less common way to approach the study of public opinion is by investigating the phenomenon as a process.

Public Opinion Process Models

There are a number of public opinion process models; several will be described briefly here.

Foote and Hart's (1953) Developmental Model.   Using Blumer's approach to understanding public opinion, Foote and Hart state that public opinion is developmental in nature and maintain that it is formed through a sequence of stages.[72] They perceive the public opinion process as one in which an individual or group moves through a decision-making process beginning with policy and proposal phases. At the end of the proposal phase there is a recognized issue and people "know what they want." Following these phases are the policy and program phases. By the end of the "program phase" an approved course of action is decided upon. The final phase is the appraisal stage, where periodic reevaluations take place. Foote and Harte see the public opinion process as a fairly orderly, sequential process resulting in informed decisions and action.

Davison's (1958) Communication and Opinion Leadership Model. Davison formulates his understanding of the public opinion process from the German poet Christoph Wieland. In one of the first formal discussions of public opinion, in 1798, Wieland wrote:

> I for my part understand by it an opinion that gradually takes root among a whole people, especially among those who have the most influence when they work together as a group. In this way it wins the upper hand to such an extent that one meets it everywhere . . . it is an opinion that without being noticed takes possession of most heads, and even in situations where it does not dare to express itself out loud it can be recognized by a louder and louder muffled murmur. It then only requires some small opening that will allow it air, and it will break out with force. Then it can change whole nations in a brief time and give whole parts of the world a new configuration.[73]

Davison's process model focuses a great deal on the role of the issue in public opinion formation. He says the process begins with issue presentation, in which many issues are discarded but a few remain. According to Davison an issue begins to take root only when it is communicated from one person to a second, who then carries it further in his own conversation. Most potential issues disappear from attention before this "human chain" grows to an appreciable length, but the few that remain form the basis for public opinion.

Davison sees the public opinion process as a process that is strongly influenced by group opinions and leaders. He also emphasizes that individuals are influenced by perceptions of others' opinions. These perceptions and concurrent emotions may affect the likelihood of people speaking out or remaining silent. He notes that when emotions run high, people may express support for positions that they privately oppose.

Davison also views communication as crucial to opinion formation. He traces the public opinion process as it expands from the level of the primary group (a group of individuals who converse together on an issue) to the wider society.[74] Most potential issues, he observes, never make it out of the primary group. Those issues that do go beyond the group find "leadership transcending the original primary group."[75] These leaders are frequently in the business of "mass manipulation" and have means of publicizing the issue at their disposal. Leaders simplify and generalize issues so that they will appeal to the largest possible audience. If many in that audience accept the new idea, public opinion may develop. Face-to-face discussion proceeds in other primary groups, and these new discussions lead to more public communication about the issue. This process is circular.

As public discussion of the issue increases, individuals begin to develop expectations about what others' opinions are likely to be. These expectations may develop as a result of individuals' "sampling" group opinions, from social projection of one's own opinion onto others or from individuals' believing that they "know" how members of a group are likely to respond to an issue. Individuals use these expectations to determine where relevant reference groups stand on an issue. They then determine their own opinions relative to the opinions of salient others. Davison argues, "A process is set up in which expectations produce behavioral adjustments, and these in turn reinforce expectations. When this has happened, public opinion has been formed."[76]

Davison's model also is the basis for many of the more recent perspectives on the public opinion process, including work by Noelle-Neumann, Price and Roberts, and Crespi.

Noelle-Neumann's Social System Process Model—The Spiral of Silence.   The "theory of the spiral of silence" was developed in the mid–1970s by Elisabeth Noelle-Neumann, a German political scientist and pollster.[77] Charles Salmon and Chi-Yung Moh note that her work is "predicated on the notion that society is a potentially intimidating environment for the individual, a setting in which intense social pressure can be brought to bear on the person who dares to test the boundaries of the crowd."[78]

Noelle-Neumann first observed what she labeled the spiral of silence phenomenon during the 1965 elections in the Federal Republic of Germany. The election was being held between two political parties, the Christian Democrats and the Social Democrats. Noelle-Neumann found that public perceptions of who would win the election showed a steady, "independent movement"[79] despite the polls, which showed equivalent levels of support from December until September. Then, during the final days of the election, 3 to 4 percent of the voters shifted their alliances in the direction of the candidate the public perceived as the winner. During the 1972 election, Noelle-Neumann noticed the same phenomenon occurring. Because these findings were so surprising to her, she decided to investigate, and her research on the spiral of silence began.

Since that time, more public opinion research has been conducted on the spiral of silence than on almost any other single public opinion approach, thesis, or question.[80] Carroll Glynn and Jack McLeod[81] note that the spiral of silence theory is important because it describes how, through social interaction, people influence each other's willingness to express opinions. The social nature of humans is an important component of the spiral of silence theory.

Noelle-Neumann relies heavily on the studies of Asch,[82] whose work we discussed in Chapter Five, to describe the relationship of conformity to her spiral of silence theory. Indeed, much of Asch's research, as well as that of Sherif[83] and Milgram,[84] provides evidence that people may be so affected by their perception of what others think that they feel pressured to conceal their own opinions.

The theory of the spiral of silence states that one's perception of the distribution of public opinion affects one's willingness or unwillingness to express opinions.[85] Individuals who notice that their personal opinions are spreading will voice these opinions self-confidently in public; those who notice their opinions are "losing ground" will be inclined to adopt a more reserved attitude and remain silent. These perceptions of reality are transformed into reality as those who feel that their opinions are not popular remain quiet and those who believe their opinions are growing in popularity hear their own views more and more often. The result is a spiral of silence.[86]

Although the label "spiral of silence" does not carry with it the implied sophistication of most social-psychological theories, the term is quite appropriate. One can envision a swirling tornado of opinion spiraling into dust and silence.

The spiral of silence theory is based on the assumption that our relationships with others are so critical to us that we will do anything, even change our opinions or become silent about them, to be accepted by others. Noelle-Neumann states that to the individual, "not isolating himself is more important than his own judgment."[87] We want others to like us, and we want to continue our relationships with others. To most of us, this is far more important than expressing an opinion that may deviate from those of our friends.

Although it is impossible here to present the details of research conducted on the spiral of silence, it is important to mention that there are four key elements that need to be considered when examining this theory: (1) one's own opinion on an issue, (2) one's perception of the predominant public opinion, (3) one's assessment of the likely future course of public opinion, and (4) one's willingness to support one's opinion with action, verbal statements, or other signs of commitment.[88]

According to the spiral of silence theory, one's opinion and one's assessment of the predominant public opinion are both assumed to influence one's judgment of the future course of opinion. Willingness to express one's opinion depends on an interaction between these two variables. That is, one's opinion (majority or minority) and one's perception of the future trend in public opinion will affect the likelihood that one will speak up on any number of issues.

There are several unique aspects of Noelle-Neumann's conception of the public opinion process, including: (1) societal functions of public opinion; (2) moral and behavioral components of public opinion; (3) the importance of perception in the public opinion process; and (4) the importance of communication in opinion outcomes. The spiral of silence theory attempts to describe impacts on public opinion that go far beyond interpersonal interaction. Noelle-Neumann also ascribes importance to the mass media's impact on the formation and presentation of the public's opinions. According to Noelle-Neumann, the key factors the media bring into play in the spiral of silence are that they are both "ubiquitous" and "consonant" with one another.[89]

And what does this mean? Noelle-Neumann says that the media are everywhere (ubiquitous) and that they repeat the same messages over and over (consonance). Clearly, this is a simple but important truth. The media are constantly bombarding us with information, constantly framing our social reality. And we constantly hear the same message—on the radio and television, in newspapers and magazines. These same messages are repeated from reporter to reporter, from medium to medium. Thus, according to Noelle-Neumann, we learn most of our societal norms, customs, and so forth from the media. What we should believe is constantly being reinforced because of these media messages.

Noelle-Neumann states that part of the problem with the ubiquitous and consonant nature of the mass media is that journalists tend to be more liberal than the rest of society.[90] She says that journalists share common norms and values and reflect their liberal points of view in the messages they present in the media. Of course, given the dramatic rise of conservative voices and ownership control for many mass media venues, at least in America, the perception of a liberal bias in the media is debatable.

It is clear that the spiral of silence is an important theory that the student of public opinion should understand. Although many researchers have found flaws or problems with the theory,[91] most scholars agree that the spiral of silence theory contributes immensely to public opinion theory. If anything, the most simple of its premises attest to its importance: We are social; others are important to us; we want others to like us; and we want to fit in. These factors clearly influence public opinion formation.

Of all the approaches discussed in this chapter, Noelle-Neumann's spiral of silence theory comes closest to being an actual theory. However, this theory and the other approaches mentioned earlier all have serious flaws that limit their usefulness. For example, none of them specifies clearly the roles that social and reference groups can play in opinion formation, there is no discussion of cultural influences, and there is little consistent theoretical thread in the research.

Price and Roberts's (1987) Communication and Reciprocal Relationships Process Model. Like Davison,[92] Vincent Price and Donald Roberts attempt to model public opinion processes at the social level.[93] There are some important similarities in the elements they consider critical and in their definitions of public opinion. Basing their model on Cooley's[94] and Davison's works, Price and Roberts viewed the public as a "communicating group." As they state, "public opinion processes form around an issue over time. In contrast, polls and election studies imply that issue opinions exist within a public at any given time."[95] Price and Roberts believe that viewing public opinion as a "process of social organization through communicating" is "well worth considering," because it restores communication to a central role. They note that there are interactions of individual and "public" opinion at each successive level.

In their model, Price and Roberts point out that (1) "a public is not organized in any fixed fashion until forced to communicate in resolving issues; and (2) public opinion is decidedly not the distribution of opinions within a public, but is instead a complex function of processes where disparate ideas are expressed, adjusted, and compromised en route to collective determination of a course of action."

According to Price and Roberts, the public opinion process may be conceptualized as communication between political actors who are pursuing public recognition and support for views and members of the interested public who are trying to understand the issue and decide who to support. Price and Roberts observe that many people "deciding their stand on a public issue are not so much deciding their own opinion (or *where* they stand on the matter) but instead deciding on their social loyalties (in other words, *with whom* they stand)" (emphasis ours).[96] They call public opinion a social process and, more specifically, a communication process. They argue that communication allows a group of people to "think together," even as individual cognition often involves "talking to yourself." The public, then, is formed by the issue, not the other way around. A public is composed of various groups, some of them interpersonal, others broadly social, "attempting through discursive means to resolve a common issue."[97] The process of forming and changing public opinion is a complex one that involves political actors, media, and an interested public, and all these elements attempt to ascertain and influence opinions on social issues. The public opinion process is a process of social accommodation.

Crespi's (1997) Multidimensional Model.   Crespi describes public opinion as a multidimensional process and insists that viewing it as a process adds needed dimensions to a complex concept.[98] He bases his model on Davison's discussion of the public opinion process.[99] However, he adds the multidimensional interaction of psychology, sociology, and political elements to this process.

Crespi believes that the process of public opinion needs to include both individual and social components and designs his model to reflect a series of continuous interactions and outcomes. By recognizing the separate significance of the individual and collective actions of the public opinion process, "we do not feel compelled, on one hand, to explain collective phenomena solely as the outcome of individual-level processes, nor, on the other hand, to assume the existence of a collective level of existence independent of those processes."[100]

Commonalities of Public Opinion Process Models

Over the past sixty years, different scholars in different disciplines have designed process models such as those described in this chapter. While the approaches range from psychological to a combination of psychological, political, and sociological, there are common threads in the models, such as inclusion of an issue, communication, perceptions of reality, and group influences.

IMPLICATIONS FOR THE FUTURE

It is clear that we need to develop useful theoretical approaches in public opinion research. For the most part, we know that psychological, social, and political factors can change or motivate public opinion outcomes, but we are not sure what these factors are or exactly when these outcomes will occur. We know that the media are important in the formation of public opinion, but we do not know enough about how people are influenced by these powerful transmitters of information.

Politicians know there are ways to manipulate the public through the media; yet public opinion scholars do not know enough about the public opinion process to be able to determine how and when this manipulation will occur. The public is more vulnerable and more susceptible because of this lack of research in this important area.

Perception has been defined throughout this chapter as a summary attitude based on all of our past and present sensory information. Perceptions are limited because they are selective. Perceptions also play a comparative role—we compare our perceptions to those of others. Socialization, the influence of what others important to us think, and social comparison, the comparison of my opinion to others to test its validity, have become important theories used to explain how individuals apply their perceptions to the larger social context.

Public opinion is clearly more than responses to public opinion polls. It is a verbal expression of culture, of social interactions, of psychological processes. Students of public opinion should understand the approaches described in this chapter but should also make sure they have a solid grasp of theories developed in other fields, especially sociology, social psychology, and psychology. It is important that we understand how public opinion works so that we can go beyond mere speculation or description. The field is young and exciting, and there is much left to learn. Public opinion scholars of the future can help us understand this important and fundamental social process that is vital to our very survival.

NOTES

1. Perry R. Hinton, *The Psychology of Interpersonal Perception* (London: Routledge, 1993).

2. Walter Lippmann, *Public Opinion* (New York: Harcourt, Brace, 1922), pp. 4, 11.

3. Charles H. Cooley, *Human Nature and the Social Order* (New York: Scribner, 1902).

4. George J. McCall and J. L. Simmons, *Identities and Interactions: An Examination of Human Associations in Everyday Life,* 2nd ed. (New York: Free Press, 1978), p. 104.

5. Ibid.

6. Ibid.

7. Jerome S. Bruner, "Social Psychology and Perception," in Eleanor E. Maccoby, Theodore M. Newcomb, and Eugene L. Hartley, eds., *Readings in Social Psychology* (New York: Holt, Rinehart and Winston, 1958), p. 86.

8. Paul R. Abramson, *Political Attitudes in America: Formation and Change* (San Francisco: W. H. Freeman and Co., 1983); M. Kent Jennings and Richard G. Niemi, *Generations and Politics: A Panel Study of Young Adults and Their Parents* (Princeton: Princeton University Press, 1981); Roberta L. Sangster and Robert W. Reynolds, "A Test of Inglehart's Socialization Hypothesis for the Acquisition of Materialist/Postmaterialist Values: The Influence of Childhood Poverty on Adult Values," *Political Psychology* 17 (1996):253–269.

9. Leon Festinger, "A Theory of Social Comparison Processes," *Human Relations* 7 (1954):117–140.

10. Ibid., p. 119.

11. Ibid.

12. V. Price and O. Hayg, "Social Psychological Perspectives on Public Opinion," in Theodore L. Glasser and Charles T. Salmon, eds., *Public Opinion and the Communication of Consent*, pp. 178–208 (New York: Guilford Press, 1995), p. 188. Part of the Guilford Communication Series, Theodore L. Glasser and Howard E. Sypher, eds.

13. A. W. Kruglanski and O. Mayseless, "Motivational Effects in the Social Comparison of Opinions," *Journal of Personality and Social Psychology* 5, 53 (1987):834–842.

14. Ibid., p. 835.

15. Hinton, *Psychology of Interpersonal Perception*.

16. Carroll J. Glynn, Ronald E. Ostman, and Daniel G. McDonald, "Opinions, Perceptions and Social Reality," in Theodore L. Glasser and Charles T. Salmon, eds., *Public Opinion and the Communication of Consent* (New York: Guilford Press, 1995), pp. 249–277.

17. Hinton, *Psychology of Interpersonal Perception*.

18. Glynn, Ostman, and McDonald, "Opinions, Perceptions and Social Reality"; Carroll J. Glynn, "Public Opinion as a Normative Opinion Process," in Brant R. Burleson, ed., *Communication Yearbook 20* (Thousand Oaks, CA: Sage Publications, 1996), pp. 157–183.

19. Ruben Orive, "Social Projection and Social Comparisons of Opinions," *Journal of Personality and Social Psychology* 54, 6 (1988):953–964.

20. Glynn, Ostman, and McDonald, "Opinions, Perceptions and Social Reality."

21. Ibid.

22. James M. Fields and Howard Schuman, "Public Beliefs About the Beliefs of the Public," *Public Opinion Quarterly* 40 (1976):427–448.

23. Glynn, Ostman, and McDonald, "Opinions, Perceptions and Social Reality."

24. Ibid.

25. Frank H. Allport, *Social Psychology* (Cambridge, MA: Riverside Press, 1924); Richard Louis Schanck, "A Study of a Community and Its Groups and Institutions Conceived of as Behaviors of Individuals," *Psychological Monographs* 43, 2 (1932) (whole issue); Hubert O'Gorman and Stephen L. Garry, "Pluralistic Ignorance—A Replication and Extension," *Public Opinion Quarterly* 40 (1976):449–458; Dale T. Miller and Cathy McFarland, "Pluralistic Ignorance: When Similarity Is Interpreted as Dissimilarity," *Journal of Personality and Social Psychology* 53, 2 (1987):298–305; D. Garth Taylor, "Pluralistic Ignorance and the Spiral of Silence: A Formal Analysis," *Public Opinion Quarterly* 46 (1982):311–355.

26. O'Gorman and Garry, "Pluralistic Ignorance."

27. Schanck, "A Study of a Community and Its Groups and Institutions."

28. O'Gorman and Garry, "Pluralistic Ignorance," p. 450.

29. Glynn, Ostman, and McDonald, "Opinions, Perceptions and Social Reality."

30. O'Gorman and Garry, "Pluralistic Ignorance."

31. Glynn, Ostman, and McDonald, "Opinions, Perceptions and Social Reality," p. 262.

32. Miller and McFarland, "Pluralistic Ignorance."

33. Norman Cameron, *The Psychology of Behavior Disorders: A Biosocial Interpretation* (Boston: Houghton Mifflin, 1947).

34. Ibid., p. 168.

35. Ibid.

36. Ibid., p. 169.

37. O'Gorman and Garry, "Pluralistic Ignorance."

38. Fields and Schuman, "Public Beliefs About the Beliefs of the Public."

39. Ibid., p. 430.

40. Ibid.

41. Carroll J. Glynn, "Perceptions of Others' Opinions as a Component of Public Opinion," *Social Science Research* 18 (1989):53–69.

42. Ibid.

43. Ibid., p. 63.

44. Ibid., p. 64.

45. Glynn, Ostman, and McDonald, "Opinions, Perceptions and Social Reality."

46. Lee Ross, David Greene, and Pamela House, "The 'False Consensus Effect': An Egocentric Bias in Social Perception and Attribution Processes," *Journal of Experimental Social Psychology* 13 (1977):280.

47. Brian Mullen et al., "The False Consensus Effect: A Meta-Analysis of 115 Hypothesis Tests," *Journal of Experimental Social Psychology* 21 (1985):262–283.

48. Ross, Greene, and House, "False Consensus Effect.'"

49. Steven J. Sherman, Clark C. Presson, and Laurie Chassin, "Mechanisms Underlying the False Consensus Effect: The Special Role of Threats to the Self," *Personality and Social Psychology Bulletin* 10, 1 (1984):127–138.

50. Lee Ross, "The Intuitive Psychologist and His Shortcomings: Distortions in the Attribution Process," in Leonard Berkowitz, ed., *Advances in Experimental Social Psychology* (New York: Academic Press, 1977), pp. 150–195.

51. Ross, Greene, and House, "False Consensus Effect.'"

52. Roger A. Drake, "Lateral Asymmetry of Personal Optimism," *Journal of Research in Personality* 18, 4 (1984):497–507.

53. Neil D. Weinstein, "Unrealistic Optimism About Future Life Events," *Journal of Personality and Social Psychology* 39, 5 (1980):806.

54. Ibid.

55. Hugh M. Culbertson and Guido H. Stempel, "Media Malaise: Explaining Personal Optimism and Societal Pessimism About Health Care," *Journal of Communication* 35 (1985):180–190.

56. Tom R. Tyler and Fay L. Cook, "The Mass Media and Judgments of Risk: Distinguishing Impact on Personal and Societal Level Judgments," *Journal of Personality and Social Psychology* 47 (1984):693–708.

57. Glynn, Ostman, and McDonald, "Opinions, Perceptions and Social Reality."

58. Weinstein, "Unrealistic Optimism About Future Life Events."

59. W. Phillips Davison, "The Third-Person Effect in Communication," *Public Opinion Quarterly* 47 (1983):1–15.

60. Ibid.

61. Ibid., p. 3.

62. Jeremy Cohen et al., "Perceived Impact of Defamation: An Experiment on Third-Person Effects," *Public Opinion Quarterly* 52 (1988):161–173.

63. James T. Tiedge et al., "Discrepancy Between Perceived First-Person and Perceived Third-Person Mass Media Effects," *Journalism Quarterly* 68, 1–2 (1991):141–154.

64. Dominic L. Lasorsa, "Real and Perceived Effects of 'Amerika,'" *Journalism Quarterly* 66 (1989):373–378.

65. George Kennan, "TV's Misguided Cold War Games," *New York Times*, January 5, 1987, p. A16.

66. Dominic L. Lasorsa, "Policymakers and the Third-Person Effect," in J. David Kennamer, ed., *Public Opinion, the Press, and Public Policy* (Westport, CT: Praeger, 1994), pp. 163–175.

67. Ibid., p. 165.

68. Ibid., p. 172.

69. Carroll J. Glynn and Ronald E. Ostman, "Public Opinion About Public Opinion," *Journalism Quarterly* 65 (1988):306.

70. W. Philips Davison, "The Public Opinion Process," *Public Opinion Quarterly* 22 (1958):91–106.

71. Carroll J. Glynn, "Public Opinion as a Social Process," in S. Dunwoody, D. McLeod, L. Becker, and J. Kosicki, eds., *The Evolution of Key Mass Communication Concepts: Honoring Jack M. McLeod* (Cresskill, NJ: Hampton Press, 2004).

72. N. N. Foote and C. W. Hart, "Public Opinion and Collective Behavior," in M. Sherif and M. O. Wilson, eds., *Group Relations at the Crossroads* (New York: Harper and Row, 1953), pp. 301–332.

73. Christoph Martin Wieland, *Gespräch unter vier Augen* (1798), p. 103.

74. W. Philips Davison, "The Public Opinion Process," *Public Opinion Quarterly* 21 (1957):103–118.

75. Ibid., p. 106.

76. Ibid.

77. Elisabeth Noelle-Neumann, "Return to the Concept of a Powerful Mass Media," *Studies of Broadcasting* 9 (March 1973):67–112.

78. Charles T. Salmon and Chi-Yung Moh, "The Spiral of Silence: Linking Individual and Society Through Communication," in J. David Kennamer, ed., *Public Opinion, the Press, and Public Policy* (Westport, CT: Praeger, 1994), pp. 145–161.

79. Glynn, Ostman, and McDonald, "Opinions, Perceptions and Social Reality."

80. Carroll J. Glynn, Andrew F. Hayes, and James Shanahan, "Spiral of Silence: A Meta-Analysis," *Public Opinion Quarterly* 61, 3 (1997):452–463.

81. Carroll J. Glynn and Jack M. McLeod, "Implications of the Spiral of Silence Theory for Communication and Public Opinion Research," in Keith R. Sanders, Lynda Lee Kaid, and Dan D. Nimmo, eds., *Political Communication Yearbook* (Carbondale, IL: Southern Illinois University Press, 1985), pp. 43–68.

82. Solomon E. Asch, *Social Psychology* (Englewood Cliffs, NJ: Prentice-Hall, 1952).

83. Muzafer Sherif, *The Psychology of Social Norms* (New York: Harper and Brothers, 1936).

84. Stanley Milgram, "Nationality and Conformity," *Scientific American* 205, 6 (1961):45–51.

85. Carroll J. Glynn, "The Communication of Public Opinion," *Journalism Quarterly* 64 (1987):688–697.

86. Elisabeth Noelle-Neumann, *The Spiral of Silence. Public Opinion—Our Social Skin* (Chicago: University of Chicago Press, 1984).

87. Elisabeth Noelle-Neumann, "Turbulences in the Climate of Opinion: Methodological Applications of the Spiral of Silence Theory," *Public Opinion Quarterly* 41 (1977):143–158.

88. Taylor, "Pluralistic Ignorance and the Spiral of Silence."

89. Noelle-Neumann, *The Spiral of Silence*; Noelle-Neumann, "Return to the Concept of a Powerful Mass Media."

90. Ibid.

91. Glynn, "Perceptions of Others' Opinions as a Component of Public Opinion"; Lasorsa, "Real and Perceived Effects of 'Amerika'"; Salmon and Moh, "The Spiral of Silence"; Glynn, Hayes, and Shanahan, "The Spiral of Silence: A Meta-Analysis"; Glynn and McLeod, "Implications of the Spiral of Silence Theory"; Carroll J. Glynn and Jack M. McLeod, "Public Opinion du Jour: An Examination of the Spiral of Silence," *Public Opinion Quarterly* 48, 4 (1984):731–740; Charles T. Salmon and F. Gerald Kline, "The Spiral of Silence Ten Years Later," in Keith R. Sanders, Lynda Lee Kaid, and Dan D. Nimmo, eds., *Political Communication Yearbook* (Carbondale, IL: Southern Illinois University Press, 1985), pp. 3–30; Charles T. Salmon and Hayg Oshagan, "Community Size, Perceptions of Majority Opinion and Opinion Expression," *Public Relations Research Annual* 2 (1990):157–171; Wolfgang Donsbach and Robert L. Stevenson, "Challenges, Problems and Empirical Evidence of the Theory of the Spiral of Silence," paper presented at the International Communication Association Conference, San Francisco, 1984; Frank L. Rusciano, *Isolation and Paradox: Defining "the Public" in Modern Political Analysis* (New York: Greenwood Press, 1989).

92. Davison, "The Public Opinion Process."

93. Vincent Price and Donald F. Roberts, "Public Opinion Processing," in C. R. Berger and S. H. Chaffee, eds., *Handbook of Communication Science* (Beverly Hills, CA: Sage Publications, 1987), pp. 781–816.

94. C. H. Cooley, *Social Organization: A Study of the Larger Mind* (New York: Charles Scribner's Sons, 1909).

95. Price and Roberts, "Public Opinion Processes," p. 785.

96. Price and Roberts, "Public Opinion Processes," p. 800.

97. Ibid., p. 803.

98. J. Crespin, *The Public Opinion Process* (Hillsdale, NJ: Lawrence Erlbaum, 1997).

99. Davison, "The Public Opinion Process."

100. Price and Roberts, "Public Opinion Processes," p. xi.

7

Economic Approaches[1]

INTRODUCTION

The last three chapters have described a number of psychological and sociological perspectives and influences on public opinion. This chapter introduces an approach from another social science—from the field of *economics*. This may, at first, seem far afield from the study of social and political attitudes and opinions, since we normally associate "economics" with behavior in the economy—in the marketplace in which the supply and demand of goods is the focus of attention, and the behavior of interest is the production and sale of goods at one end of the economy, and the purchase and consumption of goods at the other. It is not a great intellectual leap, however, to extend thinking about an economy to a social or political marketplace in which individuals make choices that are not economic ones. In markets we have consumers who make choices and purchases, whereas in the political system we have citizens and voters who choose their opinions toward issues or other political objects and who engage in political activity and ultimately directly select among parties and candidates in elections.

How does an economic approach differ from the psychological and sociological approaches that we have considered? How much does this further complicate our analysis of attitudes and opinions? We have already seen that a wide range of influences are at work in the sociological and psychological processes that produce individuals' attitudes and opinions. Indeed, there are so many possible influences that the study of public opinion may seem intractably complicated. How do students of public opinion sort through this complexity? Are some perspectives more important than others? What are the most important or, at least, the most regular and predictable influences at work? How have social scientists tried to answer this?

This chapter will take up these questions in introducing economic approaches. The chapter will focus in particular on the study of public opinion and political behavior. This discussion can be extended beyond political issues and political participation to social attitudes and behavior,[2] but our emphasis is on political opinions and behavior, for which the comparisons of different approaches have been the subject of substantial attention and debate.[3]

COMPLEXITY, INDUCTION, AND DEDUCTION

The study of public opinion and political action attempts to describe and explain complex behavior, ranging from how individuals come to express particular opinions, why they change their opinions, why some people vote or work individually or in groups, and others don't, and why they vote the way they do and choose to work for or against some political ends. The behavior to be explained can vary in its *complexity,* and any full explanation has to involve the nature of individuals' mental processes that are at work. That is, human psychology is fundamental to this, but as shown in earlier chapters, psychology is highly complex since it attempts, ultimately, to explain highly complicated behavior. In contrast, in purely sociological approaches or in economic ones, the mental processes required are assumed to be simpler. Economic approaches, in particular, try to explain complex behavior and outcomes—especially the dynamics of political behavior—by making simple assumptions about human psychology.

In addition to the varying assumptions they make, explicitly or implicitly, about the mental processes at work, social scientists can approach these research questions in one of two ways. One is to seek answers *inductively* by looking at the empirical evidence for persistent findings and regularities that lead to conclusions about what perspectives justify the most emphasis. The other is to approach this problem *deductively,* that is, to start out abstractly and theoretically without emphasizing existing evidence, and to begin with a set of principles or *assumptions* that are arguably reasonably plausible. Theoretical ideas then guide expectations regarding what influences and outcomes will occur most regularly and predictably. Whether to proceed deductively or inductively, however, should not be considered an "either/or" question, since evidence and theory should come together in the end, and both can therefore be examined together along the way, if not at the very start. Indeed, whether to proceed theoretically or empirically—or in what balance—is a question that faces physical, biological, and behavioral scientists generally, as well as social scientists.

This is the starting point for this chapter, which tries to offer a synthesis of some of the contemporary theory bearing on public opinion and political behavior. Note that this is "a" synthesis not "the" synthesis, since there are other ways of comparing and debating different social science approaches to the study of public opinion and behavior. The chapter will introduce approaches that come from economics. Advocates of an economic or what is known as a *rational choice* perspective, in particular, have argued forcefully that deductive theorizing is crucial to seeking and understanding important tendencies and regularities in public opinion and political behavior. While sociological and psychological theorizing have also attempted to be deductive, economic or rational choice approaches have done this more explicitly—and exclusively.

ECONOMIC EXPLANATIONS

While psychology attempts to explain both simple and complex forms of behavior, including the expression of attitudes, the range of the psychological explanations for the complexities of behavior may seem daunting. Indeed, they are. Chapters Four, Five, and Six provide a view of public opinion and behavior that has enormous complexity, and to explain everything about them is almost like fitting together a jigsaw puzzle with too many pieces to keep track of. But in examining political attitudes and behavior, to what extent do we really have to keep track of all the pieces—to what extent do we have to emphasize and fully track the unstructured complexity of psychological processes and also (the somewhat simpler) sociological influences? The answer, from the standpoint of economic approaches, is "not so much."

Economic reasoning provides ways of thinking about the behavior and choices made by individuals in the political realm. More precisely, it can be labeled "microeconomic" in how it focuses on and theorizes about "micro" or individual-level behavior (in contrast to "macroeconomic," regarding, for example, a nation's overall economy), and one variant of it is "rational choice" theory, which has increasingly been emphasized by its advocates in a broad range of social science research. Economic approaches seek simplicity or "parsimony" in assigning significance to, in the case of this chapter, the findings of a substantial volume of political behavioral research.[4] Moreover, this approach, in contrast with psychological and sociological approaches, can—and does—theorize not only about individuals in the mass public or the electorate, taken alone, but also, most importantly, about the behavior of the *political leaders, candidates, and political parties* that are part of the political process and that seek public—that is, voters'—support.

SELF-INTEREST, RATIONALITY, AND THE ENDS OF POLITICAL BEHAVIOR

An economic approach theorizes about the political behavior of individuals, including politicians and political parties, based on what logically follows from a limited number of facts and assumptions. At the most fundamental level, the best-known ideas from economics have emphasized the importance—both empirically and normatively—of the assumption of *self-interest*. Specifically, economists use this assumption as a powerful tool and mechanism for explaining and predicting behavior. That is, if we assume that the primary goal of individuals is to *maximize* benefits, we can assume they will behave "rationally" in this context, in a self-centered way—even selfishly. Taking this to a normative conclusion, the famous Adam Smith posited that individuals pursuing what was best for themselves in an open and free market economy ultimately led, as if guided by a "hidden hand," to prosperity and to the best outcomes for societies and nations as a whole.[5]

What does this mean—empirically—in attempting to explain and predict behavior?

The idea here is that there are some expected patterns of political choices or behavior that will occur that are manifestations of—or are at least consistent with—the existence of self-interested individuals. These patterns are expected to overshadow the effects of other possible, though presumably lesser, influences or largely random peculiarities that can be left aside. This provides a way of simplifying the analysis, and the expected pattern of difference constitutes an *"equilibrium"* outcome—an outcome toward which the choices and behavior of individuals will tend (in a sense, *on average*), and this result can reveal what influences matter most or at least substantially.

The assumption of self-interest is a very simple one about the human mind and human behavior, and it is easy to see how it provides some readily useful explanations for why individuals express some of the opinions that they do. For example, in Table 5.3, some of the opinion differences that we discussed can be explained by economic self-interest reasoning. People who are well off and as a result pay more in taxes in dollar terms express less positive attitudes about people on "welfare." We also see racial differences in opinion because whites are better off financially than non-whites. From these simple patterns of correlation, we cannot tell definitively that these are the causal processes at work, but such economic explanations are reasonable, defensible, and applicable to a wide range of opinions and behavior. (Can you explain other findings presented elsewhere in this book in terms of self-interest?)

Thus we can emphasize self-interested economic and political objectives and define "rational" behavior here as the pursuit of such goals or *ends*. In one of the first and most influential discussions of economic approaches to the study of politics, Anthony Downs in *An Economic Theory of Democracy* states: "In the long run, we naturally expect a rational man to outperform an irrational man, *ceteris paribus* [everything else equal], because random factors cancel and efficiency triumphs over inefficiency."[6] Arguably much of what constitutes psychological and sociological theorizing occurs randomly in populations of individuals, often in pursuit of other nonpolitical or noneconomic goals, but what is systematic are those influences associated with pursuing the political or economic self-interested goals of individuals or groups. Downs does not deny the existence of purely psychological, nonselfish factors, but they are considered less relevant: The economic "model in particular ignores all forms of irrationality and subconscious behavior even though they play a vital role in real-world politics."[7] Specifically, primacy is given to "the economic or political goals of each individual or group in the model,"[8] which can be established at the start.

One type of example Downs cites is of a man who prefers a particular position on an issue or who prefers a specific candidate, in pursuit of a particular goal that furthers the man's interests; but if he perceives, spontaneously and unexpectedly, that this will upset his wife, it is arguably rational for him personally to change his opinion if he also does not want to upset his wife. Such behavior would be irrational, however, given his consistent political interest, which is expected to be primary.[9] If the man's desire to maintain tranquility in his family were his primary personal interest, or if he did not in fact have political goals, then changing his opinion could be the fully rational response. We will later return to this kind of contradiction and the need to look beyond personal self-interest.

What about the role of sociological considerations versus self-interest? For example, the influences of individuals' personal interactions and the groups in which people live and associate, which we considered in Chapter Five? While acknowledging the existence of the personal and group-related influences emphasized by Paul Lazarsfeld and other sociologists, the economic approach, again, gives priority to the pursuit of more economic and political interests, "otherwise all analysis of either economics or politics turns into an adjunct of primary group sociology."[10] The justification for this, however, is compelling given the possible conflicting or "cross-cutting" group-based influences that might exist: "nearly all primary groups are influenced by general economic and political conditions; hence we may provisionally regard the peculiarities of each such group as counterbalanced by opposite peculiarities of other primary groups."[11] To the extent that such offsetting differences do not occur, the differences that remain are likely to be group-based ones that are manifestations of political or economic interests. This would be consistent, for example, with Marxist approaches that emphasize the emergence and major consequences of economic class differences.

The discussion of self-interest, at this point, may seem to most readers as a very narrow—and peculiar—description of how people are expected to behave. Focusing only on self-interest-based goals in this way has its limitations; it can only take us so far in understanding public opinion and political behavior. In reality, individuals have ends they pursue beyond those that are determined by self-interest and that can be measured in purely economic or personal terms. While many people do not have saints as their role models, people do widely behave altruistically, unselfishly, or in a public-spirited way: They donate money and time to charitable causes; many people who are well off are happy to have their tax dollars assist those in need or protect the nation's environment. While many non-whites and women have personal reasons for supporting equal employment laws and court decisions, many white males support these as well. Thus we need to look beyond self-interest.[12]

The power of the assumption that individuals will rationally pursue their self-interest is not simply the emphasis on self-interest, but rather of individuals being consistent and forward-looking in their pursuit of the goals motivating them. Individuals have interests they want to pursue and maximize, and in reality people can have varying interests. Some might be generally self-interested, while others might be largely altruistic. Or, when it comes to some issues an individual might mainly be concerned with how he or she is affected by it, but for other issues an individual might care more about how the community or the nation at large is affected. Research on the balance between self-interest and concern for the collective interest provides a very plausible mixed picture. In terms of self-interest, in addition to what we have already cited, farmers and union members are quite mindful of their economic interests, and smokers have defended their habit and reacted to threats to regulate it (they seem to be losing that battle at this writing), as have drinkers of alcohol.[13]

But what is most striking is that substantial research has failed to find what are some of the expected blatant manifestations of self-interest in individuals' attitudes and behavior. People may be influenced by certain norms and values that they may be exposed to, by how they are socialized at home, in school, or through religion. Do some of the contradictory findings concerning self-interest have to do, for example, with religious people being ostensibly more altruistic and humanitarian? With women being more altruistic and caring because of how they are brought up or because of their greater religiousness than men? Perhaps most surprising have been research findings that have shown that individuals (and their families) who might be affected most adversely by particular policies do not express the greatest opposition to these policies. In the case of the military draft, young adults of draft age have not been the most opposed to conscription, nor were young adults the ones most likely to oppose the United States' entry into the wars in Korea, Vietnam, Afghanistan, and (both wars in) Iraq. Studies of opposition to racial desegregation through busing do not systematically find greater opposition simply among parents who have children who might be bused; adults' opinions are more influenced by their racial and other related attitudes. Self-interest does manifest itself in motivating opponents of busing to become politically active when their children are imminently affected, and it does directly evoke opposition among taxpayers when new taxes appear at hand.[14]

Perhaps most striking is what has been the "common wisdom" regarding purely personal *pocketbook* voting, which apparently occurs to a much lesser extent than expected. There is substantial evidence that the state of the *national* economy can affect voting and elections, but the process by which this occurs does not simply follow the expected pattern in which individuals vote for particular parties or candidates based on how well the economy is affecting their own personal financial situations. Rather, the somewhat greater tendency is that voters are influenced by their perceptions of how well the nation—the *collective* as a whole—is doing. The economy, then, is a national issue, not only a personal one: It is the nation's interest that matters apparently more than individuals' own personal interests.[15]

Thus, an economic approach that emphasizes rational self-interest in determining the ends individuals seek is not as useful as might be expected in explaining public opinion and political behavior. As one set of researchers conclude in their review of this topic: "To summarize, self-interest ordinarily does not have much effect on the mass public's political attitudes. There are occasional exceptions as when there are quite substantial and clear stakes (especially regarding personal tax burdens) or ambiguous and dangerous threats. But even these conditions only infrequently produce systematic and strong self-interest effects, and then, ones that are quite narrowly specific to the interest in question. The general public thinks about most political issues, most of the time, in a disinterested frame of mind."[16]

RATIONAL CHOICE: RATIONALITY OF MEANS

Self-interest aside, individuals' interest or motivations, whatever they are, can be strong, consistent, and knowable, and once known, it should be a direct task to predict and explain a range of opinions and behavior without directing much attention to the various psychological and sociological processes that distract from the application of the consistent interests at work. We return to our earlier assertion that the hallmark of an economic approach is its emphasis on deduction and what deductive logic leads it to predict based on an initial set of principles or assumptions. The goal, again, is to derive theoretically informative and important *equilibrium* outcomes concerning public opinion and political behavior. The assumptions we focus on will no longer emphasize the rationality of the ends that individuals seek defined in terms of self-interest. The economic approach we turn to is *rational choice theory.*

What is rational choice theory and what kinds of assumptions does it make? In what is arguably its strongest form, rational choice theorizing has assumed self-interest in the ends that individuals pursue, and predictions can be derived from this. But this is not central to the rational choice approach: Rational choice theory is not concerned with the rationality of the goals or ends of behavior; rather, its emphasis is the rationality of the *means* that individuals choose to reach their desired goals. It assumes that individuals have goals, and "it is taken as fundamental that individuals have beliefs and preferences." Given this, "A rational individual is one who combines his or her beliefs about the external environment and preferences about things in that environment in a consistent manner."[17] Individuals are assumed to be persistent and directed in their efforts to achieve their goals. It does not matter whether they are self-interested, collectively or altruistically oriented, or have a mix of these motives. What is central to rational choice theory is *how* the goals are pursued. Rational choice theory asks: Given a particular desired end, what political choices and behavior can we expected in rational pursuit of such ends? Thus we are interested in how individuals pursue their goals—the *means* that they use.

Putting this more formally, in pursuing their goals we expect individuals to do so *instrumentally* rationally by minimizing their costs and maximizing their benefits—that is, by using "the least possible input of scarce resources per unit of valued output."[18] In the case of political opinion holding and behavior, individuals will have opinions and behave in ways that efficiently pursue their interests. In the case of opinions that are expressed choices, "If Mr. i is given the opportunity to choose among x, y, and z, then we say that his choice is rational if it is in accord with his preferences. Thus a choice is rational if the object chosen is at least as good as any other available object according to the chooser's preferences. Put differently but equivalently, an object is a rational choice if no other available object is better according to the chooser's preferences."[19]

In emphasizing the means individuals use to work toward their goals, rational choice theorizing distinguishes itself from other approaches by the way it assumes that individuals work toward consistent goals, and that they engage in planning and forward-looking behavior, taking into account and *anticipating* the opinions and behavior of other individuals or political actors involved. The purported strength of rational choice approaches is in these kinds of dynamics, strategic choices, and *interactions*. Analytically, this includes *formal mathematical models* and also what is known as *game theory* or game theoretic models of behavior.[20]

We can hardly do justice to the applications of rational choice theory and the debates about its overall usefulness in the confines of a single chapter. In the remainder of this chapter, we will compare it further with sociological and psychological approaches, offer some examples of its applications, and discuss some limitations or challenges to it.

Because rational choice theory is deductive, given sets of assumptions, rational choice theory can produce specific explanations and predictions that can then be examined empirically. In contrast, the discussions of sociological and psychological explanations in Chapters Four, Five, and Six present a variety of causal mechanisms and processes that can influence public opinion and political behavior. Some are more complex than others, and they provide intuitively appealing, highly plausible, and arguably accurate explanations for different cases of opinion holding and particular behavior. Psychologists in particular want to wrestle with the full complexity of mental processes to understand fully the most complicated kinds of behavior.

There are some limitations, however, in applying sociological and psychological explanations to explain opinion formation and change, as well as political behavior: It is possible to have competing, if not outright conflicting, explanations for the *same* behavior, and these approaches do not attempt to disentangle the complexity of the *political context*. As a result it is often difficult to reach a conclusion as to what is the main influence at work in a particular case.

For example, when a new political issue emerges, what opinions will people express? From a sociological perspective, we would look to individuals' characteristics and their social environment, as discussed in Chapter Five (see also Chapter Eight) and as we considered earlier in this chapter with regard to self-interest. One complication here is that people have characteristics or are subject to influences that may pressure them in different directions. In the case of sociological factors, what if individuals in fact have a very *diverse* range of family members, friends, and coworkers? Would their opinions be somewhere "in-between" those of others who are situated in a more homogeneous set of personal relationships or networks? This would be a case of cross-pressures in which individuals are pulled in different directions because of different attributes. What prediction would we make about opinions of those who have to deal with such cross-pressures? Sorting out such multiple influences is difficult.

We can add to the sociological explanations a variety of psychological considerations. The wide range of these are described or alluded to in Chapters Four and Six (see also Chapter Eight). Regarding a new issue, theories of attitudinal and behavioral "balance" and cognitive dissonance would all seem to apply. Understanding what influences predominate here requires finding out about individuals' attitudes toward other related issues, their political ideology and partisanship, and their attitudes toward leaders or other persons toward whom they may perceive tensions or disagreements regarding the issue. There also may be influences related to past socialization and learning that need to be considered as well. In terms of sorting out the priority that we might give to different influences, the "Michigan model" described in the next chapter (Chapter Eight) emphasizes, in particular, the expected influences of political partisanship (party identification) on individuals' issue opinions, where partisanship is acquired through socialization and intergenerational transmission and learning (involving feelings or *affect* toward one's parents, "identity," and related processes).

One of the most important political examples to consider here is the case of voters' choices in elections, for which there has been substantial theorizing and research involving sociological, psychological, and rational choice approaches and theory. The earlier discussion regarding sociological and psychological explanations still applies. The "Columbia model," emphasizing sociological influences on voting, is described at greater length in Chapter Eight. The Michigan model that emphasized the strong psychological effect of partisanship provided what was known as a "normal vote" analysis. In this normal vote model, partisanship predominantly affected how Democratic and Republican Party identifiers voted, with short-term forces having some effect, potentially decisive, especially on "independent" voters. It was with respect to these more variable and dynamic short-term influences that the sociological and psychological approaches have had less to say. In contrast, rational choice theory is better able to grapple with these, along with how political actors and the political environment interact with individuals and voters. Rational choice theory also considers further, in a deductive fashion, the possible role of sociological and partisanship influences.

How, then, does rational choice theory approach public opinion toward some new issue that arises? Beyond the assumptions and implications about the interests and goals that individuals pursue as noted earlier (i.e., individuals have goals that they attempt to pursue consistently and efficiently), what is crucial to rational choice theorizing are the assumptions that are made about the constraints that individuals and political leaders and others face in the political process. The specific constraints are the costs of information, the costs of participating in politics, and the uncertainty that voters and other political actors face.[21]

The basic calculus in rational choice theory involves calculating the benefits—or "utility" in economic language—and costs of some behavior, and making the prediction concerning an individual's behavior for which the *net* benefits, that is, the result of the calculation of "benefits *minus* costs," are greatest. It is important to note that a net benefit of "zero" is greater than a *negative* benefit, which would result when costs are greater than benefits. The simplest, though unrealistic, set of assumptions is that everyone—individuals in the electorate as well as parties, candidates, and all other political actors—has *complete information* about issues and also about each others' political positions and behavior. They are all-knowing, by assumption, or equivalently we can assume that they have information readily available to them at literally no (zero) cost and that they consume all relevant information that is free. The expressed choices of members of the public are targeted toward goals that they seek, which follow directly from their beliefs and preferences.

Table 7.1 presents the choices of eleven individuals concerning government spending on some policy—"Program X," for example, defense spending. Table 7.1 is an example of an ordered "spatial" distribution of individuals (voters) along a policy space (in this case a budgetary spending continuum). The distribution is assumed to be what is known formally as "single peaked," which means that while individuals prefer most the position (the dollar amount here) that they have expressed (e.g., Voter A prefers to spend $100 million), they prefer positions that are spatially

TABLE 7.1   Preferred Spending on Program X

Voter	Most preferred spending (millions of $)	
A	100	
B	90	
C	80	
D	70	
E	60	
F	*50*	middle, or *median*, voter
G	40	
H	30	
I	20	
J	10	
K	0	

Note: Spending preferences of eleven voters (A to K) on Policy X. The "median voter" is voter F, who prefers to spend $50 million. See text.

closer to them than those that are further away (Voter A prefers $60 million over $50 million). This is intuitively appealing and may seem like common sense, but it is an important assumption.[22] It follows from the assumption of complete information that individuals can express a level of preferred spending that maximizes their utility (e.g., the level of national defense they want). Thus their expressed opinion will reveal information about the benefits that have been maximized, and it is possible to discern who is benefiting. This formal statement is straightforward, but it is (as you may already sense) not particularly interesting or informative by itself.

It is more interesting and useful to consider this in the context of voters participating in politics, where we have parties and candidates seeking votes. We continue to assume that voters and political actors have complete information and there are no costs to participation. With no costs to participation, we assume everyone will vote, and we focus on their vote choice. Everyone is expected to vote, even though any one vote cast has very little chance in being decisive in the election; but since there are no costs, any expected very small gain from voting still exceeds the zero cost.

To illustrate how rational choice theorizing plays out concerning elections, we will focus on the standard example of electoral competition involving two parties or candidates, "A" and "B." Rational choice theory, to start, assigns primacy to issues and policies. We can think of these as a single issue or a catch-all ideological or partisan policy continuum, such as policy *liberalism or conservatism* or a *left–right* policy continuum, conceptualized the way we see politics described in journalistic discourse in the United States or elsewhere. Issues and policies are assumed to matter in a big way since this is how individuals appraise the benefits of voting for one party rather than another. This is particularly plausible under the assumption of complete information. Voters will therefore most prefer to choose the party that takes issue or ideological positions that are exactly the same as their own, since that will give them the maximum benefit from their vote if their party or candidate wins the election. If no party takes exactly their position, because voters' preferences are single-peaked, as noted earlier, they would prefer a party that takes a position *closest* to their position. Rational choice approaches bring theory to bear on the behavior of the parties as well. It is assumed that parties want to maximize their utility, which means ultimately the rewards and power of office holding, and they need to maximize their votes to win elections. Therefore, given that voters have established their policy preferences, in the way, for example, illustrated in Table 7.1, and assuming that the issue shown influences how voters vote, a party will need to take a position that will enable it to win the election.

To understand what would happen in this case, we can simply treat this like players—in this case voters and parties—in a game. The voters have already staked out their positions that maximize their utility. What will the parties do? Each party will first take a position that it prefers based on its own policy goals, and this is illustrated in Figure 7.1. While parties ultimately want to win elections, they do have issue and policy goals that they want to pursue; but they can only achieve them if elected. Figures 7.1a and 7.1b expand upon Table 7.1 to show examples of distributions of larger number of voters. The horizontal axis shows the policy positions and the vertical axis shows the numbers of voters located at each position on the horizontal axis. Once parties A and B take their initial positions, they can observe (as we are assuming they have complete information concerning where the voters stand) how close they are located to the voters, knowing that the voters will choose the party they are closest to. It should be apparent that given the distribution of voters, it is the centermost location, "M", that is the spot toward which the parties will both ultimately want to move (you can play out the game by moving each party as they try to position themselves so they are closer than the other party to the most voters). As Table 7.1 and Figures 7.1a and 7.1b

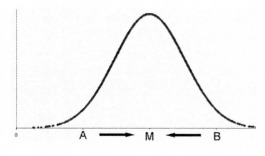

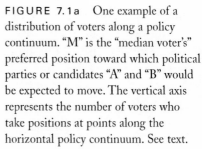

FIGURE 7.1a   One example of a distribution of voters along a policy continuum. "M" is the "median voter's" preferred position toward which political parties or candidates "A" and "B" would be expected to move. The vertical axis represents the number of voters who take positions at points along the horizontal policy continuum. See text.

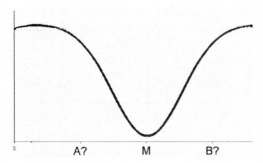

FIGURE 7.1b   Another example of a distribution of voters along a policy continuum. "M" is the "median voter's" preferred position toward which political parties or candidates "A" and "B" would be expected to move—or would they? The vertical axis represents the number of voters who take positions at points along the horizontal policy continuum. See text.

show, this center position, which is called the "median," is the one above and below which half the voters are located, and the voter located there is called the "median voter." Thus the parties converge on the median voter, and this is the equilibrium outcome.

If the parties converge at the median, then what do the voters do? They cannot distinguish the benefits that they would get from either party. They can do equally well (or badly) by choosing either party. In this situation, further decision rules are needed, and one that has been widely used instructs voters to make a prospective judgment regarding how well the parties will perform in office, based on information concerning how the incumbent party (the one currently in office) has recently performed. If it has done well, voters should choose to keep it in office; if it has done poorly, they should vote for the other party.

Note that the equilibrium holds for both Figures 7.1a and 7.1b, even though we see in Figure 7.1b that both parties can attract substantial numbers of voters by diverging toward the clusters of voters at each side of the distribution; that is, there are a lot of voters who would like the parties to distinguish themselves more and to locate closer to them to provide greater benefit to voters if the parties are elected. But the parties cannot afford to do this since the other party could simply move toward the middle and so win the election. As we will see, this situation can change readily under different assumptions. In the current case, the equilibrium outcome remains that both parties are predicted to converge at the median voter, and the voters would then have to resort to the performance-based tie-breaking rule.

What, then, happens to this rational choice modeling when we relax the assumptions and assume, more plausibly, that there may be substantial real-world information costs and costs of participation, and that this introduces uncertainties into individuals' political behavior? First, whether individuals will vote becomes less certain when there are costs entailed in casting votes and in participating in politics, and when individuals incur costs in becoming informed. The expected effect on the election outcome of any one vote is minuscule, and a voter's costs will enormously exceed the expected benefit from voting one's policy preferences. Further, given that one vote will not be decisive, any collective benefit that might be obtained from a voter's preferred party winning the election would be obtained by the voter regardless of whether he or she votes. This is the "free rider" outcome that applies to all manner of political activities and joining of groups or organized interests where the outcomes ultimately at stake are collective or "public goods."[23]

Taking into account the benefits relative to costs and free riding, the equilibrium regarding voting is that no one would vote (except those for whom voting involves essentially no costs; who might those voters be?) and the only people who would become informed about policies, parties, and candidates are those for whom this information gathering is virtually costless—incidental to other things they do. However, in reality, many individuals do vote for reasons outside this simple rational choice model or as the result of more complex rational choice considerations, involving repeated elections (as "repeated games"), how individuals observe and react to the behavior of others, and other factors that are beyond what we can cover in this chapter.[24] In the context of elections and politics in which voting occurs, rational choice theorizing leads to plausible expectations for which we can cite empirical support, such as the finding that voter turnout is typically higher in elections that voters perceive as close and in institutional contexts in which there are fewer or weaker voter registration and other impediments, and hence lower costs, to voting.[25]

Given that many individuals will vote (even with incomplete information and costs to voting), what will influence these voters and what will be decisive in elections? Rational choice theory provides a way of thinking about what will matter most in different election contexts. Figures 7.1a and 7.1b are still highly relevant, but the political behavior and concomitant theorizing are more complicated. First, since voters incur costs in voting, if they see themselves located too far from any party in the issue space, they will become less likely to vote. That is, they may become *alienated* and choose not to vote since their preferred party, if elected, will offer little benefit to them. As a result, the parties will ignore or write off voters at the extremes in Figure 7.1a. In the more polarized distribution in Figure 7.1b, the parties would have reason to move away from the median voter toward their respective preferred sides of the distribution to capture voters there who might otherwise choose not to vote.

That voters do not have complete information changes the dynamics of voter choice in other important ways. It is no longer the case that voters' preferred positions in the issue space are fixed and taken as given by the parties. It is now possible for parties and candidates, when they have policy goals that they also wish to pursue, to attempt to get voters to *move* their positions. The theorizing now allows for the possibility of *persuasion*—for parties, candidates, and other political actors to attempt to lead—or manipulate—public opinion, in addition to responding to it (see Chapter Nine).[26] The less information people have and the less salient and visible particular issues are, the more susceptible to persuasion voters may be. Further, as we return to in Chapter Eight, voters seek out information shortcuts, and what parties are perceived to stand for generally due to the ideologies they have established and adhered to can be used by voters to cut their information costs in choosing their preferred parties or candidates. They may be more likely to resort to this when they are uninformed and gathering information incurs significant costs. (Note too that sociological influences might come into play in a similar way.)

The behavior of parties and candidates is also expected to be affected in other ways. On those issues where they take positions noticeably different from those of voters, they have incentives not to take visible positions on these issues or to obscure their positions. Faced with such invisibility and ambiguity, voters would then become more likely to ignore these issues or misperceive where the parties or candidates stand in a manner more favorable to these political actors. The end result would then likely be that on those issues for which voters do have information—albeit not necessarily accurate information—regarding where two parties or two candidates stand, the voters overall will not likely perceive much difference between them. This outcome, perhaps surprisingly, is strikingly similar to the expected outcome under the assumption of complete information. Voters would then, once again, base their choice on the incumbent party's perceived past performance in office in estimating how well the parties would do in the future after (re)taking office. Research has shown that this kind of performance-based retrospective voting occurs, and the Michigan model has been adapted to take this into account (see Chapter Eight).[27]

Figure 7.2 shows how useful empirically these kinds of spatial comparisons can be, as these played out across several issues at once in the 2000 presidential election. While this spatial modeling approach, technically speaking, does not formally lead to an equilibrium when we have more than two issues or multiple ideological dimensions, Figure 7.2 does provide a sense that presidential candidates George W. Bush and Al Gore, while not appearing enormously different from each other on the issues (as we would expect!), were each closer to the voters on about the same number of issues shown (three each) and were approximately equidistant from them on one. This suggests that, if these represented the main issues of concern to the electorate, neither candidate would likely be a clear winner in the election based on spatial voting criteria. Other factors, therefore, could (and evidently did!) affect the election at the critical, decisive margin. While these other variables could include perceptions concerning the incumbent party's performance in office, as noted earlier, these may well be sociological or psychological influences of the sort that rational choice theory downplays, perceptions of the personal qualities of the political leaders that may or may not have bearings on perceptions of likely performance in office, or random or otherwise unsystematic factors.

RATIONAL CHOICE AND PSYCHOLOGY:
A FURTHER LOOK

The preceding discussion suggests that rational choice theory provides a systematic approach to understanding important influences on public opinion and political behavior. Its strength lies in its emphasis on deduction in attempting to explain important aspects or parts of political behavior. It too,

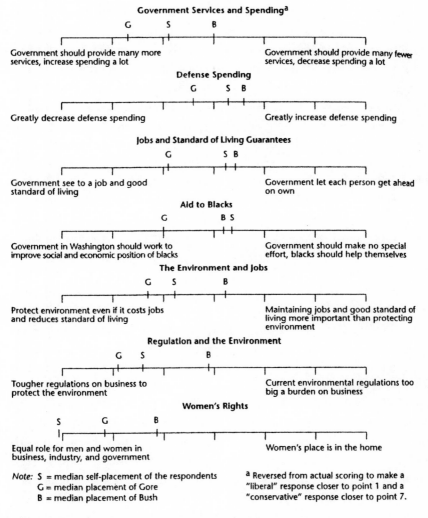

FIGURE 7.2 Median Self-Placement of the Electorate and the Electorate's Placement of Candidates on Issue Scales, 2000.

SOURCE: Paul R. Abramson, John H. Aldrich, and David W. Rohde, *Change and Continuity in the 2000 and 2002 Elections* (Washington, D.C.: Congressional Quarterly Press, 2002), Figure 6–3, p. 134.

however, falls well short of explaining everything we would like to explain, and in the end we need to look toward other models and variables, including the ones emphasized in sociological and psychological approaches.

Still, the simplicity of the human psychology assumed in rational choice theorizing and how far rational choice theorists can get with it is compelling. Rational choice theorists are content not to be sufficiently complex to attempt to explain everything, but rather focus on important and interesting patterns and differences. This has great theoretical appeal and it is persuasive as long as the behavior and outcomes that occur do so through ostensibly unimpeded rational processes involving cost/benefit-like estimations. What has been shown increasingly and persuasively in recent years, however, is that certain psychological processes have consequences for rational behavior in ways that appear to be predictable, systematic, and of direct concern. Some of these processes are *affective*, involving feelings and emotions. Others are cognitive and they have been found to be increasingly compelling and are the subject of exciting new research in psychology and economics.

AFFECT AND EMOTIONS

Some recent research on affect has reemphasized the importance of feelings and emotions in understanding public opinion and behavior. For example, one group of researchers, examining what they call "affective intelligence," has argued and offered evidence that processes involving anxiety or fear, in particular, can enhance processes of rational choice and complement conventional rational choice explanations. This psychological approach and some of its theorizing is summarized in Table 7.2, which compares models of the normal vote, rational choice, and affective intelligence. What the last two columns of the table assert and the authors' research shows is that the kinds of behavior that are central to rational choice—attentiveness or exposure to new information, receptiveness to such information, the importance of issues and policies, the levels of knowledge acquired, and the relationship of issue positions to voting decisions (see Chapter Eight)—are all sharpened when individuals experience anxiety, especially when new and unfamiliar or threatening situations arise. Rational choice theory assumes a minimal degree of attentiveness by individuals to what's around them, but increasing anxiousness or fear can lead people to be more attentive, thereby increasing their engagement in rational choice behavior. While we might have expected anxiety to make individuals more erratic and even irrational, this may only be the case in certain extremes.

Other perspectives on the role of emotions and feelings argue for greater attention to them for more sweeping reasons. While acknowledg-

TABLE 7.2 Comparing Models of the Normal Vote, Rational Choice, and Affective Intelligence

	Normal Vote Model	*Rational Choice*	*Affective Intelligence*
Who is attentive?	Partisans	Everyone	The habituated attentive and the anxious voter
Who is receptive to new information?	Independents and weak partisans	Everyone	Those for whom new information generates anxiety
View of partisanship	Ingrained commitment to historical learning	Not particularly relevant	Provides reliable cues to guide recurring political choices
View of issues and policies	Effective to mobilize supporters and to seduce the inattentive and weakly informed	Always relevant	Important when anxious voters seek information and also also to articulate habituated commitments
View of information levels in electorate	Curvilinear relationship between partisanship and knowledge gathering	Information readily available though "costs" may limit the number of people who are well informed	Information levels highly dynamic and responsive to the strategic importance of information
Voting decision	Dependent on partisanship and especially for independents "short-term" forces	A self-interested comparison among salient issue positions, with the candidate choice reflecting the candidate who takes the position closest to the voter	Either reliance on habituated cues or reasoned considerations when unfamiliar or threatening situations preclude routine reliance on habit

SOURCE: George E. Marcus, W. Russell Neuman, and Michael MacKuen, *Affective Intelligence and Political Judgment* (Chicago: University of Chicago Press, 2000), Table 7.1, p. 132.

ing that emotions may enhance rational choice processes in certain contexts, they see emotions as profoundly important in their separate independent effects on behavior; in their relationship, thus far unresolved, with interests; and in how emotions and interests interact (i.e., are contingent on each other) in their influence on people's lives. Emotions may be critical to understanding the *causal mechanisms* that produce a wide range of human behavior.[28]

COGNITION AND BEHAVIORAL ECONOMICS

In contrast to the role of affect, certain cognitive processes pose substantial challenges to rational choice theory at its core. Specifically, it has been found that in certain kinds of situations that should be explicable from a rational choice perspective, *misperceptions* can occur that lead to unexpected irrational behavior. In such cases, psychological considerations have to be accounted for directly in the theorizing. While this poses a challenge to rational choice theory, it has also been seen as a social scientific opportunity to advance the study of human behavior. Within the field of economics this has led to an extension of economic theory—the development of the field of *behavioral economics*—that takes into account psychological processes that affect economic reasoning.

Research in the field of behavioral economics has identified a number of types of systematic distortions that defy straightforward rational choice prediction and explanation and require understanding psychology and perception. Two important examples have to do with what is called the principle of invariance, which is an essential condition for rational choice theory, and with the *framing* of *risks* in choice situations.[29]

"Invariance" is the idea that the choice made between options should not be affected by how the options are represented; that is, it is the content of the options that matters, not how they are described or depicted—or *framed*. An example of how invariance can fail owing to psychological processes can be found in a study of choices between medical treatments.[30] The same statistics were described to two sets of survey respondents in different ways and this led to strikingly different responses to the same substantive choices. Respondents were asked whether they preferred surgery or radiation in the following identical situations, with the two groups of respondents differing in whether the outcomes were described to them in terms of "survival" or "mortality":

Survival frame asked of one group of respondents:
Surgery: Of 100 people having surgery 90 live through the post-operative period, 68 are alive at the end of the first year and 34 are alive at the end of five years.

Radiation Therapy: Of 100 people having radiation therapy all live through the treatment, 77 are alive at the end of one year and 22 are alive at the end of five years.

The result here is that 18 percent of respondents chose radiation. In contrast, when framed in terms of mortality, as described next, this more than doubled to 44 percent preferring radiation:

Mortality frame asked to the other group of respondents:
Surgery: Of 100 people having surgery 10 die during the surgery or the post-operative period, 32 die by the end of the first year and 66 die by the end of five years.
Radiation Therapy: Of 100 people having radiation therapy none die during treatment, 23 die by the end of one year and 78 die by the end of five years.

The difference in responses by the two groups has to do evidently with the advantage of radiation *appearing* greater when the threat of death drops from 10 percent to 0 percent rather than the increase from 90 percent to 100 percent in terms of survival. What is also noteworthy is that this *framing effect* was *not* less for physicians or statistically knowledgeable business students than for a group of clinic patients.

Risk aversion and *risk seeking* can play out in different ways by changes in the labeling of outcomes in the following survey experiment in which one group of respondents was asked to choose between Programs A and B, and another group was asked to choose between Programs C and D:

Imagine that the U.S. is preparing for the outbreak of an unusual Asian disease, which is expected to kill 600 people. Two alternate programs to combat the disease have been proposed. Assume that the exact scientific estimates of the consequence of the programs are as follows:
If Program A is adopted, 200 people will be saved. [72 percent chose this]
If Program B is adopted, there is a 1/3 probability that 600 people will be saved, and a 2/3 probability that no people will be saved. [28 percent chose this]

For these respondents, the majority choice is clearly *risk averse:* They prefer the "prospect" with certainty of saving 200 lives to the risky prospect that has the same "expected value" (on average, if this were a re-peated situation, we would expect 1/3 × 600 = 200 to survive).

The second group of respondents was asked to choose one of the fol-lowing options, identical to the above choices:

> If Program C is adopted 400 people will die. [20 percent chose this]
>
> If program D is adopted there is a 1/3 probability that nobody will die, and 2/3 probability that 600 people will die. [78 percent chose this]

In contrast to the descriptions of Programs A and B, the outcomes here are described in negative terms (death) and the majority choice is *risk seeking*. The certainty of death for 400 people is preferred less than a two-thirds chance that 600 people will die. The choices between pro-grams are the same as between A and B but the descriptions are framed differently; the choice problem is the same but the responses are differ-ent, which requires an explanation outside rational choice theory—in psychology.

CONCLUSION

Sorting out social science theorizing is not a simple task. The good news is that there is no lack of theories, but the downside is, ironically, the same: We often have multiple explanations for why people hold the opin-ions they do and behave the way they do. Economic theorizing has at-tempted to offer a rigorous deductive approach to studying political be-havior. Its strength has been its effort to cut through the complexity of individual-level psychology and social relations to untangle regular and important influences that are at work, and also to take into account and theorize about the behavior of elite political actors—parties and politi-cians—in their interaction with the public at large as voters in the politi-cal process. The most useful conclusion we can offer at this juncture is that no one type of theorizing provides a complete explanation for opin-ion holding and political behavior. It is important to consider and apply sociological, psychological, and economic approaches to explain the broadest range of attitudes and behavior. In turning to evidence bearing on questions concerning the public's competence and democracy and their normative implications, we consider further all three types of approaches in Chapter Eight. (Readers should note that the use of the term "rationality" in this chapter is different from the rationality of collective opinion described in later chapters.)

NOTES

1. We thank Charles Cameron for his comments in drafting this chapter.

2. See Gary S. Becker, *The Economic Approach to Behavior* (Chicago: University of Chicago Press, 1976).

3. See Donald P. Green and Ian Shapiro, *Pathologies of Rational Choice Theory: A Critique of Applications in Political Science* (New Haven: Yale University Press, 1994); *Critical Review. Special Issue: Rational Choice Theory and Politics* 9 (Winter-Spring, 1995).

4. See Anthony Downs, *An Economic Theory of Democracy* (New York: Harper & Row, 1957), pp. ix–x.

5. See Adam Smith, *The Wealth of Nations* (New York: Random House, 1937 [1776]).

6. Downs, *An Economic Theory of Democracy*, p. 6.

7. Downs, *An Economic Theory of Democracy*, p. 34.

8. Downs, *An Economic Theory of Democracy*, p. 6.

9. Downs, *An Economic Theory of Democracy*, p. 7.

10. Downs, *An Economic Theory of Democracy*, p. 8.

11. Downs, *An Economic Theory of Democracy*, p. 8.

12. For example, see Jane J. Mansbridge, ed., *Beyond Self-interest* (Chicago: University of Chicago Press, 1990).

13. See Benjamin I. Page and Robert Y. Shapiro, *The Rational Public: Fifty Years of Trends in Americans' Policy Preferences* (Chicago: University of Chicago Press, 1992), pp. 285–286.

14. See Page and Shapiro, *The Rational Public,* pp. 285–286, 304–305; David O. Sears and Carolyn L. Funk, "Self-interest in Americans' Political Opinions," in Mansbridge, ed., *Beyond Self-interest,* pp. 147–170.

15. For a summary, see Sears and Funk, "Self-interest in Americans' Political Opinions," pp. 156–157.

16. Sears and Funk, "Self-interest in Americans' Political Opinions," p. 170.

17. Kenneth A .Shepsle and Mark S. Bonchek, *Analyzing Politics: Rationality, Behavior, and Institutions* (New York: W.W. Norton, 1997), p. 17.

18. Downs, *An Economic Theory of Democracy*, p. 5.

19. Shepsle and Bonchek, *Analyzing Politics,* p. 25.

20. On game theory and how it might be best used to explain individuals' behavior from the standpoint of what is called *behavioral economics,* as described later in the chapter, see Colin F. Camerer, *Behavioral Game Theory: Experiments in Strategic Interaction* (New York and Princeton: Russell Sage Foundation and Princeton University Press, 2003). This area of study recently received some attention in popular culture in the book and movie *A Beautiful Mind,* about the life of Nobel Prize-winner John Nash.

21. The discussion that follows draws heavily on and offers further interpretation of Part I and Part II of Downs, *An Economic Theory of Democracy,* and Benjamin I. Page, *Choices and Echoes in Presidential Elections: Rational Man and Electoral Democracy* (Chicago: University of Chicago Press, 1978).

22. These ideas were originally put forth by economists Harold Hotelling, Arthur Smithies, Duncan Black, and Anthony Downs. See Downs, *An Economic Theory of Democracy*, pp. 114–119; and, for example, Melvin J. Hinich and Michael C. Munger, *Analytic Politics* (New York: Cambridge University Press, 1997), pp. 24–27.

23. See Mancur Olson, *The Logic of Collective Action* (Cambridge, MA: Harvard University Press, 1965).

24. Cf. Susanne Lohmann, "The Poverty of Green and Shapiro," *Critical Review. Special Issue: Rational Choice Theory and Politics* 9 (Winter-Spring 1995):127–154.

25. On the usefulness of rational choice theorizing in restrictive contexts like these, see Morris P. Fiorina, "Rational Choice, Empirical Contributions, and the Scientific Enterprise," *Critical Review. Special Issue: Rational Choice Theory and Politics* 9 (Winter-Spring 1995):85–94.

26. See Lawrence R. Jacobs and Robert Y. Shapiro, *Politicians Don't Pander: Political Manipulation and the Loss of Democratic Responsiveness* (Chicago: University of Chicago Press, 2000).

27. See Morris P. Fiorina, *Retrospective Voting in American National Elections* (New Haven: Yale University Press, 1981), and Warren E. Miller and J. Merrill Shanks, *The New American Voter* (Cambridge, MA: Harvard University Press, 1996).

28. See Jon Elster, *Alchemies of the Mind: Rationality and Emotions* (New York: Cambridge University Press, 1999).

29. The discussion that follows is taken from Amos Tversky and Daniel Kahneman, "Rational Choice and the Framing of Decisions," in Robin M. Hogarth and Melvin W. Reder, eds., *Rational Choice: The Contrast Between Economics and Psychology* (Chicago: University of Chicago Press, 1987), pp. 67–94.

30. B. J. McNeil, S. G. Pauker, H. C. Sox, Jr., and A. Tversky, "On the Elicitation of Preferences for Alternative Therapies," *New England Journal of Medicine* 306 (1982):1259–1262.

PART THREE

PUBLIC OPINION
IN CONTEXT

8

Public Opinion and
Democratic Competence

In Chapter One, the first reason we gave for studying public opinion was that "policy, in democratic states, should rest on public opinion." Now that we have examined some of the processes that influence people's opinions and attitudes, it is time to return to that claim. Some observers argue that, actually, policy should have little if anything to do with public opinion. Dean Acheson, who served as U.S. Secretary of State from 1949 to 1953, reportedly once said, "If you truly had a democracy and did what people wanted, you'd go wrong every time."[1] Echoing other leaders and political writers, Acheson was vigorously denying the public's *democratic competence*.

What is democratic competence? Our answer may depend on the role we want public opinion to play in guiding policy. Some theories of representative democracy assume that people need only enough wisdom to vote for responsible political leaders. Then it is up to the leaders to govern in the public interest. For instance, Acheson obviously didn't think much of most Americans' policy ideas, but he probably thought that they had acted sensibly in electing the president (Truman) who asked him to serve as Secretary of State! This line of thought—that the *only* important political role of citizens is to choose their leaders—is sometimes called "democratic elitism." Few people fully embrace it. Some doubt that citizens even have the judgment to choose responsible political leaders, although it is not obvious who could better be trusted with that choice. Many others have higher (but not always much higher) views of average people's political judgment, and higher standards for government responsiveness to public opinion. Probably most citizens of the United States and other democratic states agree that governments should generally do what most people want—at least if what most people want is reasonable.

This statement opens up many questions, both about values and about facts. The value questions include: When and why should the government do what most people want? What desires count as "reasonable"? How should the political system protect the rights or interests of minorities? Once we better understand the dimensions of these questions, we can try to sort out the facts about democratic competence (or the lack of it) and their political implications. For instance: How much do people know about policy issues? How many people have well-considered opinions about policy issues? Do people even have reasonable grounds for deciding whom to vote for? How much respect do people have for minority rights and other democratic values? What policy issues evoke the sharpest disagreements, and how bitterly do people disagree about them? Finally, how often *does* the government do what most people want—or, more generally, how strongly does public opinion influence policy and in what ways?

These questions of value and fact have inspired countless projects in political philosophy and empirical research. We will spend much more time on the empirical research than on the philosophy, but we are especially interested in how the two areas are related. Also, we will continue to focus almost exclusively on the United States—partly because that is the democratic country that we and most of our readers know best, partly because the theme of democratic competence seems complex enough without trying to do justice to the similarities and differences among many different countries.

Here is our plan. First we will take a somewhat closer look at some of the value questions lurking within the broad issue of democratic competence. Then we will look at evidence about the quality of people's opinions—what they know, how well considered their views are, and how closely their votes reflect their views. Then we will step back and look at the American people's basic values—in particular, their support for democratic norms, and how their views set broad channels for political debate in the United States. Finally, in the next chapter, we will look intensively at evidence about the various impacts of public opinion on policy.

THE PUBLIC ROLE IN GOVERNMENT:
A PHILOSOPHICAL SKETCH

In Chapter Two, we briefly traced some historic disagreements about public opinion and government. Plato and Cicero were among the ancient scholars who challenged democratic competence. Here, although we can only scratch the surface, we want to consider more directly the question: What are the possible roles of the public in government and policymaking?

At one extreme, we can imagine a direct or pure democracy in which every citizen has a direct and equal voice (or at least equal right to a voice) in every policy decision. However, in a country of some 300 million people, it is impractical to allow every person to vote on every policy issue—much less to expect them to participate in informed debate. You might wonder: As more and more people gain access to the Internet, isn't it at least possible that they could have the right to vote on every proposed law? Certainly they *could*, although thousands of bills are introduced in the U.S. Congress every year. But each law includes many distinct policy decisions—not even considering all the provisions that could have been written in but weren't. If we could somehow frame every one of these decisions, or even the "most important" ones, as Internet plebiscites, it is hard to imagine millions of people wanting to vote on all of them, or knowing enough to vote wisely, or being able to discuss them before they vote. (Americans do vote on certain policy decisions at state and local levels, but not many decisions. Even in small towns, most people seem more than willing to leave most of the decisionmaking to a few other people.) Here is one (not the only!) crucial rationale for representative democracy rather than pure democracy: Citizens simply lack the time and desire to participate in every decision.[2]

At the other extreme, we can imagine a dictatorship in which the ruler or ruling party intends to pay no heed to public opinion in determining policy. We say "intends" because, in reality, not even a dictatorship can entirely disregard the wishes of its subjects. No army or police force can regulate every aspect of every citizen's life. Moreover, most dictatorial regimes argue that they are legitimate because they serve the people's interests. Many even claim democratic legitimacy.[3] But dictators cannot be trusted to serve the interests of their citizens. Dictators' distinctive character traits—often some combination of fervent ideological belief and desire for personal power—hardly equip them for careful attention to citizens' needs. We cannot trust dictators to want only the best for their citizens, or to understand the citizens' interests better than the citizens themselves do.

Between the extremes of pure democracy and dictatorship, we find wide and muddy middle ground. While no one political leader can be trusted to promote the interests of all citizens, we have found no means for citizens to act on their political interests directly. In fact, we doubt that citizens grasp the many specific policy decisions facing government nearly well enough to know what choices to favor. But the problem is even worse than that. This talk of "acting in citizens' interests" implies that citizens all share the same interests and values. Obviously they do not. To mention just a few clashes of interest and value, which we will examine more closely later:

1. Some Americans believe that people with high incomes should be taxed at a considerably higher percentage rate than other citizens (progressive taxation); others believe that everyone should be taxed at the same rate (a "flat tax"). As you might expect, people with higher incomes are more likely to support a flat tax, or at least lower taxes for themselves than people with lower incomes think they should pay. However, in this and many other apparently straightforward economic conflicts, many people state opinions that go against their apparent self-interest. These opinions appear to be rooted in their values about, for instance, how equal society should be and what sorts of things the government should do to promote equality.

2. In the past, many white Americans held and acted upon a system of values and beliefs that held blacks to be inherently inferior. Whites often discriminated against African-Americans, even when this discrimination did not necessarily serve whites' economic interests. Now large majorities of white Americans repudiate racial discrimination. Yet racial polarities remain in American politics. White and black Americans, in particular, tend to disagree sharply on a wide range of policy issues for a variety of reasons—and observers often disagree sharply on which reasons are actually most important.

3. Whether abortion should be legal is a perennial value-based dispute in U.S. politics. Many Americans believe that abortion amounts to murder and should always be illegal. Many others believe that abortion is a personal (and health-related) choice and should be legally protected. Still others believe that abortion should be legal in some circumstances but not in others—and many Americans are ambivalent or inconsistent about the nuances of their opinions.

These examples suggest, first of all, that the American public often is far from agreeing on the "public interest" or "common good." They further point to the dangers of what Tocqueville called *tyranny of the majority*: Under a system of simple majority rule, what is to stop the majority from imposing onerous conditions on the minority? (For Tocqueville, the risks of majoritarian tyranny in the United States encompassed the subtle suppression of dissent; indeed, he claimed that there was less "independence of mind and real freedom of discussion" there than in any other country he knew.)[4] The framers of the Constitution were especially worried about protecting prosperous minorities against poor majorities. James Madison, in *The Federalist* #10, famously argued that the federal government would be better able to resist a "rage for . . . an abolition of debts, an equal division of property, or for any other improper or wicked project," than individual states would be. Many critics complain that the Constitution is slanted toward the rich—but the power to take away people's property (or freedom) is inherently dangerous, and the framers were right to worry about it. Of course, the survival of slavery for almost eighty years after the Constitution, and the subsequent "Jim Crow" laws discriminating against Southern blacks, underscore that nothing in the Constitution guaranteed justice for minorities. The U.S. system is designed, among other purposes, to protect minorities against transitory public passions; it is less effective at protecting against enduring and widely felt hostility.

The U.S. system is often described as a representative democracy—in which citizens elect the people (especially the president and the members of Congress) who directly make policy. One argument for representative democracy is that it gives all citizens some say in government, while acknowledging that not everyone can participate directly in policy decisions. But there are other important rationales for the U.S. system.

We have just alluded to one: to delay action based on popular pressure. Madison and the framers argued that the public was subject to intense paroxyms of passion, which could lead people to support not only infringements on the rights of minorities, but other misguided changes in policy. It may seem strange that one purpose of representative democracy is, in effect, to *limit* how closely (or at least how quickly) the government represents public opinion—and even stranger that the framers of the U.S. Constitution would openly say so. In *The Federalist* #63, Madison or Hamilton (we are not sure which) wrote to justify the proposal for a Senate:

> As the cool and deliberate sense of the community ought, in all governments, and actually will, in all free governments, ultimately prevail over the views of its rulers; so there are particular moments in public affairs when the people, stimulated by some irregular passion, or some illicit advantage, or misled by the artful misrepresentations of interested men, may call for measures which they themselves will afterwards be the most ready to lament and condemn. In these critical moments, how salutary will be the interference of some temperate and respectable body of citizens, in order to check the misguided career, and to suspend the blow meditated by the people against themselves, until reason, justice, and truth can regain their authority over the public mind?

Thus, the author argued that while the "cool and deliberate sense of the community" should prevail in the long run, in the short run the people sometimes need to be protected from themselves. The Senate is buffered from rapid changes in public opinion because senators are elected to six-year terms, and only about one-third of senators are chosen in any one election. Originally—and in many states until the ratification of the 17th Amendment in 1913—senators were elected by members of state legislatures rather than directly by citizens, providing another buffer against changes in public opinion. (In fact, these indirect elections are a buffer against even *stable* public opinion, although the framers argued that ultimately the state legislatures would surely be consonant with the public's desires.)[5]

While the United States' representative scheme was said to protect the public against its own worst impulses, it had a more positive purpose:

to facilitate *deliberation* on policy decisions. Members of Congress do not simply vote bills up or down; they are supposed to learn about public issues, weigh the possible consequences of various policies, and finally approve the policies that seem best to them on balance. The U.S. Congress certainly does not always live up to this idealized goal,[6] yet deliberation is a crucial purpose of the institution. The six-year terms of senators, and the two-year terms of representatives in the House—twice as long as most state legislators' terms—were intended in part to give members time to learn what they needed to know in order to deliberate wisely. As the U.S. government has grown more complicated, Congress has developed an elaborate system of committees and subcommittees to help it handle issues.

To many political philosophers throughout history, the idea of public-spirited *nonelected* experts has had even more appeal than representative democracy. One famous example is Plato's concept of the "philosopher-king"—although, at first glance, it may not be obvious why a philosopher-king is any kind of expert. In book 6 of the *Republic*, Plato recommends that the state should only be entrusted to the sort of person "who has the gift of a good memory, and is quick to learn—noble, gracious, the friend of truth, justice, courage, temperance. . . ." Plato's ideal ruler thus combines expert knowledge and intelligence with a range of noble virtues. Nowadays, our image of an expert tends to emphasize knowledge rather than nobility—but, to the (varying) extent that we trust experts to make good decisions about policy, we must trust them to act selflessly in the service of a greater good. During the Progressive era of the early twentieth century, many observers argued for a greater policymaking role for experts. Walter Lippmann, in his 1922 book *Public Opinion,* argued that representative government can only work well if there is "an independent, expert organization for making the unseen facts intelligible to those who have to make the decisions."[7] From here it is a small step to giving experts considerable discretion to make the decisions themselves.

The U.S. government has always incorporated some aspects of expert power insulated from public pressure. We have already discussed the indirect election of presidents and senators, and the rationale for extending (in particular) senators' terms to allow them to develop expertise. Members of the federal judiciary—Supreme Court justices and federal judges—are more dramatically insulated from public pressure. Once nominated by the president and ratified by the Senate, they serve for life unless Congress votes to impeach them and remove them from office. One rationale for lifetime judicial service is positive: What job in government requires more expertise than mastering constitutional law? Another is negative: Who needs more protection from public opinion than people who are entrusted with judging justly, without fear or favor? The Federal Reserve, which controls important aspects of the U.S. money supply, is a striking example of a major policymaking institution that is deliberately buffered from direct public pressure. (The chairman of the Federal Reserve is chosen by the president and serves a seven-year term.) The federal government depends on the expertise of many civil service employees who are hired, at least in principle, on the basis of ability and usually keep their jobs indefinitely.

While almost everyone concedes that direct democracy is unfeasible, and that dictatorship is indefensible, observers vary in their degree of comfort with representative democracy and expert rule. For some, the public seems to act most often as a barrier to responsible policymaking, and/or as a spur to truly bad decisions. (Remember the Acheson quotation with which we began.) Others place more emphasis on the flaws of the elected officials and experts. These policymakers differ from most citizens in several ways, not all of which lend themselves to the interests of the public at large. They tend to be highly educated and relatively prosperous (many members of Congress are lawyers), interested in public policy, and—for better or worse—intent on increasing their own power to influence that policy. As federal employees, they enjoy certain benefits that many U.S. citizens do not, such as excellent health insurance. Even when these people have the best interests of the broader public at heart, critics say, their life experience may shelter them from understanding the public's deepest needs.[8] President George H. W. Bush's 1992 reelection campaign was undermined when the *New York Times* (misleadingly) reported that he had been "amazed" by the sight of a supermarket price scanner—which was widely cited as a metaphor for Bush's isolation from most people's lives and problems. The widespread public suspicion that elected officials are "out of touch with" their constituents helps to explain why candidates so often tell stories of how they worked their way up from poverty—or, failing that, how their parents or grandparents did. (Civil servants and other "bureaucrats" rarely get to plead their connections with The People.) Many observers simply do not believe that elected officials have the public interest in mind.

Notice that there is no real contradiction between believing that the public cannot be trusted with much policymaking influence, and believing that government officials (elected or unelected) cannot be trusted either. As Madison famously put it in the *Federalist* #51, "If men [*sic*] were angels, no government would be necessary. If angels were to govern men, neither external nor internal controls on government would be necessary. In framing a government which is to be administered by men over men, the great difficulty lies in this: you must first enable the government to control the governed; and in the next place oblige it to control itself." Luckily for us, this is a book about public opinion, not a treatise on how to create the perfect governmental system (which we doubt exists). So the questions facing us are a bit more tractable, although we believe still rather complex, interesting, and important. Many of these questions, as should be clear by now, hinge on the public's democratic competence—whether the citizenry's complement of knowledge, beliefs, and values lends itself to relatively positive influences on policy.

In the end, our evaluations of democratic competence will shape our preferences about the public role in political decisionmaking. At this time in the United States, there is little debate about the public's *formal* role, which is primarily to vote for candidates at various levels of government. Walter Lippmann wrote in 1925 that "to support the Ins when things are going well; to support the Outs when they seem to be going badly, this . . . is the essence of popular government." Lippmann probably believed that voting for the Ins or the Outs was the most that the public can be expected or hoped to do well.[9] (Some doubt that the public can do even this much.) Voters sometimes can vote directly on proposed state or local laws, through initiative and referendum processes that allow citizens or legislatures to place these proposals on the ballot. Some observers would like to increase these possibilities, while others would like to limit them. But more debate concerns the public's *informal* role: the ways in which policymakers' perceptions of public opinion influence their decisions. Should policymakers do their best to ignore public opinion? Or should they pay careful attention to public opinion, or public opinion of a certain kind?

THE PUBLIC'S LOW LEVEL OF POLITICAL KNOWL-
EDGE: A PROBLEM?

One suspicion that haunts many political observers is that most Americans simply know very little about politics in general—far too little for their thinking (such as it is) about political issues to be other than profoundly misguided. The first part of this suspicion is, more or less, clearly true. Back in Chapter 1, Box 1.4 illustrated some contemporary areas of ignorance. Table 8.1 goes further, showing that political knowledge has not grown since the 1940s, even as the average level of schooling in the United States has increased.[10]

As Table 8.1 shows, not even half of survey respondents could correctly provide the name of their congressional representatives, a percentage that has actually declined since 1973. Further, strikingly few knew in 1964 that the former Soviet Union was not a member of NATO—which was essentially an anti-Soviet alliance. Americans do better on some of the simplest facts, such as the length of the president's term, and on certain "current events" questions. Still, overall, the data suggest massive public ignorance.

However, "the facts" here may not be as discouraging as they seem at first. Many analysts argue that these questions amount to trivia quizzes that test people's recall of numbers and names, removed from any political context. In practice, it is more important for people to recognize or find relevant names and facts when they need them, such as before elections or at the ballot box, or when an issue is actually most prominent in the news. If people showed little ability to learn about an issue as it became more salient, that would be discouraging indeed.

Table 8.2 offers reassuring evidence that the public can learn. When the mass media give extended attention to an issue, people learn more about it. Specifically, over time, more Americans learned which side the United States backed in the Nicaraguan struggle between the leftist Sandinista government and the rebel contras (probably even more Americans would have answered correctly if the term "contras" had been used in the question).[11] Nevertheless, barely more than one-half the respondents answered even this question correctly—and some of the right answers must have been lucky guesses. Surely, few Americans ever knew enough about Nicaragua to form what experts would deem "considered opinions" about policy.

TABLE 8.1 Political Information Among American Adults

Topic (in order of most recent % correct)	Year	Percentage	Survey Organization
know the length of the president's term	1989	96	SRLVCU
	1947	92	Gallup
know meaning of "veto" (presidential)	1989	89	SRLVCU
	1947	77	Gallup
identified governor of home state	1989	74	SRLVCU
	1973	89	Harris
	1945	79	Gallup
know that there are two senators from each state	2001	60	Gallup
	1978	52	NORC
know what a business (economic) recession is	1989	57	SRLVCU
	1947	51	Gallup
know which party has more members in U.S. House of Representatives	2000	55	NES
	1989	68	SRLVCU
	1947	63	Gallup
have heard or read of NATO and know that Russia is not a member	1964	38	Gallup
know that a 2/3 majority is required for the U.S. Senate and House to override a presidential veto	2002	32	CIRCLE
	1947	44	Gallup
know that the term of a U.S. House member is two years	1978	30	NORC
	1946	47	Gallup
identified both U.S. senators of home state	2000	19	Saguaro
	1989	25	SRLVCU
	1945	35	Gallup
identified U.S. congressman from home district	1989	29	SRLVCU
	1973	46	Harris

KEY: NORC: National Opinion Research Center. SRLVCU: Survey Research Laboratory, Virginia Commonwealth University. Saguaro: Saguaro Seminar at JFK School of Government, Harvard University. CIRCLE: Center for Information and Research on Civic Learning and Engagement. NES: National Election Study.

SOURCE: Based on Benjamin I. Page and Robert Y. Shapiro, *The Rational Public: Fifty Years of Trends in Americans' Policy Preferences* (Chicago: University of Chicago Press, 1992), pp. 10–11.

We also have evidence that the public can "unlearn": Knowledge levels can go down as well as up. For instance, in surveys during the 2000 presidential campaign, the Vanishing Voter Project found that respondents knew less about the issue positions of the major candidates, George W. Bush and Al Gore, in April than they had in February.[12] Scott Althaus demonstrates that respondents are more likely to know which party controls each branch

TABLE 8.2   Change over Time in Public Knowledge: The Nicaraguan Conflict, 1983–1987 (in percent)

	7/83	11/83	3/85	6/85	3/86	5/87	8/87
Rebels	29	26	37	46	59	52	54
Government	24	24	23	20	13	21	20
Neither	1	<1	1	1	1	1	1
No opinion	47	50	39	34	27	26	24

SOURCE: Page and Shapiro (see Table 1), p. 13; from data in Richard Sobel, "The polls—A report: Public opinion about United States intervention in El Salvador and Nicaragua," *Public Opinion Quarterly* 53:114–128, at 120. ABC News/*Washington Post* surveys. Question: "Do you happen to know which side the U.S. is backing in Nicaragua, the rebels or the government?" Sample size ranges from 1148 to 1509.

of Congress, and to recognize the names of political leaders, in presidential election years than in other election years—which implies that (at least some) Americans go through cycles of learning and forgetting.[13]

Even the most optimistic analysts of public opinion concede that people's general indifference to the details of politics limits their ability to participate usefully in the political process. It is hard to take comfort in the argument that it is "rational" for people to be ignorant about politics, a subject we will return to later. True, for most people, tending to family, work, and personal life has greater and more immediate payoffs than studying political issues. Yet if almost everyone ignores politics, how can the public possibly form sensible policy preferences, much less make sure the government follows these preferences?

Part of the answer, some believe, is that the public performs better as a whole—collectively—than most individual citizens do. One reason is that citizens adopt a tacit division of labor. Not only do some know more about politics than others, but different issues engage different people. A multiplicity of "issue publics" exists, each one consisting of people who follow a particular issue. Moreover, as we see in Table 8.2, issue publics can grow; more people can learn about an issue as it becomes (or remains) prominent.

Before we leave this topic, notice that the suspicious observers we mentioned at the beginning of the section have made a leap in reasoning: that if citizens are generally ignorant of politics, then their thinking about political issues will be misguided. This argument begs the question, how *do* citizens "think" about issues they know almost nothing about? This question turns out to be crucial to survey research and many other forms of public opinion research. The answer, of course, depends on the issue and the setting. But we think that people's relatively ignorant opinions at least make more sense than you might expect, and throughout this chapter we will give some reasons why people seem to be capable of making something out of almost nothing.

HOW DO PEOPLE VOTE?
THE EARLY COLUMBIA AND MICHIGAN MODELS

As we have seen, representative democracy rests on the ability of citizens collectively to choose—to elect—officials who will generally pursue the public interest, as opposed to their own. (Despite disagreement on what counts as the public interest, most people surely agree that it is something other than merely what enriches the officials themselves!) Given the centrality of elections, arguably the most important aspect of citizens' political thinking is how they decide who to vote for, or whether to vote at all. A great deal of public opinion research has focused on explaining people's voting decisions. Not only do many academics want to know how people decide whom to vote for, but of course many political actors do as well.

There are many theories of voting, but many can be traced back to two contrasting models that were developed in the early years of the modern polling era. Between 1940 and the mid-1960s, two university-based institutions, the Bureau of Applied Social Research at Columbia University and the Survey Research Center at the University of Michigan, developed what came to be called the "Columbia model" and the "Michigan model." The Columbia approach focused on *sociological* processes: how people's social environments and relationships influenced their votes. The Michigan model placed more emphasis on *psychological* variables: how people thought about the parties, candidates, and issues and how these factors influenced their votes. The models had more in common than these descriptions suggest, but the differences were real, and they inspired very different research strategies.

The Columbia model emphasized the influence of social groups and relationships on voting decisions. Paul Lazarsfeld and his colleagues conducted a pathbreaking study of Erie County, Ohio, during the 1940 presidential campaign.[14] Remarkably, as part of the study, they interviewed almost 600 respondents *seven* times from May through November, in order to trace changing opinions. (Most surveys interview respondents only once or, at most, twice.) They learned, first, that very few people—about 12 percent—changed their voting intentions from one candidate to the other at any time in the campaign, and about one-third of those

changed back by election day. Thus, the campaign did not win many con-
verts, although it apparently did get many people to "pay attention" and
eventually to vote. Many more voters moved from "don't know" to a candidate (28 percent) or from a candidate to "don't know" and then back to
the same candidate (11 percent). Thus, a small majority of voters did
change preferences at some point in the campaign.[15]

The direction of these changes was fairly predictable, at least in retrospect. People usually ended up voting as most people of their social class,
religion, and place of residence (urban or rural) did. Upper-class rural
Protestants were very likely to vote Republican, and lower-class urban
Catholics to vote Democratic. The Columbia scholars attributed these
patterns to how people's closest relationships—with family and friends,
coworkers, fellow churchgoers, and so on—affected their political views.
The intensive interview format allowed the scholars to trace, to some extent, how these influences actually worked. Some people tended to be
"opinion leaders"—highly interested in politics, usually with a distinctly
partisan outlook that colored their reactions to events. By discussing politics with opinion leaders in the same social setting, for example, Aunt
Mary or Steve at the mill, other people tended to adopt the same partisan line. (This tendency presumably comes, at least in part, from
processes we described in Chapter Five as enforcing social norms.) Of
course, some social settings were more diverse than others, and some people received mixed or opposing signals, or "cross-pressures," that might
lead them to delay voting decisions or to skip voting entirely. But most
people in the end turned in the direction of most of their social cohort.

To illustrate the power of social influences, the Columbia scholars
combined their three key social variables (class, religion, and urban/
rural residence) into a seven-point index of political predisposition
(IPP). The IPP was a very strong predictor of people's votes, as you can
see in Figure 8.1. Lazarsfeld and his associates summed up this way: "A
person thinks, politically, as he is, socially. Social characteristics determine political preferences."[16]

No one completely believed this statement, not even Lazarsfeld. First,
it said little about the processes of social *persuasion* that Lazarsfeld was
especially interested in. (As a later work put the point, uncertain voters
"turn to their social environment for guidance, and that environment
tends to support the party that is 'right' for them also.")[17] Unfortunately,
researchers usually cannot observe these processes directly: They cannot,

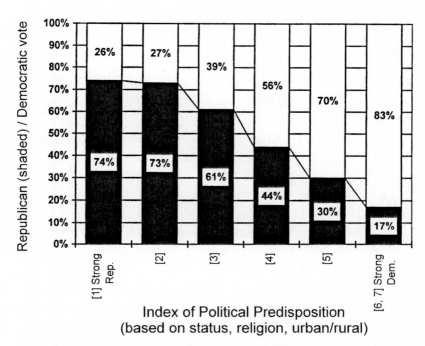

FIGURE 8.1   Index of Political Predisposition and Presidential Vote, 1940 (Erie County, Ohio). SOURCE: Paul Felix Lazarsfeld, *The People's Choice* (New York: Columbia University Press, 1968), p. 26. Copyright 1968 by Columbia University Press. Used by permission of the publisher.

Note: To calculate people's "index of political predisposition" (IPP), first each respondent's socioeconomic status was rated on a four-point scale from 1 for the highest to 4 for the lowest. Then two points were added for Catholics (versus Protestants) and one point was added for urban (versus rural) dwellers. Thus, the IPP rated from 1 to 7, with higher scorers more likely to vote Democratic.

for instance, tape-record every conversation people have during an election campaign, much less determine which of these conversations had the largest influence on people's final opinions and votes. Second, the Columbia model could not really explain how the political preferences of social groups might vary over time or in different places. Ironically, the IPP tended to direct attention away from the rich dynamics of opinion leadership—the heart of the Columbia theory—and toward the results of one election in one county. The index could not explain fluctuations between elections, much less longer-term trends such as the defection of blacks from the Republican to the Democratic Party after 1930. Thus, critics could say that the model neither explained nor predicted very well.

The Michigan school sidestepped these problems by combining two models: a powerful predictive model that arguably explained little completely or persuasively, and a complicated causal model—the "funnel of causality"—that claimed to explain just about everything. (The first comprehensive statement of the Michigan school, *The American Voter*, was over 500 pages long.)[18]

The predictive model emphasized three variables, the most important among them being party identification. Party identification (usually called "party ID" for short) is the attitude of considering oneself a Republican, Democrat, or whatever—party attachment—as opposed to being an official party member or even voting for the party's candidates. Ever since 1952, the Survey Research Center's National Election Studies (NES) have measured party identification by asking, "Generally speaking, do you usually think of yourself as a Republican, a Democrat, an Independent, or what?" Follow-up questions pin down Republicans and Democrats as "strong" or "weak" and classify independents as leaning toward one party, the other, or neither. Self-identified Democrats and Republicans, as you would expect, are very likely to vote for candidates of their favored party. In part, to use a term we introduced in Chapter Four, party ID functions as a *heuristic*, a shortcut for deciding how to vote: just vote for the candidate of your party! People's party identification is relatively stable over time, compared to their stated issue positions. In fact, in the 1992 NES, about 70 percent of people identified with or leaned toward the same party that their *parents* did.[19] One could almost say that most people's votes are determined at whatever age they internalize their parents' political views.

Party identification predicts individuals' votes better than social characteristics do—but it cannot predict or explain differences between elections. To overcome this weakness, the Michigan model also considers people's issue opinions and their images of the candidates. Of course, party identification tends to influence both these areas. As you would expect from the discussion of consistency theories in Chapter Four (and of projection effects in Chapter Six), strong partisans tend to perceive that they agree with the candidate of their party on the issues, even if they don't. Partisans also will tend to like their own party's candidates, accept positive messages about these candidates and reject negative ones—and, conversely, to think the worst of candidates of other parties.[20] Still, issues and candidates do matter in themselves, even for strong partisans, and especially for independents or weaker partisans. In 1980, 35 percent of "weak Democrats" voted for the Republican challenger, Ronald Reagan, whereas only 5 percent of "weak Republicans" voted for the Democratic incumbent, Jimmy Carter; independents favored Reagan by more than two to one.[21] Here, broad unhappiness with Carter probably accounted for much of the difference.

A model based on party ID, candidates, and issues can easily be applied to any presidential election, making better vote predictions across more places and times than the Columbia model. (Figure 8.2 shows some results from a party–candidate–issue model for the 2000 presidential election.) However, it seems to explain little beyond the obvious. People tend to vote for people they like, with positions they like, from the party they like—and party matters most. These facts are important, and maybe even reassuring ("issues" do seem to matter), but they do not seem to explain political *change* any better than the Columbia model does.

To give their analysis explanatory power, the Michigan scholars proposed their complex "funnel of causality," which incorporated a wide range of variables (see Figure 8.3). The funnel began, at the wide end, with the social sources of political cleavages, such as the conflict between North and South. These sources were often rooted in events older than the respondents and did not directly influence people's political beliefs. Yet they profoundly influenced the basic values and group loyalties that people formed in childhood and generally held all their lives. These early-formed attitudes in turn influenced people's party ID; party ID influenced people's views of the issues and the candidates—the factors nearest the "tip of the funnel," where people actually decided how to vote. Major events, election-year economic and social conditions, media coverage, campaign activities, and the opinions of friends (among other things) could also affect people's partisanship and views of the candidates and issues. Just about everything fit into the model—although, in practice, it was almost impossible to juggle all the pieces at once. Few, if any, scholars ever tried to "test" the funnel theory as a whole. Instead, many studies investigated how party ID, issue opinions, and candidate ratings influenced each other and voting decisions. Scholars recognized that how party ID changed over time might matter even more. But it would take many years of data collection to learn much about that.

Arguably, the Columbia and Michigan schools did not really disagree on much. What really set the Columbia school apart was its interest in how social relationships—with family, friends, coworkers, and other acquaintances—influenced people's attitudes. Lazarsfeld and his colleagues explored social influences by asking many people, in a limited geographic

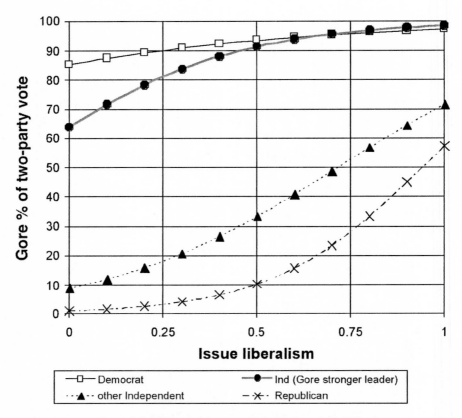

FIGURE 8.2   Party, Candidates, and Issues in the 1992 Presidential Election
The graph depicts how the 2000 presidential election was affected by voters' party
identification, candidate evaluation, and issue positions.* Most Democrats voted for
the Democratic nominee, Al Gore; most Republicans voted for the Republican
nominee, George Bush, who won the election despite receiving about 500,000 fewer
votes overall. However, some of the least issue-liberal Democrats—and many of the
(relatively rare) most liberal Republicans—voted for the other party's candidate.
Among independents, those who gave Gore a higher rating for "provid[ing] strong
leadership" were very likely to vote for Gore. Independents who gave Bush equal or
better marks for leadership were more likely to vote for Bush, but issue positions were
especially important among this group.

---

*Using 2000 NES data, five issue positions—support for government spending and services, whether
the government should guarantee jobs and standard of living, whether the government should
provide health insurance, how much the government should do to help blacks, and when abortion
should be legal—are combined to form a 0-1 scale of issue liberalism (the average score is 0.5). The
results in the graph are smoothed by calculating separate logistic regressions for each of the four
categories. (Note that votes for Ralph Nader and other candidates are excluded.) Many other
measures of candidate evaluation could be used, but the question about leadership turns out to be an
especially strong predictor in 2000.

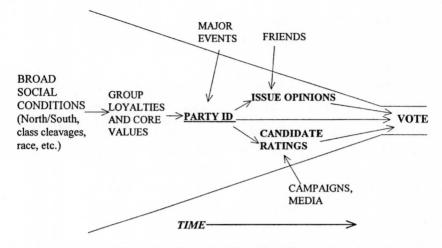

FIGURE 8.3   A Sketch of the "Funnel of Causality." SOURCE: Based on Russell J. Dalton, *Citizen Politics in Western Democracies,* 1st ed. (Chatham, NJ: Chatham House Publishers, 1988), p. 178.

Note: Many possible relationships are not shown.

area, detailed questions about their conversations with other people. (This tradition is carried on, for instance, in the research of Robert Huckfeldt and John Sprague.)[22] The Michigan scholars preferred to conduct national surveys that gathered valuable data about how people all around the country thought about politics but revealed less about the social processes that influenced people's thinking.

What did all this voter research imply for democratic competence? There is no simple answer. At first glance, the Columbia model seems to offer the bleaker view: People apparently cast their votes by following, lemminglike, the people around them. However, as Walter Lippmann noted, of course people tend to rely on the judgments of people around them: "Complete independence in the universe is simply unthinkable."[23] Moreover, people in similar settings often have the same interests at stake in an election, so voting alike—however they manage to do it—may evince good sense, not blind followership. (We hope to have convinced you in earlier chapters that social judgments and dynamics are not always bad.) The Michigan model allowed for great individuality. Its voters could form their party identifications, opinion stances, and candidate evaluations through highly sophisticated processes. But these voters could just as well be mindless machines, parroting their parents' party affiliations, their friends' opinions, and their newspapers' candidate endorsements. Although no one said that "the American voter" was mindless, the anecdotes suggested that the voter might not be thinking very hard.

RATIONAL IGNORANCE, IDEOLOGICAL INNOCENCE, AND NONATTITUDES

The suspicion that voters might not think very hard was buttressed by Anthony Downs' account in *An Economic Theory of Democracy* (1957) of "rational ignorance." Downs' economic "rational choice" approach, which we introduced in Chapter Seven, offers a rough-and-ready cost–benefit analysis of how prospective voters (and political parties) ought to behave. For citizens, Downs notes, the tangible benefit of voting is tiny, because each citizen has almost no chance of affecting the election outcome.[24] Probably most citizens who vote also derive some intangible benefit from voting, because they feel that they have fulfilled their civic duty. Against these small benefits, citizens must weigh not only the immediate costs of voting (such as the time spent going to the polls and waiting in line) but also the costs of gathering enough information to decide how to vote. *Even if* individual votes mattered a great deal, voters would want just enough information to decide which candidate would probably "pay off" best for them. But when thousands or millions of people are voting, each voter can easily afford to be wrong about which candidate best serves their interests. Therefore, no rational voter will seek out information on candidates and issues. It might sound like good citizenship, but it is a bad investment (unless it simply gives the voter personal satisfaction).

We find that many readers resist the force of the rational ignorance argument altogether, because it seems so obviously wrongheaded. Surely if most voters are wrong about which candidate is better, they will all end up worse off! But an individual voter cannot determine what "most voters" do, only his or her own actions; and if a well-informed vote is as unlikely to influence the outcome as a poorly informed vote, then there is simply no value in being well-informed. The idea of rational ignorance was not new: Tocqueville, for one, had anticipated it in his observation that "the people never can find time or means" to evaluate candidates accurately.[25] But with Downs' elegant formalization, rational ignorance appeared as the skeleton at the democratic banquet.

Rational ignorance certainly seems to explain the public's relative lack of political knowledge; just how far does it undermine democratic competence? For people to vote wisely, perhaps they do not need much "quiz-show knowledge" (like the sort in Box 1.4 or Table 8.1), but surely they should know something more than their (or their parents') party ID. Political *ideology*—liberalism, conservatism, and so forth—could plausibly be the thread connecting many people's issue stands, party ID, candidate evaluations, and votes. The most common model of U.S. ideology is a simple "spectrum," with liberals on the left and conservatives on the right. Liberals tend to support (among other things) government spending on social problems, gun control laws, and abortion rights; conservatives tend to oppose these. Conservatives tend to be more supportive of military spending, capital punishment, other policies seen as tough on crime, and prayer in the schools than liberals are. There is no logical reason that these issue positions must go together; indeed, many people stake out what they regard as more philosophically consistent positions that straddle "left" and "right."[26] Nevertheless, if a politician is described as, say, "ultraliberal" or "right-wing," any politically knowledgeable observer can make good guesses about the politician's views on many issues. To anticipate language we will use later in the chapter, ideology is one simplifying *heuristic,* or shortcut, that can help people to make good judgments based on limited information. Journalists routinely characterize politicians in terms of this liberal–conservative continuum. Do most Americans also make use of this ideological approach?

In *The American Voter,* the Michigan scholars concluded that very few Americans used ideology to judge political parties and candidates. Respondents in the 1952 National Election Study were asked to list things that they liked and disliked about the parties and presidential candidates. The researchers used these "open-ended" responses to assign people to *levels of conceptualization,* or what we might call levels of political sophistication (see Table 8.3).[27] According to the analysts, ideology mattered to only 11.5 percent of the respondents; of those, only 2.5 percent were "ideologues" who used abstract concepts such as liberalism to evaluate the parties and candidates; and the remaining 9 percent, dubbed "near ideologues," used abstract concepts, but in vague or inaccurate ways. The largest group, 42 percent, appealed to tangible group benefits (e.g., "the Democrats are for the common man"). Of the rest, 24 percent appealed to the "nature of the times": For instance, they credited or blamed President Eisenhower, who was seeking reelection, for the state of the national economy. The remaining 22.5 percent of the population could offer no

TABLE 8.3   Levels of Conceptualization, 1956

Category	Examples (excerpts)	Proportion of Sample
A. Ideology	"I think [the Democrats] are . . . a more liberal party, and I think of the Republicans as being more conservative and interested in big business" (p. 229).	11.5%
B. Group benefits	"I've just always before been a Democrat. . . . I just don't believe [the Republicans] are for the common people" (p. 238).	42.0%
C. Nature of the times	"[My husband's] stocks are up. They go up when the Republicans are in" (p. 243).	24.0%
D. No issue content	"I'm a Democrat. *(Is there anything you like about the Democratic Party?)* I don't know" (p. 247). "Parties are all about the same to me. . . . I really don't care which man is best or otherwise" (p. 249).	22.5%

SOURCE: Adapted from A. Campbell, P. Converse, W. E. Miller, and D. E. Stokes, *The American Voter*, unabridged ed. (New York: John Wiley, 1960).

issue content at all. Critics pointed out that judging Eisenhower on his economic performance or attentiveness to group interests might be at least as sensible as trying to judge his (notoriously vague) ideology. Still, the failure of the vast majority even to mention ideological principles raised doubts about their grasp of political issues—at least in the terms that political leaders and journalists grasp these issues.

Philip Converse, building upon his collaboration in *The American Voter*, argued that "ideological innocence" was widespread among the American public—and, even more disturbing, that most people had hardly any real opinions on many political issues. Converse's 1964 article "The Nature of Belief Systems in Mass Publics"[28] introduced the concept of *ideological constraint,* or the degree of consistency among a person's beliefs. The "ultraliberal" and "right-wing" politicians we described a few pages ago evince high constraint: Their beliefs across a wide range of issues are highly predictable. Converse argued that mass public opinion (i.e., most people's thinking) showed very little constraint: Many people seem unaware of what issues "go together." Mass belief systems tended to be disorganized and tended not to depend on "abstract, 'ideological' principles." People more often built their political beliefs—such as they were—around charismatic leaders, family life, and other concrete objects.

To illustrate this disregard for ideology, Converse closely analyzed in-depth interviews in which respondents were asked, "What do the terms liberal and conservative mean to you?" Fully 37 percent of the respondents could not name any difference between "liberal" and "conservative" and, beyond that, only about one-half gave answers that Converse judged even roughly correct. Only 17 percent demonstrated a "broad understanding" of the terms, by what Converse considered quite generous criteria. Subsequent analysts have enjoyed quoting examples of unsophisticated responses to the question noted above—and these are far from the weakest answers:

> Not too much really. For some reason conservative gets identified with the South—identified with drabby looking clothes vs. more something I would wear, drabby clothes, too, but it is just a different type.

> Oh, conservative. Liberal and conservative. Liberal and conservative. I haven't given it much thought. I wouldn't know. I don't know what those words mean! Liberal . . . liberal . . . liberal . . . liberal. And conservative. Well, if a person is liberal with their money they squander their money? Does it fall into that same category?[29]

Some analysts have argued that citizens may not use a liberal–conservative continuum to structure their own beliefs but nonetheless have some understanding of what these terms mean for political leaders. For instance, two-thirds of the 1988 NES respondents responded that they have something in mind when they hear that someone's political views are liberal or conservative.[30] Over one-half (54 percent) of respondents were able to locate both 1988 presidential candidates (George H. W. Bush and Michael Dukakis) on a seven-point ideology scale and to locate Dukakis to the left of Bush. (It is hard to say whether 54 percent is a "good" figure, but at least it is better than 2.5 percent!) We noted earlier that many citizens may not spontaneously remember the names of political leaders or other political facts but can easily be reminded of these facts. Likewise, it appears that many citizens do not spontaneously use the "liberal" and "conservative" categories often used by political elites, but nonetheless they can at least partly understand political debates that use these terms.

But might people have highly organized, constrained belief systems without being able to explain them in terms of "liberal" and "conservative"? Logically, people might—but Converse presented two lines of evidence that most people did not. First, he compared the opinions of an "elite" group of congressional candidates and a mass sample from the 1958 NES survey. Converse found many pairs of issues for which candidates' views on one issue powerfully predicted their views on the other—apparent evidence of ideological constraint among this elite sample. For the NES respondents, the relationships across issues were generally much weaker. This result implied that most people's issue opinions, unlike the candidates', were not well anchored in broader belief systems. If these opinions depended neither on factual knowledge nor on belief systems, perhaps they were no more than whims that people might change at the slightest pretext. Worse, perhaps people made up these "opinions" on the spot when asked, in which case they could hardly be called opinions at all.

Converse pointed to evidence that people's policy opinions—if they merited that name—were in fact remarkably unstable. Converse examined an NES "panel" in which a group of potential voters were asked the same questions (among many others) in 1956, 1958, and 1960. He found that on each issue, so many people's responses changed from one survey to the next that many respondents seemed to be answering at random. Especially discouraging was the pattern of change over time. For instance, on one question about job guarantees, about 40 percent of respondents changed their basic response (support, opposition, or "not sure") from 1956 to 1958. Suppose that most of these people had really changed their political opinions in this time. Even more people would change their views from 1958 to 1960 (and perhaps some people would return to their 1956 position). Overall, we should find that from 1956 to 1960, considerably more than 40 percent of respondents changed their position on job guarantees. But in fact, only about 42 percent did. It looked as if many, even most, of the people who changed *answers* over time might not really have changed *opinions*.

Converse suggested a simple explanation: A small number of people—around 20 percent—answered the question identically each time, while the vast majority answered pretty much *at random*. This "black and white" model of sages and fools did not fit the data perfectly (although for some questions it came very close) and could not be literally true. Nevertheless, Converse was convinced that many, indeed most, respondents were answering the questions essentially at random. They could not consult their considered opinions on, for instance, whether "the government should leave things like electric power and housing for private businessmen to handle," because they had never formed any opinions. As Converse summed up his argument: People's policy attitudes were in fact largely *nonattitudes*.[31]

The proposition of "nonattitudes" posed a challenge not only to democratic competence, but to public opinion analysis itself. If people had no real opinions, why attempt to study them? And how could government be accountable to public opinion if public opinion did not exist? Today, many, if not most, analysts find Converse's emphasis on nonattitudes overdrawn. They see more stability and coherence of various sorts in public responses across issues and over time. Nonetheless, Converse's 1964 essay (which we have only skimmed through here) remains persuasive and compelling on many points. Any account of people's political opinions must reckon with Converse—and with the Downsian logic of "rational ignorance" that helps us make sense of Converse.

COLLECTIVE DELIBERATION: THE RATIONAL PUBLIC?

It is useful to understand how people's beliefs differ systematically among various dimensions, as in the typologies described earlier. However, if we are asking whether government policy is—or should be—responsive to overall public preferences, then typologies are somewhat beside the point. The more urgent question is whether the public as a whole (or majorities of the public) distinctly agrees on specific political positions that could guide policy. Opinion surveys are the most prominent way of trying to identify public policy preferences, although certainly not the only way (see especially Chapter Three, and the discussion of deliberation at the end of this chapter). But are citizens competent to guide policy? And do opinion surveys reveal which policies citizens would support if they participated directly in politics?

Benjamin Page and Robert Shapiro strongly affirm that citizens can and should steer policy—and, implicitly, that surveys are useful to identify public preferences. They argue that "the American public, as a collective body, does seem to have a coherent set of policy preferences that fit with people's basic values and that respond to changing realities and changing information. Lacking a supply of philosopher kings or a reliable means of identifying them, it is not easy to find a better source of guidance on what a government should do than the preferences of its citizenry."[32]

Page and Shapiro draw on the aggregate opinion of many people, expressed in many surveys over time, as opposed to individual responses. They find, first of all, that aggregate public opinion is generally stable. That is, if a question about policy preferences is asked repeatedly over several years' time, overall opinion is unlikely to bounce around sharply and unpredictably. This typical stability in aggregate public opinion comes as a surprise to many observers who expect to find that public opinion is *volatile*–continually changing for no good reason. You might think that if individuals mostly respond at random to survey questions, then overall opinion should change at random too. Indeed it might, but only very slightly. (For instance, suppose that *everyone* answers a particular question by flipping a coin. Individual responses will be completely random and unpredictable—but the overall split will always be about 50–50, give or take a few percentage points.) So, by itself, the finding that overall opinion is usually stable doesn't tell us much about its rationality. Actually, if overall opinion were perfectly stable, that would imply that people were paying no attention to new events and information that might be expected to change their minds.

In fact, Page and Shapiro's trend data do show that public opinion sometimes "moves." Page and Shapiro argue that these moves seem to happen for identifiable, and usually sensible, reasons. For instance, during the Cold War, when people expressed greater or lesser fear of the Soviet Union, they were apparently responding to new information about Soviet power and intentions. (Sometimes the new information may have been wrong, but that was not the public's fault.) Moreover, Page and Shapiro observe that various demographic groups usually respond similarly—as "parallel publics"—to changing circumstances. This parallel movement suggests that members of these various groups are interpreting new information in the same way (on average), using common standards of judgment. Much of this new information is transmitted by the mass media, but some of it amounts to people's personal experience of a changing society. For instance, the spread of "feminist" attitudes can be seen as

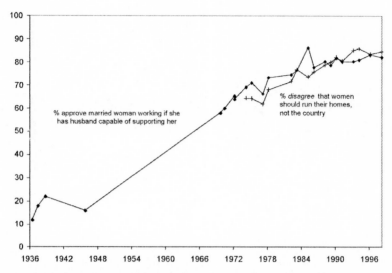

FIGURE 8.4   Women Working Outside the Home, 1936–1998
QUESTION (Gallup, NORC-General Social Survey): "Do you approve or
disapprove of a married woman earning money in business or industry if she
has a husband capable of supporting her?" or "Do you approve of . . . ."
Survey dates: (Gallup) 6/37, 10/38, 9/69, 6/70, 9/75; (NORC) 3/72–3/98.
QUESTION (NORC-General Social Survey): "Do you agree or disagree with
this statement: Women should take care of running their homes and leave
running the country up to men?" Survey date: 3/74–3/98.

a response to decreasing birth rates and increasing numbers of working
women—as well as, perhaps, encouraging these trends. Page and Shapiro
argue that survey trends reveal a *rational public* that responds to new evidence in reasonable ways.[33]

Figures 8.4 through 8.6 illustrate the rational public at work. Figure
8.4,[34] which bears on the role of women, shows the largest opinion change
that Page and Shapiro found—about a 70-percentage-point increase in
public support for allowing a married woman to work if she has a husband
to support her. It may be hard nowadays to imagine this as a burning policy issue, but in the economic depression days of the 1930s, Illinois and
Massachusetts considered laws that would ban most married women from
working.[35] Judging from the polls, such laws would have been fairly popular! The enormous change in opinion from 1936 to 1998 can readily be
explained by changes in the lives and roles of women. While people's
views on these questions may not be entirely considered, some aspect of

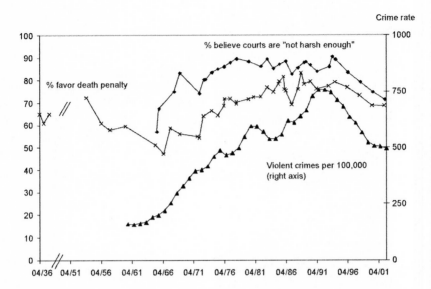

FIGURE 8.5   Capital Punishment and Courts' Treatment of Criminals, 1936–2002
QUESTION (Gallup, NORC-General Social Survey): "Are you in favor of the
death penalty for persons convicted of murder?" Variant question in 1936 and
1937: ". . . death penalty for murder?" Survey dates: (Gallup) 4/36, 12/36, 11/37,
11/53, 3–4/56, 8–9/57, 3/60, 1/65, 5/66, 6/67, 1/69, 10–11/71, 3/72, 11/72, 4/76,
3/78, 1/81, 1/85, 11/85, 1/86, 9/88 ("Do you favor or oppose the death penalty
for persons convicted of . . . murder?"); (NORC-GSS): 3/72, 3/02. QUESTION
(NORC-GSS): "Do you favor or oppose the death penalty for persons convicted
of murder?" Survey dates: 3/74–3/96. QUESTION (Gallup, NORC-GSS, *Los
Angeles Times*): "In general, do you think the courts in this area deal too harshly
or not harshly enough with criminals?" Survey dates: (Gallup) 4/65, 8–9/65, 2/68,
1/69, 12/72, 6/89 (". . . in your area . . . "); (Gallup/CNN/*USA Today*) 10/93 ("in
your area . . ."); (NORC-GSS) 3/72–3/02; (LAT) 1/81. The violent crime figures
are rates per 100,000 inhabitants. See Benjamin I. Page and Robert Y. Shapiro,
The Rational Public (Chicago: University of Chicago Press, 1992), pp. 90–94.

prevailing beliefs obviously has changed fundamentally and dramatically.
(Later we will consider changes in people's attitudes toward frequently
stigmatized groups, including communists and homosexuals.)

Figure 8.5[36] traces an issue often on the public agenda—crime and
criminal punishment. It shows three general trends, each one explainable
and reasonable. First, we see a decline in support for capital punishment
in the 1950s and early 1960s, associated with concerns that some capital
defendants would not get fair trials. At this time, people generally felt
safe on dark city streets and in their homes. Beginning in the 1960s, vio-

lent crime rates (and corresponding news reports) increased sharply. In response, public support for capital punishment rose, as did support for less lenient treatment of criminals by the courts. As violent crime rates began to decline sharply after 1992, public support for capital punishment and harsher sentencing also declined, although it remained (like the crime rates) far above the levels of the early 1960s.

While the opinion *trends* on criminal justice issues seem reasonable, the percentages themselves should not be taken at face value: Here, as elsewhere, question wording may greatly influence the results. For instance, according to both the 1994 and 1996 General Social Surveys, over 80 percent of the public believed that courts in their area did not deal harshly enough with criminals. Yet, in a 1995 study conducted by Texas A&M researchers, only 39 percent believed the courts were not harsh enough. Why such a huge disparity? In the GSS, respondents are given two choices—"too harshly or not harshly enough." Some respondents volunteer a third answer, that the courts are doing about right; in 1996, about 12 percent of respondents volunteered this answer. But the 1995 Texas A&M study offered "about right" as a third choice, and 57 percent of all respondents chose it.[37] Thus, the GSS question arguably overstates public support for tougher sentencing. Similarly, some question wordings evoke less support for capital punishment, while others evoke more support.[38]

Figure 8.6 is an example of the movement of "parallel publics" in a period of great political change. The figure shows parallel opinion changes by region in support for increased defense spending. (Note that the South is consistently most supportive.) The low level of support in 1973 could be seen as a national reaction to the costly, unsuccessful, and intensely controversial U.S. involvement in the Vietnam War. The "spike" in 1980 occurred after the Iran hostage crisis and the Soviet invasion of Afghanistan. This was a time of widespread and plausible concern about the country's military capability, concern fed by political rhetoric that expressed hostility toward the Soviet Union and criticism of the Carter administration. The subsequent reversal of opinion was a response to three factors: an easing of political rhetoric, the fact of an actual increase in defense spending (which had already begun under President Carter), and the advent of the 1981–1982 recession, in which the public gave lower priority to defense spending—preferring fewer "guns" and more "butter," so to speak. The results for 2000 and 2002 show increasing support for greater defense spending, although not nearly at 1980 levels.

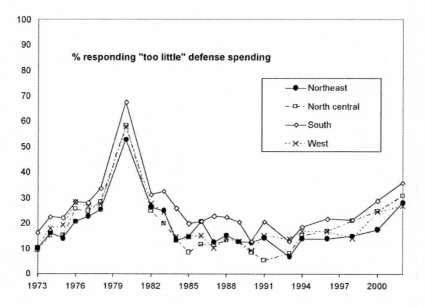

FIGURE 8.6   Defense Spending, 1973–2002: Opinion by Region
QUESTION (NORC-General Social Survey): "We are faced with many
problems in this country, none of which can be solved easily or inexpensively.
I'm going to name some of these problems, and for each one I'd like you to tell
me whether you think we're spending too much money on it, too little money,
or about the right amount. . . . Are we spending too much, too little, or about
the right amount on . . . the military, armaments, and national defense?" Survey
dates: (NORC-GSS) 3/73–3/02.

Crucially, the striking opinion changes of Figures 8.4 through 8.6 are
possible only if large numbers of people have, in some sense, meaningful
opinions. Aggregate opinions change when many people are exposed to
new information, pay attention to this information, and change their
opinions (i.e., their survey responses) as a result. As the example of defense spending showed, these changes are often similar across smaller
subgroups, showing just how pervasive exposure and response to new information can be, at least in the modern United States. However, the
"parallel publics" argument has limits. For instance, as we have already
suggested, strong partisans may respond very differently to new political
information than independents do, given their predispositions to favor
their own party. Moreover, some people receive new information much
faster than others do. For instance, in 1994, Larry Bartels pointed out

that after the end of the Cold War, views on defense spending had diverged. Politically informed respondents expressed substantially less support for defense spending than they had during the Cold War, while there had been relatively little change among the 60 percent of the public with the least information about politics.[39]

Other major studies have established the importance, and buttressed the reasonableness, of trends in American public opinion. James Stimson has elaborated the concept of "public mood," or the overall trend in public opinion to support more or less liberal policies. As we discuss in the next chapter, the research of Stimson and colleagues indicates that these general public policy preferences tend not only to influence national policy but also to respond to changes in national policy.[40] William Mayer presents evidence that various opinion trends are in large part influenced and explained by objective changes in conditions.[41] These works contain some distinct differences of interpretation—for instance, Mayer argues that Page and Shapiro overstate the degree of stability in public opinion, and that Stimson's idea of a single "public mood" is too simple.[42] Still, all these studies can be read as supporting the notion of a rational public that responds to new information in reasonable ways.

If most people know very little about political issues, how do their aggregate or collective responses manage to make sense? Page and Shapiro argue that people participate (to varying degrees) in a process of *collective deliberation*. Policymaking elites and expert analysts often provide much of the substance of this collective debate. However, they do not supply the results. In the end, the public makes "a multitude of individual decisions about who and what is right."[43] For better or worse, sometimes a prevailing public decision emerges that goes sharply against most "expert" opinion.

Even if public opinion influences policy (as will be seen in the next chapter), collective deliberation is no democratic panacea—especially if political elites can control the terms of the debate. In Page and Shapiro's own words, "Government responsiveness to the public would constitute a hollow victory, for example, if public opinion were itself manipulated by elites or interest groups in such a way that policy followed the mistaken wishes of a deceived public."[44] Many people may be sufficiently attentive and "informed" to react to such manipulation, though not nearly knowledgeable enough to resist it. Here Page and

Shapiro hearken back to Key's warning that "the voice of the people is but an echo"—although the case of Zoë Baird suggests that maybe it is not always just an echo.

Page and Shapiro conclude that the public's collective policy preferences are intelligible and important. In other words, analysts can tell coherent stories about "what Americans really think" about the issues[45] because Americans really do think about the issues, or at least (in the aggregate) they answer polls as if they do. And if we are serious about democracy, public opinion as measured in polls should be taken seriously. Unfortunately, the public's collective policy preferences do not always emerge very clearly. Earlier we noted the case of public opinion on sentencing of criminals: The GSS indicated that huge majorities of the public favored stricter sentencing, while a Texas A&M survey in the same time period indicated that a majority actually thought the status quo was "about right." Similar conundrums emerge on many other issues, including fairly mainstream ones.

For instance, in the mid-1990s, political controversy swirled around a proposed constitutional amendment that would require the federal government to balance its budget. Many surveys showed strong support for such an amendment. For instance, a CBS News survey at the end of January 1997 asked, "Would you favor or oppose a balanced budget amendment to the Constitution that would require the Federal Government to balance its budget by the year 2002?"; fully 76 percent said they favored such an amendment.[46] But another survey just two weeks earlier evoked a very different result. The earlier survey asked, "Do you think requiring the Federal Government to balance the budget is the kind of issue you would like to change the Constitution for, or isn't balancing the budget that kind of issue?" Only 39 percent said that it was.[47]

How could people express such seemingly contradictory views on a prominent policy issue? The only clear substantive difference between the two balanced budget amendment questions is the reference to 2002, which may have sounded gradual and responsible to some respondents (as opposed to merely "requiring the Federal Government to balance the budget"). Probably more important was that in responding to the "favor or oppose" question, people tended to focus on the desirability of a balanced budget; in responding to the "that kind of issue" question, they focused on the seriousness of changing the Constitution. Here is an example of a "framing effect," which we discuss further below. (Similarly, a survey in March 2004 found that a sizable majority supported a constitutional amendment to allow marriage only between a man and a woman, while another sizable majority said that the issue was not "important enough . . . to be worth changing the Constitution for"!)[48] Survey results like these have some meaning, but they do not seem to state any clear public mandate. What, then, does "meaningful opinion" mean? We return to this issue (but do not settle it) in the next section.

MAKING DO: "GUT RATIONALITY," HEURISTICS, AND POLITICAL JUDGMENTS

Whereas Page and Shapiro investigate what they call "collective deliberation," Samuel Popkin's *The Reasoning Voter* offers one effort to make sense of voters' individual deliberations. Popkin draws on the insights of the Columbia school, the "information shortcuts" noted by Downs, and findings from cognitive psychology to make the case for gut rationality in presidential voting. He argues that people can and do make decent voting decisions without having to conduct systematic research into presidential candidates.

> People learn about specific government programs as a by-product of ordinary activities. . . . They obtain economic information from their activities as consumers, from their workplace, and from their friends. They also obtain all sorts of information from the media. Thus they do not need to know which party controls Congress, or the names of their senators, in order to know something about the state of the economy or proposed cuts in Social Security or the controversies over abortion.[49]

Similarly, and sensibly, voters use "campaign competence as a proxy for competence in elected office—as an indication of the political skills needed to handle the issues and problems confronting the government." And voters "use evaluations of personal character as a substitute for information about past demonstrations of political character."[50] If certain candidates have made a mess of their campaign or their personal life, maybe they should not be trusted to direct the national government. (Bill Clinton, as president, challenged this equation during the Monica

Lewinsky scandal of 1998: Many voters approved of his job performance even as they deplored his personal conduct. By then, of course, people had five years of job performance to evaluate, so they were not forced to depend on evidence about Clinton's personal character.) Because it is hard to pin down candidates on the issues and because presidents often cannot enact their policy preferences anyway, basing votes on "personalities instead of issues" makes more sense than policy experts may want to admit. In fact, research indicates that well-informed people are at least as likely as less-informed respondents to weigh personalities more heavily than issues.[51] Thus, voters use shortcuts, or heuristics, in gathering and analyzing information, so that they can make good (or at least better than random) votes without much hard (or impossible) work.

Although Popkin's analysis is limited to voting, other researchers have found that people employ heuristics in making all kinds of political judgments—such as taking positions on policy issues.[52] Different people use different heuristics, depending on their political sophistication and their cognitive styles. Some heuristics are group based and follow the logic of attitudinal consistency ("balance theory") we discussed in Chapter Four. A person may "reason" as follows: "Blacks like affirmative action, and I like (dislike) blacks, so I like (dislike) affirmative action." "Republicans favor lower taxes on capital gains, and I am a Democrat, so I oppose them." Similar heuristics can be based on individuals: "Ralph Nader endorsed this referendum, and I respect Nader, so I will vote for it."[53] Other heuristics engage simple values: For instance, Sniderman and colleagues argue that people evaluate some social policies by asking whether the likely beneficiaries are deserving (a "desert heuristic"). For some people, although (as we have seen) not very many, ideological beliefs such as liberalism or conservatism serve as powerful heuristics. Heuristics, by definition, do not require very much thought, but this does not mean that they are merely "emotional," "irrational," or arbitrary. On the contrary, heuristics may be very reasonable, in the sense that they sometimes enable people to reason and act effectively without very much knowledge or effort.

One especially powerful heuristic for voting decisions, which we encountered in Chapter Seven, is *retrospective voting*, or voting on the basis of incumbent performance (rather than issue positions or other criteria). Earlier in this chapter, we quoted Lippmann's view that the essence of democratic governance is "to support the Ins when things are going well; to support the Outs when they seem to be going badly." Many studies indicate that voters do weigh incumbent performance, as well as economic conditions, very heavily in determining their presidential votes.[54] Unfortunately, retrospective voting may entail holding incumbents responsible for economic conditions that are not actually their fault. For instance, some observers believe that President George H. W. Bush was defeated by Bill Clinton in 1992 because people faulted Bush for an economic recession and a tax increase. The recession was arguably beyond Bush's control; the tax increase, while it went against Bush's pledge of "no new taxes," was arguably necessary to avoid large increases in the federal budget deficit. So, while voters were apparently judging Bush on his record, it is debatable whether they were judging him fairly.

Yet another form of heuristic is called *on-line tallies.* A broad and impressive body of research on on-line tallies posits that people judge candidates by keeping an internal count of "pros" and "cons"—but not necessarily recalling the content of these likes or dislikes![55] Thus, heuristics can take a wide array of forms—and, just as there is no overarching and widely accepted "theory of core values," there is no single "theory of political heuristics."

Several studies show that heuristics do not resolve all the problems of limited political information. Delli Carpini and Keeter find that the presidential votes of politically knowledgeable respondents are powerfully predicted by their ideology and issue positions. For the least knowledgeable respondents, however, issue positions have little predictive power, and ideology has hardly any at all.[56] This result implies, of course, that uninformed voters do not use issues and ideology to decide their votes. But it also implies something more disturbing: that, despite whatever heuristics these voters use, they are more likely than informed voters to vote contrary to their stated preferences. Unfortunately, not all such heuristic failures "wash out" at the aggregate level. Larry Bartels, studying presidential elections from 1972 through 1992, estimates that incumbent presidents on average won about 5 percent more of the vote—and Democratic candidates about 2 percent more—than they would if all voters were fully informed.[57] In individual elections (and perhaps especially in congressional elections), voters' lack of information could lead to even more dramatic distortions.

The policy opinions expressed in opinion surveys may also be crucially distorted by many respondents' lack of information. As a dramatic example, Scott Althaus examines responses to a 1992 NES question on whether married women should be required to notify their husbands before having an abortion. Overall, almost two-thirds of respondents supported spousal notification requirements. However, the respondents with the most factual knowledge were roughly evenly divided on this requirement, whereas those with the least knowledge favored it by about 4 to 1. This gap apparently cannot be explained by other social, economic, or political differences. It appears that the most knowledgeable respondents are better able to think out the arguments on both sides of this issue, leading more of them to oppose spousal notification requirements—and revealing much more controversy than the raw results would indicate. Althaus finds many other (albeit less extreme) gaps between informed and uninformed respondents.[58] Clearly, heuristics do not necessarily allow people to vote or to respond to survey questions as if they were fully informed. However, analysts are far from a consensus on how well heuristics work in general.

Some analysts emphasize not heuristics, but *schemas*. Schemas are "mental prototypes, images, metaphors, 'scripts,' or categories that provide a frame of reference against which experience is compared and interpreted."[59] In some ways, schemas create expectations just as stereotypes do (see Chapter Four). Schemas will also make particular concerns, rather than others, appear relevant. According to schema theory, people interpret new information in terms of their existing schemas. Unlike heuristics, schemas are not really reasoning shortcuts. Rather, schemas "tell" people how to reason about the matter at hand.

For instance, when Iraq invaded Kuwait in the summer of 1990, many people used a schema inspired by the Munich Pact of 1938. After Nazi Germany had invaded Czechoslovakia in 1938, Great Britain and France attempted to appease Adolf Hitler by ceding some territory to Germany without Czechoslovakia's consent. The "appeasement schema" (or "Munich schema") holds that such conciliatory responses to aggression only encourage further aggression—such as Germany's invasion of Poland in 1939. President Bush invoked the appeasement schema when he publicly compared Iraqi president Saddam Hussein to Adolf Hitler. Other observers relied on the "Vietnam schema," in which the use of force to punish a much weaker opponent leads to a military quagmire with heavy casualties. A stream of public commentaries related the Gulf crisis to either the appeasement or the Vietnam schema, illuminating some aspects of the crisis while obscuring others. The appeasement schema evoked considerations about what territory Iraq might attempt to seize next; it implied that stopping Iraqi aggression now would be simpler and less costly than trying to do so later. By contrast, the Vietnam schema encouraged people to consider the possibility of a long-term military involvement, the risk of heavy American casualties, and the chance that military action would not achieve U.S. policy goals.

Similarly, various people draw on different schemas in thinking about welfare programs. Some people tend to think of hardworking parents temporarily down on their luck who deserve help to get back on their feet again. Others think of lazy or spoiled women who would rather live on the dole than work to support themselves and their children. Again, countless public commentaries invoke one schema or the other, often at great length. Many thoughtful and detailed discussions of welfare are heavily influenced by one of these schemas. Logically, these schemas are not mutually exclusive; neither are the appeasement and Vietnam schemas. However, when schemas point in opposite directions, people often favor one at the expense of the other. (We can understand this tendency as an effort to reduce cognitive dissonance or affective inconsistency, as described in Chapter Four.)

A weakness of schema theory is that we generally cannot predict very well which schema a person will apply to new information. Sometimes, to be sure, we can make some predictions. For instance, someone who lived through World War II should be more likely to rely on the appeasement schema than someone who did not—although other events could lead someone to a similarly jaded view of appeasement. This ambiguity points to another weakness of schema theory, one it shares with many other psychological theories. Since we cannot "see" schemas directly, it is hard to pin down what they are or how they influence people's thinking in a way that would convince a skeptic. Still, many political psychologists find schema theory a useful way of understanding why many political debates seem to restate a few arguments over and over. These debates often hinge not on "new ideas" but on efforts to persuade people to apply one widely held schema instead of another. In the short run, schemas themselves are generally stable and largely impervious to rational argument. It may be much easier to convince people that, for example, the Vietnam schema applies to the Gulf crisis than to persuade them of a new and unfamiliar way of thinking about such crises.

THE ZALLER SYNTHESIS

Let us go back to John Zaller's work, discussed in earlier chapters, and see how it wrestles with ideas from Converse and others. Zaller flatly agrees with Converse that people do not have predetermined "true" (crystallized) attitudes on many, if any, survey questions.[60] Yet he argues that people do have predispositions (values, interests, and ideological views) that have important implications for the issues treated in political surveys. Zaller also implicitly agrees with Page and Shapiro that public opinion as reported in polls, in the aggregate, is generally stable and responds sensibly to new information (to the extent that this information is received). Yet he does not believe that public opinion should be as influential in policymaking as Page and Shapiro would like. Zaller relates these views to a theoretical framework different from anything we have seen so far in this chapter, although it has deep roots in political psychology.

If people do not have established opinions on, say, defense spending, how do they answer survey questions about it? Zaller argues that they make up these responses on the spot, based on whatever relevant consideration first comes to mind. (A consideration is simply "any reason that might induce [someone] to decide a political issue one way or the other.")[61] However, for considerations to "come to mind," they have to be in the mind first! To review, Zaller proposes a three-step "receive–accept–sample" (RAS) model that pivots on *political awareness*.

1. People who pay closer attention to politics—who are more politically aware and knowledgeable—are more likely to *receive* new political messages that can serve as considerations.[62] When President Bill Clinton argued in 1993 that a new national health care program was needed to protect the uninsured, some people "got the message," whereas others never tuned in. (Political messages often do not come from politicians. Many "messages" about AIDS, for in-

stance, come from TV news stories that may not mention politicians or even specific policy issues. Other political messages come from talk and variety shows, TV situation comedies, rap music, advertisements of various kinds, and many other sources.)

2. Politically aware respondents are also more likely to *accept* messages that suit their predispositions—and to reject messages that do not. Thus, knowledgeable liberals were more likely to "buy" President Clinton's argument about the uninsured than either unknowledgeable liberals or knowledgeable conservatives. Conversely, knowledgeable conservatives were more likely to accept the opposing argument that Clinton's proposal would create a wasteful, oppressive bureaucracy. However, most people accepted some considerations on both sides. Bear in mind that not all considerations are arguments (or depend on ideology). For instance, a person might simply figure, "Clinton supports this plan, and I like/hate him, so that's a reason to support/oppose it."

3. Come survey time, people *sample* from among whatever considerations they have received, pro and con, that are "accessible" and seem relevant to the question. In the case of a yes-or-no question, it is almost as if people throw all these considerations into a hat, then pull one out at random to decide how to answer. (For more complicated questions, it is as if people "average" the accessible considerations.) Of course, neither Zaller nor anyone else thinks that we can really count up all of someone's considerations. Considerations (like many concepts in social science) seem "real" but cannot be counted or measured very precisely. Here, Zaller's argument sounds like the idea of "on-line tallies" mentioned earlier, but there is a crucial difference: his discussion of what goes into the hat—which considerations are accessible.

Accessibility depends on several things. One is political knowledge. Liking or hating President Clinton wouldn't help you answer a question on health care reform unless you knew (or thought you could guess) whether Clinton supported the reform. Another important influence is how recently the consideration has been called to mind. Survey designers can actually manipulate (deliberately or accidentally) which considerations are called to mind by the way in which they *frame* their questions.

Indeed, a growing body of research focuses on frames as a crucial element in understanding how people respond to survey questions.[63] In the terms of schema theory, we can think of frames as cues in the question text that encourage people to apply one schema or another, and thus to use particular considerations when they answer.

As an example of how "frames" could function in the health care debate of 1993–1994, consider the question, "Do you support the health care proposal now before Congress?" Rewording it—"Do you support Bill Clinton's health care proposal, now before Congress?"—would encourage people to "sample" their view of Clinton. Alternatively, changing "Bill Clinton's" to "President Clinton's" or even "the president's" might bring to some people's mind the consideration that "presidents deserve the benefit of the doubt," and thus evoke more support. (You might argue that these wordings are not just changes in "frame," but actually add *information* to the original question, which did not mention Clinton. That is quite true. Frames can be thought of as a kind of information, and there is no way to supply information—even "balanced" information—without influencing a question's frame.) By altering the wording and order of *earlier* questions in the survey, designers could profoundly influence what people are thinking about when they answer a question on health care reform. These question-wording and "context" effects have long troubled survey analysts, in part because they seem to complicate the task of finding "true public opinion." Zaller argues, however, that these effects amount to important evidence about the nature of public opinion. His elegant theory of these effects, rooted in the idea of "considerations," is a major advance.

Now we can see how Zaller can agree, more or less, with all the authors mentioned above. If people are pulling their survey answers out of a hat, it is pointless to ask what answer is their "real attitude." However, based on their awareness and their predispositions, some people will be much more likely to offer (for instance) a pro-defense-spending opinion than others. (We might think of someone's "real attitude" as the average answer she would give if asked a question repeatedly—although even this average would be affected by nuisance factors such as question order.)

Moreover, based on people's predispositions and awareness, we can predict to some extent how they will respond to new information (political messages). Most important for Page and Shapiro's argument, we can predict that the public as a whole *will* respond to new messages, although some people will either ignore or reject them.[64] If most major sources of political information agree that the United States needs a military buildup, public opinion will probably move in that direction, as it did in 1980—in what Zaller calls a "mainstream effect." We can also expect that if there are no new and strong messages, public opinion will be fairly stable. This view is compatible with a fairly rational public, although some parts of the public are more rational than others.

Although Zaller's model seems compatible with Page and Shapiro's argument, he has a strikingly different view of democratic competence. Where Page and Shapiro emphasize the "good news" about stability and change in public opinion, Zaller underscores the bad news: "Many citizens . . . are blown about by whatever current of information manages to develop the greatest intensity. . . . [M]ost of the rest [i.e., the politically aware] respond mechanically on the basis of partisan cues," tending to rely upon elites that share their predispositions.[65] This view leads Zaller to the question, "If, as I have implied, only specialists are competent to conduct political debate, why bring the public into it at all?" Why not just leave government to the experts? Zaller answers: because "government, in the absence of checks, invariably goes astray and becomes overbearing or worse. . . . It is the collective ability of citizens in a democracy to pressure leaders in useful directions and, when necessary, to remove the leaders, more than the collective wisdom of the people, that seems to me critical."[66] Thus Zaller's view is similar to Lippmann's—the public's role is to choose between the Ins and the Outs—although "pressur[ing] leaders" may allow for a somewhat larger role. Although the public cannot *conduct* political debate, at least it can tell when its leaders go astray.

Even so, Zaller is more like Page and Shapiro in his concerns than he is different in his conclusions. None of these authors sees the public as inherently capricious, rash, authoritarian, or otherwise dangerous. They worry more that elite debate might become one-sided: In Zaller's closing words, "The real problem is guaranteeing the existence of . . . [a] vigorous competition among opposing ideas."[67] As long as elite debate thrives and is accessible to the public, reasons Zaller, the public will be able to support the side that matches its own prevailing predispositions. Page is less optimistic: He worries that no matter what policy experts are saying and no matter what the public believes, nothing can force the major political parties to adopt public preferences.[68] Either way, clearly it is possible for the government to go against public predispositions. The next chapter investigates policy responsiveness to public opinion in great detail.

AMERICANS AND DEMOCRATIC IDEALS

So far, we have examined the American public's democratic competence primarily by evaluating its rationality: What do Americans know about politics? How do they decide who to vote for, and how reasonable is the basis of their decisions? How reasonable or reasoned are the views they express on policy issues? Now we focus on the content of the American people's beliefs about democracy and policy issues: How far do they support democratic institutions and norms—for instance, free speech or minority rights? On what issues are they most sharply divided, and how do they contend with these disagreements?

Americans consistently express considerable pride in their political system. Typically, in a 2000 survey, 89 percent of respondents agreed (and 71 percent "strongly" agreed) that "Whatever its faults, the United States still has the best system of government in the world."[69] (Americans express less satisfaction in how their political system actually functions—a point we will discuss at some length later on.) In particular, Americans say that they support *democracy*. In a 1999 study, 93 percent of U.S. respondents said that democracy should be taught as a value in the public schools (only "honesty" was considered more important).[70] In the 1995 World Values Survey, 91 percent of U.S. respondents agreed with the statement, "Democracy may have problems but it's better than any other form of government."[71]

If Americans support the U.S. political system because it is democratic, what do they understand by "democratic"? The most obvious "democratic" aspect of the system is free elections for the president, Congress, and many state and local offices. Americans do place a high value on free elections. In a 1999 survey, 84 percent said that free elections were a "major reason" for America's success in the twentieth century—more than any other reason offered except "the Constitution" (cited as a major reason by 85 percent).[72] However, perhaps surprisingly, when most Americans think of democracy, they do not first think of free elections. Apparently they perceive free elections as one means, or method, to help achieve various democratic values. But what values are "democratic"? Americans most often identify democracy with the ideals of *liberty* and *equality.*[73]

Americans generally consider the United States a bastion of liberty, the "home of the free." In the United States at its best, they believe, people are free *from* governmental tyranny, free *to* speak their minds, practice their religions, and pursue happiness and prosperity in any way that does not infringe on the rights of others. The Bill of Rights, which comprises the first ten amendments to the U.S. Constitution, defends freedom of speech, freedom of religion, freedom of the press, freedom from arbitrary punishment, and other crucial aspects of liberty.

Americans also believe that the United States is (or should be) committed to political and social equality. The Declaration of Independence affirms the "self-evident" proposition that "all men are created equal"; each person is entitled to a vote and to some say in political decisions; no one should be subservient to anyone else because of differences in social class or condition. Equality also extends, in part, to the economic realm. Americans clearly are not equal in wealth or income, and most Americans do not support "levelling" economic conditions (which would entail considerable restraints on freedom). However, most Americans do affirm support for equal *opportunity* to succeed in whatever field one chooses. For many Americans, equal opportunity entails a substantial role for government; most, for instance, support public schools in order to provide citizens with a basic education. Most Americans even support a wide range of assistance to the poor, although they tend to oppose "welfare" by that name.[74]

To some Americans, it is obvious that the United States stands for liberty and equality—perhaps more decisively than any other country in the world. But some observers question whether Americans themselves are fully committed to the ideals of liberty and equality, as they have been described here. One editorialist denies the American public's commitment to *civil liberties:* "Public opinion polls clearly indicate . . . that strong majorities of Americans—when read the Bill of Rights, without being told it's the Bill of Rights—oppose full freedom of the press, full freedom of speech, protections against warrantless searches, the prohibition on cruel and unusual punishment and so on."[75] Questions are also raised about

Americans' commitment to equality in various forms. Political equality in the sense of "one person, one vote" has been contested throughout U.S. history: Most strikingly, in the South most blacks were effectively denied voting rights until the 1960s. Other aspects of political equality remain contested: While people tend to support the abstraction of "equal rights," they often disagree sharply on how it should be applied. Disagreements about social and economic equality are even more complex. In some cases, it may seem fair to say that public opinion on various issues contradicts "democratic ideals"; in other cases, we may need to reserve judgment.

One thing that Americans typically do *not* identify as a key democratic ideal is public participation in decisionmaking. This omission may seem strange, given that "democracy" seems literally to mean that the public rules, or takes part in decisions. Many critics believe that the American people should play a larger role in decisionmaking at all levels of government than at present. However, John Hibbing and Elizabeth Theiss-Morse forcefully and persuasively argue that Americans are not inclined to obey these critics. According to Hibbing and Theiss-Morse, most Americans are not interested in politics, dislike political debate and compromise, and do not want to spend more time following political issues. "As a result, people most definitely do *not* want to take over political decision making from elected officials. . . . Americans do not even want to be placed in a position where they feel obligated to provide input to those who *are* making political decisions."[76] What Americans would like best, Hibbing and Theiss-Morse argue, is rule by experts who are selflessly devoted to the common good—or, as they put it, "empathetic, non-self-interested decision makers (ENSIDs)."[77] From the standpoint of rational ignorance, as we discussed earlier in the chapter, it is easy to understand why Americans do not want to participate more in politics than they do. If Americans believed that their political leaders were ENSIDs, they might participate in and think about politics even less.

CIVIL LIBERTIES AND POLITICAL TOLERANCE: THE "STOUFFER SHIFT"

Political theorists have often argued that *political tolerance* for dissenting views, manifested in freedom of speech and of the press, is a basic principle of representative democracy. If people are not allowed to express dissenting opinions, then elections cannot truly hold the government responsible. If political tolerance is central to democracy, and if democratic government is responsive to public opinion, then we might expect that democracy will only thrive if the public substantially embraces political tolerance. Or to put it another way, if the United States stands out for its commitment to political liberty, then we might expect that Americans are strongly committed to political tolerance. But in the 1950s, many observers doubted Americans' commitment to political tolerance.

Social scientists of the 1950s were haunted by memories of the Nazi Party's rise to power in Germany, and its aftermath. The relationship between the German public and the Nazis remains controversial even today. Adolf Hitler's rise to power was not, as some people imagine, a democratic excess: Hitler was appointed chancellor in early 1933 after twice losing elections for president in 1932. (Hitler's first outright electoral victory came in a 1934 plebiscite, more than a year after all other political parties had been outlawed.)[78] However, the Nazi party did win a plurality with 37 percent of the votes in the parliamentary (*Reichstag*) elections of July 1932. After Hitler came to power, his popularity seems only to have increased, largely due to the effectiveness of Josef Goebbels' propaganda efforts and the suppression of dissenting voices. The Nazi regime's plans, which included military conquest and the extermination of German Jews, proceeded with little evident opposition from the German public. Reflecting on these events, political observers and social scientists wondered whether some flaw in German *political culture* was to blame for the demise of democracy and the advent of a ruthless dictatorship—and many worried about the long-term prospects in other countries, including the United States.

One team of researchers, led by German émigré Theodor Adorno, related the collapse of democracy in Germany to a generalized *authoritarian personality* (as we mentioned in Chapter Four).[79] The authoritarian mind-set, according to Adorno and his colleagues, was marked by rigid adherence to conventional values, excessive submissiveness to authority, and a propensity to condemn and even punish deviants. Writing in 1950, the researchers saw these traits as ominously widespread among Americans. The concept of authoritarianism has provoked much debate over the years, but never did the debate seem more urgent than in the shadow of World War II. If authoritarian values were widely held, could democracy survive?

For many observers, the rise of "McCarthyism" underscored the threat to democracy. In February 1950, Senator Joseph McCarthy claimed to have evidence of 81 people "whom I consider to be Communists in the State Department." Over the next four years, McCarthy launched several Congressional investigations into suspected Communists in federal jobs. McCarthy also opened a campaign against what he considered anti-American books in American libraries, and an investigation into "Communist thinkers" in colleges and universities. Although many of McCarthy's charges were completely unsubstantiated, he had considerable public support—as well as strong public opposition. McCarthy's critics argued that he had created a climate of suspicion in which merely associating with accused Communists, or even denying the truth of particular accusations, could expose patriotic Americans to charges of treachery. For McCarthy's detractors, "McCarthyism" became, in Richard Rovere's words, "a synonym for the hatefulness of baseless defamation, or mudslinging"; McCarthy himself said in 1952 that "McCarthyism is Americanism with its sleeves rolled."[80]

In the midst of this controversy, in mid-1954, came the study that became Samuel Stouffer's book *Communism, Conformity, and Civil Liberties.* In Stouffer's words, the study examined Americans' reactions to two dangers: "One, from the Communist conspiracy outside and inside the country. Two, from those who in thwarting the conspiracy would sacrifice some of the very liberties which the enemy would destroy."[81] The study interviewed almost 5,000 ordinary Americans, plus 1,500 selected local community leaders in medium-sized cities. Respondents were asked a variety of questions—including open-ended questions about threats facing America, questions about Communists in America, and questions about possible restrictions on "nonconformists" such as Communists, Socialists, and atheists.

The results painted a complex and troubling picture of American views on political tolerance. The community leaders were generally more tolerant—more inclined to express support for civil liberties—than the public at large. For instance, 64 percent of community leaders said that a speech "against churches and religion" should be allowed, compared with only 39 percent of other respondents in the same cities. On other questions, solid majorities of both groups supported civil liberties. For instance, respondents were asked whether an accused Communist "who swears under oath he has never been a Communist" should be fired from a high school teaching job. Only 16 percent of community leaders, and 22 percent of the national sample, said that he should be fired.[82] But admitted Communists received much less tolerance. Fully 89 percent of community leaders, and 91 percent of the national sample, said that an admitted Communist should be fired from a high school teaching job. Almost the same percentages favored firing an admitted Communist who taught in a college. Indeed, 66 percent of community leaders, and 77 percent of the national cross-section, favored stripping admitted Communists of their American citizenship. Also, 54 percent of community leaders, and 66 percent of the national sample, thought that a book by an admitted Communist should be removed from the public library. Similar percentages thought that he should be fired if he were a store clerk or a radio singer.[83]

How was the government supposed to find who the Communists were? Sixty-two percent of community leaders, and 64 percent of the national sample, thought "the government should have the right to listen in on people's private telephone conversations, in order to get evidence against Communists"—although the question did not ask whether any limits should be placed on that power. Somewhat larger majorities—65 percent of community leaders, 73 percent of the national sample—said it was a "good idea . . . for people to report to the F.B.I. any neighbors or acquaintances who they suspect of being Communists."[84] This idea becomes unnerving when one considers some of the reasons that various respondents gave for suspecting that someone they knew might be a Communist: "He was always talking about world peace." "He brought a lot of foreign-looking people into his home." "During the war I used to say Russia was our enemy and he got mad at me." "He had a foreign camera and took so many pictures of the large New York bridges." "My husband's brother drinks and acts common-like. Sometimes I kind of think he is a Communist."[85] Stouffer emphasized that such responses were uncommon, but he also quoted community leaders who felt that they could not speak their minds for fear of having their loyalty questioned.

What did these results mean for civil liberties in the United States? Stouffer, whose sympathies clearly lay with the civil libertarians, emphasized that the community leaders were generally more tolerant—although, as we have seen, not always much more so. As he put it, "the community leaders, being especially responsible and thoughtful citizens, are more likely than the rank and file to give a sober second thought to the dangers involved in denying civil liberties to those whose views they dislike."[86] Stouffer also found that younger people, people with more education, and city-dwellers were more tolerant of political nonconformists than their older, less educated, and rural counterparts. Stouffer argued that the increase in access to higher education, increased geographic mobility and the influx into cities, and the communications revolution were among the "social, economic, and technological forces" that worked to spread "the idea that 'people are different from me, with different systems of values, and they can be good people, too.'"[87] As we will see, Stouffer was basically right in his expectation that political tolerance would increase—certainly for the groups (communists, socialists, and atheists) that he considered.

Some observers, perhaps less willing than Stouffer to look to the future, took a darker view of what they saw as a widespread willingness to abridge basic rights. Granted, if American Communists had foresworn loyalty to the United States and were potential spies and saboteurs, then one might reasonably support some abridgements of their rights—although that judgment was open to debate. Abridgements of the rights of *accused* Communists were harder to stomach. Abridgements of the rights of avowed atheists seemed to violate the core principle of free speech—and yet, most respondents thought that speeches and books "against churches and religion" should not be permitted in their communities.[88] To the extent that community leaders supported civil liberties, or at least did not act to turn repressive sentiments into policy, they could be seen as bulwarks of democratic values against a profoundly undemocratic public. This argument became a strong form of what we have referred to as *democratic elitism*, or elite democratic theory: the apparent paradox that democracy, at least in the United States circa the mid-1950s, depended on ordinary citizens not taking too strong an interest in what the government actually did.[89]

James Gibson later presented evidence that while political elites might generally be more politically tolerant than the public at large, the actual course of anticommunism depended more on elites than on the public.[90] Gibson started from the fact that the fifty states varied in the anticommunist legislation they adopted. Some states banned the Communist Party and Communists outright; others took no action against Communists at all; and others adopted intermediate policies, such as banning Communists from holding public office. Gibson rated the states based on the severity of their repressive policies. Then, he tallied the results of the Stouffer study, state by state. Gibson showed that the states with the least tolerant *elites* (community leaders) tended to have the most repressive policies, while the tolerance or intolerance of the mass public seemed to make no difference. Gibson conceded that "elites tend to be relatively more tolerant than the masses." Yet he insisted, "it is difficult to imagine that the repression of the 1950s was inspired by demands for repressive public policy from a mobilized mass public"—especially because (as Stouffer also had pointed out) very few among the public identified Communism as a major issue.[91] Mass intolerance may have *permitted* anticommunist repression, but it did not drive it.

Recall that Stouffer had expected political tolerance—and, indeed, the general belief that "people are different from me . . . and they can be good people, too"—to increase over time. Since 1972, the General Social Survey has repeated many of the questions on Stouffer's tolerance scale, enabling us to track trends over time. For the most part, Stouffer's expectation has held true. Willingness to "tolerate" anti-religionists, Communists, militarists, and homosexuals as speakers, college teachers, and authors in a local library all have increased dramatically since 1976 (the first year all these categories were asked about). The increases in tolerance range from 12.5 to 26.4 percentage points, with homosexuals registering the greatest gains in tolerance. (Figure 8.7 shows trends for college teachers.) In the 2002 survey, solid majorities "tolerate" each of these groups in each of these contexts, although support is weakest for allowing militarists and Communists to teach in college (57 percent and 62 percent, respectively). Of the groups that the GSS asks about, only "racists" have evoked little increase in tolerance since 1976. In 2002, about 53 percent of respondents said that racists should be allowed to teach in college—the first time a majority expressed support for this view, and only about 13 points above the 1976 level. Solid majorities did say in 2002 that racists should be allowed to speak in the community (64 percent) and that their books should not be removed from local libraries (67 percent)—but these figures have changed only slightly from 1976.

Why are trends in tolerance toward racists different than trends in tolerance toward Communists, homosexuals, or anti-religionists? Certainly

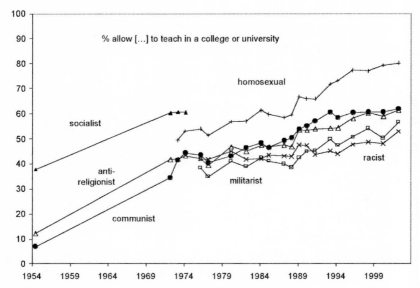

FIGURE 8.7   Civil Liberties of College Teachers, 1954–2002

QUESTION (Joint NORC-Gallup, NORC-GSS): "There are always some people whose ideas are considered bad or dangerous by other people. ("Atheist" or "Anti-Religionist") For instance, somebody who is against all churches and religion. . . . Should such a person be allowed to teach in a college or university, or not?" ("Socialist") "Or consider a person who favored government ownership of all railroads and all big industries. . . ." ("Racist") "Or consider a person who believes that Blacks are genetically inferior. . . ." ("Communist") "Now I would like to ask you some questions about a man who admits he is a Communist. . . . Suppose he is teaching in college. Should he be fired, or not?" ("Militarist") "Consider a person who advocates doing away with elections and letting the military run the country. . . . Should such a person be allowed to teach in a college or university, or not?" ("Homosexual") "And what about a man who admits he is a homosexual? . . . Should such a person be allowed to teach in a college or university, or not?" Survey dates: (NORC-Gallup) 6/54; (NORC-GSS) 3/72–3/02.

prevailing views about homosexuals and anti-religionists have warmed considerably over this time period. Some scholars have questioned whether the upward trends in Figure 8.7 should be considered increases in "tolerance." As Sullivan et al. put it, political tolerance "implies a willingness to permit the expression of those ideas or interests that one opposes," and thus "presumes opposition or disagreement."[92] Arguably some of the apparent growth in tolerance is better understood as a decline in opposition or disagreement! By the same token, since (as we will demonstrate below) support for racist beliefs has declined since 1976, the fact that "tolerance" for racists has not actually *decreased* may imply an increase in actual tolerance for these now unpopular views.

To some extent, these trends can be interpreted as supporting the idea of a rational democratic public: specifically, a public that balances the value of free speech against specific threats posed by various groups. Why were Americans in 1976 more willing to allow a racist to speak than a Communist, while in 2002 they were more likely to allow a Communist to speak than a racist? Especially since the collapse of the Soviet Union in 1990, it has become increasingly hard to imagine that a Communist speaker could pose a serious threat. On the other hand, it is easy for many to imagine that a racist speaker could at least incite a riot. This widespread perception of race as a dangerous issue leads us to a closer examination. But before we turn to racial divisions in American public opinion, we want to consider something widely regarded as more fundamental: money. That is, we will briefly explore the role of economic self-interest in American public opinion, which proves to be rather modest.

AMERICANS AND MONEY: ECONOMIC SELF-INTEREST AND SOCIOTROPIC VOTING

As we noted earlier, the authors of the Constitution worried how to prevent the relatively poor majority from seizing the wealth of a few. One might imagine that "soaking the rich"—if not seizing their property, then at least taxing the dickens out of them—would seem like an unambiguously good idea to the vast majority of Americans. Likewise, you might think that people with high incomes would generally support sharply reducing taxes—at least their own taxes—and cutting government services that do not benefit them directly. Indeed, a "rational choice" perspective such as was presented in the preceding chapter might seem to demand a high degree of conflict along economic lines. Simply put, poor people should strongly favor reducing income differences between rich and poor, and rich people should strongly oppose it.

The actual relationship between economic standing and support for income redistribution is considerable, but weaker than many people expect. For instance, one General Social Survey question asks respondents to place themselves on a seven-point scale, where 1 implies strong support for "reduc[ing] the income differences between rich and poor" and 7 implies no support.[93] In the three GSS studies between 1998 and 2002, 25 percent of respondents with family incomes under $20,000 expressed strong support for redistribution (1 on the seven-point scale), compared with 8 percent of respondents with family incomes of $110,000 or more. (We will call these two income groups "low-income" and "high-income," respectively.) At the other end of the scale, 11 percent of the low-income respondents and 26 percent of the high-income respondents replied "7" for no support. Statistically, these differences are very strong. Practically, however, the differences are not so strong. On average, low-income respondents leaned slightly toward income redistribution and high-income respondents leaned slightly against it.[94]

On specific issues, income often has even less—and sometimes apparently no—effect on people's views. Some more examples from the 1998–2002 GSS: A 70 percent majority of low-income respondents, and a more modest 56 percent majority of high-income respondents, said that "we're spending . . . too little money" on "assistance to the poor."[95] (Since many of the low-income respondents do not consider themselves poor, neither group seems to be answering this question out of narrow self-interest.) You might imagine that prosperous respondents would worry less about the nation's education system because they can more easily afford private schools. But in fact, the high-income respondents expressed even a higher level of support for more education spending than the low-income respondents.[96] On the other hand, environmental protection is often described as a "middle-class issue" that low-income people cannot afford to care about. Yet, if anything, low-income respondents expressed stronger support for higher environmental spending than high-income respondents did.[97] Of course there are many other ways to look for self-interest effects, and some will indicate a greater role of self-interest than others, but it is hard to argue that diverging understandings of self-interest dominate Americans' policy views.

A long line of research indicates that economic self-interest does not dominate Americans' voting decisions, either. One important strand of research has considered how people's personal economic experience, and their perceptions of the nation's overall economic conditions, influence their voting decisions. In short, people's personal circumstances matter much less than how they perceive the overall economy. This phenomenon is called *sociotropic voting*: voting influenced by the entire society, rather than personal conditions alone. Sociotropic voting is not necessarily al-truistic (self-sacrificing): Voters certainly could reason that what is good for the entire country is, in the long run, good for their own interests. What many observers find surprising, however, is the extent to which Americans routinely equate the overall public interest with their own in-terest. Across the income spectrum, Americans seem to have similar views about what the government should and should not do. As we will see next, the "race divide" is often wider.

UNDERSTANDING AMERICAN ATTITUDES ABOUT RACE

Discussions of racial attitudes often seem sharply polarized. At one ex-treme, some observers argue that U.S. politics is dogged by the continued preeminence of white racism, which blights the life chances of blacks, Latinos, and other historical minorities. Other observers see the United States as rapidly moving beyond the racial conflicts of the past. The liter-ature on racial attitudes is vast, and we will not attempt to survey it; we will simply note some major themes that illustrate challenges for the practice of American democracy.

What do we mean by "race," anyway? Race and ethnicity both are so-cial rather than biological concepts. (One of us recently heard an ac-quaintance from Barbados bitterly criticizing all the lazy, irresponsible blacks in her neighborhood—even though her skin was darker than that of most African-Americans, and she was probably as likely to encounter white racism as they were.) In particular, some groups that used to be dis-tinct—and stigmatized—ethnic minorities within the United States, such as the Irish, now tend to blend with the "white" majority. From our perspective as public opinion observers, racial and ethnic differences are precisely as real and important as people think they are. We can imagine a future in which Americans are truly indifferent to racial and ethnic dif-ferences, but we do not live in it.

Some basic facts about race and ethnicity in America condition our discussion. In the 1970 census, blacks made up about 11 percent of the U.S. population, and people of Hispanic origin constituted less than 5 percent. By the 2000 census, Hispanic or Latino respondents outnum-bered black respondents, 12.5 percent to 12.3 percent. Setting aside several complications,[98] you can see that the Hispanic population has grown rapidly. The Asian-American population has also grown rapidly, although not as much in absolute terms: from 0.8 percent of the population in 1970 to 3.6 percent in 2000. Meanwhile, over much of the twentieth century, African-Americans were moving out of southern rural areas into southern and northern cities. All these changes (among many others) have altered Americans' experience of racial and ethnic difference. They have also altered the shape of survey research: As racial and ethnic minorities grow larger, it becomes easier to conduct national surveys of these groups. Here we will focus primarily on certain aspects of white–black relations. At that, we will pay more attention to white attitudes, partly because more is known about them (because they dominate typical national samples by sheer numbers), and partly because majority beliefs have special political importance.

Unquestionably, whites' attitudes toward African-Americans have warmed over time. In 1963, 31 percent of white respondents "tend[ed] to agree" that "Negroes are inferior to white people."[99] In itself this figure was probably much smaller than it would have been at the beginning of the twentieth century, when white racism was supported by scientific theories of the day. Such a blunt question has not been asked in many years. We do know that in a 1997 survey, only 6 percent of white respondents agreed that black Americans' social disadvantages were "mainly because most blacks have less inborn ability to learn."[100] White support for outright discrimination against blacks has dropped precipitously. One measure of this transformation is attitudes toward racial intermarriage. In a 1963 survey, 60 percent of respondents favored laws banning "marriages between Negroes and whites."[101] When the GSS began in 1972, 39 percent of white respondents supported such laws. By 2000, only about 4 percent of white respondents did.[102] Similarly, in 1972, 40 percent of white respondents agreed that whites "have a right to keep [African-Americans] out of their neighborhoods"; in 1996, only 13 percent agreed.[103] In 1944, fewer than half of white respondents believed that "Negroes [should] have as good a chance as whites at any kind of job"; by 1972, almost all whites said that Negroes should have as good a chance.[104]

Some observers argue that while American whites express abstract support for the proposition that blacks should be equal, they less often support actual policies to promote equality. In the 1996 NES, only 42 percent of white respondents—but over 90 percent of black respondents—agreed that the government should "see to it that black people get fair treatment in jobs."[105] So-called "affirmative action" policies are even less popular among whites, although their popularity varies depending on the specific proposal (and question wording). In 2000, only 9 percent of white respondents—but 56 percent of black respondents—agreed that "blacks should be given preference in hiring and promotion" due to past discrimination.[106] Notice that both whites and blacks express much stronger support for "fair treatment" than for racial preferences in hiring. Many observers argue that racial preferences amount to "reverse discrimination" and are inherently a poor way of seeking equal opportunity. However, the gap between whites and blacks on these and many other policy issues is, in the words of Donald Kinder and Lynn Sanders, "a divide without peer": an exceptionally wide disagreement across demographic groups.[107]

Kinder and Sanders probe beyond race to explore racial *attitudes* that may explain whites' frequent opposition to various policies designed to benefit racial minorities. They assert a central role for what they call *racial resentment*—not the outright belief that blacks are inferior to whites, but a more general belief that blacks are getting more than they deserve. For instance, one indicator of racial resentment is agreement with the following statement: "Irish, Italian, Jewish and many other minorities overcame prejudice and worked their way up. Blacks should do the same without any special favors." In the 2000 NES, 71 percent of white respondents agreed with this statement. Kinder and Sanders combine several questions to create their measure of racial resentment.

Kinder and Sanders show that racial resentment more strongly predicts (and, presumably, affects) whites' attitudes toward a wide range of social policies than do ideological measures of people's commitments to equality or individualism. Some of these social policies are obviously race-related, as in affirmative action. Others are not: Whites who score high in racial resentment are much less supportive of spending on "welfare" and food stamps. Martin Gilens has shown that whites tend drastically to exaggerate the proportion of welfare recipients who are black.[108] Apparently, then, the racially resentful tend to perceive antipoverty programs as "black programs" and to oppose them on that basis.

If the extent of racial resentment powerfully predicts whites' support for affirmative action, does this mean that racial resentment *explains* why most whites oppose affirmative action? Probably not. First, we should mention that the statements used to measure (white) racial resentment are statements that many black respondents also agreed with. For instance, while 73 percent of white respondents agreed in 2000 that blacks should work their way up "without any special favors," 46 percent of black respondents also agreed (while 41 percent disagreed). Interestingly, however, for black respondents there was almost no relationship between this question and support for racial preferences in hiring—while for whites, the two issues were strongly connected. Apparently, whites are much more likely than blacks to think of hiring preferences as a "special favor," rather than a counterbalance against discrimination in the past or present.

Nevertheless, much of the gap between whites and blacks cannot be explained by racial resentment, at least as measured by Kinder and Sanders. For instance, even most whites who strongly *disagree* that blacks should work their way up without "special favors" also oppose racial hiring preferences. It might be that whites understate the true extent of their racial resentment—indeed, evidence suggests that some do.[109] But much of the racial divide can (at least arguably) be explained without attributions of bitterness or outright prejudice. First, consider the obvious divergence of *group interests*. White respondents presumably tend to perceive that preferences for blacks are preferences against whites; perhaps we should be surprised that whites *ever* support such preferences. (We say "group interests" rather than "personal interests" because—much as we saw earlier with respect to income—people's attitudes toward race-targeted policies do not seem to depend very much on whether they or their family have been or are likely to be directly affected.) More subtly, people's life experiences—which, in the United States, tend to vary considerably depending in part on their race—influence their perceptions of social causality and social justice. For instance, blacks are more likely to know stories of (black) friends and relatives who feel they have been hurt by white racial discrimination; whites are more likely to know stories of (white) friends and relatives who feel they have been hurt by affirmative action. Without any conscious prejudice on anyone's part, these differing experiences are likely to lead to different policy beliefs.

The racial divide is real and wide, but far from absolute. While blacks and whites disagree sharply on race-targeted policies, the differences narrow or disappear for many other issues. Nevertheless, the black–white divide has high political salience because it carries over dramatically into vote decisions. In the 2000 presidential election, according to exit polls, 90 percent of black voters voted for Democratic candidate Al Gore, compared with only 42 percent of white voters.

WOMEN'S ROLE, WOMEN'S RIGHTS

As we saw earlier in the chapter, attitudes about the proper role of women changed dramatically over the second half of the twentieth century. Now, overwhelming majorities of Americans generally agree in principle that women are entitled to the same rights as men and should play many of the same roles. (In 1972, 74 percent of GSS respondents said they would vote for a qualified woman for president; in 1998, 94 percent did. Interestingly, across this entire period, there was no real difference between men's and women's answers.) Nevertheless, women's social role remains a matter of contention; abortion rights are a perennial focus of political dispute; and men and women often have very different political preferences.

Among married couples, double-income households have become much more common over the past fifty years. Americans, both men and women, remain ambivalent about women's increasingly common dual role as income-earners and mothers. (Ambivalence about men's common dual role as income-earners and fathers seems to be less intense.) In the 1996 GSS, 67 percent of men and 68 percent of women agreed that "both the husband and the wife should contribute to the household income." Yet many Americans worry about the effect of women's work on family life. In the 2002 GSS, 45 percent of men and 34 percent of women agreed that a "pre-school kid is likely to suffer if his or her mother works"; 41 percent of men and 39 percent of women agreed that "all in all, family life suffers when the woman has a full-time job." Here and in other questions, the differences between men's and women's responses are strikingly (often vanishingly) small.

Abortion is widely considered one of the most controversial issues in American politics. One reason is that the public is—depending on the exact wording of the question—so evenly divided. In one 2003 survey, 44 percent of respondents said they were "more pro-life"; 44 percent said they were "more pro-choice."[110] But this result is misleading if it conjures the image of two opposed camps with nobody in the middle. In another 2003 survey, 26 percent of respondents said that "abortions should be legal under any circumstances," 55 percent that they should be "legal only under certain circumstances," and 17 percent that they should be "illegal in all circumstances."[111] This question begs another: In what circumstances do Americans think abortion should be illegal? In yet another 2003 survey (see Figure 8.4), respondents were asked about a variety of situations in which abortion might be considered. Fully 85 percent said that it should be legal when the woman's life was endangered; only 35 percent said it should be legal "when the woman or family cannot afford to raise the child."

At face value, these results mean that while Americans support legal abortion in several circumstances, most reject the view that women should have the right to choose abortion regardless of their reasons (often referred to as "abortion on demand"). The General Social Survey reveals similar results. While there is strong support for legal abortion in many circumstances, modest majorities say that abortion should not be legal if a woman is unmarried, if she is poor and can't afford any more children, if she is married and wants no more children, or—most generally—if she wants it for any reason.[112]

These results seem to place modest but definite majorities in opposition to the 1973 Supreme Court ruling in *Roe v. Wade*, which gave women the right to an abortion at any time during the first three months of pregnancy (first trimester).[113] However, when people are asked about *Roe* directly, distinct majorities generally *support* it. One such question asked, "The U.S. Supreme Court ruled in 1973 that a woman can have an abortion if she wants one at any time during the first three months of pregnancy. Do you favor or oppose that ruling?" In January 2003, 54 percent said they favored the ruling, and 44 percent said they opposed it.[114] Thus, it appears that a crucial minority of Americans would say *both* that abortion should not be allowed for certain reasons, and that abortion should be allowed for *any* reason in the first trimester. Here is another example of how Americans can express apparently wildly inconsistent views even on very prominent policy issues.

Two aspects of these questions on abortion contribute to these inconsistent responses. One is called a *prestige effect:* Many people are somewhat inclined to support whatever side the Supreme Court happens to be on.

The other is sometimes called the *forbid/allow asymmetry:* People may be reluctant to endorse either "forbidding" abortion (which sounds harsh) or "allowing" it (which sounds permissive). For instance, in a 1941 study, when asked, "Do you think that the United States should allow speeches against democracy?" only 25 percent of respondents said that such speeches should be allowed. Yet, when asked, "Do you think that the United States should forbid speeches against democracy?" only 54 percent said that they should be forbidden, while 46 percent said that they should not be forbidden. Apparently over 20 percent of the public felt (or would have said) that such speeches should neither be forbidden or allowed![115]

Interestingly, the abortion issue—like the questions we considered earlier in this section—evokes little overall difference between men's and women's views. In General Social Surveys between 1998 and 2002, 42 percent of men and 40 percent of women said that abortion should be legal if the woman wants it for any reason. Abortion is an important political issue not because it separates men from women, but because it separates the parties: Supporters of abortion rights overwhelmingly support the Democratic Party, and opponents of abortion rights overwhelmingly support the Republican Party. The ideological divide between these "pro-choice" and "pro-life" camps is stark. Yet most Americans, both women and men, seem to seek a middle ground.

So far we have emphasized general agreement between women and men—yet, in recent presidential elections, the "gender gap" has been large (although not nearly so large as the racial gap). In the 2000 election, 54 percent of female voters voted for Al Gore and 43 percent voted for George W. Bush. The male electorate was almost a mirror image: 53 percent voted for Bush, 42 percent for Gore. If the gender gap doesn't hinge on obvious "women's issues," where does it come from? The answer is somewhat controversial. We know that women tend to be more supportive of social welfare spending than men are. Also, women appear to place more weight on national economic conditions while men place greater weight on personal economic circumstances—in other words, women vote more sociotropically than men do. Thus, the Republican Party's emphasis, especially since Ronald Reagan's 1980 campaign, on tax cuts and reduced social spending has more appeal to men than to women.[116] Although the gender gap is large enough to interest political observers (and candidates!), it is much smaller than the racial divide we considered earlier.

CONSIDERED OPINIONS AND
DELIBERATIVE RESEARCH

As you have noticed, a shadow hangs over most discussions of public opinion as it relates to policy. Most Americans, judging from the results of various surveys and experiments, do not have anything like fixed opinions on most policy issues. As we will underscore in the next chapter, there is evidence that policymakers do respond to public opinion, but it simply is not possible for them to slavishly obey opinions that do not exist. It *is* often possible for them to claim public support for their policies, even when those policies disagree. For instance, in 2001 and again in 2003, Congress approved large packages of tax cuts supported by President George W. Bush. Supporters of the tax cuts cited polls that indicated, for instance, that most Americans thought their taxes were too high. Opponents of the tax cuts cited other polls that showed, among other things, that most Americans would rather "protect Social Security" than reduce taxes. We do not mean to imply that survey respondents are infinitely malleable: They aren't. It would be hard to argue from survey results that most Americans oppose Social Security, believe the government should own all large businesses, or favor invading Canada. But considering that these tax cuts have been estimated to reduce government revenues by at least $2.3 trillion over a ten-year period, it is discomfiting to find that political observers cannot agree whether the public generally supports or opposes these tax cuts—quite possibly because many citizens do not know. Perhaps even more disturbing, in early 2003 (before the second round of tax cuts), only 50 percent of respondents in one survey knew that federal taxes had recently been reduced![117]

Some observers have proposed and experimented with *deliberative research* as a way to give citizens an intelligible voice in public policy debates. The term "deliberative research" is ours, not theirs; deliberative researchers use a variety of conceptual languages and methods. Deliberation most broadly means "thinking"; what we call deliberative research attempts to probe beneath people's top-of-the-head survey responses to evoke and record their *considered opinions* on policy issues. Not all research on deliberation is designed to give the public a clearer voice; for instance, James Kuklinski and colleagues have investigated the effects of deliberation on political tolerance judgments, and these experiments were not intended to affect policy debates.[118] The impetus for policy-relevant deliberative research has mostly come from people outside academia, and it is debatable whether deliberative research can be done with academic objectivity.

Deliberative research often, but not always, falls into one of two categories: survey-based research that hinges on the individual, or group-based research that emphasizes a search for consensus. This very word "deliberation" fosters this duality. Sometimes deliberation refers to the individual act of carefully considering the consequences of a decision before one decides. At other times, it means a group activity of attempting to come to a decision together through mutual persuasion, as when a jury deliberates about a defendant's guilt. These meanings lend themselves to different ways of exploring people's beliefs.

The Americans Talk Issues (ATI) surveys represent a relatively pure example of individual survey research. The ATI surveys try to go beyond the limitations of most surveys by asking many questions about a policy issue, by providing important information about the issue, and by presenting a balance of arguments on all sides of the issue. (For instance, in January 1991, when many surveys were asking one or two questions about the impending Gulf War, ATI fielded an entire survey with over sixty questions about the Gulf crisis.) As with other surveys, all the participants (respondents) receive the same questions, and they do not talk with each other.

In contrast, the Jefferson Center's Citizens Juries illustrate a group-based model of deliberative research. A citizens jury typically brings together anywhere from twelve to twenty-four people, chosen to be broadly representative of the public, for three to five days of discussion on a single issue. The jurors hear expert testimony, ask questions of the experts, discuss the issue at length, and ultimately try to arrive at a group consensus on policy recommendations. For instance, a 1993 citizens jury on federal budget issues ultimately recommended a budget incorporating over $70 billion per year in tax increases—although, at the outset, eleven of the twenty-four jurors had favored *cutting* taxes.

These two broad models of deliberative research—one in the survey tradition, the other rather like an extended focus group—have complementary strengths and weaknesses. In the survey model, unlike the group-based model, the large number of participants and the scripting of the interviews make the results fairly reliable. (As we noted in Chapter Three, reliability is quite distinct from validity. Reliability means that the survey would be expected to yield similar results each time, unless people's actual beliefs or "considerations" change. Whether deliberative surveys offer a *valid* and useful measure of "considered opinions" on policy issues is open to debate.) But the limits of a telephone survey assure that people will not have much time to think through difficult issues, and by design, they have no opportunity to discuss their differences face to face. A group-based model can offer abundant time and opportunity for mutual persuasion as well as individual thought. However, because a group discussion is influenced by many factors that are hard to control or even to measure—such as the role of the moderator, the influence of de facto group leaders, and even the body language of the expert witnesses—the results are less reliable. In other words, we cannot tell whether five different groups would come to five radically different conclusions.

James Fishkin's "deliberative public opinion polls" are an especially interesting foray into deliberative research. The 1996 National Issues Convention led by Fishkin was the most ambitious and expensive such effort, and the one involving the most "pure" academics, as well as an attempt to combine some of the strengths of individual- and group-based approaches. Fishkin, a political philosopher at the University of Texas, argues that a well-done deliberative poll can intensify the processes of collective deliberation that shape ordinary public opinion, yet leave it with an uncertain voice on policy issues.

> An ordinary poll models what the electorate thinks, given how little it knows. A deliberative opinion poll models what the electorate would think, if, hypothetically, it could be immersed in intensive deliberative processes. The point of a deliberative opinion poll is prescriptive, not predictive. It has a *recommending force,* telling us what the entire mass public would think about some policy issues or some candidates if it could be given an opportunity for extensive reflection and access to information.[119]

Fishkin does not quite define "recommending force," but clearly he believes that the results of a well-done deliberative poll should be valued by other citizens and by policymakers as an indication of—so to speak— what people would think about an issue if they thought about the issue.

The National Issues Convention (NIC), held in January 1996, brought over 400 citizens together in Austin, Texas, for a weekend of intense engagement with a variety of domestic and foreign issues: They received carefully prepared briefing books; heard talks by policy analysts; and engaged in extended discussions with each other. Fishkin cites participants' views on a "flat tax" as an example of the NIC's importance. A "flat tax" is an income tax in which everyone pays the same percentage rate, as opposed to the existing "progressive" income tax in which people with higher incomes pay a higher rate. Steve Forbes, a wealthy publisher who was among the ten Republican presidential challengers of incumbent Bill Clinton, advocated the flat tax. Forbes argued that a progressive tax punished entrepreneurs while a flat tax would encourage them, and would also be simpler to administer. Many political observers expected the flat tax idea to be popular and influential in the campaign. At the beginning of the NIC, 43 percent of participants favored the flat tax. At the end, after hearing Forbes defend the proposal and other speakers criticize it, only 29 percent favored it. It is hard to say whether or how these shifts mattered; no one claims that the "whole country" was glued to the PBS coverage of the NIC in search of recommending force. However, the NIC may have convinced the journalists who covered it that the flat tax was more likely to lose than to gain support over the course of the campaign, as indeed it did. More generally, Fishkin argues that the NIC serves as one model for promoting democratic discussion: "To the extent that a serious public dialogue occurs not just on television but also in communities around the country, deliberative democracy has a chance of taking hold."[120]

CONCLUSION

We end this chapter with a conundrum. In terms of their basic values, Americans seem reasonably democratic: generally favorable to civil liberties (although, for better or worse, far from being doctrinaire civil libertarians); generally inclined to seek and to support some sort of common good; more often similar than sharply divided in basic policy priorities. However, Americans are not well equipped for much of the work of democracy, if that work goes beyond merely "supporting the Ins [or] the Outs." Many do not know much about political issues; their votes are often not closely related to their expressed issue positions, and those positions are often changeable and inconsistent almost to the vanishing point. Indeed, as mentioned earlier, many Americans explicitly shy away from political debate and disagreement, which makes it hard to judge whether they do or could have meaningful positions on the most difficult decisions facing the country.[121] Nevertheless, we will argue in the next chapter that public opinion palpably does have an ongoing influence on government policy—an influence that we generally believe is for the better.

NOTES

1. Quoted in Walter LaFeber, "American Policy-makers, Public Opinion, and the Outbreak of the Cold War, 1945–50," in Yônosuke Nagai and Akira Iriye, eds., *The Origins of the Cold War in Asia* (New York: Columbia University Press, 1977), p. 60.

2. Even in the U.S. Congress, much of the detailed work of drafting legislation is left to the staffs, and members of Congress sometimes complain that they do not really understand the bills they are voting on.

3. For instance, Saddam Hussein, who controlled Iraq from 1979 until 2003, claimed to have won 99.96 percent of the vote in a 1995 plebiscite—and 100 percent of the vote (with 100 percent turnout) in a second plebiscite in 2002.

4. Alexis de Tocqueville, *Democracy in America*, Book I, Chapter XV.

5. To this day the president is chosen by an electoral college, not directly by the citizens—a civics lesson that many Americans relearned in 2000, when George W. Bush ultimately was elected despite receiving about 500,000 fewer votes than his opponent, Al Gore. The original idea was that electors in each state would meet to form their own judgments about who was best suited to be president. Now, the electors are pledged in advance to support specific candidates (although every so often an elector votes for someone else).

6. David Mayhew, in *Congress: The Electoral Connection* (New Haven: Yale University Press, 1974), offers one famous account of members of Congress as driven primarily by the desire to be reelected, rather than to serve the public good. Joseph Bessette's *The Mild Voice of Reason* (Chicago: University of Chicago Press, 1994) argues that to a great extent, Congress really does engage in public-spirited deliberation.

7. Walter Lippmann, *Public Opinion* (1922; New York: Free Press, 1965), p. 19.

8. For instance, political scientist and philosopher Robert Dahl writes, "No intellectually defensible claim can be made that policy elites (actual or putative) possess superior moral knowledge or more specifically superior knowledge of what constitutes the public good. Indeed, we have some reason for thinking that specialization, which is the very ground for the influence of policy elites, may itself impair their capacity for moral judgment." Robert Dahl, *Democracy and Its Critics* (New Haven: Yale University Press, 1989), p. 337.

9. Walter Lippmann, *The Phantom Public* (New York: Harcourt, Brace and Company, 1925), p. 189.

10. A thorough survey of the evidence appears in Michael X. Delli Carpini and Scott Keeter, *What Americans Know About Politics and Why It Matters* (New Haven: Yale University Press, 1996), especially Chaps. 2 and 3. Stephen Earl Bennett and colleagues find similar results for public knowledge of foreign policy in several nations, although Germans stand

out as the most knowledgeable Stephen Earl Bennett, Richard S. Flickinger, John R. Baker, Staci L. Rhine, and Linda L. M. Bennett, "Citizens' Knowledge of Foreign Affairs," *Harvard International Journal of Press/Politics* 1 (1996):10–29.

11. Some Americans surely confused Nicaragua with the neighboring country of El Salvador, where the United States backed the *government* against the Marxist rebels there.

12. Vanishing Voter Project, "Americans Are Forgetting Some of What They Knew About Bush and Gore." http://www.vanishingvoter.org/W2000/Press_Releases/04–21–00.shtml (accessed 4/27/2004).

13. Scott L. Althaus, *Collective Preferences in Democratic Politics: Opinion Surveys and the Will of the People* (New York: Cambridge University Press, 2003), p. 208. (We are also indebted to Althaus for the Vanishing Voter Project example above, which he cites on p. 203, although we have updated the URL.)

14. Paul F. Lazarsfeld, Bernard R. Berelson, and Hazel Gaudet, *The People's Choice* (New York: Duell, Sloan, and Pierce, 1944).

15. Ibid., pp. 65–66.

16. Ibid., p. 27.

17. Bernard R. Berelson, Paul F. Lazarsfeld, and William N. McPhee, *Voting: A Study of Opinion Formation in a Presidential Campaign* (Chicago: University of Chicago Press, 1954), p. 293. This book describes a 1948 study in Elmira, New York.

18. Angus Campbell, Philip E. Converse, Warren E. Miller, and Donald E. Stokes, *The American Voter,* unabridged edition (New York: Wiley, 1960; Chicago: University of Chicago Press, 1976).

19. Of course, some people may misremember which party their parents supported. Also, "relatively stable" does not mean "fixed in stone": Often people's party ID does change—slowly or quickly—over time. The transmission of partisanship and how partisanship can change over time is examined by M. Kent Jennings and Richard Niemi in *Generations and Politics* (Princeton: Princeton University Press, 1981) and *The Political Character of Adolescence* (Princeton: Princeton University Press, 1974).

20. An ambitious account of how partisanship influences people's political thinking and voting is Donald P. Green, Bradley Palmquist, and Eric Schickler, *Partisan Hearts and Minds: Political Parties and the Social Identity of Voters* (New Haven: Yale University Press, 2002).

21. These figures—which exclude votes for independent candidate John Anderson—come from the 1980 National Election Study. Here we combine all self-described independents, including those who said that they leaned toward one or the other party.

22. Robert Huckfeldt and John Sprague, *Citizens, Politics, and Social Communication: Information and Influence in a Presidential Campaign* (New York: Cambridge University Press, 1995).

23. Walter Lippmann, *Public Opinion* (1922; New York: Free Press, 1965), p. 143.

24. In fact, the likelihood was so small that to explain why so many people vote anyway, Downs argued—somewhat murkily—that they consider voting a form of "insurance" against the collapse of democracy (p. 268). However, if it is unlikely that one person's vote could determine an election, it is nearly unimaginable that it could save democracy! Downs did not even mention the intangible benefit that we mention in the text.

25. Alexis de Tocqueville, *Democracy in America* (New York: HarperPerennial, 1988), Vol. 1, Chap. 5 (at p. 198).

26. For instance, the U.S. Catholic bishops oppose both abortion rights and capital punishment, in what is sometimes called a "consistent pro-life" or "seamless web of life" ethic.

Interestingly, people who favor abortion rights while opposing capital punishment (liberals) or vice versa (conservatives) often criticize their counterparts' inconsistency but see no inconsistency in their own views. Actually, philosophically consistent arguments can be made for any of these positions.

27. This chapter touches on several measures of political sophistication, but in limited detail. A good overview can be found in Robert C. Luskin, "Measuring Political Sophistication," *American Journal of Political Science* 31 (1987):856–899.

28. Philip E. Converse, "The Nature of Belief Systems in Mass Publics," in David E. Apter, ed., *Ideology and Discontent* (New York: Free Press, 1964), pp. 206–261.

29. Cited in W. Russell Neuman, *The Paradox of Mass Politics: Knowledge and Opinion in the American Electorate* (Cambridge: Harvard University Press, 1986), pp. 19–20.

30. Richard Herrera, "Understanding the Language of Politics: A Study of Elites and Masses," *Political Science Quarterly* 111 (Winter 1996–1997):619–637. Notice that Converse obtained a similar result (37 percent were not able to name any difference between liberal and conservative, meaning that 63 percent were—although Converse rejected some of these answers as obviously incorrect).

31. See Philip E. Converse, "Attitudes and Non-attitudes: Continuation of a Dialogue," in Edward R. Tufte, ed., *The Quantitative Analysis of Social Problems* (Boston: Addison-Wesley, 1970), pp. 168–189. This paper was originally presented in 1963.

32. Benjamin I. Page and Robert Y. Shapiro, "The Rational Public and Democracy," in George E. Marcus and Russell L. Hanson, eds., *Reconsidering the Democratic Public* (University Park: Penn State University Press, 1993), p. 61.

33. Benjamin I. Page and Robert Y. Shapiro, *The Rational Public: Fifty Years of Trends in Americans' Policy Preferences* (Chicago: University of Chicago Press, 1992). We emphasize here, as we will again, that "information" is not necessarily factual.

34. See Page and Shapiro, *Rational Public*, pp. 90–97, for further discussion.

35. See the 1939 Gallup surveys cited in Page and Shapiro, *Rational Public*, p. 100.

36. See Page and Shapiro, *Rational Public*, pp. 100–104 and 378–379, for further discussion.

37. The full question wording: "In general, do you think the courts in this area deal too harshly, not harshly enough, or about right with criminals?" Survey conducted by the Public Policy Research Institute at Texas A&M, June 1995 (Roper Center accession number 0300366).

38. See Mark Warr, "Poll Trends: Public Opinion on Crime and Punishment," *Public Opinion Quarterly* 59 (1995):296–310; Greg M. Shaw, Robert Y. Shapiro, Shmuel Lock, and Lawrence R. Jacobs, "Trends: Crime, the Police, and Civil Liberties," *Public Opinion Quarterly* 62 (1998):405–426.

39. Larry M. Bartels, "The American Public's Defense Spending Preferences in the Post-Cold War Era," *Public Opinion Quarterly* 58, 4 (Winter 1994):479–508.

40. See James A. Stimson, *Public Opinion in America: Moods, Cycles, and Swings* (Boulder: Westview Press, 1991); Robert S. Erikson, Michael B. Mackuen, and James A. Stimson, *The Macro Polity* (New York: Cambridge University Press, 2002).

41. William G. Mayer, *The Changing American Mind* (Ann Arbor: University of Michigan Press, 1992).

42. See, more recently, the debate in Jeff Manza, Fay Lomax Cook, and Benjamin I. Page, eds., *Navigating Public Opinion: Polls, Policy, and the Future of American Democracy* (New York: Oxford University Press, 2002).

43. Page and Shapiro, *Rational Public,* p. 365.

44. Page and Shapiro, "Educating and Manipulating the Public," in Michael Margolis and Gary A. Mauser, eds., *Manipulating Public Opinion: Essays on Public Opinion as a Dependent Variable* (Pacific Grove, CA: Brooks/Cole, 1989), p. 294. Benjamin Ginsberg argues that mass opinion in the Western democracies has been tamed and harnessed to increase the power of the state. See Ginsberg, *The Captive Public: How Mass Opinion Promotes State Power* (New York: Basic Books, 1986).

45. Barry Sussman, former director of polling for the *Washington Post,* wrote a book called *What Americans Really Think—and Why Our Politicians Pay No Attention* (New York: Pantheon Books, 1988*).* Of course, the title only makes sense if Americans really do think something.

46. CBS News, field dates 1/30/97–2/1/97 (Roper Center accession number 0272753); 76 percent responded "favor," 17 percent "oppose."

47. CBS News and *New York Times,* field dates 1/14/97–1/17/97 (Roper Center accession number 0271190); 39 percent responded "the kind of issue," 49 percent "not the kind of issue."

48. CBS News and *New York Times,* field dates 3/10/04–3/14/04 (Roper Center accession numbers 0449530 and 0449533). "Would you favor or oppose an amendment to the U.S. Constitution that would allow marriage *only* between a man and a woman?" 59 percent favor, 35 percent oppose. "Do you think defining marriage as a union only between a man and a woman is an important enough issue to be worth changing the Constitution for, or isn't it that kind of issue?" 38 percent "important enough," 56 percent "isn't . . . that kind of issue."

49. Samuel Popkin, *The Reasoning Voter* (Chicago: University of Chicago Press, 1991), p. 213.

50. Ibid.

51. David P. Glass, "Evaluating Presidential Candidates: Who Focuses on Their Personal Attributes?," *Public Opinion Quarterly* 49 (1985):517–534; Ester R. Fuchs and Robert Y. Shapiro, "Government Performance as a Basis for Machine Support," *Urban Affairs Quarterly* 18 (1983):537–550.

52. A major collection of studies on this theme is Paul M. Sniderman, Richard A. Brody, and Philip E. Tetlock, *Reasoning and Choice: Explorations in Political Psychology* (New York: Cambridge University Press, 1991*).* A useful overview of the heuristics literature is Jeffery J. Mondak, "Cognitive Heuristics, Heuristic Processing, and Efficiency in Political Decision Making," *Research in Micropolitics* 4 (1993):117–142. See also Richard R. Lau and David P. Redlawsk, "Advantages and Disadvantages of Cognitive Heuristics in Political Decision Making," *American Journal of Political Science* 45 (2001):951–971.

53. See Arthur Lupia, "Short Cuts Versus Encyclopedias: Information and Voting Behavior in California Insurance Reform Elections," *American Political Science Review* 8 (Spring 1994):63–76.

54. Morris P. Fiorina, *Retrospective Voting in American National Elections* (New Haven: Yale University Press, 1981), makes the case most extensively at an individual level. Michael B. Mackuen, Robert Erikson, and James Stimson have argued that future economic prospects matter more than "retrospective" evaluations, in "Peasants or Bankers? The American Electorate and the U.S. Economy," *American Political Science Review* 86 (1992):597–611.

55. Rich discussions of the on-line tally theory and related models can be found in Milton Lodge and Kathleen M. McGraw, eds., *Political Judgment: Structure and Process* (Ann

Arbor: University of Michigan Press, 1995). A more recent test and extension of the theory is David P. Redlawsk, "You Must Remember This: A Test of the On-line Model of Voting," *The Journal of Politics* 63 (2001):29–58.

56. Delli Carpini and Keeter, *What Americans Know About Politics,* pp. 256–257.

57. Larry M. Bartels, "Uninformed Votes: Information Effects in Presidential Elections," *American Journal of Political Science* 40 (1996):194–230. Here Bartels uses only demographic characteristics, not political attitudes, to predict vote choice. Although this choice is limiting, it spares him from the objection that information may also affect people's political views, as argued by Althaus below.

58. Scott L. Althaus, "Information Effects in Collective Preferences," *American Political Science Review* 92 (September 1998):545–558; Scott L. Althaus, *Collective Preferences in Democratic Politics: Opinion Surveys and the Will of the People* (New York: Cambridge University Press, 2003).

59. James DeNardo, *The Amateur Strategist: Intuitive Deterrence Theories and the Politics of the Nuclear Arms Race* (New York: Cambridge University Press, 1995), p. 181. A useful overview of schema theory is David O. Sears, Letitia Anne Peplau, Jonathan L. Freedman, and Shelley E. Taylor, *Social Psychology,* 6th edition (Englewood Cliffs, NJ: Prentice-Hall, 1988), pp. 101–115.

60. John R. Zaller, *The Nature and Origins of Mass Opinion* (New York: Cambridge University Press, 1992); John Zaller and Stanley Feldman, "A Simple Theory of the Survey Response: Answering Questions Versus Revealing Preferences," *American Journal of Political Science* 36 (1992):579–616.

61. Zaller, *Nature and Origins,* p. 40.

62. What we call "political messages," Zaller usually calls "information"—but he emphasizes that he does *not* mean neutral facts. Notice, however, that there is no neat distinction between "political" and "nonpolitical" messages.

63. See Donald R. Kinder and Lynn M. Sanders, *Divided by Color: Racial Politics and Democratic Ideals* (Chicago: University of Chicago Press, 1996), Chap. 7.

64. These messages can affect public opinion in two ways. They can add new considerations, or they can change the way that people "sample" among their existing considerations, by priming or framing (see the further discussion in Chapter Eleven).

65. Zaller, *Nature and Origins,* p. 311; see also p. 328.

66. Ibid., pp. 331, 332.

67. Ibid., 332.

68. See Page, *Who Deliberates?*

69. ABC News/*Washington Post* survey, field dates December 14–15, 2000 (Roper Center accession number 0375554).

70. Gallup Poll survey on Attitudes Toward the Public Schools, field dates May 18-June 11, 1999 (Roper Center accession number 0337561).

71. Results courtesy of the University of Michigan's Numeric & Spatial Data Services Web site, http://nds.umdl.umich.edu/cgi/s/sda/hsda?harcWEVS+wevs. 49 percent of U.S. respondents "strongly agreed," and 42 percent "agreed." This level of agreement is comparable to that of many other countries who participated in the World Values Survey; in fact, the highest level of agreement was in Norway, where 72 percent "strongly agreed" and 22 percent "agreed." However, only five other countries besides Norway (out of about fifty) evinced greater agreement with this statement.

72. The People & the Press 1999 Millennium Poll conducted by Princeton Survey Research Associates for the Pew Research Center for People & the Press, field dates April 6–May 6, 1999 (Roper Center accession number 0331729).

73. For instance, a 2000 survey asked respondents, "In one word, could you tell me what democracy means for you?" Fully 49 percent said "liberty"—about two-thirds of those who answered. Just 6 percent said "equality," but this was the second most common response. Later, respondents were asked, "Do you think that democracy has more to do with liberty or equality?" 52 percent answered liberty, 34 percent answered equality, 9 percent volunteered "both," 2 percent volunteered "neither," and 3 percent did not know or did not answer. So, while both results indicate that liberty is more important than equality, people seem to place greater emphasis on equality when they are asked about it specifically than when they are not.

74. An excellent introduction to this complex issue is Martin Gilens, *Why Americans Hate Welfare: Race, Media, and the Politics of Antipoverty Policy* (Chicago: University of Chicago Press, 2000). On the question of whether and how Americans extend equality to the economic realm, see also Jennifer L. Hochschild, *What's Fair?: American Beliefs About Distributive Justice* (Cambridge, MA: Harvard University Press, 1981).

75. *Las Vegas Review-Journal,* "Rule by Polls," 12/28/98. Accessed on-line at http://www.reviewjournal.com/lvrj_home/1998/Dec–28Mon–1998/opinion/10303514.html.

76. John R. Hibbing and Elizabeth Theiss-Morse, *Stealth Democracy: Americans' Beliefs About How Government Should Work* (New York: Cambridge University Press, 2002), pp. 130–131.

77. Hibbing and Theiss-Morse, p. 161.

78. Under Germany's Weimar constitution of 1919, the popularly elected president appointed a chancellor, who was the head of government. The World War I hero Paul von Hindenburg was elected chancellor in 1925, and defeated Hitler to win reelection—at age 85!—in 1932. After von Hindenburg died in August 1934, Hitler arranged for the offices of president and chancellor to be combined in a new position, officially called Führer und Reichskanzler (Leader and Reich Chancellor). In a plebiscite, 88 percent of German voters approved of this change.

79. T. W. Adorno, Else Frenkel-Brunswik, Daniel J. Levinson, and R. Nevitt Sanford, *The Authoritarian Personality* (New York: Harper & Brothers, 1950).

80. Richard H. Rovere, *Senator Joe McCarthy* (New York: Harper & Row, 1959; 1973), pp. 7–8.

81. Samuel A. Stouffer, *Communism, Conformity, and Civil Liberties: A Cross-section of the Nation Speaks Its Mind* (Garden City, NY: Doubleday & Co., 1955), p. 13.

82. Stouffer, p. 38.

83. Stouffer, pp. 40–43.

84. Stouffer, pp. 44–45.

85. Stouffer, pp. 176–178.

86. Stouffer, p. 27.

87. Stouffer, p. 220.

88. Stouffer, pp. 32–34.

89. Berelson, Lazarsfeld, and McPhee, in their 1954 study, asked, "How could mass democracy work if all the people were deeply involved in politics? . . . Extreme interest goes with extreme partisanship and might culminate in rigid fanaticism that could destroy democratic processes if generalized throughout the country." Berelson et al., *Voting,* p. 314.

90. James L. Gibson, "Political Intolerance and Political Repression During the McCarthy Red Scare," *American Political Science Review* 82, 2 (June 1988):511–529.

91. Gibson, pp. 518–519.

92. John L. Sullivan, James Piereson, and George E. Marcus, "An Alternative Conceptualization of Political Tolerance: Illusory Increases 1950s–1970s," *American Political Science Review* 73, 3 (Sept. 1979):781–794, at p. 784.

93. "Some people think that the government in Washington ought to reduce the income differences between the rich and the poor, perhaps by raising the taxes of wealthy families or by giving income assistance to the poor. Others think that the government should not concern itself with reducing this income difference between the rich and the poor. Here is a card with a scale from 1 to 7. Think of a score of 1 as meaning that the government ought to reduce the income differences between rich and poor, and a score of 7 meaning that the government should not concern itself with reducing income differences. What score between 1 and 7 comes closest to the way you feel?"

94. The low-income respondents averaged 3.30 on the 7-point scale, and the high-income respondents averaged 4.75.

95. This battery of questions begins, "We are faced with many problems in this country, none of which can be solved easily or inexpensively. I'm going to name some of these problems, and for each one I'd like you to tell me whether you think we're spending too much money on it, too little money, or about the right amount. Are we spending too much money, too little money, or about the right amount on . . ." While most respondents say we are spending too little on "assistance to the poor," "welfare" is less popular. In 2002 only 21 percent thought we were spending too little on "welfare," and 41 percent thought we were spending too much. Gilens, *Why Americans Hate Welfare,* discusses this and related points at length.

96. In the 1998 through 2002 GSS, 68 percent of low-income respondents and 78 percent of high-income respondents said we were spending too little on "improving the nation's education system." Overall, there was no clear relationship between income and support for higher spending on education.

97. In the 1998 through 2002 GSS, 61 percent of low-income respondents and 56 percent of high-income respondents said we were spending too little on "improving and protecting the environment"—not a statistically significant difference.

98. For instance, the 2000 census was the first census that allowed people to identify themselves as multiracial, as about 2.4 percent of respondents did. Also, because the Census Bureau treats race and Hispanic origin as distinct concepts, it happened in the 2000 census that about 2 percent of self-identified Hispanics also identified as black. A growing percentage of respondents do not identify with any of the census's five racial categories: the percentage of "some other race" respondents reached 5.5 percent in 2000, up from 0.3 percent in 1970.

99. "[Now let me ask you some questions about Negroes as people. Leaving aside the whole question of laws or civil rights, I'd like to know how you feel as an individual. Do you personally tend to agree more or disagree more with these statements?] . . . Negroes are inferior to white people." 31 percent agree more, 69 percent disagree more. Louis Harris and Associates, fielded October 1963 (Roper Center accession number 0246069).

100. "[On the average, black Americans/African-Americans have worse jobs, income and housing than white people.] Do you think these differences are . . . mainly because most blacks have less inborn ability to learn?" Among white respondents: 6 percent yes, 89 percent no, 1 percent sometimes (volunteered), 4 percent not sure. Yankelovich Partners for *Time*/CNN, field dates 9/23/97–10/2/97 (Roper Center accession number 0288173).

101. "Do you think there should be laws against marriages between Negroes and whites?" 60 percent yes, 36 percent no, 3 percent don't know. National Opinion Research Center, fielded December 1963 (Roper Center accession number 0199107). These results include respondents of all races.

102. "Do you think there should be laws against marriages between [Negroes/Blacks/African-Americans] and whites?" (The wording has varied over the years.)

103. "White people have a right to keep [Negroes/Blacks/African-Americans] out of their neighborhoods if they want to, and [Negroes/Blacks/African-Americans] should respect that right."

104. "Do you think Negroes should have as good a chance as white people to get any kind of job, or do you think white people should have the first chance at any kind of job?" In 1944: 42 percent as good, 51 percent whites first, 1 percent qualified responses (volunteered), 6 percent don't know. National Opinion Research Center, fielded May 1944 (accession number 0093810). In 1972: 96 percent as good, 3 percent whites first, 1 percent don't know. General Social Survey, fielded Feb.-April 1972 (accession number 0089800).

105. "Should the government in Washington see to it that black people get fair treatment in jobs, or is this not the federal government's business?"

106. "Some people say that because of past discrimination, blacks should be given preference in hiring and promotion. Others say that such preference in hiring and promotion of blacks is wrong because it gives blacks advantages they haven't earned. What about your opinion—are you for or against preferential hiring and promotion of blacks?" National Election Study, 2000.

107. Donald R. Kinder and Lynn M. Sanders, *Divided by Color: Racial Politics and Democratic Ideals* (Chicago: University of Chicago Press, 1997), p. 27.

108. Gilens, *Why Americans Hate Welfare.*

109. James H. Kuklinski, Paul M. Sniderman, Kathleen Knight, Thomas Piazza, Philip E. Tetlock, Gordon R. Lawrence, and Barbara Mellers, "Racial Prejudice and Attitudes Toward Affirmative Action," *American Journal of Political Science* 41 (1997):402–419.

110. "On the issue . . . pro-choice?" FOX News/Opinion Dynamics survey, field dates July 15–16, 2003 (Roper Center accession number 0435847).

111. CNN/*USA Today*/Gallup Poll, field dates October 24–26, 2003 (Roper Center accession number 0440288). The question has evoked very similar answers in 17 surveys going back to July of 1996.

112. Combining GSS results from 1998 through 2002, between 56 and 59 percent of respondents said that abortion should be illegal in each of these circumstances.

113. Specifically, *Roe v. Wade* states that the state may not regulate abortion decisions "prior to approximately the end of the first trimester," because during that period "mortality in abortion may be less than mortality in normal childbirth."

114. ABC News/*Washington Post* survey, field dates January 16–20, 2003 (Roper Center accession number 0419809).

115. D. Rugg, "Experiments in wording questions: II," in *Public Opinion Quarterly* 5 (1941):91–92, here cited from Hans-J. Hippler and Norbert Schwarz, "Not Forbidding Isn't Allowing: The Cognitive Basis of the Forbid–Allow Asymmetry," *Public Opinion Quarterly* 50, 1 (Spring 1986):87–96, at 87–88.

116. Three somewhat distinct recent accounts of the gender gap are: Carole Kennedy Chaney, R. Michael Alvarez, and Jonathan Nagler, "Explaining the Gender Gap in U.S. Presidential Elections, 1980–1992," *Political Research Quarterly* 51 (1998):311–339; Barbara Nor-

rander, "The Evolution of the Gender Gap," *Public Opinion Quarterly* 63 (1999):566–576; Karen M. Kaufmann and John R. Petrocik, "The Changing Politics of American Men: Understanding the Sources of the Gender Gap," *American Journal of Political Science* 43 (1999):864–887.

117. "First, to the best of your knowledge, in the past two years has there or hasn't there been a federal income tax cut?" 50 percent has, 33 percent has not been, 17 percent don't know. NPR/Kaiser/Kennedy School of Government, field dates 2/5/2003–3/17/2003 (Roper Center accession number 0428162).

118. See, for instance, James H. Kuklinski, Ellen Riggle, Victor Ottati, Norbert Schwarz, and Robert S. Wyer, Jr., "The Cognitive and Affective Bases of Political Tolerance Judgments," *American Journal of Political Science* 35 (1991):1–27.

119. James S. Fishkin, *Democracy and Deliberation: New Directions for Democratic Reform* (New Haven: Yale University Press, 1993), p. 81. See also James S. Fishkin, *The Voice of the People: Public Opinion and Democracy* (New Haven: Yale University Press, 1997).

120. Fishkin, *Voice of the People,* p. 184.

121. Nina Eliasoph, *Avoiding Politics: How Americans Produce Apathy in Everyday Life* (New York: Cambridge University Press, 1998); John R. Hibbing and Elisabeth Theiss-Morse, *Stealth Democracy: Americans' Beliefs About How Government Should Work* (New York: Cambridge University Press, 2002).

9

Public Opinion and Policymaking

COAUTHORED WITH LAWRENCE R. JACOBS

Unless mass views have some place in the shaping of policy, all the talk about democracy is nonsense. As [Harold] Lasswell has said, the "open interplay of opinion and policy is the distinguishing mark of popular rule."

V. O. KEY JR.,
Public Opinion and American Democracy

V. O. Key, Jr., firmly emphasizes what we observed in the first chapter: When we talk about democracy we must talk about public opinion.[1] By definition, in a democracy (from the Greek word *demos*), the people are supposed to rule. This expectation pervades American history; it is an important symbolic hope—if not a realistic aspiration—from the Declaration of Independence to the Constitution to reminders by Abraham Lincoln and others who have emphasized government "by the people" as well as "for the people."

The influence of public opinion on government is a central normative question (concerning the way things should be) as well as an empirical question (concerning the way things are) about democracy and politics. How much influence the public should have is a philosophical question that requires, as we saw in Chapter Eight, that we evaluate the basic competence of the mass public. One major challenge to any aspirations for democracy is the possibility that V. O. Key, Jr., himself feared: "that democratic government only amounts to a hoax, a ritual whose performance serves only to delude the people and thereby to convert them into willing subjects of the powers that be."[2]

How much effect the public actually has on government policymaking is, in fact, a question we can try to answer. Specifically, we can point to evidence that boldly shows that public opinion affects what government does to some more than minimally important degree. This may surprise some readers who are skeptical, or even cynical, about what happens in politics. Others may be puzzled that we even consider the question; from American history or social studies classes in high school, they may have learned that "of course, public opinion affects public policy in the United States." But we do not accept these assumptions without evidence that government does or does not respond to public opinion. Furthermore, if we find support for the assertion that government policies have in some noticeable ways responded to public opinion, whether this responsiveness will continue and whether we would want to call this government responsiveness "democratic" are other questions. We will return to these questions at the end of the chapter.

PUBLIC OPINION ONLY CONSTRAINS POLICY?

In considering the causal impact of public opinion on policy, it is useful to consider three possibilities: Public opinion constrains public policy; public opinion exerts strong pressure to direct or redirect government policy; public opinion is ignored in government policymaking.

In Chapter One, we observed how public opinion can ultimately at least constrain policymaking. (Attentive readers will note that we use "constrain" here in a context different from the term "ideological constraint" in Chapter Eight.) This occurred in the case of foreign policy issues such as aid to the contras in Nicaragua after a long period in which public opinion was ignored when the issue was not particularly salient and important. By "salient," we mean widely visible to the public, particularly in the mass media, or felt directly by people and their families and friends, as a poor economy might be. The issue of support for the contras in Nicaragua increased in visibility and prominence in the media as it was divulged that funds secretly obtained from the sale of arms to Iran were used to supply aid to the contra rebels, whom the United States was supporting against the leftist Nicaraguan government. This was the "Iran–Contra Affair," the event that catapulted U.S. marine Oliver North into the public eye as the allegedly heroic "fall guy" for the Reagan administration.[3]

To take another case, in the Gulf War period from late 1990 to 1991, President George Bush had the public's backing in his decision first to help defend Saudi Arabia against Iraq and then to lead a multinational, though largely American, attack against the Iraqis in Kuwait and Iraq. Similarly, in 1964–1965, Lyndon Johnson went to war in Vietnam initially with substantial public support. Much later, as we will discuss later in this chapter, the United States decreased its level of participation in the war after public opposition gathered momentum. Another case in point occurred when the United States supported the admission of the People's Republic of China (then commonly referred to as "Communist China" or "Red China") to the United Nations in 1971 only after public support very gradually—reflecting a long-standing reluctance—increased for this controversial decision.

On the domestic policy front, too, we can readily cite cases of government policies responding to public opinion. The Supreme Court initially legalized abortion in the United States (the well-known *Roe v. Wade* decision in 1973) after a ten-year period of declining public opposition to the legalization of abortion. The historically important Civil Rights Act of 1964 and Voting Rights Act of 1965 passed after public opinion became increasingly supportive of desegregation and of liberalizing "civil rights" policies broadly. Capital punishment was ruled unconstitutional in the early 1970s, following increasing public opposition to it from the 1950s on, as is shown in Figure 8.5 in Chapter Eight. But then in the 1970s, public opinion moved decisively in the opposite direction, and a subsequent ruling by the Supreme Court made capital punishment legal once more.[4] Ironically, in these cases of abortion and capital punishment, the government institutions changing these policies were the courts. In the end, the Supreme Court, which is supposed to be more insulated from shifts in public opinion than the other branches of government, which are held directly accountable to the electorate, made the final decision.

In focusing the discussion on the public's constraining influence, it is ambiguous whether the word "constrain" gives too little credit to the power of public opinion.[5] In the examples just cited, the public was often an important driving force that attempted to end racial inequities, fight crime, and either send American troops abroad or bring them home. These are, in part, subjective judgments: One person's "constraining effect" is another's "powerful effect." We will let the cases and data speak for themselves, so that the reader may judge. The authors of this chapter would argue that public opinion is more than a constraint, since the force of public opinion can be used to push policies through and to continue them. Clearly, to take some later examples, public support was critical to the passage in 1996 of welfare reform (which the public had long wanted in some form);[6] to increasing the minimum wage that same year; and to enacting at the same time some modest incremental health care reforms and regulations (the requirement that "preexisting conditions" be covered by insurance policies and that health insurance be "portable" as people change from one job to another). The public's second thoughts about enacting major health care reform, evoked by sharp congressional and organized group opposition, helped stop dead in its tracks the Clinton administration health care reform plan in 1994 (the plan was voted down in committee, never making it even to floor debate in Congress). Last, in the case at this writing (in the spring of 2004) of the occupation of Iraq by American troops at the end of the second Gulf War, increasing uncertain public support has been politically important in maintaining what has become a precarious policy.

In sharp contrast to these cases, we can also point out noteworthy instances in which the government has not done what public opinion (as revealed by opinion polls) has ostensibly wanted. This clearly happened in the case of aid to the contras for a significant period of time. There were also widespread public perceptions from 1970 to 1996 that "too much" was spent on foreign aid, and also on the space program, but there was not any responsive government reaction to this. But foreign aid, as a single general and amorphous policy, and the space program during that time had not been among the most urgent and salient issues in the mass media and thus not high on the public's radar screen.

There have been some well-known and widely debated examples of the failure of government to respond to what have been clear public preferences as reported in national opinion surveys. These include support for allowing some form of prayer in schools, as well as support for more stringent gun control laws (short of actually banning the possession of rifles or even handguns), although we have seen the enactment of restrictions on the sale of assault weapons and the requirement of a waiting period before a gun sale is permitted (the Brady Bill, named after President Reagan's press secretary, who was shot during an assassination attempt on the president). In the cases of both school prayer and gun control, however, questions have been raised about how responding to public opinion would lead to conflicts with the Constitution concerning the "separation of church and state" and the "right to bear arms." On gun control, political pressure from lobbies of gun owners (mainly the National Rifle Association) and gun and ammunition manufacturers have come into play—occurring so extensively that it has been widely criticized.

President Clinton's decision to invade Haiti during the 1994–1995 period clearly went against public opinion and against the preferences of most members of Congress in both parties. Nor did Clinton's decision to work vigorously for the passage of the North American Free Trade Agreement (NAFTA) initially have clear public support. In one of the most politically charged and polarizing issues in recent years (perhaps only topped by the controversy over the outcome of the 2000 presidential election), the Republicans in the House of Representatives went beyond the preferences of the majority of Americans in pursuing the impeachment of President Clinton (i.e., the House passed two articles of impeachment). Neither the House nor the Senate opted to vote on "censure," the option that the public supported. In the end, it was only the two-thirds vote required for Clinton's conviction by the Senate that prevented Congress from defying public opinion.[7]

Clearly, the public's wishes are not always followed, and we will return to this later. This apparent lack of responsiveness, however, may not mean a decision is, in the end, "undemocratic." We will also return to the question of what is "democratic" and what is not.

THEORIES

The problem in drawing general conclusions about the responsiveness of policymaking to public opinion is that we can point to different examples supporting different conclusions. The way political scientists attempt to resolve this is to consider theories about what to expect in American politics and to look as sweepingly as possible at what the available evidence shows.

Theoretically, there is good reason to expect a noticeable pattern of responsiveness of policymaking to public opinion. Specifically, we can identify political processes at work that should contribute to responsiveness.

First and foremost, the reason to expect some minimum—and observable—responsiveness in the United States has to do with periodic elections of government officials, when voters have the chance to voice their approval or disapproval of the actions of these leaders. Because elected leaders know that they (or, if they are not running for reelection, their party's candidate) will be held accountable at election time, they have reason to anticipate public opinion, so their attention to such opinion is not reserved only for election campaigns (see related discussion of rational choice theory and voting in Chapter Seven). Studies have tried to confirm in different ways that policy responsiveness increases as elections near.[8] We can also point again to the passage in the wake of the 1996 election of a modest health care reform bill, an increase in the minimum wage, and welfare reform. At election time, leaders ignore public opinion at their own peril; at other times, they know that they or their party may have to answer for their past acts at the next election.

Another possible reason to expect policy responsiveness is that voters elect leaders who are simply like themselves in enough ways that the leaders happen to share the opinions of the those who elect them. The leaders share the wants and values of the public.[9] This might also occur if leaders were chosen simply by random lottery among voters, which is an idea that has been given some consideration historically.[10] It is not clear, however, how similar political leaders actually are, individually or as a group, to ordinary citizens. These leaders self-select to be very active in politics, and they are clearly of upper status in terms of education, income, and occupation (disproportionately lawyers, today). For a long time, women and members of minority groups rarely held important public offices. So it is more likely that other processes and pressures occur that lead to responsiveness.

In addition to electoral pressure, there may be social pressure to comply with the public's wishes. There may be a feeling among elected representatives that they should represent those who have elected them. These representatives may feel that they are obligated to do what their constituents or voters have delegated them to do. In fact, representative who adopt this as a style of representation have been called "delegates." Other leaders—elected or appointed—feel that they have been chosen to act as their own consciences dictate, to do what they think is best for the public. There is no reason to expect these "trustees," as they have been called, to respond more to the demands voiced by the public than to other types of information related to policy decisions.[11] It is possible that the style of representation that leaders use may vary by issue or at different times. The term "political" or "politico" has been used to describe representatives who adopt varying styles for political or other reasons.

The critical question that we have to address here is how the public's preferences are determined by policymakers and then brought into, or linked to, the policymaking process. It has become popular in recent years to talk about how opinion polls and, in the 1990s, how "focus groups" have become increasingly important as ways candidates and political leaders learn about public opinion (though the latter had long been used, but less visibly; see the earlier discussion in Chapter Three).[12] In fact, with information about public opinion so widely available, we would have reason to expect more responsiveness in the 1990s and in the future than ever before. But politicians and government officials of the past as well as the present have long had other sources of information about public opinion available to them: constituency mail; various informants who report what they observe, including staffs, advisers, and even friends and acquaintances; information from political party leaders and others in the party; reports, editorials, and commentaries in the mass media; and the opinions and information conveyed by organized groups.

Political scientists have long thought that interest groups play a major, if not a critical, role in processes by which public opinion influences, or fails to influence, policymaking. Groups have the capacity to (as political scientists say) "aggregate and articulate"—that is, to find out about and widely communicate—opinions found among the public. A powerful theory was offered by political scientists to show how interest groups helped represent public opinion in politics and thereby facilitate democracy. This theory of "democratic pluralism," or "pluralism," essentially maintained that over time and across all issues that arise, we can expect public opinion to be fully represented. This would occur through existing groups and by new groups that would be formed as new issues arose or as segments of the public who felt unrepresented began organizing them.[13] Later, we will examine how political parties, as organized groups, might also provide this linkage between the public and government through processes of selecting candidates and by developing policy stances that are supported by party members and party loyalists in the electorate.

Some readers may be suspicious about the role of "special interests" and "lobbyists" in American politics. Not surprisingly, a number of critics of democratic pluralism have presented counterarguments to any expectations that organized groups act democratically. In short, these critics argue that in the case of seemingly open group processes, there have still been ample opportunities for nondemocratic influences to occur; that is, there are influences at work on policymakers that prevent the public from getting what it wants or getting what is in its best interest.

For one thing, according to these critics, not all opinions have groups to represent them. And in particular, it is not so easy for groups to organize and become effective at communicating the opinions of previously unrepresented interests into the political process. Further, the groups that are likely to form and remain influential are those that are small, have substantial wealth or other resources, and have much to gain, which motivates them to organize and act.[14] If there are no groups to pick up the banner of unrepresented opinions as they emerge from a dormant, inactive, or "latent" stage,[15] this clearly has devastating consequences for a pluralist or group-based form of democracy. If those who were well-off financially and in other ways from the start were also the most likely to organize their interests (and contribute money to political parties and candidates, to be sure), then the "heavenly chorus" of public opinion would clearly have an upper-class bias.[16]

In contrast to democratic pluralism and the preceding criticisms of it, other theorists have argued that policymaking is dominated by powerful elites—individuals or small groups (such as business leaders, military leaders, and specific political leaders who have connections to each other)—who dominate all areas of policymaking, nationally and locally. These individuals and groups have been given various political labels such as "the power elite."[17]

Another theory has maintained that American democracy was thwarted by particular powerful groups that exerted political control not over all areas of public policymaking but rather over the narrow, but important, policy areas that were of special interest to them. Thus, different groups controlled specific areas of policymaking, especially in different states and localities. For example, farmers controlled farm policy in their states, if not nationally; power and utility companies influenced how states and localities regulated their enterprises; and the like. As a result of this dominance by different private centers of power, it is rare for public opinion to be very influential.[18]

One way elites or special interests dominate and thwart public opinion is by keeping issues off the visible political agenda. As a result, the public is not aware of what is happening and thus does not mobilize against these groups or elites.[19] Clearly here, the role of the mass media in making issues widely visible is very important (see Chapter Ten). It has even been claimed that policymaking is dominated by the influences of business and industry or the need for government or "the state" to act in business's interest in order to strengthen both the nation and state by enhancing economic growth.[20] Other arguments emphasize the blatant dominance of money in interest group activity and in political campaigns, which further reduces the influence of ordinary people, who, even collectively, may have fewer financial resources to contribute.

Overall, then, there are different types of political processes at work that have different consequences for the public's influence on government. Electoral accountability, how political leaders see their roles, and group-based democratic pressures can lead the public to have substantial influence on policymaking. In direct conflict with this are other processes that can sharply limit the public's ability to constrain or drive what government does.

EVIDENCE

But what is the reality here? As we will see, there is considerable evidence that although the public does not always rule, it is often able to move—or maintain—government policies in desired directions.

Thanks to the expansion of survey research and the recently increasing number of studies that have focused directly on the opinion–policy relationship, students of public opinion are now in a much better position than in the past to examine these matters. But the general issues and expectations have not changed, especially with respect to whether public opinion is a constraint or a director of policymaking. V. O. Key, Jr., wrote in 1961:

> The anxieties of students about their inability to gauge the effects of opinion rest on an implicit assumption that public opinion is, or in some way

ought to be, positively directive of government action. Our analyses suggest that the relationships between government and public opinion must be pictured in varied ways, none of which requires solution of the problem of the precise measurement of the weights of opinion in the governing process. Mass opinion may set general limits, themselves subject to change over time, within which government may act. In some instances opinion may be permissive but not directive of specific action. In others opinion may be, if not directive, virtually determinative of particular acts.[21]

To examine these effects of public opinion we need to consider a variety of research strategies. To start, how do we broadly compare public opinion and government policies to get a sense of the results of democratic procedures in action? This is the simplest and most fundamental question, but it is one that took political scientists a long time to analyze directly in a social-scientific fashion. Some of the earliest empirical studies of this, which were the first to be widely cited in public opinion textbooks, had to do with representation in Congress. These studies of constituency representation, as we will see later on, examined the votes cast by legislators on proposed laws; they did not directly compare public opinion with government policies that were ultimately fully enacted.

Students might quickly—and quite correctly—think that a simple way to study the effect of public opinion on policy in a democracy would be to compare majority public opinion with subsequent government policy, given that we have majoritarian rules and we make simple favor-or-oppose decisions on policies in our Madisonian or constitutional tradition. The simplest question to ask is this: How often does majority opinion get what it wants from government? One way to try to answer this directly would be to count how frequently national government policies have corresponded with prior public opinion. We say "prior" opinion since we are interested in the responsiveness of government to prior public demands (or lack thereof). To keep matters simple, by "public opinion" here, we again mean majority opinion that we could measure through responses to questions in opinion polls that ask explicitly about identifiable government policies.

Although this would appear to be a relatively simple research task, it has actually been more difficult than expected. Modern scientific opinion polling began in the United States in 1935, but many of the polls that be-

TABLE 9.1   Public Preference and Policy Outcome for All Nonspending Cases

	Preference	
Outcome	Status Quo	Change
Status quo	56 (76%)	61 (41%)
Change	18 (24%)	87 (59%)
Total	74 (100%)	148 (100%)

NOTE: Consistent = 64%; N = 222

SOURCE: A. D. Monroe, "Consistency Between Public Preferences and National Policy Decisions," *American Politics Quarterly* 7, p. 9. Copyright 1979 by Sage Publications. Reprinted by permission of Sage Publications.

came available to researchers were not designed with this type of study in mind. That is, the surveys did not ask many questions that were worded in ways that would enable researchers to study the effect of majority opinion on a wide range of government policies. It took thirty years or more for enough public opinion data to become available. At that point, a handful of researchers—most notably Donald Devine, Robert Weissberg, and Alan Monroe[22]—developed appropriate strategies for using these data to examine government responsiveness to public opinion. These were the first and broadest studies of aggregate national opinion.

Monroe's study was the largest one to compare majority opinion and policy in the United States. His research design compared public support for proposed changes in policy with subsequent policies themselves. For example, if in response to a survey question, 51 percent or more of survey respondents opposed our establishing diplomatic relations with Cuba and the government did not establish such relations up to four years later, this would be a case in which government policy was consistent or "congruent" with public opinion. In this case, too, we would have majority support for existing policy, or the "status quo," in Monroe's terms. If majority opinion had favored the establishment of diplomatic relations and the government had subsequently complied, this would be a case of congruence with a "change" in policy. Table 9.1 summarizes Monroe's results for a large number of policy issues. Clearly, the 64-percent level of consistent cases is striking for 222 cases of majority support for particular policies. It is far more than 50 percent of the time, which would be expected through chance alone.

Monroe, however, cautioned against concluding too quickly that there is a cause-and-effect relationship between public opinion and policy. The data clearly pointed in that direction, but this was still incomplete evidence. Adopting a similar method for comparing majority opinion and policy, other researchers found less evidence of this sort for responsiveness, particularly in other countries.[23] Additional studies using different research methods and other data were clearly needed to confirm or challenge Monroe's finding. Examining such other studies, we find further evidence of the impact of public opinion on policymaking in the United States.

Taking a different approach, Benjamin Page and Robert Shapiro undertook a project somewhat larger in scope than Monroe's.[24] One part of their study used a method similar to Monroe's and confirmed a comparable level of "majoritarian" opinion–policy congruence. But they were much more interested in finding out how often changes in policy occurred after changes in public opinion. Specifically, they wanted to see how frequently they found cases in which a change in opinion from one time point to another was followed by a corresponding or parallel change in government policy. In this case, they ignored whether the level of support for a policy was a majority or not; they examined only the direction of opinion change and the direction of policy change. For example, if support for increasing spending on health care increased (by more than survey sampling error) from 1980 to 1982 and government spending increased (in real dollars, adjusting for inflation) from 1980 to 1983, then this was considered a case of "covariational congruence" between policy change and opinion change. Had spending decreased from 1980 to 1983, this would have been classified as an instance of noncongruence. To put it simply, the idea was to count how often public opinion and policy changed in the same direction.

In their analysis of 231 instances of changes in policy preferences and changes of policy, Page and Shapiro found that policies one year later moved in the same direction as opinion 66 percent of the time. These results are shown in Table 9.2. Note that the 66-percent figure depended on their excluding 120 cases of "no change in policy," which included, according to the authors, a great many cases in which policy (the "status quo" in Monroe's term) was already maximally congruent with opinion; cases in which congruent policy changes occurred more than one year after public opinion changed; and cases in which even with some noticeable opinion change, there was still only small minority support for a policy change, so that a change in policy could not yet plausibly be expected to occur.

Table 9.3 shows further that these data clearly pick up the responsiveness of policy to the degree of change in public opinion: Larger opinion

TABLE 9.2   Congruence Between Opinion and Policy, 1935–1979

	Total Cases		Cases with Policy Change	
	%	N	%	N
Congruent change in opinion and policy	43	(153)	66	(153)
Noncongruent change in policy	22	(78)	34	(78)
No change in policy	33	(120)		
Uncertain	2	(6)		
Total	100	(357)	100	(231)

NOTE: Each case is an instance in which public policy preferences changed significantly, according to repeated administration of identical survey items.
SOURCE: Benjamin I. Page and Robert Y. Shapiro, 1983, table 1, p. 178.

TABLE 9.3   Frequency of Congruence for Opinion Changes of Different Sizes

Size of Opinion Change in Percentage Points	Direction of Policy Change					
	Congruent		Noncongruent		Total	
	%	N	%	N	%	N
6–7	53	(25)	47	(22)	21	(47)
8–9	64	(32)	36	(18)	22	(50)
10–14	62	(40)	38	(25)	29	(65)
15–19	69	(22)	31	(10)	14	(32)
20–29	86	(18)	14	(3)	9	(21)
30+	100	(10)	0	(0)	4	(10)
Total	65	(147)	35	(78)	100	(225)

NOTE: Gamma = –.29.
SOURCE: Benjamin I. Page and Robert Y. Shapiro, 1983, table 3, p. 180.

changes made corresponding policy changes more likely, with congruent policy change (53 percent) not much more likely than chance (50 percent) for a 6- or 7-percentage-point change, and a near certainty (86 percent or more) with opinion changes of 20 percentage points or more. Similarly, Monroe had found congruent policy changes more likely when there was larger majority support.[25] Page and Shapiro (as well as Monroe) also show that congruence was more likely for the most salient issues. Thus, this kind of "covariational" (over time) congruence occurred in ways consistent with theories about when we would expect changes in policy to correspond to changes in opinion. This kind of issue-by-issue correspondence between public opinion and policy has been confirmed by other types of research that we will turn to next.

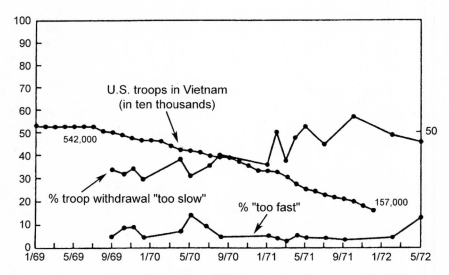

FIGURE 9.1a   Opinion–Policy: Troop Withdrawals from Vietnam, 1969–1972.
SOURCE: Robert Y. Shapiro and Benjamin I. Page, "Foreign Policy and Public Opinion,"
in David A. Deese, ed., *The New Politics of American Foreign Policy* (New York: St.
Martin's Press, 1994), Figure 10-8a, p. 232. Copyright 1993 by St. Martin's Press, Inc.
Reproduced by permission of St. Martin's Press, Inc.

Response in the figure is to the following: QUESTION: (Harris): (Version A) "In
general, do you feel the pace at which the president is withdrawing troops from Vietnam
is too fast, too slow, or about right?" Survey dates: 10/69, 12/69. (Version B) adds
"Nixon." Survey date: 8/70. (Version C) omits "from Vietnam." Survey date 10/69.
(Version D) adds "U.S." Survey date: 4/70. (Version E) puts "slow" first. Survey date:
1/71. (Version G) substitutes "think." Survey dates: 5/70, 7/70. (Version H) adds "Nixon"
and "slow" first. Survey dates: 3/71, 4/71. (Version I) omits "in general," puts "slow" first.
Survey date: 10/71. (Version J) long prologue on Nixon plan, substitutes "more rapid
rate," "slower rate," "satisfactory." Survey date: 10/71. (Version K) "Do you feel the pace
of withdrawal of U.S. troops from . . . ? Survey dates: 2/72, 5/72. Source for U.S. troop
data: SS–2 Unclassified Statistics on Southeast Asia, Comptroller, Office of the Secretary
of Defense, Table 6. Reported in Raphael Littauer and Norman Uphoff, eds., *The Air
War in Indochina* (Boston: Beacon Press, 1972), pp. 265–272, Table 6.

There have been "time series" studies comparing trends in public opinion and public policy on particular issues. Figures 9.1a and 9.1b and Figure 9.2 show these trends for cases of U.S. troop withdrawal in Vietnam
and changes in defense spending. In Figures 9.1a and 9.1b, the rate of
troop withdrawal from Vietnam was sensitive to public attitudes toward
the war in general and toward the rate of troop withdrawal in particular,
as shown by the parallel and relatively synchronized opinion and policy

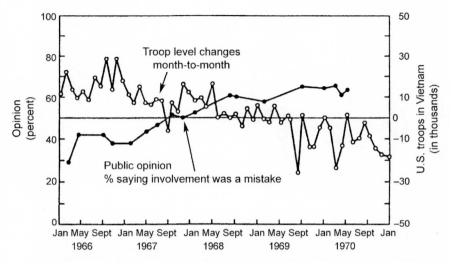

FIGURE 9.1b Opinion—Policy: U.S. Involvement in Vietnam. SOURCE: Robert Y. Shapiro and Benjamin I. Page, "Foreign Policy and Public Opinion," in David A. Deese, ed., *The New Politics of American Foreign Policy* (New York: St. Martin's Press, 1994), Figure 10-8b, p. 233. Copyright 1993 by St. Martin's Press, Inc. Reproduced by permission of St. Martin's Press, Inc.

Response in the figure is to the following: QUESTION: (Gallup): "In view of the developments since we entered the fighting in Vietnam, do you think the U.S. made a mistake sending troops to fight in Vietnam?" Survey dates: 8/65, 3/66, 5/66, 9/66, 11/66, 2/67, 5/67, 7/67, 10/67, 12/67, 2/68, 3/68, 4/68, 8/68, 10/68, 2/69, 9/69, 1/70, 3/70, 4/70, 5/70, 1/71, 5/71.

trend lines. Figure 9.2 shows an even more impressive correlation (which is well documented and also analyzed by other researchers) between the level of U.S. defense spending and public support for increasing such spending.[26] The most immediate interpretation of this graph is that the public helped give defense spending a big boost in the early 1980s, then reversed the process; this hardly appears to be a passive role for public opinion.

These time-trend analyses are arguably the best quantitative method for evaluating whether there is a possible cause-and-effect type of correlation between opinion and policy. But good time series data like those shown in Figures 9.1a, 9.1b, and 9.2 have not been widely available, so that other data typically from only one or two time points were analyzed in the case of the majoritarian (Monroe) and covariational congruence (Page and Shapiro) studies described earlier.

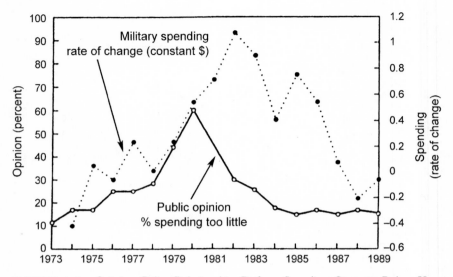

FIGURE 9.2   Opinion–Policy Relationship: Defense Spending. SOURCE: Robert Y. Shapiro and Benjamin I. Page, "Foreign Policy and Public Opinion," in David A. Deese, ed., *The New Politics of American Foreign Policy* (New York: St. Martin's Press, 1994), Figure 10-7, p. 231. Copyright 1993 by St. Martin's Press, Inc. Reproduced by permission of St. Martin's Press, Inc.

Response in the figure is to the following: QUESTION: (NORC-GSS): "Are we spending too much, too little, or about the right amount on . . . the military, armaments, and national defense?" Defense spending data were obtained from The Budget of the United States and were deflated.

Another common statistical method that has been used to compare public opinion and indicators of policymaking or related behavior is shown in Figure 9.3 and described further in Box 9.1. This is a method that can be used for comparing data for different geographic units such as legislative districts or states or even different countries at the same point in time. These are "cross-sectional" data, in contrast to time series data. (Similarly, when we study data from a single public opinion survey, we are comparing the responses of different people representing a "cross-section" of the American public at a single time point.) In time series analysis of the relationship between public opinion and policy, we compare the same unit—the country as a whole, in the case of Figures 9.1a, 9.1b, and 9.2—at several time points to see how policy changes and opinion changes are related.

In contrast, Figure 9.3 is an illustration of cross-sectional data analysis. For purposes of explaining this method clearly, Figure 9.3 presents

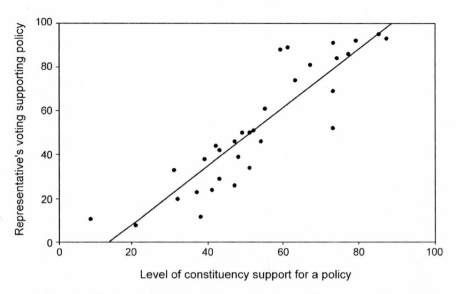

FIGURE 9.3   Relationship Between District Opinion and Congressional Voting.

hypothetical data. Here, we can examine any variation in policymaking activity by comparing one congressional district with a certain level of constituency support for a policy to another district with a different level of public support, to see if congressional representatives' voting records differ in ways consistent with responsiveness. That is, if constituency opinion is more supportive of a policy in District A than District B and if representatives were responsive, we would expect District A's representative to be more supportive of the policy than District B's. This is in fact the case we present in Figure 9.3. If such differences were widely prevalent, then we would see the upward sloping pattern of districts also shown in the figure. We see that the more supportive public opinion is in a congressional district, the more supportive the voting record of the representative in Congress. Using this comparative method, for which there are ways of calculating statistical correlations, we can study public opinion and policymaking across states, counties, cities, regions, or even countries. If we find no upward or downward slope (i.e., if a flat line fits the data better than any other), then policymaking would be unrelated to opinion; if the slope were downward ("negative," not "positive"), we would see that policymaking is consistently the opposite of what citizens in the units want (see Box 9.1).

BOX 9.1   "SCATTER PLOT" AND STATISTICAL CORRELATION

In this chapter, we cite studies that examined the relationship between public opinion and policy by explicitly or implicitly drawing on "scatter plots" and statistical correlations of the sort shown in the graphs that follow. In these scatter plots, each point on the graph represents a unit such as a congressional district, a state, or a policy issue. In our first example, each point represents data plotted for congressional districts. The horizontal axis (X-axis) is the level of public or constituent support in a district for some policy such as economic welfare or civil rights; the vertical axis (Y-axis) is a congressional representative's roll-call voting record or score supporting the corresponding policy in question.

Graph A shows a "positive correlation," in which the points cluster close to a line sloping upward; that is, in districts in which there is a high level of public support for a policy, the district's congressional representative has a more supportive voting score than representatives in districts where there is less public support for the policy. Graph B shows a "negative correlation," in which the points cluster close to a line sloping downward. Graph C shows the case of "no correlation," in which the points do not cluster around either an upward- or a downward-sloping line but where a horizontal line fits best. In this case, districts with high levels of public support for a policy do not tend to have congressional representatives who disproportionately favor or oppose the policy.

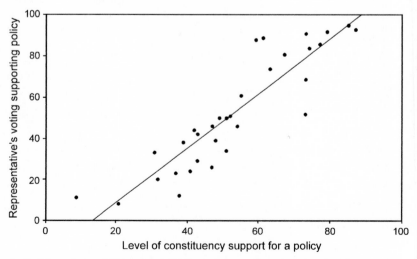

A. Positive relationship between district opinion and congressional voting.
   Note: Hypothetical data.

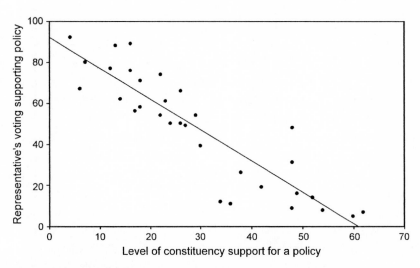

B. Negative relationship between district opinion and congressional voting.
   Note: Hypothetical data.

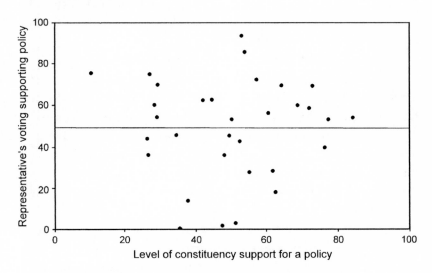

C. No relationship between district opinion and congressional voting.
   Note: Hypothetical data.

The reason for presenting the illustration in Figure 9.3 is that the first classic study of representation of pubic opinion used this method to study representation in Congress. In addition, this method has been used extensively to study the effect of public opinion on policymaking by state governments in the United States.

The case of representation in Congress does not allow us to examine the actual enactment of policies per se but rather to observe a political mechanism or process that "links" public opinion and policy. The path-breaking Warren Miller and Donald Stokes study of 1963, "Constituency Representation in Congress," used this correlational method to examine both the relationship between public opinion and roll-call voting in Congress and also the processes and linkages by which public opinion was perceived and consequently influenced voting by individual legislators.[27] Miller and Stokes found modest correlations of the sort (though not so well-defined) shown in the scatter plot in Figure 9.3. It was clearly the case that the votes cast by legislators were more supportive of a policy when a greater proportion of the public in their districts favored that policy. Miller and Stokes found a greater correlation (which would be shown by a steeper line and by the points on the scatter plot falling closer to the line) for the highly salient civil rights issues of the 1950s than for economic issues. The correlation was least for foreign policy (a less steep line, with points falling further away from it), which was less salient than civil rights and economic issues at the time.

This kind of domestic–foreign policy distinction has long been debated. The difference between foreign and domestic policies is largely in their relative salience and complexity and in the speed with which important events affect both mass and elite opinion and the main policymakers involved. The White House is expected to act first in the case of many foreign policy and most national security issues, with Congress weighing in subsequently, so that the linkages between district-level public opinion and the behavior of individual members of Congress may be weaker on foreign policy than domestic issues.

Later studies of constituency representation using the Miller and Stokes methodology found similar and stronger patterns of constituency representation. Interestingly, this did not necessarily indicate an increase in responsiveness but, rather, less measurement error than in Miller and Stokes's original data. The cause of measurement error was not only the small sample sizes (numbers of respondents) from the selected congressional districts but the fact that the sampling method used did not guarantee representative samples within each district.[28]

The method of statistical correlation illustrated in Figure 9.3 has also been used in interesting and informative ways to study specific policies across U.S. states. In a wide range of studies, noticeable correlations be-

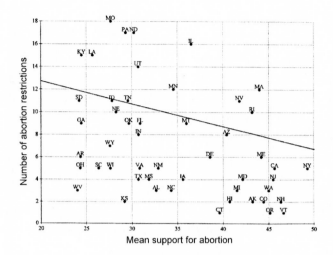

FIGURE 9.4   Abortion Policy Restrictions and Support
for Abortion in the States, 1988. SOURCE: M. E. Wetstein,
*Abortion Rates in the United States: The Influence of Opinion
and Policy* (Albany: State University of New York Press,
1996), Figure 10, p. 89.

tween state policies and various indicators of state-level public opinion
have been reported. In such studies, good measures of public opinion
have been hard to come by, since there have been few national surveys
with samples large enough to even approximate state-level public opinion. Some innovative studies provide good illustrations. Using some large
Gallup poll samples from the mid-1930s, Robert Erikson in 1976 cleverly showed a relationship between state public opinion and policy in the
cases of the enactment of child labor laws (some states had them and others did not, until national legislation settled the issue) and of allowing
women to serve on juries (some states did not allow this, despite the fact
that women by then had the right to vote).[29]

On a more visible contemporary issue, Figure 9.4 shows Matthew Wetstein's findings for the issue of abortion in 1988, for which states have had
some discretion with respect to the restrictiveness of regulations.[30] This
and Wetstein's other analyses, as well as a similarly apt study by Malcolm
Goggin and Christopher Wlezien,[31] showed that public opinion had some
effect on states' policies concerning abortion. The correlation shown is no
more than modest, which has been fairly typical for studies of the opinion–policy connection on specific issues at the state level. The points for
each state cluster around an expected downward-sloping line, representing

a negative correlation, since a high level of support for permitting legal abortions is associated with a state having fewer procedural restrictions on abortions. One reason for the weakness of the relationship may be the result of error in measuring state-level public opinion (due to small and not ideally representative samples, as in the Miller and Stokes study, as well as errors due to survey question wording). But it is also quite possible that states are limited in their responsiveness, issue by issue, to public opinion. State-level policies may not be particularly salient (though abortion may be atypical in this regard), and often the issues involved may not be perceived and associated with state government action alone, compared to national issues such as abortion that have been widely covered in the press. State policymaking may also be affected heavily by organized groups and other influences described earlier.

RESPONSIVENESS TO SPECIFIC ISSUES VERSUS PUBLIC MOOD OR IDEOLOGY

One question that these studies of specific issues raise is whether policymakers respond to public opinion issue by issue or whether they respond to a more general sense of public sentiment. In terms of the behavioral process at work by which political leaders learn about and respond to public opinion, we need to ask whether they do so one issue at a time or whether they focus on the overall "mood" of the public. Responsiveness to specific issues is very plausible for the most salient issues, about which policymakers are likely to receive some clear indications of the public stance. But for other policy questions or for a range of issues toward which opinions represent broad liberal to moderate to conservative moods, policymakers are less likely to be concerned with opinions on each issue separately. A general sense of liberalism or conservatism may be sufficient.

The appeal of focusing on the public mood is that this is what leaders may be more likely to sense if they do not have other detailed information about public opinion on specific issues. Some political leaders may not think or perceive that the public has identifiable and specific attitudes and opinions on many—or even any—issues. Both political leaders and citizens may use ideology as a shortcut in making judgments about issues and about where others stand on them (see the discussion in Chapter Eight; but as we will see later, political leaders are more likely now than in the past to have information about particular attitudes and opinions based on polls and other information and analyses). Just as journalists and political leaders themselves typically talk about political issues, so Democrats define and take liberal stances and Republicans describe and claim conservative positions on economic and social issues.

Recent studies of the effect of the "public mood" in comparing both state and national public opinion and policymaking bear out yet another observation by V. O. Key, Jr., on how broad public mood and government action matter most:

> Parallelism between action and opinion tends not to be precise in matters of detail; it prevails rather with respect to broad purpose. And in the correlation of purpose and action time lags may occur between the crystallization of a sense of mass purpose and its fulfillment in public action. Yet in the long run majority purpose and public action tend to be brought into harmony.[32]

The studies of the public mood or liberal–conservative ideology have shown clear and pronounced effects of public opinion on policymaking. These studies have examined the effect of liberal–conservative mood on state policymaking and on trends in national policymaking. They have used innovative and persuasive measures of the degree of the public's ideological liberalism or conservatism.

Figure 9.5, taken from Robert Erikson, Gerald Wright, and John McIver's 1993 study *Statehouse Democracy*,[33] shows a strong correlation between states' opinions and policy liberalism. State-level opinion was measured by combining responses to a question about self-identified liberalism (survey respondents were asked whether they consider themselves "liberal," "conservative," or "moderate") from many years of the CBS News/*New York Times* polls. The overall responses for individual states were compared with different policies and a combined policy measure. The systematic variations that are apparent in state-level opinions and policies are suggestive, indeed, of how the "devolution" of welfare and other policies from the national government in Washington to the states in the 1990s and into the new century may play out, as even greater reliance occurs on the states that have been expected to act as policy innovators and as "laboratories" for policy experimentation.[34]

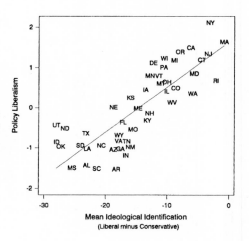

FIGURE 9.5
State Policy and Public Opinion.
SOURCE: R. S. Erikson, G. C.
Wright, and J. P. McIver, *Statehouse
Democracy: Public Opinion and
Policy in the American States* (New
York: Cambridge University Press,
1993), Figure 4.2, p. 79.

Although the *Statehouse Democracy* results are impressive, more striking and important for national politics and policymaking is the major study by James Stimson, Michael MacKuen, and Robert Erikson on *dynamic representation* at the national level.[35] Using a measure of public mood developed earlier by Stimson that combined numerous issue-specific opinion trends over time (thus showing that there has been an identifiable public mood),[36] this research shows how liberal mood and policymaking by different national institutions and actors track each other in a way indicating long-term policy responsiveness to opinion. These basic trends are shown in Figure 9.6. Different institutions have different political dynamics, with trends in policymaking by the House of Representatives looking most like trends in the public opinion.

You might pause for a moment and think about why this would be the expected result. Similar cyclical patterns in all institutions provide significant support for responsiveness being substantially connected to policymakers' sensitivity to a general public mood.[37] The summary graph "e." in Figure 9.6 shows how changes in liberal–conservative mood precede changes in the overall measure of policy activity (a composite of the policy activity measures in graphs a through d) and the numbers of important new "liberal" laws that were enacted. There was increasing opinion and policy liberalism into the 1960s, declining liberalism into the early 1980s, followed by some increasing liberalism. This responsiveness to general ideological shifts does not, of course, preclude responsiveness to salient policies on an issue-by-issue basis, since not all opinion trends track in complete synchronization with the public's overall ideological

Public Opinion over Time: Domestic Policy Mood, 1956–93

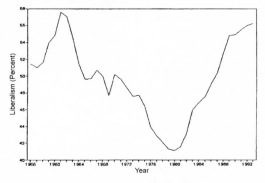

Indicators of Public Policy Change in Four Parts of American Government (Three Year Moving Averages)

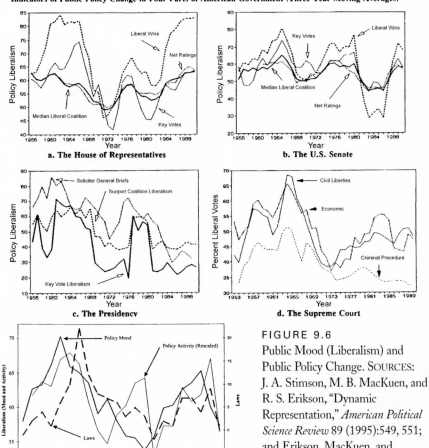

a. The House of Representatives

b. The U.S. Senate

c. The Presidency

d. The Supreme Court

e. Policy Mood, Policy Activity, and Laws

FIGURE 9.6
Public Mood (Liberalism) and
Public Policy Change. SOURCES:
J. A. Stimson, M. B. MacKuen, and
R. S. Erikson, "Dynamic
Representation," *American Political
Science Review* 89 (1995):549, 551;
and Erikson, MacKuen, and
Stimson, *The Macro Polity* (New
York: Cambridge, 2002), Figure 9.1,
p. 332.

mood.[38] In the mid-1990s, for example (not shown in Figure 9.6), welfare reform can be interpreted as a response to a conservative shift in
opinion since 1992,[39] but the passage of the minimum wage increase and
incremental health care reform can be associated with liberal opinions on
these particular issues. The point here is that policy is not completely explained by liberal or conservative mood.

Having reviewed the evidence, what do we conclude overall about the
relationship between public opinion and policy? On balance, though it is
hardly a social-scientific law that government policies consistently (policy
by policy) reflect public opinion, government policymaking in the United
States has reflected ideological shifts in public opinion and also, noticeably, "what the people want in those instances where the public cares
enough about an issue to make its wishes known."[40]

LOOKING FURTHER AT LINKAGES: PARTIES, POLLING, AND IN-DEPTH CASE STUDIES

The preceding sections describe striking patterns of correlations between
public opinion and policies. But this evidence is in most respects still circumstantial, since the cause-and-effect linkage processes are not fully
traced, although some have been mentioned. In particular, in social science language, the analysis has focused on only opinion and policy variables. Certainly, we need to look at other variables that could affect both
public opinion and policy to avoid attributing an influence to public
opinion when some other causal influence may actually be at work. In addition the relationships that are based on cross-sectional data, in contrast
to time series evidence, do not allow us to observe which moved first—
opinion or policy. This leaves the direction of any causal effect in doubt.
That is, the correlation between opinion and policy could represent the
effect of policy on opinion, a situation in which the public ratifies or just
goes along with government-enacted policies. To be persuaded that opinion is affecting policy requires evidence concerning processes that solidly
link public opinion to subsequent policy decisions.

If we take electoral motivation as the critical driving force that pressures political leaders to respond to public opinion, one point of consensus can be found in the research on the opinion–policy linkage: Political
parties, as we alluded to earlier, can play a major part in this process. A
number of different studies have shown how party activists, leaders, and

TABLE 9.4   Convention Delegates to the 1996 Party Conventions: How They Compare on Issues

	Democratic Delegates (%)	Democratic Voters (%)	Republican Voters (%)	Republican Delegates (%)
Scope of government				
Government should do more to:				
Solve the nation's problems	76	53	20	4
Regulate the environment and safety practices of business	60	66	37	4
Promote traditional values	27	41	44	56
Social Issues				
Abortion should be permitted in all cases	61	30	22	11
Favor a nationwide ban on assault weapons	91	80	62	34
Necessary to have laws to protect racial minorities	88	62	39	30
Affirmative action programs should be continued	81	59	28	9
Organized prayer should be permitted in public schools	20	66	69	57
International				
Trade restrictions necessary to protect domestic industries	54	65	56	31
Children of illegal immigrants should be allowed to attend public school	79	63	46	26

SOURCE: *New York Times*, August 26, 1996, p. A12.

government officials convey or magnify the preferences of their fellow partisans among the mass public. There is evidence of this in the policy stances of political party delegations to the national conventions for presidential elections and also in the party platforms adopted at these conventions.[41] We also find this in Congress and in American state legislatures, as well as in evidence for Western Europe.[42]

In particular, we can trace processes by which delegates to party conventions in the United States tend to represent the opinions of party identifiers in the electorate. We also find that party platforms tend to represent the preferences of the mass public. Table 9.4 and Figures 9.7a–9.7e present data for the 1996 Republican and Democratic convention delegates. When we compare across issues—that is, each case plotted in Fig-

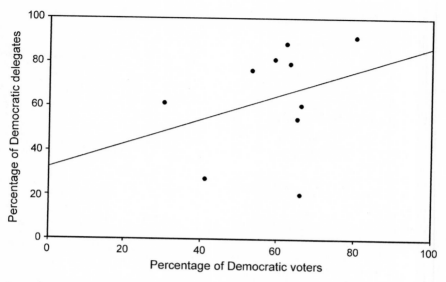

FIGURE 9.7a   Relationship Between Democratic Voters and Democratic Delegates
on Issues

ures 9.7a–9.7e is an issue, with party voters' opinions on the horizontal
axis and party delegates' opinions on the vertical axis—we find that voters' opinions are more strongly correlated (positively) with the opinions of
their own party's delegates than with those of the other party. The opinions of each parties' delegations are negatively correlated (downward-
sloping line) with those of the other party. Therefore, the party delegates
magnify existing opinion differences in the electorate, in a sense representing them by overrepresenting them.

As part of this linkage process or as part of a separate process by which
American political parties attempt to appeal to the broad electorate and
not just to their own partisans, parties attempt to appeal to public opinion through their platforms or through the promises their presidential
candidate makes and attempts to keep. They do this by following through
on the preferences of their partisans on some issues or by moving to the
overall center of public opinion (as we might expect from parties con-
verging toward the "median voter" according to the theoretical discussion
in Chapter Seven).[43]

Table 9.5 presents Alan Monroe's data showing how both parties
across the issues he examined tended to adopt party platform pledges that

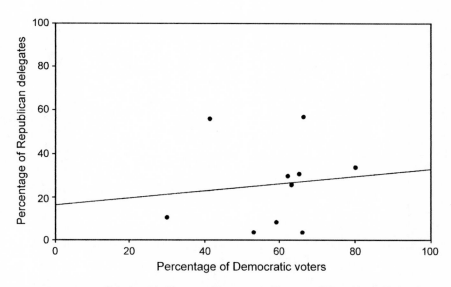

FIGURE 9.7b   Relationship Between Democratic Voters and Republican Delegates on Issues

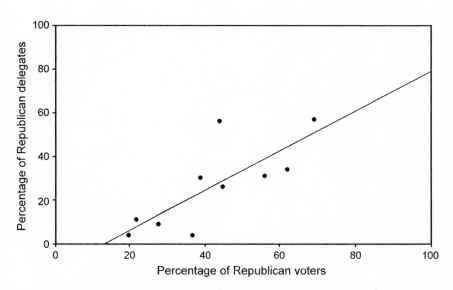

FIGURE 9.7c   Relationship Between Republican Voters and Republican Delegates on Issues

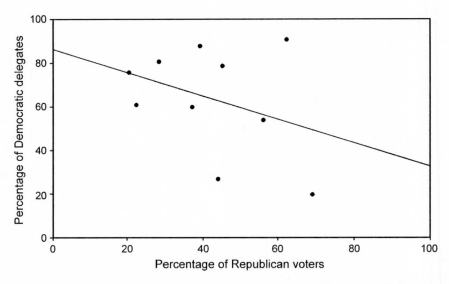

FIGURE 9.7d   Relationship Between Republican Voters and Democratic Delegates on Issues

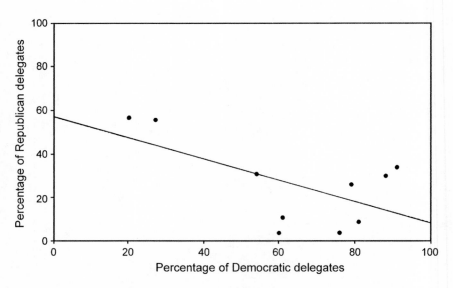

FIGURE 9.7e   Relationship Between Democratic Delegates and Republican Delegates on Issues

TABLE 9.5   Majority Opinion and Party Pledges

Party Pledges	Percentage of Majority Opinion Favors		Percentage Consistent
	Change	*Status Quo*	
Republican			
Change	65	39	64
Status quo	35	61	
Total	100	100	
N	94	44	
Democratic			
Change	79	41	74
Status quo	21	59	
Total	100	100	
N	117	46	

SOURCE: From Alan D. Monroe, "American Party Platforms and Public Opinion," *American Journal of Political Science*, 27 (February 1983), table 5, p. 32. Reprinted by permission of the University of Wisconsin Press.

were consistent with majority opinion; this occurred 64 percent of the time for Republican pledges and 74 percent of the time for Democratic Party positions. Although this shows that both parties appear to be sensitive to public opinion, perceptive readers will note that we cannot tell directly from these data whether the Republican and Democratic platform pledges are more responsive to Republican and Democratic Party identifiers, respectively, within the public.

The data in Tables 9.4 and 9.5 and Figures 9.7a–9.7e concerning the behavior of political parties and their activist delegates also fit in well with another development. As parties have remained weak in the electorate, there is the possibility that the frequency of opinion–policy congruence has declined since the 1980s (though, as we will consider below, there are other processes linking public opinion to policymaking that may have become stronger but may not have offset the declining role of parties).

Emphasizing the role of political parties in this way is useful, but politics involves complex processes in which a variety of other influences are at work at the same time. Additional evidence and analysis are required in order to strengthen any conclusions we wish to make about cause and effect. Even if parties provide an important linkage, there may be other political mechanisms at work. We must look further for other processes that can connect the public to policymakers and policymaking.

Additional evidence and insight comes from historical and in-depth case study research. This type of research takes longer to do, requiring archival, interview, and secondary analyses, as well as other ways of gathering information, that directly allow researchers to track how policymakers learn about and respond to public opinion. The case studies that have been done have helped complement and supplement the wide range of research that has already been described and that has made a strong circumstantial case for a significant effect of public opinion on policymaking in the United States. These include, for example, Lawrence Jacobs' 1993 study of health care policy in Britain (the establishment of its National Health Service after the war) and the United States (the passage of Medicare in 1965).[44] In particular, Jacobs uncovered what has been called a "recoil effect" (see Box 9.2), by which political leaders wound up responding to public opinion despite their original intentions to track public opinion for the purpose of manipulating it.

BOX 9.2   "RECOIL EFFECT"

This chapter discusses next how American presidents have used opinion polls and other information about public opinion in regular and institutionalized ways, constituting what might be called a "public opinion apparatus." The opinion polling that presidential administrations do is actually part of political campaign and party activity and spending; this is not paid for by the American government.

Lawrence Jacobs studied this increasing attention to public opinion in Great Britain as well as the United States.[1] He traced the history of how public opinion analysis became institutionalized and, in particular, how this attention to public opinion has appeared to backfire or "recoil" in a way that has sometimes led to more democratic policymaking than was actually intended. Jacobs found that this occurred in the establishment of Britain's National Health Service after World War II and in the passage of Medicare in 1965 in the United States. These changes in health care policy were notably responsive to particular values and attitudes of the British and American people.

The way the process of tracking public opinion began in Britain is quite telling. According to Jacobs' research:

During the war government officials created the first administrative structures to track public opinion systematically. The purpose of building an intelligence gathering capacity was to "provide . . . [an] effective link between the people of the country and the government . . . convey[ing] the thoughts, opinions, and feelings of the public . . . [so that they were] constantly in the minds of administrators." In particular, the Ministry of Information produced two distinct types of data on public opinion: a qualitative survey conducted by the ministry's Home Intelligence Division and a statistical report by its Social Survey Division. Over the course of the war, the focus of intelligence gathering shifted from assessing the effectiveness of government publicity efforts and measuring general "morale" to studying public preferences toward particular government policies, especially as they related to postwar reconstruction.[2]

The creation of the British National Health Service was part of this postwar reconstruction. Further, for the executive branches of the British and later the U.S. government,

the public opinion apparatus equipped government officials with two capabilities, the ability to *manipulate and to respond* to public opinion. The aspect of the apparatus that was developed first and most extensively was the capacity to conduct public relations campaigns aimed at shaping popular preferences. The second capacity involved gathering intelligence on public opinion; in particular, polling became a central aspect of government efforts to gain a regular and reliable grip on public opinion. The development of these two capacities was tied to the struggle for political power and institutional position; the apparatus became integrated into the policymaking process when executive branch officials recognized that it presented opportunities to offset advantages possessed by others, the legislature as well as nongovernmental groups and individuals.

The evolution of the public opinion apparatus had a profound effect on policymakers' perspective toward the public; [and quoting the phrase used by Marjorie Ogilvy-Webb,[3] an authority on public administration in Britain during the period discussed,] its "*recoil effect* is greater than its blast." In striving to have an outward effect on public opinion, the creation of this apparatus has an inward effect; it educated government officials to be aware of and sensitive to public opinion. Thus, while the apparatus originated as an attempt to manipulate popular preferences through public relations campaigns, its development over time increased senior government officials' interest in tracking and responding to public popular preferences. This new outlook among politicians and civil servants involved a shift from a preoccupation with secrecy and seclusion to a recognition of public opinion as an important factor in administrative decision making. (emphasis added)[4]

NOTES

1. Lawrence R. Jacobs, "The Recoil Effect: Public Opinion and Policy Making in the United States and Britain," *Comparative Politics* 24 (1992):199–217; Lawrence R. Jacobs, *The Health of Nations: Public Opinion and the Making of American and British Health Policy* (Ithaca: Cornell University Press, 1993).

2. Jacobs, "The Recoil Effect," p. 205.

3. Marjorie Ogilvy-Webb, *The Government Explains: A Study of the Information Services: A Report of the Royal Institute of Public Administration* (London: George Allen and Unwin, 1965), p. 196.

4. Jacobs, "The Recoil Effect," p. 200.

Among the other case studies that have been done, foreign policy issues—the area of policymaking in which presidents and their administrations may feel less compelled than in domestic policy to follow public opinion—have provided important illustrations of policy responsiveness. Studies of specific foreign policy issues and processes have confirmed that public opinion has mattered in identifiable ways in U.S.–Chinese relations, such as in the admission of China to the United Nations, as we noted earlier;[45] in U.S. policymaking toward the contras in Nicaragua, as we have also discussed;[46] and in foreign policymaking during the Reagan–Bush years, in which one author observed that it was imprudent for policymakers to ignore public opinion.[47]

Further, although specific case studies have been informative, including those of the issues highlighted at the beginning of the chapter,[48] more systematic evidence has come from efforts that synthesize in-depth research in order to unravel historical and current trends in the causal relationship between public opinion and policy. This strategy requires, first, finding trends over time in the extent to which policymakers seek out (or otherwise get information on) public opinion; and, next, determining how political leaders respond to or are otherwise affected by this information. Jacobs did this in the case of health care policy and Thomas Graham did the same for nuclear arms control from the beginning of the Cold War to the 1980s, a period in which he found that more attention was paid to public opinion than political leaders would admit.[49] Philip Powlick found that there has been an increase in serious and responsive attention to public opinion in the State Department.[50] This represented a change in what Bernard Cohen had found earlier: Officials in the State Department had explicitly seen their role as one of shaping public opinion, not responding to it.[51] However, the most recent trend that Powlick found appeared to move back in that direction for the Reagan and Clinton administrations, which tended to place more institutional emphasis in foreign policymaking on leading rather than following public opinion. The same has appeared (at this writing) to be the case for the second Bush administration as it has engaged the United States in foreign affairs as the preeminent world power. We will not know more about leadership and responsiveness in foreign policy of recent administrations until further research is done.[52]

Other historical research that has focused on finding out how presidents and others directly used information about public opinion has revealed that there is a reciprocal relationship between public opinion and policymaking. There is evidence that the government has attempted to lead as well as respond to public opinion. This is consistent with the many correlational studies cited earlier, since most of them had not ruled out that there was also an effect of policy on opinion. These effects need not be mutually exclusive. Clearly, it is necessary to track these relationships and processes over time, in order to see if particular trends or tendencies have been more likely at some times than others.

In this spirit, using archival and other primary sources, some recent research examined the increasing "institutionalization" of public opinion analysis by American presidents, which refers to the establishment and continuation of what can be called a "public opinion apparatus" in each presidential administration. One objective of this work was to see what impact this routine public opinion analysis had on the overall opinion–policy relationship. The opinion–policy process that has evolved is one in which presidents have increasingly, since Kennedy, assembled and analyzed their own information on public opinion. Indeed, political leaders are now far more likely than in the past to have this information, based simply on the widespread availability of polls and analyses of public opinion. Although presidents and politicians had long used unscientific methods to estimate where the public stood on issues, and scientifically gathered public opinion data had found their way into the White House beginning with Roosevelt,[53] only since Kennedy has the entire process been routinized by each succeeding president.

The evidence indicates that the driving force for this has been elections, as once in office, presidents strive to be reelected. In the 1960s, presidents started to use their own pollsters and public opinion consultants or staff, with private polls being paid for by the political parties or other nongovernmental sources.[54]

Table 9.6 summarizes the extensiveness of private polling by the White House from Kennedy to Nixon. The most important data are the numbers of polls done by Johnson and Nixon during their first terms in office, when they were governing and not also campaigning for reelection, which shows that this polling activity became substantial. It continued to be extensive for later presidents, involving substantial expenditures by the Republican National Committee, the Democratic National Committee, and presidential reelection committees.

Figure 9.8 graphs the payments made to presidential pollsters during the Carter, Reagan, George H. Bush, and Clinton administrations. These data show that even after taking into account that they served two terms in office, in contrast to Carter's and Bush's one-term presidencies, Presidents Reagan and Clinton spent the most money on—and devoted the most attention to—polling and public opinion analysis, especially between elections. The result of this institutionalization of public opinion analysis is that the White House has become increasingly better positioned than in the past to respond to, or to attempt to lead or manipulate, public opinion.[55] As Figure 9.8 shows, however, while a substantial polling capacity has been institutionalized within the White House, presidential administrations have varied in how much they have used this capability.[56]

With respect to the choices faced by presidents Kennedy, Johnson, and Nixon to lead or to follow public opinion, research has found evidence that has shown the following: government responsiveness to public opinion; cases of opinion leadership; and cases of presidents working against public opinion for particular reasons. As might be expected, responsiveness occurred on salient issues, especially those that clearly had potential electoral consequences.[57]

TABLE 9.6   The Number and Distribution of Private Polls During the Kennedy, Johnson, and Nixon Presidencies

	Kennedy	*Johnson*	*Nixon*
Total number of private polls	93 (1958–1963)	130 (1963–1968)	233 (1969–1972)
Number of polls during presidential election periods	77 (1958–1960)	48 (Fall 1963– 1964, and 1968)	153 (1972)
Number of polls during governing period	16 (1961–1963)	82 (1965–1967)	80 (1969–1971)

SOURCE: L. R. Jacobs and R. Y. Shapiro, "The Rise of Presidential Polling: The Nixon White House in Historical Perspective," *Public Opinion Quarterly* 59 (1995), table 1, p. 167. Data derived from archival records in the presidential archives of John Kennedy, Lyndon Johnson, and Richard Nixon.

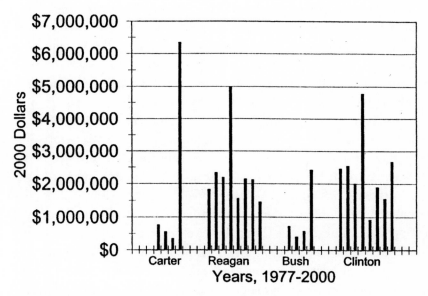

FIGURE 9.8   Payments to White House pollsters. SOURCE: S. K. Murray and P. Howard, "Variation in White House Polling Operations: Carter to Clinton," *Public Opinion Quarterly* 66 (2002), Figure 1, p. 533. Data Source: Federal Election Commission, Party Disclosure Documents, 1977–99. Figures are from the Republican National Committee or the Democratic National Committee and from all presidential reelection committees. Congressional campaign committees are not included.

Although Kennedy was the first president to run for office using the services of a publicly known pollster and political consultant—Louis Harris—polling and analysis of public opinion did not become a regular part of White House operations until the Johnson and Nixon administrations. Johnson had available to him information obtained by pollster Oliver Quayle, and Nixon (privately and through the Republican Party) commissioned full polls devoted to the president's desire for particular information. During the Johnson administration, the 1964 election provided an important juncture in how the president used information on public opinion. Concerned about being reelected, Johnson at first tended to respond to the public's wishes, emphasizing the popular desire to pursue disarmament and peace, in sharp contrast to the widely perceived positions of his Republican opponent, Barry Goldwater. On the basis of his polling reports, Johnson made sure to distinguish himself regarding the use of U.S. military force, including the use of nuclear weapons in Vietnam. But Johnson, like Kennedy before him, attempted to lead rather than respond to the public on the issue of foreign aid. Johnson's apparent strategy of responding to public opinion was particularly pronounced on domestic issues as well. Johnson continued this responsive behavior even after it became clear he would easily defeat Goldwater. He did so for the purpose of solidifying his public support for the purposes of leading the public on his racial and social policy agenda in his new full term as president.[58]

Beginning after the election in 1965, Johnson chose to lead, not follow, the public. His domestic proposals, especially the War on Poverty, had not been demanded by the public, but the public came to support this effort. In the case of foreign policy, the Vietnam War became an issue of extreme contention, and here Johnson had no intention of letting the public influence his actions. There was a clear break in this opinion–policy relationship between 1964 and 1965–1966, with responsiveness declining and leadership increasing from the first to the second period, with Vietnam being the dominant issue in foreign policy. In the end, however, after 1965–1966, the failure to respond to what Johnson knew to be public opinion on particular aspects of the Vietnam War had increasingly adverse effects on his presidency.[59]

The Nixon administration greatly expanded the institutional organization and sophistication of White House–directed polling and public opinion analysis. Despite his claims that political leaders should not be

influenced by polls, Nixon and his advisers used polling data to avoid taking unpopular positions and to enhance their ability to lead the public on
policies that they wanted to pursue, especially in the area of foreign policy, in which Nixon clearly wanted to leave his historical mark. The
archival evidence shows that in struggling with how to deal with the
Vietnam War, Nixon responded to public opinion in a manner that explains the relationship between the trends in public opinion and the
withdrawal of troops shown earlier in Figure 9.1.[60] Clearly, the Vietnam
War was regarded as a most crucial election issue in 1972, even as Nixon
maintained a substantial and steady lead over his Democratic opponent,
George McGovern, in preelection polls.

The research further shows that the Nixon administration was persistent in tracking public opinion on a wide range of policy and political
concerns (especially approval of the president).[61] An important case of
both opinion responsiveness and leadership in foreign policy concerned
the admission of Communist China to the United Nations, paving the
way for the formal recognition of China by the United States. Drawing
on publicly reported and other information about public opinion, Nixon
and his advisers could detect the softening of the public's hostility toward
Communist China in 1971, making it more receptive to efforts to lead it
further in a less belligerent direction. The result was Nixon's trip to China
and China's admission to the UN, which Nixon and his administration
did not finalize until there was further public support for it in opinion
polls.[62] At the same time, Nixon raised the visibility of this issue in a way
that enhanced his own and his party's electoral appeal. We find evidence
here and in the cases discussed earlier for presidential responsiveness to
public opinion that can be directly associated with actual or anticipated
electoral advantages, during a period in U.S. history in which Cold War
foreign policies could become major election-year issues.

CHANGES AND VARIATIONS IN
RESPONSIVENESS TO PUBLIC OPINION?

Given the increase in presidential polling since the Kennedy administration, the possibilities for recoil effects, and, more broadly, the prolifera-
tion and coverage of polls in the mass media, one might conclude that
government responsiveness to public opinion that we have observed will

persist and perhaps even increase. Some recent research, however, has suggested that the attention to public opinion depicted in Figure 9.8 may have occurred in tandem with some *decline* in government responsiveness to public opinion. When Monroe updated his findings reported in Table 9.1 for the period after 1980, he found a decline—to 55 percent (still significantly above the 50 percent threshold that could be attributed to chance)—in overall responsiveness.[63]

In their book *Politicians Don't Pander: Political Manipulation and the Loss of Democratic Responsiveness,* Jacobs and Shapiro offer a provocative thesis explaining what they see as a systematic decline in responsiveness.[64] They cite Monroe's replication as well as other long-term evidence of the changing impact (as measured by correlations similar to those depicted in Figure 9.3 and Box 9.1) of constituency opinion on congressional ideological positioning.[65] They theorize persuasively that while politicians wish to be elected and reelected, they also have policy goals that they attempt to pursue between elections. Further, they see the balance of concern shifting more in the direction of pushing for the policies they and their parties want, as the parties in Congress became more ideologically polarized since the mid-1970s. While the increase in polling that occurred may have been motivated in part or substantially by the desire to respond to the preferences of voters in order to get their support, politicians and their advisors and consultants had incentives to use information about public opinion from polls, focus groups, and other sources to determine how to lead, persuade, or otherwise redirect public opinion, rather than respond to it. Jacobs and Shapiro's own research on the Clinton administration and the behavior of the administration's Republican opposition revealed that the administration largely developed policies based on its policy or political objectives, as in the case of the unsuccessful Clinton health care reform initiative. It used opinion polling in its effort to figure out how to sell their plans and proposals to the public. The congressional Republican opposition, after it ascended to legislative power after the 1994 midterm elections (which the failure of health care reform contributed to), engaged in similar behavior in developing its conservative political agenda.

Whether this represents a genuine and persistent change in the relationship between public opinion and policymaking remains to be seen. Further, as Jacobs and Shapiro and others have argued, we should not expect the opinion–policy relationship to be a persistent and stable one. The relationship may vary over time and may be contingent on the kinds of policies at issue and political context.[66] It is important to determine whether political leaders have policy goals or objectives—or reasons related to ideology, partisanship, or their view of what would constitute effective policymaking—that differ from those of the public at large. As the result of these differences, or even if these differences do not exist, political leaders may not be responsive to public opinion because they may *misperceive* where the public stands on particular issues. Such misperceptions can occur when leaders do not have available to them, or choose not to rely on, reliable and valid measures of public opinion that (as we and others would argue) might best be found in well-constructed opinion polls.[67]

IS GOVERNMENT RESPONSIVENESS TO PUBLIC OPINION *DEMOCRATIC*?

Notwithstanding some of these developments and contingencies, the evidence we have examined and discussed in this chapter shows that government in the United States is more than minimally responsive to public opinion. The apparent effect of public opinion is more than just a constraint of last resort that is effective only because political leaders and their parties have to face elections. But based on this, do we want to claim that we have largely democratic policymaking in the United States? As we noted in earlier discussions, it is not only democratic governments that pay attention to public opinion. Indeed, as V. O. Key, Jr., stated in the very first sentence of his classic *Public Opinion and American Democracy*, "Governments must concern themselves with the opinions of their citizens, if only to provide a basis for repression of disaffection."[68] At this extreme, opinion may then be repressed or forcibly reshaped, so that it comes into line with what a government has done and will do. In this case, the agreement between public opinion and policy that appears can hardly be pronounced "democratic" responsiveness.

But short of this extreme case, which we would expect to find in authoritarian governments, to make judgments about democracy we need to consider both what has influenced public opinion and the quality of the opinion that has resulted. The quality of the policies that are enacted also matter to the extent that "democracy" involves holding up certain norms and values. Many of us would be reluctant to call "democratic" those policies that violate what we have cherished as fundamental civil liberties and rights (see Chapter Eight). Thus, the lack of government responsiveness on the issue of prayer in public schools and other proposals that might violate constitutional protections may still be interpreted as democratic— that is, consistent with liberal-democratic norms that have been established and supported for all time, even though they might be opposed by the public at a given moment.

As we saw in Chapter Eight, the public itself is not omniscient; individuals do not walk around with all the information they need to make judgments about issues that arise and to decide what government should do about it. They depend on information from others, and when it comes to national issues, the public is heavily dependent on political leaders, other elites, organized groups, and others; the positions and ideas and other information these sources have to offer are conveyed to the public through the mass media. The mass media themselves, too, can have some independent impact on public opinion based on what news outlets—depending on the decisions made by reporters, editors, publishers, and others—choose to report about, including the sources they select for news stories and any personal opinions that reporters or editors themselves offer.

What matters here is the quality of the information that is provided and whether the process involved is one that we would call political leadership or education, as opposed to manipulation or deception. Leadership and education are processes that could fit in well with a responsiveness to public opinion that is worthy of being called democracy. If, in one case, the public is influenced by accurate facts and persuasive stances that do not distort reality, so that the public is able to pursue its interests, we would find this very different from a case in which public opinion is influenced by incomplete information, distortions, or outright falsehoods from self-serving elites or other interests, so that the public did not have the best available information to pursue its interests. In the latter case, the quality of public opinion would be problematic and the responsiveness of government to this opinion would not be "democratic."

Clearly, making judgments of this sort is not easy and can be politically charged as well. What is true or false is sometimes not easy to determine. The same holds especially for judging whether information provides a "biased" presentation of reality (what would "unbiased" presentations look like?). But in order to make judgments about whether a policy decision is democratic, we have to wrestle with these questions. Some cases are easier to draw conclusions about than others.

For example, what some now call an infamous case of policy responsiveness involving political manipulation that defied democracy occurred when President Lyndon Johnson marshaled support for escalating U.S. involvement in Vietnam. Johnson initially rallied public support to expand American military involvement in Vietnam by misrepresenting alleged attacks on two ships, the *Maddox* and the *Turner Joy,* off the coast of North Vietnam in 1964. Public support rose for increased military action in Vietnam, and the Johnson administration responded by going to war. Other cases, again subject to further debate, might include observations about how prior to the U.S. entry into World War II, the Roosevelt administrations essentially goaded the Germans to attack American ships that engaged in naval reconnaissance for the British;[69] how the first Bush administration misrepresented American options prior to the start of all-out fighting in the first Gulf War against Iraq;[70] or how (based on the evidence available at this writing) the second Bush administration, in the short period leading up to the second Gulf War, misled the public about the Iraqi leader Saddam Hussein's progress toward obtaining "weapons of mass destruction."[71] Although the validity of these examples may be a subject for debate, it is no accident that they are foreign policy issues: It has been argued that there is danger to democracy in foreign policymaking because the public has fewer competing sources of information available to it (i.e., the source is overwhelmingly the government) than in other areas.[72]

Standing in contrast, though also not beyond further debate, is the case of the passage of an increase in the minimum wage in 1996. This had overwhelming public support and might be hailed as a triumph for democracy. For one thing, this was a case in which the public could make an independent judgment that the prior minimum wage of $4.25 per hour was not an adequate living wage for an individual or family. Political leaders and others could echo this through the press. Opponents might claim—and did claim—that the public was being misled and that raising the minimum wage would adversely affect small business and low-end employment. But a good case can be made that these trade-offs were widely acknowledged (the fact that it took so long to pass an increase in the minimum wage is an indication of this), and in the end, the public made value judgments based on the trade-offs and decided that raising the wage would lead to a better outcome for the nation overall.

Taking a more controversial issue, opponents of welfare reform legislation in 1996 might readily claim that the public was misinformed: that Aid to Families with Dependent Children (AFDC) spending was not enormous; that fraud was less rampant than portrayed in the media; and that reforms would in fact have clear adverse effects, so that any government responsiveness to widespread support for reform was hardly democratic. However, to the extent that the public had simply made value trade-offs and concluded—perhaps correctly—that there is substantial uncertainty regarding how to deal with welfare (especially given limited resources), the passage of welfare reform could be considered democratic.

To take this even further, since the quality of public opinion is so central to reaching such normative conclusions about the opinion–policy relationship, we should also not dismiss policymakers' failure to respond to public opinion as undemocratic. There can be cases in which policymakers feel they must make policy decisions that do not have public support (when acting as the "trustees" we described earlier), because they feel (and they think there is evidence that) the public has been misled or manipulated or has not yet become fully informed about a policy at issue. Ideally, such policy decisions should be delayed until the public is more fully engaged in them, but even when this delay does not occur, persuading the public after the fact of the merit of a policy need not be dismissed as undemocratic, that is, only as long as deceit or manipulation has not occurred.

CONCLUSION

We have covered a lot of new ground in this chapter. Thanks to the expansion of public opinion research, there is much more evidence than ever before to tell us about the relationship between public opinion and policymaking and the workings of democracy. We have offered answers about the basic degree of correspondence or correlation between what the public has wanted and what the government has done. To make judgments about calling this "democracy at work" has required that we interrogate the evidence further in ways that are not simple and straightforward. This may be yet another frustration for students of public opinion.

But in everyday life, we now see a more direct and dynamic role than ever before of public opinion in politics and policymaking. We see this in the reporting of opinion polls and in the continual appeals to public opinion (often referred to as "going public")—including all types of political advertising—that are made through the mass media by presidents, members of Congress, political parties, organized groups, and others interested and active in the political process.[73] Some see this as a bad development that detracts from institutional consultations and deliberations among political leaders and experts who may be best able to formulate effective policies. Others see this as bad because it gives the public itself a false sense that what government does is democratic, even as the public is then manipulated in ways that do not necessarily serve the public's interests. Short of regulating public discourse, political leaders will have to adjust to this more visible role for the public (although the "recoil effect" may lead elites unknowingly to respond to public opinion in their attempts to control it!).

Here, as in other areas of research, there is still some uncertainty in the findings and evidence we have reported, as well as in what to make of them, concerning how much actual public control of policymaking there is. Further archival research and interviews with former policymakers and government officials (when they are free to reflect honestly) should help decrease the uncertainty, along with further tracking of trends in public opinion and policymaking. Whether we conclude that the public only loosely constrains policymaking or that the public at times forcefully pushes the government to act in different ways, there is evidence that government policies are responsive to public opinion in the United States.

Whether there is "enough" or "too much" responsiveness and whether we should call this responsiveness to public opinion "democratic" depends on the quality of public opinion and the information received and on the independent capabilities of policymakers. Even with the optimism that can be found in the assessment of the public's competence in Chapter Eight, it is still of great importance to try to improve the public's level of attention to politics and its level of knowledge about policy issues, so that the citizenry can constrain and influence its leaders in ways that can ultimately improve government policies and American democracy.

NOTES

1. V. O. Key, Jr., *Public Opinion and American Democracy* (New York: Alfred A. Knopf, 1961). See also Harold D. Lasswell, *Democracy Through Public Opinion* (Menasha, WI: Banta, 1941).

2. Key, *Public Opinion and American Democracy,* p. 7; see also Benjamin Ginsberg, *The Captive Public: How Mass Opinion Promotes State Power* (New York: Basic Books, 1986). For related discussion about mass opinion and government, see Susan Herbst, *Numbered Voices: How Opinion Polling Has Shaped American Politics* (Chicago: University of Chicago Press, 1992), and James A. Morone, *The Democratic Wish: Popular Participation and the Limits of American Government* (New York: Basic Books, 1990).

3. See Amy Fried, *Muffled Echoes: Oliver North and the Politics of Public Opinion* (New York: Columbia University Press, 1997).

4. On some of these issues and other related research, see Paul Berstein, *Discrimination, Jobs, and Politics: The Struggle for Equal Employment Opportunity in the United States Since the New Deal* (Chicago: University of Chicago Press, 1985); Benjamin I. Page and Robert Y. Shapiro, "Effects of Public Opinion on Policy," *American Political Science Review* 77 (1983):175–190; and Benjamin I. Page and Robert Y. Shapiro, *The Rational Public: Fifty Years of Trends in Americans' Policy Preferences* (Chicago: University of Chicago Press, 1992).

5. Compare Richard A. Sobel, *The Impact of Public Opinion on U.S. Foreign Policy* (New York: Oxford University Press, 2001).

6. R. Kent Weaver, Robert Y. Shapiro, and Lawrence R. Jacobs, "The Polls—Trends: Welfare," *Public Opinion Quarterly* 59 (1995):606–627; Greg. M. Shaw and Robert Y. Shapiro, "The Polls—Trends: Poverty and Public Assistance." *Public Opinion Quarterly* 66 (Spring 2002):105–128.

7. Lawrence R. Jacobs and Robert Y. Shapiro, *Politicians Don't Pander: Political Manipulation and the Loss of Democratic Responsiveness* (Chicago: University of Chicago Press, 2000), pp. xi–xii.

8. See James H. Kuklinski, "Representation and Elections: A Policy Analysis," *American Political Science Review* 72 (1978):165–177; and Edward R. Tufte, *Political Control of the Economy* (Princeton: Princeton University Press, 1978).

9. On the "sharing model," see Robert S. Erikson and Kent L. Tedin, *American Public Opinion,* 5th ed. (Boston: Allyn and Bacon, 1995), pp. 18–19, 281–286.

10. See James S. Fishkin, *The Voice of the People: Public Opinion and Democracy* (New Haven: Yale University Press, 1995).

11. See John C. Wahlke, Heinx Eulau, William Buchanan, and Leroy C. Ferguson, *The Legislative System* (New York: Wiley, 1962).

12. See Michael X. Delli Carpini and Bruce Williams, "The Method Is the Message: Focus Groups as a Means of Social, Psychological, and Political Inquiry," in Michael X. Delli Carpini, Leonie Huddy, and Robert Y. Shapiro, eds., *Research in Micropolitics,* Vol. 4, *New Directions in Political Psychology* (Greenwich, CT: JAI Press, 1994).

13. See David B. Truman, *The Governmental Process: Political Interests and Public Opinion,* 2nd ed. (New York: Alfred A. Knopf, 1971); and Robert A. Dahl, *Who Governs: Democracy and Power in an American City* (New Haven: Yale University Press, 1961).

14. See Mancur Olson, *The Logic of Collective Action: Public Goods and the Theory of Groups* (Cambridge, MA: Harvard University Press, 1965).

15. On "latent opinion" or latent interests, see Truman, *The Governmental Process,* and Key, *Public Opinion and American Democracy.*

16. See E. E. Schattschneider, *The Semi-Sovereign People* (Hinsdale, IL: Dryden Press, 1960); and Kay Lehman Schlozman and John T. Tierney, *Organized Interests and American Democracy* (New York: Harper and Row, 1986).

17. See C. Wright Mills, *The Power Elite* (New York: Oxford University Press, 1956); Floyd Hunter, *Community Power Structure* (Chapel Hill: University of North Carolina Press, 1953).

18. See Grant McConnell, *Private Power and American Democracy* (New York: Random House, 1966).

19. See Schattschneider, *The Semi-Sovereign People*; and Peter Bachrach and Morton S. Baratz, "Two Faces of Power," *American Political Science Review* 56 (1962):947–952, and "Decisions and Nondecisions: An Analytical Framework," *American Political Science Review* 57 (1963):632–642.

20. For example, see Charles E. Lindblom, *Politics and Markets: The World's Political-Economic Systems* (New York: Basic Books, 1977).

21. Key, *Public Opinion and American Democracy*, p. 97.

22. Donald J. Devine, *The Attentive Public: Polyarchical Democracy* (Chicago: Rand McNally and Company, 1970); Robert Weissberg, *Public Opinion and Popular Government* (Englewood Cliffs, NJ: Prentice-Hall, 1976); Alan D. Monroe, "American Party Platforms and Public Opinion," *American Journal of Political Science* 27 (1983):27–42.

23. Compare Devine, *Attentive Public*; Weissberg, *Public Opinion and Popular Government*; Joel E. Brooks, "Democratic Frustration in the Anglo-American Polities: A Quantification of Inconsistency Between Mass Public Opinion and Public Policy," *Western Political Science Quarterly* 38 (1985):250–261, and "The Opinion–Policy Nexus in France: Do Institutions and Ideology Make a Difference?" *Journal of Politics* 49 (1987):465–480.

24. Page and Shapiro, "Effects of Public Opinion on Policy"; Robert Y. Shapiro, *The Dynamics of Public Opinion and Public Policy*, Ph.D. diss., University of Chicago, 1982.

25. See also Thomas W. Graham, "Public Opinion and U.S. Foreign Policy Decision Making," in David A. Deese, ed., *The New Politics of American Foreign Policy* (New York: St. Martin's Press, 1994).

26. See Thomas Hartley and Bruce Russett, "Public Opinion and the Common Defense: Who Governs Military Spending in the United States?" *American Political Science Review* 86 (1992):905–915; Christopher Wlezien, "The Public as Thermostat: Dynamics of Preferences for Spending," *American Journal of Political Science* 39 (1995):981–1000, and "Dynamics of Representation: The Case of U.S. Spending on Defence," *British Journal of Political Science* 26 (1996):81–103; Charles W. Ostrom, Jr., and Robin F. Marra, "U.S. Defense Spending and the Soviet Estimate," *American Political Science Review* 80 (1986):819–841; Larry M. Bartels, "Constituency Opinion and Congressional Policy Making: The Reagan Defense Buildup," *American Political Science Review* 85 (1991):457–474. Wlezien has recently compared time series results for different policy areas in "Patterns of Representation: Dynamics of Public Preferences and Policy," *The Journal of Politics* 66 (2004):1–24.

27. Warren E. Miller and Donald E. Stokes, "Constituency Influence in Congress," *American Political Science Review* 57 (1963):45–56.

28. See Robert S. Erikson, "Constituency Opinion and Congressional Behavior: A Reexamination of the Miller–Stokes Data," *American Journal of Political Science* 22 (1978):511–535; Benjamin I. Page, Robert Y. Shapiro, Paul W. Gronke, and Robert M. Rosenberg, "Constituency, Party, and Representation in Congress," *Public Opinion Quarterly* 48 (1984):741–756.

29. Robert S. Erikson, "The Relationship Between Public Opinion and State Policy: A New Look Based on Some Forgotten Data," *American Journal of Political Science* 20 (1976):25–36.

30. Matthew E. Wetstein, *Abortion Rates in the United States: The Influence of Opinion and Policy* (Albany: State University of New York Press, 1996).

31. Malcolm L. Goggin and Christopher Wlezien, "Abortion Opinion and Policy in the American States," in Malcolm Goggin, ed., *Understanding the New Politics of Abortion* (Newbury Park, CA: Sage Publications, 1993).

32. Key, *Public Opinion and American Democracy*, p. 553.

33. Robert S. Erikson, Gerald C. Wright, and John P. McIver, *Statehouse Democracy: Public Opinion and Policy in the American States* (New York: Cambridge University Press, 1993).

34. David Osborne, *Laboratories of Democracy: A New Brand of Governors Creates Models for National Growth* (Cambridge, MA: Harvard Business School, 1988).

35. James A. Stimson, Michael B. MacKuen, and Robert S. Erikson, "Dynamic Representation," *American Political Science Review* 89 (1995):543–565, and Robert S. Erikson, Michael B. MacKuen, and James A. Stimson, *The Macro Polity* (New York: Cambridge University Press, 2002).

36. James A. Stimson, *Public Opinion in America: Moods, Cycles, and Swings* (Boulder: Westview Press, 1991).

37. For a review of studies of the responsiveness to public opinion by different institutions and levels of government, see Robert Y. Shapiro and Lawrence R. Jacobs, "The Relationship Between Public Opinion and Public Policy: A Review," in Samuel Long, ed., *Political Behavior Annual*, Vol. 2 (Boulder: Westview Press, 1989).

38. See Page and Shapiro, *The Rational Public*; Elaine B. Sharp, *The Sometime Connection: Public Opinion and Social Policy* (Albany: State University of New York Press, 1999); Lawrence R. Jacobs and Robert Y. Shapiro, "Politics and Policymaking in the Real World: Crafted Talk and the Loss of Democratic Responsiveness," in Jeff Manza, Fay Lomax Cook, and Benjamin I. Page, eds., *Navigating Public Opinion: Polls, Policy, and the Future of American Democracy* (New York: Oxford University Press, 2002)

39. See Weaver, Shapiro, and Jacobs, "Poll Trends: Welfare."

40. Paul Burstein, "The Sociology of Democratic Politics and Government," in Ralph H. Turner and James F. Short, eds., *Annual Review of Sociology*, Vol. 7 (Palo Alto, CA: Annual Reviews, 1981), p. 295.

41. Alan D. Monroe, "American Party Platforms and Public Opinion," *American Journal of Political Science* 27 (1983):27–42.

42. See Erikson, Wright, and McIver, *Statehouse Democracy*; Page et al., "Constituency, Party, and Representation in Congress"; Russell J. Dalton, *Citizen Politics: Public Opinion and Political Parties in Advanced Western Democracies* (Chatham, NJ: Chatham House Publishers, 1996).

43. See Anthony Downs, *An Economic Theory of Democracy* (New York: Harper and Row, 1957); Benjamin I. Page, *Choices and Echoes in Presidential Elections: Rational Man and Electoral Democracy* (Chicago: University of Chicago Press, 1978); Gerald M. Pomper with Susan S. Lederman, *Elections in America: Control and Influence in Democratic Politics*, 2nd ed. (New York: Dodd, Mead, 1980); Kelly D. Patterson, *Political Parties and the Maintenance of Liberal Democracy* (New York: Columbia University Press, 1996); Jeff Fishel, *Presidents and Promises: From Campaign Pledge to Presidential Performance* (Washington, DC: Congressional Quarterly Press, 1985).

44. Lawrence R. Jacobs, *The Health of Nations: Public Opinion and the Making of American and British Health Policy* (Ithaca: Cornell University Press, 1993).

45. Compare Leonard A. Kusnitz, *Public Opinion and Foreign Policy: America's China Policy, 1949–1979* (Westport, CT: Greenwood Press, 1984).

46. See Richard Sobel, ed., *Public Opinion in U.S. Foreign Policy: The Controversy over Contra Aid* (Lanham, MD: Rowman and Littlefield, 1993).

47. See Ronald H. Hinckley, *People, Polls, and Policymakers: American Public Opinion and National Security* (New York: Lexington Books, 1992).

48. On employment and civil rights, see Burstein, *Discrimination, Jobs, and Politics.*

49. Jacobs, *Health of Nations*; Thomas W. Graham, *The Politics of Failure: Strategic Nuclear Arms Control, Public Opinion, and Domestic Politics in the United States, 1945–1985,* Ph.D. diss., Massachusetts Institute of Technology, 1989, and "Public Opinion and U.S. Foreign Policy Decision Making," in David A. Deese, ed., *New Politics of American Foreign Policy.*

50. Philip J. Powlick, "The Attitudinal Bases of Responsiveness to Public Opinion Among American Foreign Policy Officials," *Journal of Conflict Resolution* 35 (1991):611–641, and "Public Opinion in the Foreign Policy Process: An Attitudinal and Institutional Comparison of the Reagan and Clinton Administrations," paper presented at the Annual Meeting of the American Political Science Association, Chicago, 1995.

51. Bernard C. Cohen, *The Public's Impact of Foreign Policy* (Boston: Little, Brown, 1973).

52. See Robert Y. Shapiro and Lawrence R. Jacobs, "Who Leads and Who Follows? U.S. Presidents, Public Opinion and Foreign Policy," in Brigitte L. Nacos, Robert Y. Shapiro, and Pierangelo Isernia, eds., *Decisionmaking in a Glass House: Mass Media, Public Opinion, and American and European Foreign Policy in the 21st Century* (Boston: Rowman and Littlefield, 2000), and other essays in this volume; Robert Y. Shapiro and Lawrence R. Jacobs, "Public Opinion, Foreign Policy, and Democracy: How Presidents Use Public Opinion," in Manza, Lomax Cook, and Page, eds., *Navigating Public Opinion.*

53. Robert M. Eisinger, *The Evolution of Presidential Polling* (New York: Cambridge University Press, 2003).

54. Some of the history of this is described in Lawrence R. Jacobs and Robert Y. Shapiro, "The Rise of Presidential Polling: The Nixon White House in Historical Perspective," *Public Opinion Quarterly* 59:163–165; see especially the new books Robert M. Eisinger, *The Evolution of Presidential Polling* (New York: Cambridge University Press, 2003), and Diane J. Heith, *Polling to Govern: Public Opinion and Presidential Leadership* (Stanford, CA: Stanford University Press, 2004).

55. See John G. Geer, *From Tea Leaves to Opinion Polls: A Theory of Democratic Leadership* (New York: Columbia University Press, 1996); Eisinger, *The Evolution of Presidential Polling*; and Heith, *Polling to Govern.*

56. Shoon Kathleen Murray and Peter Howard, "Variation in White House Polling Operations: Carter to Clinton," *Public Opinion Quarterly* 66 (Winter 2002):527–558.

57. See Lawrence R. Jacobs and Robert Y. Shapiro, "Public Decisions, Private Polls: John F. Kennedy's Presidency," paper presented at the Annual Meeting of the Midwest Political Science Association, Chicago, 1992; "The Public Presidency, Private Polls, and Policymaking: Lyndon Johnson," paper presented at the Annual Meeting of the American Political Science Association, Washington, DC, 1993; "Issues, Candidate Image, and Priming: The Use of Private Polls in Kennedy's 1960 Presidential Campaign," *American Political Science Review* 88 (1994):527–540; "Lyndon Johnson, Vietnam, and Public Opinion: Rethinking

Realist Theory of Leadership," *Presidential Studies Quarterly* 29 (September 1999):592–616; and especially the theoretical analysis in Geer, *From Tea Leaves to Opinion Polls.*

58. Jacobs and Shapiro, "The Public Presidency, Private Polls, and Policymaking: Lyndon Johnson."

59. Jacobs and Shapiro, "The Public Presidency, Private Polls, and Policymaking: Lyndon Johnson," and "Lyndon Johnson, Vietnam, and Public Opinion: Rethinking Realist Theory of Leadership."

60. For a detailed account of this, see Andrew Z. Katz, "Public Opinion and Foreign Policy: The Nixon Administration and the Pursuit of Peace with Honor in Vietnam," *Presidential Studies Quarterly* 27 (1997):496–513.

61. Lawrence R. Jacobs and Robert Y. Shapiro, "The Rise of Presidential Polling," and "Presidential Manipulation of Polls and Public Opinion: The Nixon Administration and the Pollsters," *Political Science Quarterly* 110 (1995–96):519–538.

62. See Page and Shapiro, *Rational Public,* pp. 242–251; compare Kusnitz, *Public Opinion and Foreign Policy.*

63. Alan D Monroe, "Public Opinion and Public Policy 1980–1993," *Public Opinion Quarterly* 62 (1998):6–28.

64. Jacobs and Shapiro, *Politicians Don't Pander.*

65. See Stephen D. Ansolabehere, James M. Snyder, Jr., and Charles Stewart III, "Candidate Positioning in U.S. House Elections," *American Journal of Political Science* 45 (2001):136–159.

66. On the importance of understanding the variations in the opinion–policy relationship and under what circumstances responsiveness occurs, see several essays in Manza, Cook, and Page, eds., *Navigating Public Opinion*; Sharp, *The Sometime Connection*; Jeff Manza and Fay Lomax Cook, "A Democratic Polity? Three Views of Policy Responsiveness to Public Opinion in the United States," *American Politics Research* 30 (November 2002):630–667.

67. Steven Kull and I. M. Destler, *Misreading the Public: The Myth of a New Isolationism* (Washington, D.C.: Brookings Institution Press, 1999).

68. Key, *Public Opinion and American Democracy,* p. 3.

69. On these and other ostensible cases of manipulation of public opinion, see Page and Shapiro, *The Rational Public,* Chap. 9.

70. On political communication during the first Gulf War, see the essays in W. Lance Bennett and David L. Paletz, eds., *Taken by Storm: The Media, Public Opinion, and U.S. Foreign Policy in the Gulf War* (Chicago: University of Chicago Press, 1994), and Benjamin I. Page, *Who Deliberates? Mass Media in Modern Democracy* (Chicago: University of Chicago Press, 1996).

71. For example, see Barton Gellman and Walter Pincus, "Errors and Exaggerations: Prewar Depictions of Iraq's Nuclear Threat Outweighed the Evidence," *Washington Post National Weekly Edition,* August 18–24, 2003, pp. 6–8.

72. See Page and Shapiro, *The Rational Public,* Chaps. 5, 6, and 9; Shapiro and Jacobs, "Who Leads and Who Follows? U.S. Presidents, Public Opinion and Foreign Policy."

73. In the case of presidents, see Samuel Kernell, *Going Public: New Strategies of Presidential Leadership,* 3rd ed. (Washington, DC: Congressional Quarterly Press, 1997).

10

Communicating, Campaigning, and the Public

In Chapter One, we looked at many ways of defining public opinion, based on what the term means to different people in different contexts. We have established that public opinion is not a static, immobile object that holds a constant shape and mass over time. Rather, it is a highly dynamic, fluid process that reflects how people think, interact with one another, and deal with the bodies politic into which they have organized themselves.

We have seen how, at the individual or personal level, citizens constantly change and reassess their attitudes and opinions, the better to fit new knowledge and experience. At the macro, or mass, societal level, politically salient events occur that transform political coalitions, the nature of issues, and the appropriateness of given policy options. At the level of group interaction and networking, the everyday give and take of political talk at the dinner table, at the workplace, and over the phone or the Internet reshapes what we think of one another and about politics. At each of these levels, the development and generation of public opinion require active communication processes to be at work. Recall from Chapter Six how mass and interpersonal communication interplay to promote such phenomena as the spiral of silence and third-person effects from media. We have also learned that when people do learn new things or change attitudes or behaviors as a result of what they see or hear from others, complex psychological processes are involved, some involving highly logical steps, some based more on whims of the moment.

This chapter begins by examining how our thinking about the role of communication in the public opinion process has progressed. We will emphasize the interplay of mass media and public opinion, where most of the gains in our knowledge have taken place over recent decades. We will also, however, demonstrate the obvious but sometimes overlooked importance of interpersonal communication in the mix.

COMMUNICATION, MASS MEDIA, AND PUBLIC OPINION: EARLY DEVELOPMENT AND PERSPECTIVES

Communication serves many functions to keep our diverse society working well enough to maintain basic equilibrium. The sociologist Harold Lasswell defined three key functions of communication for societies, each of which also has clear ramifications for public opinion.[1] The first is surveillance, or keeping one another abreast of what is taking place in the world, especially events that may be threatening to the common good. Print and electronic news media have become a ritualized force to which we entrust much of this responsibility. A second function, correlation, serves to keep us in touch with what others are thinking about what is going on, how events are being interpreted, and the opinions of others toward various topics. Lasswell saw this correlation among views and building of consensus as a social "glue" necessary to getting things done in a community or society. Such a correlating function helps develop democratic consensuses out of conflict situations, a central tenet of modern democratic theory. A third function is transmission, or the passing of the norms and morals of the culture to others entering the social system, most obviously the young. Formal education fills much of this role for the society as a whole. Other more informal communication channels often help transmit norms within groups, initiating new members into the rituals that keep organizations together over time.

Lasswell was thinking as much or more about interpersonal as mass communication channels in defining these three functions. Other scholars have added specific additional functions for modern mass media— entertainment being one, economic enhancement another.[2] The modern advertising–marketing multiplex driven by media enterprises has been claimed as necessary for keeping our present consumer-based economy operating.

Historically, we see a distinct change in thinking about the social purposes of communication as mass media developed in the late nineteenth century and on into the twentieth. It became popular—and sometimes convenient—for social critics and scholars to blame the new media technologies for a host of other changes occurring about the same time, many of them viewed as threatening. Much of that concern was likely grounded in fear of the unknown—of novel, mysterious, and seemingly unrestricted technologies that might be challenging and changing not only the political but the social and cultural worlds of the time.

Not coincidentally, this was also the era in which mass society theories of public opinion began to emerge.[3] Western industrialized societies were viewed as moving away from clusters of closely knit communities with close personal linkages toward becoming more transient, urbanized, and impersonal. The basic economically driven movement of people from rural communities and farms to centralized factory-driven cities was a key component here. This was seen as leading to breakdowns in community structure and personal relationships, with individuals becoming more anonymous and isolated. Such isolation, it was feared, could result in publics that acted as more of a "mass" of less socially tied and responsible citizens. Such masses, lacking closer social ties, could be more amenable to various forms of propaganda and demagoguery. The new media of the era were thus even more feared as a catalyst that could sway these masses. At this time, communication about politics per se was rapidly moving away from a largely interpersonal pursuit—buttressed by printed materials available to the relatively well-educated and affluent few. It was becoming a more institutionalized system, involving more free-flowing information from a variety of sources to huge audiences.

The development of higher-speed printing technologies in the early and mid–1800s made inexpensive daily newspapers available to millions of urban dwellers, giving them up-to-date local and telegraph-fed national news and commentary. The technology also greatly reduced the cost of and increased the availability and visual appeal of magazines, books, pamphlets, catalogs, and other print items. Motion pictures became a mainstream entertainment medium in the early 1900s, with such popular fare as D. W. Griffith's *Birth of a Nation* showing the potential political and social clout of film. By midcentury, radio blossomed into a mature technology capable of reaching into every U.S. home, providing a diverse mix of popular to more sophisticated entertainment, commentary, and news, including live coverage of war, disasters, political speeches, and elections.

Television entered the scene on a grand scale in the 1950s and, within a decade, became the dominant mass medium for entertainment as well as a medium heavily depended on for national and international news. By the 1980s, telecommunication via satellite had greatly expanded television's content capabilities to include dozens of cable-cast and direct satellite channels covering a much wider range of interests. The same satellite capabilities, attended by rapid innovation in the computer industry, allowed greatly enhanced personal interactive communications in the 1990s, relying on Internet capabilities and far more sophisticated telephone systems that were soon to be linked with television. E-mail and World Wide Web sites have emerged as significant communication channels, bridging mass communication with interpersonal communication, blurring many distinctions between the two concepts.

Each of these developments caused a certain amount of awe at its potential for opinion-shaping power. Concerns rose about the impact of each new communication technology on public opinion and often about its influence on the cultural and moral fabric—and social behavior—as well. Political debate was thought to be cheapened by many nineteenth-century newspapers' penchant for sensationalism, called "yellow journalism" (meaning in part unfair, biased coverage), and often crude, close-to-libelous attacks on public officials. *Birth of a Nation* displayed a popular motion picture's ability arguably to misrepresent the post–Civil War South in a way blatantly unfair to black citizens. Radio's ability to provide live access in the homes of its audiences to the words of political leaders—champions and demagogues alike—caused considerable concern. Moreover, the propagandistic value of radio as an international medium via shortwave broadcasting was quickly discovered by many countries. This perhaps peaked during World War II and the subsequent Cold War battles for the airwaves among the Voice of America, the British Broadcasting Corporation, and Radio Moscow. The onset of television appeared to some to take the more persuasive and perhaps more odious elements of all of the above channels and drop them into the laps of citizens in their living rooms. Many critics see the relatively unrestricted accessibility of the Internet as aiding political radicalism and pornography and as a threat to individual privacy.

In sum, each of these new technologies in its own way fueled concerns that it had the power to sway public opinion unduly, to influence or propagandize large groups of people to believe or act in ways somehow unhealthy for themselves and their society. Taking these media as a group and coupling them with the concurrent large-scale economic, political, and social changes taking place in the United States and elsewhere, it is not surprising that legitimate questions have been raised by social observers about their influence. Others have vehemently attacked media at various times, having found a convenient scapegoat for war, economic depression, the social upheavals fermented by industrialization, and related ills.

But how much have these new media really mattered? How much of a difference did they make in how public opinion is developed and shaped? In truth, we will probably never really know what their consequences were in previous decades. Nevertheless, we can hazard some well-educated guesses and, at the least, frame the questions in ways that will help us more successfully figure out the influence of communication media in our present environment and what we should make of that. Perhaps in its most simplistic—if not too simplistic—terms, the ongoing debate is between (a) scholars, social critics, and policymakers concerned that mass media have an edge over the publics or audiences they reach, unduly influencing them, and (b) those who argue that these publics can resist such influences and indeed use media in largely beneficial ways.

Before turning to the evidence on either side of that debate, we should carry the thread from previous chapters a bit further and say more about who decides what kinds of information media carry with respect to public opinion and who decides what that information is. Recall that Chapter Nine discussed how elites try to influence more general publics directly on political issues, with interpersonal opinion leadership being a key concept. Here, we will first consider how elites—and others—try to use mass media as agents of influence and then, from the point of view of the public, consider the evidence concerning how successful such manipulation may be.

WHO DECIDES WHAT THE MEDIA PRESENT?

A critical question is how issues, events, and, indeed, personalities come into media view in the first place. It is worth recalling here Lippmann's point that

FIGURE 10.1   The media give us representations of the world beyond our experience. SOURCE: © Tom Tomorrow. *Greetings from This Modern World* (New York: St. Martin's Press, 1992).

at their best, the media give us representations, pictures of an outside world we do not directly see or experience (see Figure 10.1).[4] Someone is preparing those pictures or stories for us—of events, of issues, of personalities—that we will likely never encounter "live" on our own. Who prepares those pictures, with what biases, and with what intents are critical questions.

In its most basic form, the evidence shows that for most major public issues, most of the public begins to pay them more heed after they have been reported in newspapers and on television.[5] How much the public is interested in events and issues is for the most part proportional to how much news coverage the issues get. But journalists seldom report on issues or events unless they see some compelling public interest or need to be served by doing so. Even in reporting the most trivial or sensational stories, reporters are driven by an assumption that audiences will want to know about it and will "buy" the story by reading or watching it. Hence, the news agenda may be set in large part by the press's expectations of what audiences want or need. It becomes not quite so surprising that audiences eventually place those topics higher on their own agendas. There are likely instances in which the news media discover stories about events that are already priorities on the public agenda. More localized community or grassroots issues come to mind here—concern generated by neighbors about a landfill problem may be presented to a city council hearing or lead to organized protest, attracting news media attention. In fact, this is becoming a more common tactic used by citizens to gain attention for issues that occupy them.

It is also commonplace for organized interest groups—including corporations and government agencies and other elites—to try to influence the press and by that the public agenda.[6] A cursory scan of mainstream daily newspapers or news broadcasts suggests that most of the information presented in them originates from governmental organizations, lobbying groups, corporations, and other institutions with their own agendas and influence strategies. These can include efforts by, say, Federal health agencies to inform citizens of how to protect themselves from a new disease outbreak or attempts by a tobacco company to put the best possible light on the risks involved in cigarette smoking. An environmental group holds a press conference on what it regards as a major threat by Congress to watershed protection; a U.S. senator alerts a *New York Times* reporter of the possibility that his election opponent has a campaign slush fund. Although we count on the press to sort out the merits of these episodes, report on them as appropriate, and assemble them into the day's news agenda, it seems undeniable that the news that is produced is in part a function of the agendas of others.

Much of the U.S. public relations industry is built around encouraging the press to give more play to a company, personage, issue, or event. Anecdotal evidence suggests that political candidates can significantly influence news play during campaigns and that incumbents can be highly successful at it. Research shows that presidents in particular can use the power of their office to sway the news agenda,[7] more likely when they are more popular with the public and the press.[8] Officeholders and other individuals who are regarded by the media as public spokespersons typically have a major influence simply in the access they have to the media and journalists, who often seek their opinions and reactions to events. Such elites are also able to frame or develop the context of media presentations and stories, which can lead reporters to emphasize certain aspects of an event or issue at the expense of others.[9] Such framing, as explained by Robert Entman, can exaggerate particular aspects of political problems, leading to suggested solutions to those problems that may be slanted toward particular political biases or moral judgments. Entman offers the global example of the Cold War between the United States and the Soviet Union, which dominated most news accounts of world events from the 1950s through the 1980s. Civil wars in developing countries, for example, tended to be reported in U.S. news media more in the context of whether a possibly "Communist" or Soviet-leaning faction was involved and how that had happened, rather than on issues and causes perhaps more germane to the country in question.

Another example would be whether a story about decreased Medicare support for the elderly is framed more in terms of its impact on the health of the elderly, on spiraling health care costs that affect the quality of health care in the U.S. overall, or on the contribution of Medicare costs to the Federal spending deficit. Depending upon which frame is chosen and by whom, the line of argument for solutions and the moral issues involved can be quite different. Part of this process includes attempts by elite spokespersons to "spin" stories, or emphasize angles of issues that will put themselves or their viewpoints in the most favorable light.

As Clarice Olien, George Donohue, and Phillip Tichenor remind us, these and other influences on the news media render them far from being independent, autonomous, "objective" observers.[10] The press can be viewed as a socially controlled institution in the same sense that executive government agencies, the courts, schools, and higher education are. All respond to and are constrained by other societal forces, notably including one another, and the public.

At the core of most approaches to how communication and public opinion relate is the notion of public issues that people agree or disagree about. Inherent in the concept of an issue is conflict, the grist not only of public opinion but of everyday news coverage as well. A series of studies by Olien, Donohue, and Tichenor on the role of the press in community conflict and public opinion have suggested that news media may too often report conflict in ways that satisfy established, powerful political and social groups.[11] This may be at the expense of the less potent, and perhaps of the public trust.

The First Amendment protections accorded the press imply that it serves something of a "watchdog" role, alerting the community at large to potentially conflicting intrusions. Olien and associates challenge this and argue that in too many cases, the news media act more as a "guard dog," favoring more powerful and influential community interests. This does not imply that the press favors individuals or organizations when they behave inappropriately, which could be more of a "lap dog" role. Rather, the news establishment is seen as having developed power relationships with other community institutions and focuses more on maintaining those relationships and on exploiting conflicts that work toward that end. Olien and associates suggest that such reporting emphasizes conflict between individuals within power structures rather than opposition to the power structure itself. More ritualistic controversies, such as election campaigns, are played up, as opposed to threats to the political system. Olien and colleagues offer the example of the 1972 presidential election, in which "ritualistic" coverage of McGovern versus Nixon on traditional candidate and campaign topics displaced coverage of the system-threatening Watergate affair until after the election.

More critical observers such as Edward Herman and Noam Chomsky view most contemporary media as being conservatively bound up in the marketplace of commerce rather than in the marketplace of ideas, reluctant to examine problems and issues that could push the economic or political status quo too far off center.[12]

THE EFFECTS OF MASS MEDIA ON PUBLIC OPINION

Do these efforts at influence and manipulation through the media work? Is public opinion affected? A succinct answer might be a rephrasing of Harold Lasswell:[13] Some of the messages on some of the media have some effects on some audiences some of the time. Here we will consider four broad categories of possible effects on (1) the public agenda for issues; (2) how informed the public is about issues; (3) public opinions, attitudes, and behaviors; and (4) public values and norms.

The Media and the Public Agenda

A major and often underestimated force in public opinion dynamics is how and why people choose to direct their attention to one issue at the expense of another, to spend more time and effort thinking about one problem than another. Awareness of and attention to issues precede the shaping of opinion positions about them. Our attention spans, as well as the scope of issues we can deal with at any one time, are limited. Some of us may find ourselves giving much attention to gender discrimination, and others to U.S. involvement in international conflicts; some may be concerned over animal rights, and still others over global environmental issues. But few if any of us can give equal attention to all of those and others; rather, we "agendize" and prioritize our concerns. The news media appear subtly and consistently to influence the agenda of issues we have opinions about. As succinctly put by political scientist Bernard Cohen, "The press may not be successful much of the time in telling people what to think, but it is stunningly successful in telling its readers what to think about."[14] A multitude of studies have validated this agenda-setting function of the news media. The more play and emphasis newspapers or television news give to particular events or issues, the more likely are audiences of those media to regard them as more salient, more important. Recall the status-conferring ability of the media discussed previously: The mechanism may be quite the same, but here it is spread across the larger workings of the entire news-dissemination process.

Early work on agenda setting in the 1970s, primarily by communication scholars Maxwell McCombs and Donald Shaw of the University of North Carolina, found direct links between the ranking of issues as treated in the news media and the ranking of importance given to those issues by the public in opinion polls (Table 10.1).[15] When citizens were asked which issue or issues they regarded as most important, the order of those issues corresponded quite well with the degree of news play they had received. How audiences of specific news media ranked Vietnam War issues or the economy or race issues was presaged by how much news coverage those issues had received. News coverage in these studies is typically measured by content analysis of newspapers, magazines, and television news. Individual topics are rated according to how much coverage they get in terms of space in print media or time in broadcast news. Account is also taken of the prominence of coverage

TABLE 10.1   Correlations of Voter Emphasis on Issues with Media Coverage

	Major Items	*Minor Items*
Newsweek	.30	.53
Time	.30	.78
New York Times	.96	.97
Raleigh Times	.80	.73
Raleigh News and Observer	.91	.93
Durham Sun	.82	.96
Durham Morning Herald	.94	.93
NBC News	.89	.91
CBS News	.63	.81

SOURCE: Based on Maxwell E. McCombs and Donald Shaw, "The Agenda-Setting Function of the Mass Media," *Public Opinion Quarterly* 36 (1972), table 4, p. 183.

given a topic, for example, by how much front-page coverage it received in a newspaper or how close to the beginning of a newscast it was in the case of television.

Some of the research has carefully traced the time order of this relationship, a critical point in demonstrating that the news helps form audience agendas, rather than the other way around. For the most part, issues appear to be first emphasized in the news agenda, which then leads to their being ranked more highly by the public, rather than vice versa. Laboratory experiments involving television newscasts across a number of topics have borne this out.[16] Governmental policymakers may also be influenced by news agendas, independently of their influence on citizens.[17] Recalling the discussion of third-person effects in Chapter Six, we can speculate on whether public officials and policymakers may be prompted to act in anticipation of the impact they think news will have on the public. The implications of this become problematic if policymakers think the news media have a greater effect on the public than is actually the case and make decisions based on that assumption.[18]

If news media influence which issues people think about, how does the news provide cues to prompt or focus that thinking about any one issue? Some clues to this can be found in Iyengar and Kinder's use of the concept of priming touched on earlier in this text.[19] When faced with an often bewildering array of complex information about an issue, citizens need to choose which facets of it they will consider as most relevant. The news helps them do that, Iyengar and Kinder hypothesize, by priming, or drawing greater attention to some aspects of an issue at the expense of others.

This psychological phenomenon may become most relevant when linked to a soon-to-happen decision or behavior. I may be primed to choose one movie over another at the video shop by happening to see a display ad emphasizing that a favorite actor is in it. If I am driving to the polls to vote in a major election, I may be swayed by hearing an effective radio spot linking a political candidate to a cause I believe in, especially if it is in a lesser contest involving candidates I know little about. An important point about priming phenomena is that they are usually short-lived, almost inevitably replaced by the next attracting stimulus that grabs our attention (see Box 10.1).

BOX 10.1   PRIMING TIME FOR TELEVISION?

Shanto Iyengar and Donald Kinder ran a series of experiments examining what role "priming" played in the way people make judgments about the performance of the president. Different groups of subjects were shown different television newscasts, each emphasizing a particular national issue. One newscast dealt primarily with national defense, another with inflation, another with energy, and so forth. The subjects were then asked to rate the president on several attributes, including his performance in each of the issue areas that had been experimentally manipulated.

The subjects put more weight on the particular issue to which they had been exposed when they made their judgments of the president: Those who had seen the national defense newscasts rated the president based more on how good a job they thought he was doing on national defense; those who had seen the inflation news judged him more on the inflation issue, and so on. Also bearing out the priming hypothesis was the finding that the various newscasts had no influence on how the subjects rated the president's overall character, a judgment presumably based on a much wider array of personal and performance traits less touched by one issue or another.

SOURCE: Shanto Iyengar and Donald R. Kinder, *News That Matters: Television and American Opinion* (Chicago: University of Chicago Press, 1987), Table 4.2, p. 38.

However, in some contexts, including political ones, they may prove somewhat longer term. Jon Krosnick found, for example, that former

President George H. W. Bush was more likely to be assessed on the basis of his handling of the Persian Gulf War in 1991 following the massive press coverage of it than on his handling of the rather unchanged domestic economy and other foreign affairs issues.[20] These latter issues had been paramount in citizen judgments of Bush prior to the war. One might argue they returned to greater importance as the 1992 election neared, contributing to Bush's defeat. President George W. Bush was facing the same duality of public assessment regarding the war in Iraq and the economy in mid–2004.

This power of the press to shape the public agenda has its limits. It is not quite clear how much the news media may determine citizens' agendas without their knowledge or consent, versus how much citizens purposely use the media to help them prioritize the complex aggregations of issues they confront on a daily basis. In many cases, individuals are clearly quite aware that they rely on media for a sense of what is important in the world, and in fact, they may occasionally rebel if they think they are not getting what they need. Poll questions asking whether respondents think the media are giving "too much attention" to some events—the 1995 O. J. Simpson murder trial is a case in point—often draw substantial numbers of affirmative replies. Moreover, there is evidence that more vivid, dramatic, and emotionally driven news coverage does little to enhance the agenda-setting effect on citizens.[21]

Maxwell McCombs and Tamara Bell reported that citizens with a higher need for political orientation—those who are politically interested but less knowledgeable—had agendas more closely matching those of news media, presumably because they were more actively seeking such input.[22] Despite a wide range of studies exploring other aspects of agenda setting, firm conclusions as to the conditions under which it is likely to be greater or weaker are few. Some research indicates that interpersonal discussion of issues diminishes agenda setting,[23] but other findings conclude that the more involved citizens are with particular issues, the greater the media agenda setting.[24] Individuals may be more disposed to such media influence when it reinforces their own interests or experience.

The Media and an Informed Public

How people become informed as citizens and how well informed they become are two critical aspects of public opinion dynamics. The level of information and knowledge underlying public thought, discussion, and debate obviously constrains the quality of the process, drawing from Lasswell's surveillance function of communication in society. These are also consequences of communication that until quite recently have been uncritically "assumed to happen" rather than having been studied as an active process. It is ironic that the most obvious effect of interpersonal and mass-mediated communication—the gain of information or knowledge—has been examined less than the more debatable communication effects of attitude and behavioral change.

We know in the most rudimentary way that citizens gain information about public issues from one other and from institutions such as schools, governmental and political organizations, and mass media. From studies of election campaigns in recent times, we assume that these campaigns are an important educational tool for voters in the sense that they learn not only about candidates and their positions but also about issues of the day. We also assume that major news events very quickly inform the public about issues of consequence, whether involving war, natural disasters, violent protest, assassinations, major medical discoveries, or economic booms or busts. We can also assume that in cases involving political persuasion or change, at least something in the form of information is conveyed. But we still have little understanding of how information gets transferred, from what sources, through which channels, and to which audiences or publics.

Media As Information Sources

Certain myths about how people gather information in today's multimedia environment have been called into serious question, however. One is that television is the main and most effective purveyor of political and other kinds of information. Several studies summarized by John Robinson and Mark Levy argue to the contrary.[25] For one thing, research indicates that television news viewers did not gain any more information about current events than users of other media; in fact, in some cases television news viewers were less well-informed. In terms of understanding or comprehension of news, television viewers ranked a poor third behind newspaper and magazine readers. Moreover, the extent to which people discussed the news more often with others was as good a predictor of news comprehension than use of any mass media source.

FIGURE 10.2   Princess Diana's life and death were avidly followed by the media. (Photo courtesy of Associated Press/Elvis Barukcic)

In the end, most people use a variety of news sources for different purposes, and it makes little sense to regard any one medium as the most predominant. There has been some concern, however, that among the minority who use only one source, television news is most likely to be the one chosen. That, coupled with significant declines in newspaper readership—especially among the young—could signal the emergence of a less news-conscious public.[26] Nonetheless, recent years have also seen increases in at least the quantity of television news content and the growth of Internet news sources and other electronic channels. However, a 1994 follow-up analysis by Robinson and Levy of people's news sources and what they knew about current events showed little change from their study of the previous decade: Television news produced the least learning.[27] Debate continues over the quality of news, especially the increasing trend in the 1990s toward sensationalizing news, including a renewed focus on personal incidents in the lives of public figures (see Figure 10.2).

The twin questions "How much do people know about current events?" and "How much should they know?" have forever plagued observers of public opinion. We simply do not have a very good handle on either question. With respect to the first question, opinion polls and surveys by and large have not provided a useful overview of either the quantity or quality of civic knowledge that citizens hold, likely in part because scholars and even most critics are reluctant to overly proscribe answers to the second question. There is probably agreement in these times that we do not need more knowledge of the deepest personal revelations of public figures or of campaign-constructed pseudo-events or outright falsehoods; accurate, reflective knowledge of germane elements of political issues and values of the day would be welcome. Nevertheless, how far do we go in arguing against knowing the character attributes of our leaders and in favoring perhaps minute dollars-and-sense detail of health care cost coverage?

Indications of possible decline in public familiarity with traditional political knowledge or civic facts by Delli Carpini and Keeter are noted in Chapters One and Eight.[28] One caution here is that knowledge of civic facts should not be considered the only or even the optimal indicator of being politically informed. For instance, the complexity or depth of knowledge and the ability to use it in discussion and decisionmaking are also factors to consider; unfortunately, these are also more difficult to assess across the population.[29]

Media and Knowledge Gaps

We have confirmed, however, that the learning of politically relevant information occurs unequally across society: Some people have greater access to information; but even among those with quite equal access, learning may differ substantially. The pioneering campaign studies of the 1940s and 1950s established that voters selectively attended to political information, with the more interested citizens being more exposed to it and presumably becoming more informed as a result. Logically, politically attentive, active, and involved people were more motivated to get more information, and did so. Studies since then have found that characteristics of the social system—especially social class and education levels in particular—may affect the rate at which citizens acquire information. This has led to the development of the knowledge gap hypothesis: As the rate of information flow into a social system increases, groups with higher socioeconomic status acquire the information at a faster rate than lower-status groups, widening the knowledge gap between them.[30]

Several studies have supported this tendency across a wide range of content areas, including politically relevant ones. The mechanics of the process are not yet quite clear, but a key factor is that the status variable of education is a major player. People with more education appear to acquire information at an accelerated rate for a number of reasons—because they have greater access to it, greater skill in processing it, more motivation to seek it out, or greater use for it, or some combination of those factors.[31]

This hypothesis has subtle but significant consequences for the flow and distribution of knowledge across society and, in turn, for public opinion processes. We have often previously assumed that increasing the flow of information in a democracy would help promote more equal levels of awareness and knowledge across the system, reducing differences between "information rich" and "information poor" segments of society. Mass media have been an integral part of this thinking, leading to childhood television programs such as *Sesame Street* and massive public education efforts aimed at voter participation, public safety, disease prevention, and the like. Presumably, such public efforts could help reduce information disparities brought on by circumstances of social class and lack of education. However, the knowledge-gap hypothesis predicts the exact opposite—that the more information that gets put "out there," the information rich get richer and the poor get poorer.

Media and Public Knowledge and Public Opinion

Recent research also shows that the more someone already knows about political affairs, the more likely that person is to learn about current news events.[32] The best predictor of people's having learned about a range of topics in the news—from abortion debates to primary elections to celebrity trials—was how much they already knew about politics, despite the specific ways in which they used news media. The conclusion here is that there is a "general news audience," consisting of citizens who are more politically astute, who use news media more, and who gain more information from that use.

BOX 10.2   CAN TELEVISION NEWS SWAY OPINIONS?

Benjamin Page, Robert Shapiro, and Glenn Dempsey traced changes in opinion poll answers to numerous public policy issues between 1969 and 1983. They particularly looked for changes in answers to the same question asked in polls a few months apart in order to find out whether the public support for specific policy options had shifted over a fairly short time. They then analyzed television news coverage of these issues over the same short time periods and noted the extent to which statements presented on the news about those issues had been supportive.

It is also important that they noted the *source* of each statement, that is, whether it was made by a news reporter or commentator, by the president or administration members, other officeholders, policy experts, interest groups, and so forth. They then statistically traced how well such statements about issues predicted changes in public opinion on the same issues. All in all, the televised news statements strongly predicted changes in public response to specific poll items. The more "pro" statements made on television about a policy option, the more likely public response was to swing to a more "pro" stance on that option. But it made a difference *who* made the statement. If the statement had been made by a television commentator or by an "expert" on the particular topic, the public swing was more pronounced than if the viewpoint had been voiced by a politician or interest group member. It is likely that commentators or experts are viewed as less biased and therefore more credible sources. There is also a possibility that television commentators could be reflecting consensus opinions being formulated by elite groups—including other journalists—compounding their impact on the public, but this is a more speculative conclusion.

SOURCE: Benjamin I. Page, Robert Y. Shapiro, and Glenn R. Dempsey, "What Moves Public Opinion?" *American Political Science Review* 81 (1987):23–43.

Equally important here is how mass media may frame facts or issues for public presentation and the impact that may have on audiences. Another series of experiments by Iyengar demonstrates the potential for framing effects.[33] Television news has often been criticized for too much emphasis on stories that are "episodic," or event-based, without providing adequate context or explanation—the garden variety "murder-and-mayhem" syndrome of much local news coverage being one example. However, more thematic stories that develop issues and show more complex relationships across events or policies may be more broadly informative, but news producers—and viewers as well—may shun them as deadly dull talking-heads video. Do these two different ways affect how audiences respond to and interpret them? Iyengar's studies suggest they do.

He showed audiences newscasts depicting six issues—crime, international terrorism, poverty, unemployment, racial inequality, and the 1980s Iran–Contra scandal. Different audience groups received different treatments of each—some saw episodic versions about particular issues, others viewed thematic ones. Audience members were then asked in various ways where responsibility for the problems depicted in the stories should lie. In other words, individuals were asked to form political judgments about the causes of these problems, just after having seen the stories. In most but not all cases, audiences who saw the episodic versions of the stories tended to attribute responsibility more to the individuals involved in them, whereas groups seeing the thematic stories placed more responsibility on societal or policy-related causes (see Figure 10.3).

This was particularly true for stories dealing with poverty. When the issue was framed by stories depicting the plight of poor people—examples of coping by the homeless, for example—audiences were more likely to hold the poor responsible for their situations. But when the stories centered on the economics of the rise of poverty and cuts in Federal programs, audiences were more apt to blame societal conditions. When the news subject was unemployment, however, the type of frame did not matter: Audiences laid the cause to economic conditions whether the frame was episodic or thematic. Mixed results were found across the other subject areas, depending to some extent on specific story content; nonetheless, episodic frames were tied more often than not to attribution of responsibility to individuals.

Iyengar argues that implications from this include—in the case of poverty, for example—more willingness by television news viewers to fault individual shortcomings than societal conditions or policies for problems. Like Zaller, Iyengar relates this to accessibility bias in the way in which we recall information from memory, arguing that the more often such stories

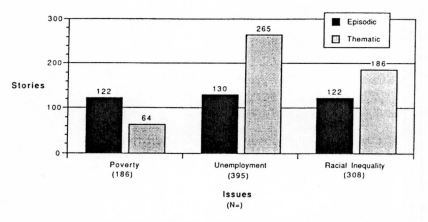

FIGURE 10.3   Episodic and Thematic Coverage of Poverty, Unemployment, and Racial Inequality, 1981–1986. SOURCE: S. Iyengar, *Is Anyone Responsible? How Television Frames Political Issues* (Chicago: University of Chicago Press, 1991), Figure 5.1, p. 47.

are viewed on television, the more likely information and conclusions drawn from that information will be more accessible in our memory systems and more easily recalled when prompted. Although the body of evidence for such media effects on our cognitions is interesting and useful, we need to keep in mind the focus on television news here, remembering that it is but one unit in the mix of information sources people use.

Newspapers and magazines, for example, likely deal far more with thematic frames and may well counter television effects, providing a better-balanced information diet to the public. Somewhat overlooked in this controversy is the simple fact that audiences carry out their own framing exercises as they observe and communicate, putting information into the perspective of their own cognitive experience.[34]

Media Effects on Change in Public Opinions, Attitudes, and Behaviors

Studies of what people learn from media and how they process such information are surprisingly recent, having come about only since the 1970s or so. Earlier research on media effects focused on the somewhat more propagandistically driven questions about whether media were directly impacting changes in our opinions, attitudes, and behaviors. From the early 1900s through the 1940s, many thought the media to be quite powerful in directly affecting citizen views and behaviors. An analogy was drawn between the media and a hypodermic needle, with the media "injecting" members of an increasingly atomized mass public with whatever thoughts and opinions the media manipulators wanted inscribed. Fanciful, yes, but the hypodermic model made the point that media did have previously unheard of direct access to individuals—in their homes, providing information unfiltered and uncensored by other human interaction or dialogue. Likely adding to the speculative fear was the seeming ease with which the Nazi political party gained leadership in Germany during the 1930s, with extensive and sophisticated use of radio, film, and print media.

Anecdotal evidence of powerful media effects in the United States was fanned by events such as Orson Welles' 1938 radio broadcast of "The War of the Worlds," a fictional invasion from Mars that reportedly scared countless listeners (see Box 10.3). U.S. involvement in World War II led to heavy investment in wartime propaganda, some of which was thought to succeed in the highly stressed and focused wartime culture.

BOX 10.3   MARS INVADES

On October 30, 1938, the night before Halloween, the CBS radio network program *Mercury Theater of the Air* broadcast a "virtual journalism" version of H. G. Wells' classic science-fiction novel *The War of the Worlds.* The novel details an invasion of England by Martians, including the mass destruction of major cities and their inhabitants, with national military forces defenseless in the onslaught. (The novel generated the 1996 movie thriller *Independence Day* and a host of lesser films, television series, and stories.)

To many of the estimated 6 to 12 million listeners of the 1938 radio version, however, the story rang too true and produced episodes of mass panic in several parts of the country. The program, produced by Orson Welles, took the approach of beginning the show as a typical live orchestra program, popular in those days. Then, a news bulletin interrupted with the announcement of a "flaming object" falling to the earth in the New Jersey countryside, followed later by more detailed announcements of Martian creatures emerging from the object and others in other locales wreaking havoc and death. The production of the show was excellent, with top-flight scripting, actors, and special effects.

Thousands of listeners across the country were drawn into the fantasy enough to swamp police and radio station switchboards, call relatives and friends to spread the panic, and flee their homes in areas close to those identified on the program as being under attack. As reality sank in over the next several hours, the network came under sharp attack, issued strong apologies, and the Federal Communications Commission put out guidelines against such mixing of news and fiction. Press stories over the next several days described hundreds of accounts of sheer terror on the part of listeners.

A pioneering group of broadcast researchers at Princeton University quickly undertook a more formal study of the panic, interviewing people who had been affected and trying to pin down the scope of the event, in an attempt to understand why some people had reacted but others had not.[1] They estimated that perhaps 10 to 20 percent of the listeners had been genuinely frightened by the broadcast, with smaller, undetermined numbers acting out their fear by calling others, trying to escape their communities, or generally becoming panicked. Many of these people had not heard the introduction to the broadcast that set the stage for the imaginary news coverage and either did not hear or ignored later statements indicating that it was a fictionalized account. To some extent, the lesser educated, the more insecure, and those with stronger religious beliefs were more inclined to panic.

In retrospect, we can also emphasize the tenor of the times and the reliance on radio during that era.[2] The United States was just emerging from a turbulent economic depression, and fear of war was building as Germany threatened more of Europe. People had learned to turn to the relatively new medium of radio as a source of credible, updated news, with live reports of major national and global events. Many audience members who may not have been listening that closely or critically at first may have been primed by other events of the times or by their own circumstances to react with fear and panic.

NOTES

1. Hadley Cantril, *The Invasion from Mars: A Study in the Psychology of Panic* (Princeton: Princeton University Press, 1940).

2. Sharon A. Lowery and Melvin L. DeFleur, *Milestones in Mass Communication Research* (New York: Longman, 1988).

However, when scholars later reexamined these and other supposedly strong media effects, the evidence became much less clear, and other important mitigating factors became apparent.[35] This was also the era in which survey research entered the picture, as did other more sophisticated social science tools, including content analysis, focus groups, and field experiments (see Chapter Three). These techniques allowed a more valid and accurate depiction of potential communication influences and of public opinion per se. Despite several notable efforts, scholars of that era came up short of finding a significant effect for mass communication on public views and actions.

A Revised View: Media's Limited Power

Two of these studies, led by Paul Lazarsfeld and his colleagues at Columbia University during the 1940s, pioneered the use of scientific surveys to improve understanding of electoral behavior and have already been noted in Chapter Eight.[36] Recall that Lazarsfeld was expecting something of a rational, information-based model for voting decisions, in which people would weigh information they received from the candidates and news media, then make their final electoral decisions as the November election day neared. He proposed that mass media would serve such important functions as converting undecided and wavering voters to particular candidates, reinforcing voters who had already firmly decided, and activating people to get out and vote.

Instead, Lazarsfeld discovered that the vast majority of voters knew for whom they would vote all along and that political party affiliation far overwhelmed direct media effects in choosing candidates. Although most voters followed the campaigns in newspapers and magazines and over radio, they attended more to content that supported their own chosen candidates. The small minority of undecided voters appeared to be among the least knowledgeable citizens and the least attentive to the campaign as well.

In cases where individuals did make up their minds to vote for a candidate during the campaign or decided to switch support from one candidate to another, interpersonal influence seemed to hold more sway. The opinions of a spouse or respected, knowledgeable neighbor appeared more likely to carry weight than campaign news coverage, candidate speeches, or editorials. Primary reference groups, consisting of family and close friends, and secondary ones (e.g., party, union, church) appeared to far outreach media in terms of influence. This gave rise to the popular two-step flow hypothesis of social influence mentioned in Chapter Eight, with more politically aware and active opinion leaders passing information and perhaps influence from the media to other citizens. This hypothesis struck yet another blow against the presumed power of the media to sway political opinions or behaviors.

The Era of Minimal Media Effects

All in all, these studies supported what came to be known as a model of "indirect" or "minimal effects" of the media on public opinion and behaviors. This view also gained support from several other studies of that time—particularly ones on public information programs aimed at promoting social change on a variety of topics. According to sociologist Joseph Klapper, media influence was slight because when people encounter media messages, they are already armed with strong predispositions—personal beliefs, attitudes, and behaviors—that cause them to selectively expose themselves primarily to messages they already agree with.[37] Selective perception and retention of messages may also be factors: People were viewed as capable both of easily distorting what they see and hear to match their own biases and of remembering what they find agreeable and forgetting that which they do not.

Thus, the media in effect end up mainly reinforcing the existing views of audience members. Voters more exposed to campaign media were less likely to change their minds. Interpersonal interaction was seen as a much stronger—and difficult to counteract—form of influence, more likely to stimulate change. To the extent that the two-step flow proposition was valid, any media effects would have to be indirect, being filtered through opinion leaders to the more general populace.

This view of media effects has a fair amount of commonsense appeal; it was also probably reassuring to hear that media could not easily propagandize citizens into unwanted or bizarre positions or behaviors. Perhaps that is one reason that the view was so readily accepted and indeed persisted as the dominant model of media influence until well into the 1960s—despite some, though not a great deal, of empirical evidence.

More recent and critical evaluations of the two-step flow, selective exposure, and other lynchpins of the model have found they do not quite hold up—at least not across enough contexts and time frames to be regarded as healthy scientific generalizations that can be relied on from situation to situation. We will consider some specific reasons for this later in the chapter. For now, it is important to consider these factors: (1) Lazarsfeld's and related studies dispelled the myth of the omnipotence of mass media as a force affecting public opinion—simple audience exposure to a message did not necessarily mean it would have an effect; (2) media were not having much persuasive influence on political—and perhaps social—behavior in elections of the 1940s and may be unlikely to in situations paralleling those of that period; (3) we cannot look at mass media as isolated from other social forces, especially interpersonal conversation and discussion; and (4) in all of the foregoing cases, we are dealing with a media system offering competing messages within the political framework—no one party had significant control over what was presented.

Research on the impact of mass media—and of personal communication, for that matter—on public opinion entered the doldrums throughout the 1950s and 1960s in the United States. This was of course ironic, since on the campaign trail the new and arguably most exciting political medium to date—television—was being quickly adopted, adapted, and often co-opted by candidates of all shapes and persuasions. Television had grown into preeminence as a political news medium, with extended coverage of nominating conventions, candidate debates, the assassination of President Kennedy, and the "living-room war," Vietnam.

RECONSIDERATIONS OF MEDIA EFFECTS: TELEVISION AND SOCIAL CHANGE

The growth of television paralleled an array of changes in U.S. society that had potentially significant consequences for public opinion processes. Social unrest and protests in the 1960s accompanied the rise of the post–World War II baby boom generational bulge, pushing a proportionally greater number of teens and young adults into the populace than had been witnessed in decades. They were also more educated and more affluent than their predecessors, with a less-constrained, more mobile lifestyle.

People in general moved around more, usually toward urban and suburban centers, reducing the pull of traditional family, neighborhood, and community affiliations. Attitudes and behaviors regarding politics became more fluid, witnessed most readily in increasing numbers of undecided voters in election campaigns, in greater fluctuation of voter turnout, and most notably in a significant rise in independent, non-party-affiliated voters and "ticket-splitting" voting for candidates of different parties on the same ballot. By the early 1970s, such volatility made it quite hard to safely predict voting behavior from party affiliation alone or to predict opinions and attitudes across a range of issues. (Ironically, the public perhaps more closely resembled what Lazarsfeld and his colleagues had expected in the 1940s.) Political communication researchers finally began catching up with these trends in the 1970s, and several new perspectives on the relationship between mass media and public opinion emerged.

Videomalaise

Two novel and intriguing approaches to mass media effects were developed at the time that seemed to put much of the blame for more negative communication influences back into the hands of the media—and especially television. In an effort to link the increased political disaffection and distrust that arose in the 1960s and 1970s directly to television news, political scientist Michael Robinson coined the concept of videomalaise. Robinson argued that the roots of videomalaise were in the then heavily watched evening television network news reports of ABC, CBS, and NBC.[38] These programs, he contended, contained reports that were often too interpretive and that placed too much emphasis on negative events and explanations. Robinson analyzed the overall themes of these programs as anti-institutional, claiming that they placed too much emphasis on violence and conflict. (Such content analysis and interpretation of news programming is not in of itself novel and has likely been around in various forms since the first attempt by a correspondent to record an observation in a way that someone else objected to.)

Robinson's content analysis was quite rigorous, and a case may be made that the television networks and other news media have placed greater emphasis on overt interpretation of events over the past two or three decades than they did previously. However, the extent to which news and interpretation of events may be more "negative" than the "reality" being depicted in a "real" fashion is a far more subjective call, often open to much legitimate argument. Recall that much of the news being reported at this time was on the Vietnam War and opposition to it, such government scandals as then Vice President Spiro Agnew's resignation under influence-peddling accusations, and, ultimately, President Nixon's resignation over the Watergate affair. These were indeed hard times for government credibility.

In any case, perhaps the more intriguing aspect of Robinson's thesis is his linking the impact of the "negative" television network news to a somewhat passive and overly trusting news audience. Network television news had a largely "inadvertent" audience, according to Robinson, many of whom watched out of habit. Moreover, the nature of television news led audience members from one story to another, despite their level of interest in particular story topics. Viewers less interested in politics thus received a steady diet of disturbing, negative information about political issues they were not familiar enough with to counterassess, leading to doubt and malaise about the system. Furthermore, the high credibility of the evening news anchors was seen as enhancing this effect. Newspapers were judged as less culpable. Regardless of the biases newspaper stories may have displayed, readers of political news more actively chose to read them. In doing so, they were probably more critical of them, not to mention that the more politically interested and astute were more likely to be active readers in the first place.

Robinson offered some intriguing support for this hypothesis from surveys and an experiment, but subsequent studies have largely not supported it. Generally, people who are exposed to more television news, to newspapers, or to other media for political information have been found to be more confident in political figures and institutions.[39] Nonetheless, Robinson's proposition had enough intuitive appeal to make one wonder if it might apply with the right audience, under the right circumstances, in some present or future setting (see Figure 10.4).

Cultivating the Public

A second and more holistic approach to television's impact on public opinion is known as the cultivation perspective, and it proposes far-

FIGURE 10.4
TV: The Electronic Hearth?
Do the negative images of the
world portrayed in television
news produce videomalaise?
Cultivation effects? The
evidence is mixed. SOURCE: ©
Tom Tomorrow. *Greetings from
This Modern World* (New York:
St. Martin's Press, 1992).

reaching influences of the medium on virtually all aspects of audience perceptions and attitudes. Developed by George Gerbner and his colleagues at the University of Pennsylvania, the proposition asserts that television has become the "common storyteller of our age," providing our diversified society with consistent and repeated messages and images.[40] This integrated content reaches across all levels of our society, cultivating shared views and conceptions of reality among otherwise diverse social groups.

Extensive analyses of television content since 1967 support the notion that television programming across the board does depict somewhat consistent portrayals of American life and values, despite differences in kinds of programs, specialized topic cable networks, and the like. Also supported is the idea that television content often does not square with what is actually going on in the "real world" of U.S. social and political life. One example is that both entertainment and news-information programming provide a relatively high dose of crime and violence, much beyond that which proportionately occurs in actual American life on a day-to-day basis. (This should not be all that surprising: One function of news is to alert the citizenry to out-of-the-ordinary events, particularly threatening ones like homicide and robbery; we do not typically define "news" as the mundane. Similarly, entertainment in the form of escapist—sometimes violent—drama is as old as theater, with little intent of showing the world as it actually is. However, the extent to which crime and violence dominate public airwaves—to the exclusion of other material—is a highly legitimate concern.)

As with Robinson's videomalaise hypothesis, the evidence on cultivation becomes less firm when attempting to show that this "unreal" array of television content has significant impact on audiences watching it. Unlike Robinson, who predicted that television news portrayals of politics would influence attitudes toward public figures and processes to become more negative, Gerbner predicts a more subtle effect: Heavier exposure to television content overall will cultivate perceptions or beliefs about social reality that are more consistent with the "television view" than with the "real-world" view. With crime, for example, individuals who watch more television would be more inclined to regard crime as more frequent and serious than it is. Some early evidence suggested that this was indeed the case and that heavier viewers of television were more fearful of crime as well. However, subsequent surveys of public opinion about crime have included more exact measures of how people view crime and have controlled for possibly confounding influences of age, gender, social class, and related demographics. These show little evidence that the overall amount of television viewing has any effect on crime perceptions or attitudes, although crime news viewing per se may have some influence.[41]

A refinement of the initial cultivation perspective posits that exceptionally heavy viewing of television—several hours per day—may override other social and cultural differences between people. That is, people who share watching great amounts of television may have more closely shared worldviews than their demographic and other social differences would suggest. This phenomenon is called mainstreaming, and Gerbner and associates have found that people who watch more television, regardless of their demographic makeup, see themselves as somewhat more moderate in their political and social beliefs. Gerbner attributes this to television's attempt to program for the middle ground, balancing countering perspectives and avoiding controversy. The cultivation approach has not been widely applied to other aspects of public opinion, and social scientists continue to debate its rationale and analytic methods.[42] The approach is useful, however, for reminding us of the potential force of television as the currently dominant mass medium in our society and of the possibilities for entertainment and other kinds of programming to influence public opinion.

MOVING TOWARD THE ACTIVE AUDIENCE

Both the videomalaise and cultivation perspectives regard audiences in a more passive light, more subject to being acted upon than acting. Emphasis has turned to the more active aspects of individuals' use of mass media in recent years. This has included a revised look at what people do with media, as opposed to what media do to people, as communications researchers Wilbur Schramm, Jack Lyle, and Edwin Parker posed the question.[43] The research findings of the 1940s and 1950s had suggested—although with little evidence—that any power of the media to persuade was effectively counterbalanced by the power of individual audience members to use media toward their own ends, for their own purposes. Individuals may be viewed as using media to perform certain psychological functions for them, including providing support for their already existing beliefs, attitudes, and behaviors. Many studies over the past three decades have put this proposition more to the test.

This view proposes that audiences are far more proactive in their dealings with media, deliberately using them to seek out such rewards or gratifications. These include reinforcement of opinions, learning new information of value, surveillance of the environment, entertainment, excitement or stimulation, companionship, diversion, passing time, and others. The approach became known as the uses–gratifications model of communication effects: People purposively use certain media contents to gratify specific needs. Individuals try to choose media content that they expect will do the best job of meeting those needs, based on previous experiences.[44] You may read editorials in the *New York Times*—or in the *Wall Street Journal*—when you get the chance because you know the views of that newspaper agree with your own on most subjects and reading them will give you the satisfaction of knowing a prestigious source is on your side. You will also likely get more facts and substantiation to buttress your case. Or you may always turn on a certain radio station in the morning because you know it will play music you like to hear then and the station gives you a little—but not too much—surveillance on what is going on in the world through its brief news and weather segments.

Obviously, however, the media chosen do not always provide the rewards people expect them to; moreover, media use may have unintended effects or consequences for the public. You may select MTV or go to a rock music Web site expecting some stimulating entertainment, which you have desperate need of after a rough day. But instead, you may catch a short documentary on involvement of musicians in a particular political cause, which may make you aware of that cause for the first time or more sympathetic to it. (Or you may so much resent not getting the entertainment you were hoping for that you will at least temporarily reject that cause.) In a more subtle way, media content can help shape our thinking even when we do get from a message much of what we had intended. It is seldom that we obtain the exact gratification or reward we seek without also getting at least a little extra baggage—the particular spin put on a point of view by a newscaster, extraneous information that alters the context of what we expected or wanted, or the putting of information into a larger context that expands our horizons.

The Audience–Media Transaction

Most theories of media influence are now generated from a view of audiences being largely active players in choosing what they hear, watch, or read, and responding accordingly. However, we cannot reject the notion that at times people are quite passive or reactive in attending to media—or in everyday conversations, for that matter, simply letting words or images wash over them, leaving themselves more open to influence or manipulation.[45] This juxtaposition of more active versus more passive possibilities for audience involvement with media has led many researchers to look at media effects on public opinion as a more interactive or transactional process. The nature of the relationship between audiences and media likely changes and shifts across different personal traits, moods, contexts, and situations.[46] Often, as audience members, we may clearly have a stronger hand in deciding what we want and get from a given communication; in other instances, we may come across unexpected messages that may motivate and move us in unexpected—and sometimes unexplained—ways. In still other situations, we may be seeking nothing in particular and get nothing in particular, so not much of consequence happens. Taking a broader political communication context, Robert Huckfeldt and John Sprague have noted the great interdependency between political information seekers and potential suppliers of it:

> The citizen is an information processor, but information is environmentally supplied, and individual choices are embedded within informational settings that systematically vary in time and space. Neither individual choice nor the environment is determinate in creating these informational settings, and hence the acquisition of political information is the end result of a complex interplay between individual choice and environmental supply.[47]

Media Dependency

How much we rely on media for such gratifications and the degree of media influence also depends on other options open to us—for information, social support, diversion, and so forth. Some people are perhaps more media dependent than others because of ease of access to such channels, or temperament, or the availability of functional alternatives for information, entertainment, and other rewards.[48] In the larger societal sense, we need to consider how necessary mass communication is to the culture and societal structure we live in. How much individuals depend on media may vary with what is taking place socially and politically in the society at any given time. Sociologists Sandra Ball-Rokeach and Melvin DeFleur have argued that in times of greater conflict and change, media dependency is apt to rise: Media may provide a mechanism for helping cope if such change challenges other more traditional social means for coping with threats to established norms and behaviors.[49]

During the late 1960s, for example, many citizens may have turned more to newspapers and especially television to try to make more sense out of a seeming explosion of social protest and turmoil. The news media were able to not only keep audiences up to date on the latest expressions of discontent but to put something of a perspective on those developments and on the reactions of other citizens to them. (There have been anecdotal suggestions that in times of crisis, it may be somehow reassuring to see those events depicted in the more familiar, institutional framework of one's regular daily newspaper or reported by a familiar voice backed by the ABC or CNN logo.) A related argument is that more immediate kinds of politically relevant information may be more salient to citizens in times of conflict, and they in turn depend on media sources more. If people sense a need to act quickly based on the facts at hand, traditional ideological considerations may be less relevant.[50] At the time of the buildup for the 1991 war in the Persian Gulf, for example, many if not most citizens appeared to be putting more weight on the immediate consequences of Iraq's takeover of Kuwait, particularly in terms of the threat to the oil supply, and on risks to American military forces, than to the ideology of party positions or patriotism.

THE INTERPERSONAL FACTOR

Oddly, most of the recent studies of communication influences on public opinion have left out the role of interpersonal conversation and discussion, the most common grounding for opinion development and change. The everyday transmission of opinions among citizens has rarely been studied, perhaps because of its ubiquity. The popular two-step flow model of the minimal media effects era still provides the jumping-off point for consideration of how personal influence works its likely considerable effects in our social system. However, that model preassumed strong, stable primary group relationships, with influentials in specific areas of expertise using established media more than other people and passing along to "followers" interpretations of media messages. Whatever the appropriateness of that model for earlier times, it is more difficult to apply it to our era of less social and political stability, with its far more diversified and widespread mass media system.

John Robinson made several inroads in redefining the model by suggesting that more attention be given to interaction among media, opinion leaders, and other citizens, noting that influence is seldom a one-way street.[51] If one person interacts with another, influence is likely to be at least somewhat shared rather than being unidirectional. The "flow" is likely to be at least somewhat "upward" as well as downward. Another issue is whether opinion leaders actually use media more than other citizens. Gabriel Weimann, in an extensive study of influential individuals in the United States, Germany, and Israel, found that although the frequency of their media use was no greater than anyone else's, they tended to use higher quality media, specifically print sources in the form of books and magazines on specialized topics.[52] Weimann also found influential people to have political news agendas that were more closely tied to those of news media, indicating that their more qualitative media use had more of an agenda-setting effect on them.

Another view of the relative interplay and impact between mass media and interpersonal discussion in election campaigns comes from Jeffrey Mondak.[53] Taking advantage of the unique opportunity of a Pittsburgh newspaper strike during nearly the entire 1992 postprimary election campaigns, Mondak studied how the loss of newspaper coverage of local races affected citizen discussion and vote decisions. Generally, he found less interpersonal discussion of the upcoming elections (as compared to discussion rates in his "control" city of Cleveland, which had no such strike and similar political characteristics). He concluded in part that news coverage provided material for topic-specific discussions of elections and that without newspapers such discussions were attenuated. However, interpersonal discussions that did occur appeared to exert more influence on vote choices in the absence of newspapers. Mondak draws from these findings an interesting model of media–interpersonal dynamics: Media coverage and personal conversation are complementary in terms of citizen exposure to campaign information but conflict with one another in terms of influence. That is, news media are necessary to provide election-based topics for discussion, in that sense complementing discussion. But in the case of influencing political decisions, media use and discussion compete, with voters likely to choose one source or the other as a basis for deciding whom to vote for.

Few would argue, however, with the sense that public opinion inherently develops out of interconnected, interacting individuals. When people confront a decision or a challenge to their existing views, they seek information and advice from the most available—and the most trusted—sources. Mass media may serve some of these functions some of the time, but social contingencies and interactions are apt to provide a more meaningful context for influence.[54]

More speculatively, many academicians and social critics have decried what they view as a loss in sense of civic community, or "sense of place" in Joshua Meyrowitz's term, and the potential role of television in that.[55] Robert Putnam has named television as a prime culprit in what he sees as a decline in "social capital," or the social networks, discussions of values, and shared participation that move citizens more effectively toward shared objectives.[56] James Carey has traced the entwined historical roots of journalism and public opinion processes throughout U.S. history and persuasively argues that mass media have become more privatized and less of a public space for democratic discussion.[57] He optimistically suggests that the turn in the 1990s to increased political uses of smaller forums such as talk radio, citizen councils, and the Internet are a reaction against the journalism establishment, an effort to reassert emphasis on public discussion and participation in civic life.

CAMPAIGNING AND OPINION CHANGE

We have made the case that changing communication styles, formats, and technologies affect public opinion processes. Mass media in particular have significantly altered how we view, think about, and respond to our political world. Now we turn to one specific media-related process— the highly visible and pragmatic issue of communication campaigns. We will dwell later in this chapter on the most obvious type of public opinion–directed campaign: promoting candidates in elections for public office. But first we put these campaigns in the broader context of more common kinds of campaigns that influence everything from our purchasing habits to health practices to cultural myths. We will first examine the overall domain of campaigns aimed at creating or altering public opinion and then focus on the central role of campaigns in elections. In both cases, we will discuss the purposes and practice of contemporary campaigns and how well they seem to work. We will also examine an underlying tension between the effects campaigns may have on individual attitudes and behaviors and their less obvious but sometimes more consequential impact upon the society as a whole.

THE CAMPAIGN ENVIRONMENT

Communication campaigns try to "(1) generate specific outcomes or effects (2) in a relatively large number of individuals, (3) usually within a specified period of time and (4) through an organized set of communication activities."[58] This definition fits a multitude of persuasive situations we are all too familiar with as media consumers.

That television commercial for, say, a new model of sport-utility vehicle is likely to be just one component of a campaign-generated and orchestrated set of communication activities. These may range from commercials to magazine ads, promotional displays at automobile dealers, reviews of the vehicle in auto trade publications and newspapers, and perhaps even the use of the vehicle in a hot new action movie. These components are tied together to push a particular theme that isolates the vehicle from its competition and puts it in the most favorable light possible.

The specific ads and other messages used to promote the vehicle will vary depending on the medium used and the type of audience being targeted. A commercial slotted for MTV may emphasize virility, power, and economy, whereas an ad for *Outside* magazine may display the model's off-road capabilities in a setting of solitude. In any case, the campaign as a whole publicizes the vehicle to varieties of individuals who may be potential purchasers. The campaign tries to make them aware of the product in a positive way, motivating them to test-drive it, and ultimately to buy it. The time frame of the campaign can be quite important—in case of the sport vehicle the campaign might peak during the heavy spring and early summer auto-buying seasons and end as newer models become available in the fall.

Similarly, the seemingly unending tape spool of public service advertisements we see around the clock on television are simply the most visible sightings of other kinds of extensive campaigns at work. "Drink responsibly," anti-smoking appeals, heart health messages, McGruff the Crime Dog, and the latest AIDS-prevention commercials are products of long-term public policy initiatives to get people to change certain kinds of behaviors for their own good, for the public good, or for the benefit of the environment (see Figure 10.5). These efforts may pro-

FIGURE 10.5   McGruff the Crime Dog is the main symbol of an
information campaign that attempts to help citizens prevent crime.
SOURCE: Registered marks of the National Crime Prevention Council.

mote social change pertinent to health, public safety, or the common
societal welfare. Such change may range from making people more
aware of a problem and the possible solutions to it to either promoting
more positive attitudes about what individuals can do or motivating
them to take actions of their own. These social marketing programs attempt to use many of the precepts of commercial marketing efforts to
promote social change.[59]

The public service ads are, like automotive or any other consumer
spots, coordinated to match specific audience characteristics and desired
responses. One AIDS-prevention advertisement, for example, may target
gay men as an audience, whereas another—using a very different approach—may focus on heterosexual at-risk high-school students. The
campaigns underlying these ads may include press releases and other
publicity efforts aimed at news media, organized community, and neigh-
borhood-level preventive efforts and at lobbying for legislation to help

remedy the problem—as with antismoking and automobile safety programs, for example.

CAMPAIGN STRATEGIES AND TACTICS

In both the commercial product and social marketing campaign situations—and as we will shortly see, for political campaigns—the strategies and tactics used are markedly similar. Marketing research is heavily relied on at first to identify potential audiences and to determine their existing ideas and behaviors regarding the product or problem. Then, potential themes and messages are tested with smaller groups of people. The targeted audiences are segmented by their demographics, awareness, and interest in the topic and by their existing behaviors, and appropriate media are then chosen to reach particular audience groups.

Modern polling and statistical analysis techniques are critical here, allowing marketers to fine-tune the audience segments they are aiming for with considerable precision. Earlier polling-based conceptualizations of American lifestyles have found their way into most major communication and marketing campaigns. Computer-based typologies of individuals can be found not only for purchasing habits but for other behaviors such as health practices and potential for various diseases, automobile safety, environmental activities, and, of course, political action, including voting choices. Psychological dispositions toward behavior change, as well as media habits, are often tied into these profiles. Marketers use such catchy terms as "Yellowstone Yuppies" to profile perhaps fortyish upper-income urbanites with a yen for expensive sport-utility vehicles and outdoor gear, backpacking vacations, gourmet foods, and socially liberal but economically conservative political leanings. Postal zip codes are often used to identify pockets of one such marketing profile or another, allowing links to U.S. census data, direct mail lists, and shopping locations.

Such data are used to focus on chosen market segments to be reached by television and radio, newspapers and magazines, billboards and posters, and direct mail. More interactive tactics may include telephone pitches, talks to civic organizations, special-interest clubs and discussion groups, and, increasingly, E-mail and the Internet. Positive news media coverage of products, services, and promoted behaviors is sought for added reach and legitimacy. Streams of messages, media, and audiences are carefully balanced to interact with one another for maximum effect within the specified time.

Campaigns have become notoriously expensive undertakings over the years, with skyrocketing research and media costs. This has led to greater concern about finding out what worked and what did not in the campaign mix to plan more efficiently for the next round. Commercial-product campaigns have an easier time measuring actual public impact, since the ultimate test is how well a product sold. But even for, say, our new sport-utility model, assessing how "well" or "poorly" the campaign itself did can be hard as sales are partially dependent on the actual advantages or shortcomings in the vehicle compared with others. Despite the sophistication of today's marketing strategies, it is still very difficult to promote or sell a genuinely poor product or idea. Two of the most heavily market-researched and cleverly promoted "innovative" products of their times were the Edsel automobile in the mid–1950s and the "new Coke" formula of the late 1980s, both of which proved to be abject failures.

Evaluating social marketing campaigns is much harder. There is no yardstick such as product sales to rely on, and doing surveys measuring changes in public awareness and attitudes can be a dauntingly expensive—and often slippery—task. Most public service campaigns operate on small budgets, especially when compared with the hefty amounts spent by industry to promote consumer goods. Many public service efforts only become possible through the willingness of media outlets—especially television—to donate free time or space. However, the few formal scientific studies carried out on public service campaign impact suggest that they can build awareness and concern among citizens and, on occasion, prompt behavioral changes.

The same mechanisms that both drive and inhibit media effects discussed earlier in this chapter are at work here. Think of a campaign as an orchestrated cluster of communication stimuli capable of prompting learning, persuasion, reinforcement, agenda setting, priming, and other vehicles leading to social influence and change. An overriding inhibition against strong campaign effects in our own society is simply that campaigns are typically competing against one another in the clamor for public attention. The automotive campaign competes against several—perhaps dozens—similar ones with the same "buy our product" goals in mind and with the same persuasive techniques being employed. The AIDS-awareness program competes against a multitude of other health prevention and other social welfare messages; antismoking ads aimed at teens stack up against a background of glitzy cigarette promotions surrounding sports and other events appealing to the young.

HOW CAMPAIGNS CAN SUCCEED

Just as it is difficult for specific campaigns to make their public mark through all the competing clutter, it becomes even harder for programs not to jump into the fray for fear of being ignored altogether. How well campaigns "work" depends a great deal on how effectively they are planned, produced, and disseminated to reach their audiences. Reviews of successful campaign strategies and tactics suggest that key factors include:

1. Using social science models of public opinion and persuasion in their design rather than relying on "gut feel" or conventional wisdoms about social influence. A prominent heart-disease prevention campaign at Stanford University in the 1980s based its rationale on the social learning theory that behavioral change can be successfully promoted through modeling the actions of others.[60] Incorporating research on source credibility, fear appeals, and audience learning capabilities can go a long way toward designing more effective programs.
2. Taking into account audiences' existing cognitions, attitudes, and behaviors and their communication patterns and habits. Knowing what audiences already know, think, and do can save wasted effort, as can knowing what information needs individuals have and the sources they use to satisfy those needs.
3. Using extensive precampaign research to examine audience perceptions and needs, then pilot-testing possible themes and messages on targeted groups. Extensive use of audience surveys, focus groups,

and copy testing can provide a more reliable image of what the campaign should attempt to change and how it would have the best chance of doing so.

4. Having clear and realistically spelled-out campaign goals, high-quality professionally produced materials, and a well-planned and orchestrated dissemination strategy. It may seem obvious that setting goals and following through on them in a professional manner is more likely to produce results, but many campaigns suffer from simple lack of knowledge about how modern media systems operate. In some cases, lack of funding leads to poor-quality advertisements and other material. Often, campaign producers do not fully think through what they really want to accomplish in the way of building awareness or behavioral change, subverting their best intentions.[61]

5. Using mass media channels early in a campaign to help build awareness and salience of an issue, while noting that interpersonal communication is more effective for stimulating action. Making people aware of problems and solutions is far easier than prompting changes in their behaviors, especially ones that individuals see as costly or effortful. Recall from the previous chapter the ability of mass media to set agendas and legitimize issues. However, this does not necessarily lead to taking action; more personal, up-close communication can be more successful at doing so.

SOCIETAL CONSEQUENCES OF CAMPAIGNS

Both commercial and public information campaigns may have influences on public opinion other than their directly intended ones. Ford's latest campaign to sell its newest Explorer may or may not successfully sway buyers away from Nissan Pathfinders, but we can be more certain that the ads promoting both companies' vehicles combined will build public awareness of and perhaps more desirability for such vehicles overall. The societal impacts of even such a seemingly innocuous product can be consequential: increased fossil fuel consumption and air pollution, land erosion from increased off-road traffic, and, as claimed in the late 1990s, increased risk of injury or death to occupants of smaller vehicles involved in accidents with the larger, often more sturdily built sportsters.

Recent arguments to ban tobacco advertising have been based upon the premise that although each cigarette ad promoted an individual manufacturer's brand, the cumulative effect was to increase the appeal of cigarettes and other tobacco products overall, especially to the young. Some social critics have extended this argument to conclude that product campaigns taken as a group inherently drive us toward being a society of consumers, more concerned with shopping and material possessions than other pursuits.[62] More economically oriented commentators hold the same view but praise advertising campaigns as helping to strengthen the market and the economy, in part by making consumers aware of new products and services.[63]

In any case, it seems undeniable that commercial campaigns help shape what is apt to be "in" or "out" of our consumer culture. How such consumer opinions may carry over into the political sphere is far less clear. But if, for example, product advertising builds expectations of goods and services that are beyond the capabilities of many individuals to obtain, the consequences may not be trivial.

The same can be said to some extent for public information campaigns. The tremendous growth in preventive health campaigns over the past thirty years, for example, may have strongly contributed to making us a more health aware and responsible society, regardless of any individual gains in fighting cancer, nutritional deficiencies, or substance abuse. The more subtle message of most public health and safety campaigns has been one of citizens taking more individual responsibility for their well-being, moving away from overreliance on governmental and quasi-public agencies.

A moderately successful example has been the McGruff "Take a Bite out of Crime" campaign, supported by the U.S. Justice Department. The program encourages citizens to take individual and collective action to prevent crime in their neighborhoods rather than relying on police alone to shoulder the task. The McGruff program raises another aspect of campaign impact—the fact that, in some cases, it is necessary for a critical mass of individuals in a community to change individually before campaign objectives can be met. In the case of crime prevention—and traffic

FIGURE 10.6   Too many information campaigns may produce confusion rather than change. SOURCE: Gary Brookins, 1997, *Richmond Times-Dispatch.*

safety and a few other instances—enough people have to take the desired action for crime to be significantly curtailed. The collective actions of block watches and neighborhood cooperation with police are needed to reduce criminal activity in a community rather than just to relocate it from a locked home to an unlocked one next door.

Concerns often rise over which "social good" programs should be promoted, since support for one can lead to neglect of another (see Figure 10.6).[64] If more media time is allocated to a crime prevention program, will that take away from an equally salient program promoting proper infant nutrition practices? And who is to set the agenda to decide which issues win out? A related concern has been that the vast majority of public information campaigns that win media acceptance are uncontroversial: Few responsible citizens would argue for more crime, drug use, or cancer. Greater media attention to such black-and-white issues may draw attention away from more controversial problems such as economic welfare benefits, government-sponsored abortion, and drug legalization.[65]

Another criticism of overreliance in particular on governmentally sponsored information campaigns is that they may promote a more "top-down" channeling of information from institutions to the public, putting less emphasis on public discussion of problems and solutions and perhaps lessening public involvement or buy-in to solutions.[66] For example, rather than being "told" by municipal information program commercials how to cut water use during a drought, more cooperation might be gained by working within neighborhoods to see what kinds of particular solutions might be optimal for particular kinds of users. Notably, the more successful programs such as McGruff and many recent health education efforts take a communitywide approach to soliciting citizen opinions and ideas for options. International development programs involving agricultural productivity and environmental protection have benefited from similar approaches.[67] Of course, these approaches all serve to involve the "public" more intimately in the process of opinion formation and change, leaving the more "elite" institutional sources such as government with a more limited charge of generating and validating research information that then enters into the mix of public debate. Campaign planners and strategists themselves face new responsibilities as more is learned about what kinds of campaign techniques work on both individuals and on the society as a whole: Knowing the kinds of impact their programs can have increases the need for these communicators to act ethically and professionally.[68]

ELECTION CAMPAIGNS

We turn now to those campaigns that have the most conspicuous consequences for public opinion: those that have as their direct, avowed intent to build or sway opinions and actions—votes—with respect to public figures or issues. Election campaigns are nothing new, going back to the infancy of the country. From George Washington's day on, candidates for all levels of office have proudly trumpeted their own virtues, roundly disparaged their opponents, and put odd twists on the "facts" regarding their positions and records on issues of concern. However, each political era has changed the context and conduct of political campaigns, the formats of which have been in part dependent upon the political and communication structures of their times (see Figure 10.7).

Political campaigns have gone through some dramatic turns during this century because of the technological developments in communica-

FIGURE 10.7 Draft Goldwater for President Rally in Washington, D.C., Armory, August 4, 1963. Rallies like this one serve a variety of functions in political campaigns. (Photo courtesy of the Library of Congress)

tion media noted earlier. Other causes of change have included shifts in the demographic, economic, and social structure of the country and, over the past few decades, the decline of political party structures and identifications and changes in nomination procedures, campaign finance laws, and the like. The influence of political party membership on voting behavior has declined markedly. By the 1990s, as many or more people were calling themselves "independents" as labeled themselves either Democrats or Republicans.

As with any other type of campaign, political campaigns are shaped by the times and places in which they occur, by the personalities and issues being promoted, and by the public temper of the day. Political campaigns include not only the highly visible national presidential election races but also those for Congress, state executive and legislative branches, and local mayoral and council contests.

An increasing number of political campaigns are based solely on issues—such as those aimed at voters in public referenda decisions. Campaign tactics are also being used more to fuel public support or opposition to legislative and executive action. Witness the rise in direct mail and television ad blitzes concerning gun control legislation, for example, or the watershed of organized health industry opposition to the Clinton administration health care proposals in 1994. Abortion also remains an emotionally charged campaign field, and many local-level issue efforts can have impacts.

As with other kinds of campaigns, the financial cost of political campaigns has risen exponentially over recent decades. These campaigns, however, also share certain characteristics that set them apart from commercial or social marketing programs. For one thing, political campaigns usually operate in a more compressed time frame, during which two or more competing campaigns are directly pitted against one another. Rarely do commercial products go head-to-head in campaigns that end on a particular date, and social marketing programs are unlikely to compete openly against one another. But in election campaigns in particular, it is all over on election day, when the targeted audience votes en masse, one way or another.

Election campaigns are also distinctive in that usually the "product" being promoted is a living, breathing candidate, full of human virtues and frailties. Thus, campaigners have to sell the complexities of a human personality to the public, along with ideological and issue-related attributes. Indeed, election campaigns have increasingly emphasized personality and image aspects of candidates, often at the expense of more issue-related appeals.[69] We do not know whether this trend has followed or led to any greater public concern with candidate character over issue positions.

HOW DO ELECTION CAMPAIGNS WORK?

Political campaign organizations are also transitory, at least as compared to corporate and public interest campaign programs. When the election is over, the losers' organizations rapidly dissipate, whereas the winners turn to the challenges of governance. (In recent decades, at least at the presidential level, governance has included careful attention to public opinion through polling and related public relations activities.)[70] This transitoriness of political campaigns, coupled with the intricate complexities of fund-raising, staffing, scheduling, polling, and message and media selection, has led to greater use of hired professional campaign managers.

FIGURE 10.8   Today many candidates hire professional staff to run their campaigns. This group managed Bill Clinton's 1992 presidential campaign. (Photo by David Burnett, courtesy of Contact Press, © 1992)

These consultants may be involved in several campaigns at once and provide key expertise in such areas as media relations, polling, and, perhaps most often, candidate marketing. Many of the tactics and strategies used have distinct consequences for traditional pluralistic democratic theory.

Consultants can be instrumental in providing candidates the latest in communication technologies and techniques and in developing strategies for pursuing funding from political action groups and votes from particular voting blocks (see Figure 10.8). As with their commercial counterparts, they rely heavily on market segmentation techniques, identifying characteristics of dominant voting segments and playing campaign messages to the needs and biases of those groups. These professional campaign planners synchronize candidate appearances and speeches, testimonials from notable individuals and organizations, planned press coverage and "staged" events, and timely reactions to the unexpected news events of the day, weaving together a web of central campaign themes and images.

There is a "good news–bad news" twist to all this, from several points of view. For one thing, it is probably good that these techniques may be quite effective at identifying for candidates what voters view as the critical issues of the day and how they would like to see them resolved. It is also a plus that a variety of political viewpoints are identified and tied to different types of people. However, it may become bad news when candidates insincerely pander to voters by espousing views they think will get them elected rather than challenging voters with evidence and logic based upon their own beliefs. It also does not serve enlightened democratic practice when candidates may try to play one voting segment against another, exaggerating the differences between blocs to manipulate votes for themselves.

Much of the foregoing suggests that it is very much an open question as to whether elites, as represented by campaign producers, lead or follow public opinion in the electioneering process. It is an interesting cycle to consider. To begin with, techniques such as polling give candidates fairly reliable estimates of what various publics want. Doubtless, this influences their decisions about how to campaign and, ultimately, how to govern if elected. In this sense, the public does affect elite leadership. Yet this information also gives candidates an edge in shaping future public opinion by designing persuasive strategies to suit their own needs. Somewhere in the middle is the press, at least to some extent trying to inform the public of what the candidates are up to, not only with respect to where candidates stand but, more recently, concerning how the candidates are trying to influence the public. One argument on the side of elites having the better of this bargain is that the press itself is often viewed as elitist, although of a somewhat different stripe; numerous recent polls documenting a loss of public respect for journalists support this. And it is the politicians and the press that have the polling and other sophisticated information-gathering capacities, not the public.

At their worst, political consultants can resemble the truth-spinning media tricksters that caused Robert Redford's all-too-successful political neophyte character to turn against his altruistic goals in the 1970s movie *The Candidate*. At their best, consultants may give candidates more reliable information about the actual concerns of voting publics, while giving voters greater access to the views and personalities of candidates.[71]

Most political campaign enterprises rely heavily on the help of troops of dedicated volunteers. Even small city elections may require a major personnel logistics plan to recruit and train such individuals, coordinate

FIGURE 10.9   Campaign volunteers are critical to a candidate's success, but much
of their work is very mundane. Here, Eugene McCarthy's campaign staff cleans up
after the Democratic National Convention in Chicago in 1968. (Photo © David
Douglas Duncan 1968)

their efforts, keep them informed and motivated, and give them adequate
psychological rewards for their work. Much of their work involves the inevitably mundane tasks of checking voter lists, preparing mailings, phone
canvassing, and leaflet dropping. These behind-the-scenes jobs are often
obscured by the glamour of catchy television ads and by the drama of
major news-event coverage. But the day-to-day hustle of countless volunteers reaching out one-on-one with the electorate is often the critical
factor in personalizing the campaign and getting out the vote.[72] It is
through such activity that the citizenry comes closest to true participation
in political campaigns, probably quite effectively. This linkage of the politically committed with one another over long hours and days or weeks
and their direct interplay with candidates or their close representatives
most likely has strong effects on staffers and candidates alike and de-
serves more attention and scrutiny (see Figure 10.9). The Internet began
playing a significant role in election campaigns in 2000, and there is every
indication that that trend will increase as we witness the buildup to the

2004 presidential campaign with candidate volunteers and professionals relying heavily on e-mail, chat lines, and more formal Web sites.

Fund-Raising

The raising of money and collateral support to run a campaign can be a time-consuming task, made even more so by the multifold financial pressures and regulations that beset contemporary campaigning. Inordinate amounts of most candidates' waking hours are spent pursuing funding, right up to—and sometimes even after—election day. Presidential campaigns offer the advantage of federal funding options throughout the primaries and into the general election; however, candidates who choose to use that support cannot exceed mandated spending limits.

In one landmark example, halfway into the 1996 Republican presidential primaries, Robert Dole found himself in trouble for having come close to having spent his $30-million-plus limit. One reason for his early excess spending was his attempt to match the television advertising blitz of multimillionaire publisher Steve Forbes, who had refused federal funding and was running his campaign on his own fortune, seemingly willing and able at the time to outspend Dole. In 1996 overall, an estimated $2 billion was spent on campaigns for the presidency and Congress, almost double the amount spent in 1992. In 2000, the total tab for all election campaigns was estimated at some $7.2 billion, including $600 million by the presidential candidates alone. The contentious November 2000 Florida recount of presidential ballots resulted in $17 million spent by Bush and Gore, the lion's share by Bush.

The dilemma from the pluralistic electorate point of view is that the emphasis on funding reduces some citizens' roles in candidate selection procedures, yet it seems unfair to forbid wealthier people from contributing to the candidates or causes of their choice. Heightened concern over campaign financing has led to moderate regulation at federal, state, and, in some cases, local levels. The basic worries are twofold: (1) that candidates will be "bought" by dominant contributors, who will expect favors from those elected; and (2) that candidates who spend the most—particularly on media—will attract the most votes, eliminating perhaps more worthy but less affluent candidate. The first problem continues to be heavily debated at all levels of government and is hardly a new issue, going back to the earliest experiments in democracy. Special-interest groups donate

enormous amounts of money to campaigns of all kinds and enthusiasti-
cally lobby the elected officials to support this cause or that on their behalf. The power of such industrial trade groups, unions, citizen action pan-
els, and the like is of genuine concern, particularly since the costs of
campaigning—and the attendant need for money to meet them—have
risen so dramatically. Federal campaign finance laws were enacted primarily to limit exceptionally large contributions by single persons or organizations that might bring undue influence to bear on candidates. In brief, the
regulations require that all donated money and expenditures need to be
carefully documented by campaign managers.

The dramatic rise of another kind of political organization—political
action committees (PACs)—over the past thirty years added more confusion to the funding situation. PACs consist of special-interest groups
ranging from public advocacy groups to corporations to trade organizations to unions.[73] Individual members may contribute freely to the committee, which is then limited in the same way as other organizations in
how much they can give to any one candidate's campaign. However,
PACs may spend as much as they choose on their own in support of a
candidate—by running their own commercials, their own direct mail
campaigns, and so forth—as long as those efforts are made independently
of the candidate's own efforts. Some PACs focus on single issues—abortion, health care, and gun control are prominent examples—and may lend
their support to a range of like-minded candidates across the country.
Such so-called soft-money contributions, especially to political parties,
were severely constrained by the Bipartisan Campaign Reform Act that
took effect in 2002. However, in the 2004 primary elections several outside groups emerged spending millions of dollars running their own partisan ads totally independent of candidates or parties.

Campaign Media

What has made fund-raising more necessary over the past forty years has
been the rise of the mass media campaign, with television absorbing the
lion's share of the expense. The cost of television spot advertising runs
from hundreds of dollars a minute in the smallest market areas to hundreds of thousands of dollars nationally.

Although buying television time is the major cost, other big expenses
include hiring professional advertising staffs to produce the material that

goes into televised messages. These include developing campaign themes, slogans, and graphic images, which need to blend into posters, as well as direct mail pieces, issue position papers, and the ubiquitous bumper stickers and buttons. Competently done political polling can be another major expense item.

Types of campaign media can be broadly separated into controlled and uncontrolled media. Controlled media are those that planners pay for and produce themselves, selecting their own themes, messages, target audiences, and schedules. Advertising is the primary format. The main form of uncontrolled media is news coverage, which is cost-free to the candidate and can offer wide and credible exposure. The downside is that the candidate has no direct control over what is reported, when, or to whom.

Controlled Media.   Controlled media include commercials and other bought-and-paid-for broadcast and cable time, newspaper advertising, direct mail, Web pages, billboards, posters, telephone canvassing, and the like. Speeches and other public appearances by or for candidates generally fall into the controlled category as well, although news media will often use portions of them, edited to their own liking. As in any campaign, controlled messages are carefully designed to influence particular kinds of audiences, and media channels are chosen to maximize impact on those audiences.

Brochures and other print pieces are useful for providing more detailed information on policy positions, past voting records, and other specifics. Often these can be tailored for direct mailing to certain zip code addresses with particular demographic or lifestyle characteristics. Residents of a neighborhood with a high proportion of retirees, for example, may be mailed highlights of a candidate's assurances about continued Social Security benefits. A heavily Hispanic area, by contrast, may be targeted with mailings in Spanish emphasizing the candidate's commitment to affirmative action standards.

Radio typically provides another vehicle for careful voter-bloc targeting. The diversity of radio stations across musical tastes, talk show politics, and other formats delivers to advertisers distinct listener types to whom campaigners can appeal. Newspaper ads reach a broader, more mainstream audience that is more inclined to be politically active and informed and more apt to vote. Internet Web sites are quickly emerging, but they primarily serve already committed political junkies.

Television commercials remain clearly the dominant form of controlled political media, and they include an interesting mix of advantages and disadvantages for candidates. A decided and obvious advantage of televised political commercials is their reach. No other medium can bring to a given message millions of viewers nationally or even tens of thousands statewide or locally, often in a single showing. Not only are these spots seen in the viewers' own homes, but they are difficult to avoid as well. It is difficult for audiences to tune out ads selectively that they might disagree with or be uninterested in. A disadvantage, however, is that such commercials are squeezed into programs in an increasingly cluttered environment, with spots of less than half a minute becoming the norm. This makes it more difficult for any type of ad to stand out on its own.

Political commercials can be aimed at some audience segments by carefully choosing the types of programs during which they appear. However, the match is not always a close one, given the diverse audiences that television draws. Also, those who watch television more heavily are among the more politically disenfranchised, and some efficiency may be wasted by aiming candidate spots at them. These disadvantages are related to the biggest one of all: the extremely high expense of airing ads during programs that draw the largest and most desirable audiences. Costs of hundreds of thousands of dollars per minute for national spots are not uncommon, and even locally shown spots can run into the thousands of dollars per showing.

The commercials' ability to convey moving sight and sound visually dramatizes not only a candidate's personal attributes but political issues and themes as well.[74] The 15- to 30-second television spot format offers a wide array of creative possibilities, ranging from focus on candidate leadership characteristics to "toughness" on crime or foreign policy to snippets of policy positions put into human, emotive terms. The mix of creative elements varies heavily with the type of candidate, the nature of the opposition, and the voter groups and concerns being addressed. Political newcomers may push their personal strengths and seek popular endorsements early in a race, whereas well-known incumbents emphasize their records in office. More telegenic contenders may show more visuals of themselves in action, with others focusing on less personal visual imagery.

Comparative ads contrast one candidate's attributes with the opposition's, often exaggerating differences in policy positions or voting records.

The fairness of these has sometimes been called into question, and some news media have run "AdWatch"-type news briefs to refute the claims of more biased ads. A trend toward more negative or attack ads on television seems to have emerged during the late 1980s, in which candidates attack their opponents on personal or policy points rather than promoting their own virtues.

Candidates have also taken advantage of the "unfiltered" opportunity to provide information to interested citizens via the Internet. Their Web pages flourish, providing biographical information, position papers, invitations to join e-mail and regular mail lists, and so forth. The use of these has clearly spread in the early 2000s beyond a small segment of hard-core (and computer literate) political activists into the mainstream of the politically interested and involved.

Uncontrolled Media.   Uncontrolled media are equally if not more important and mainly include coverage by the news media. Such coverage can provide greater reach across voters and bestow greater credibility to a candidacy—and the coverage is virtually "free" to the candidate. However, the campaign has no direct control over what messages end up on the air or in print.

Virtually all types of campaigns actively solicit news coverage of their "product," whether it be soap or safe driving or a presidential candidate. Political campaigns employ media relations specialists to provide broadcast and print news reporters with reams of press releases, position papers, and other documentation supporting the alleged virtues of the candidate. Campaign events are often timed to coincide with the schedules of evening network television programs and morning newspapers. Journalists are accorded preferential treatment in the campaign entourage and are privy to behind-the-scenes comings and goings and the occasional "exclusive" interview with a candidate.

The pace of news coverage has quickened considerably over the past decade, with the coming of around-the-clock news coverage on CNN and its competitors, instantaneous satellite transmission to local broadcast stations and newspapers, and continuous news coverage in great detail on the Internet. This has led to even greater public access to candidates, though also perhaps to a greater tendency of reporters to get the news out quickly to beat the competition. Inaccuracies can and do occur;

one notable example is the overwillingness of some television networks to jump the gun on predicting election winners before valid samplings of returns are in. News coverage varies considerably with the nature of the campaign. A candidate for alderman in a small city might revel at getting one interview in the daily newspaper over the whole course of a campaign, whereas major gubernatorial or presidential contenders may blanch at what they see as wholesale surrender of their private lives to the news media on a daily basis.

The most important drawback of press coverage is that no matter how hard the candidate tries to impress journalists, what ultimately gets reported is out of the campaign's direct control. The press chooses the content to be reported and the context in which it will appear, and often interprets the information from the point of view of other candidates or offers the media's own news judgments. An ongoing matching of wits often follows for the duration of a campaign, with politicians recognizing their own need for press coverage and trying to get the most positive spin possible along with it. Journalists, working from a different vantage point, generally recognize their own obligation to inform the public about candidates' pros and cons but need to rely on candidates to supply crucial information.

Somewhat hybrid and interactive campaign events ranging from candidate debates to talk show appearances to Internet chat lines are probably best described as a mix of both controlled and uncontrolled media: Candidates certainly have control over what they say and reach their audience directly with it, but the give-and-take of live interviewing of any sort can quickly move the locus of perceived control from interviewee to interviewer, or inquisitor.

Ideally, there should be tension between media controlled by the campaigners and the uncontrolled media, represented mainly by the press in its various forms. This tension can work to bring public interests and concerns more into the media mix—to assure that questions the public wants answered are put to the candidates. However, as noted previously, there is a risk that the press may have its own agendas to follow—and more elitist ones at that—lessening the opportunity for public influence on choosing and shaping campaign issues. In a study of news depictions of the 1991 Philadelphia mayoral campaign, for example, June Rhee found that some print stories framed the campaign more in campaign strategy terms, while others framed it more in issue terms. Using an experimental manipulation, Rhee also found that readers tended to interpret the campaign more in terms of the frames they read. Readers more exposed to strategy stories described the campaign more as a strategy process, while those reading stories framed around issues concentrated more on those.[75] Kim Fridkin Kahn offers a telling account of press coverage of female candidates and possible impact upon voters. In an analysis of gubernatorial and senatorial campaigns, Fridkin Kahn found that press coverage of campaigns of female candidates focused less on issue positions than did coverage of male candidates. Rather, personal or image attributes of women received more attention. Moreover, the press appeared to follow the lead of male candidates in covering the content emphasized by their campaigns more often than it did for female candidates. Fridkin Kahn argues that media stereotypes of women in campaigns can hinder their getting their messages over to voters, although in some contexts the stereotypes may work in favor of female candidates.[76]

IMPACT OF CAMPAIGNS ON PUBLIC OPINION AND VOTING

How do election campaign strategies and tactics actually affect voters? We will now examine what we know about what voters learn from such campaigns, how the campaigns influence vote decisions, and how campaigns might impact other political orientations of voters.

Learning from Campaigns

Voters may learn a considerable amount from news coverage of candidates. Both newspaper and television news play significant roles in informing the public about campaign issues and usually about candidate positions on them.[77] Many earlier studies suggested that newspapers did a far better job than television in informing voters.[78] Nevertheless, extent of learning from each medium can vary by the kinds of people being examined, the type of campaign, and other factors as well. A national study by political scientists Craig Brians and Martin Wattenberg of the 1992 Bush–Clinton contest showed very low levels of learning about the candidates' positions from either newspaper or television news.[79] Whether this came about from peculiarities of citizen response to the candidates, from press coverage during that particular campaign, or from other reasons is puzzling. Brians and Wattenberg suggest that a possible diminishing of coverage of substantive issues in both newspapers and television may have played a role.

As for differences in citizen response, politically interested people may learn more about candidates from newspapers than from television, but television and newspapers appear about even in informing the less involved.[80] Television has often been assumed to do a better job of giving voters "image" impressions of candidate personality attributes, but the evidence on this is less clear.[81] Thomas Patterson found television's image impact to be pertinent only in the early-impression formation stages of a campaign.[82]

Well-publicized events such as debates provide a wellspring for issue learning and impression formation[83] and may be especially effective in informing citizens not as attuned to other aspects of the campaign.[84] Some individuals may also learn from the much-maligned television commercials. Patterson and Robert McClure were the first to suggest that the ubiquitous spot ads contained enough nuggets of basic information—and were repeated often enough—to enlighten viewers as to candidates' basic policy stances.[85] The less politically involved and less news attentive who thrive more on entertainment television may find commercials to be their primary window and information source.

However, there was little research support to back up this controversial claim until the 1992 presidential election, when Brians and Wattenberg found that watching campaign spots was highly associated with learning more about candidates' issue positions—and clearly more predictive of learning than either newspaper or television news use (see Table 10.2). This could be particularly true for such situations as Republican presidential candidate Steve Forbes' multimillion-dollar television advertising blitz in the early 1996 primaries. Although many of Forbes' spots attacked other candidates, voters also arguably learned of his "flat" income tax plan from them. Brians and Wattenberg found that viewing negative campaign ads—those that attack or bash the opponent's positions or personal characteristics—was also associated with knowing more about issues. This finding is partially backed up in a series of studies of the 1992 presidential campaign and of a number of California state and local campaigns by Steven Ansolabehere and Shanto Iyengar, who also note that the strength of the effect differs across a wide range of candidates and

TABLE 10.2   Predicting Issue Knowledge and Issue-Based Candidate Evaluation by Media Sources[a]

	Knowledge of Candidates' Positions	Candidate Evaluation Issue Salience
Political ad recall	.247[c]	.363[d]
	(.084)	(.101)
Newspaper index	.010[b]	.003
	(.005)	(.006)
TV news index	.011[b]	.004
	(.005)	(.006)
Education	.268[d]	.024
	(.028)	(.034)
Sex (female)	−.079	−.004
	(.082)	(.098)
Age in years	−.016[d]	−.018[d]
	(.002)	(.003)
Campaign interest	.183[d]	.260[d]
	(.033)	(.039)
General political knowledge	.449[d]	.291[d]
	(.030)	(.036)
Interview date	−.088	.028
	(.080)	(.096)
Constant	1.410[d]	.978[d]
	(.183)	(.219)
Adjusted R^2	.39	.16
Standard error	1.64	1.96
Number of cases	1,809	1,809

NOTE: Figures are unstandardized OLS regression coefficients: standard errors are in parentheses.

[a] Variables defined and missing data cases explained in the appendix in Brians and Wattenberg.

[b] $p < .05$.

[c] $p < .01$.

[d] $p < .001$.

SOURCE: From Craig L. Brians, and Martin P. Wattenberg, "Campaign Issue Knowledge and Salience: Comparing Reception from TV Commericals, TV News, and Newspapers," *American Journal of Political Science*, 40 (1) (February 1996), table 2, p. 181. Data derived from 1992 American National Election Study. Reprinted by permission of University of Wisconsin Press.

voters.[86] One argument goes that the negative ads attract more attention and whatever issue information is contained in them may be better remembered.

Whether citizens learn more about candidates from newspapers, debates, televised news, or televised ads is likely to depend on the type of campaign, what voters already know about the candidates, and how well news media and campaign media managers carry out their jobs. A recent study of how people learn about candidates and issues over six different campaigns found television news to generally be the main source, but televised ads surpassed news in one Senate campaign in which both candidates spent huge sums on airing the spots.[87]

How Persuasive Are Campaigns?

Election campaigns work their influences on public opinion in several ways. "Strong" effects, such as causing dramatic changes in voter moods or preferences, are unlikely, but "weaker" influences on citizen perceptions and opinions are probable, given the relatively intensive stimuli campaigns bring to bear on politically charged preelection environments.

One significant impact that campaigns are often assumed to have, but that is actually the least likely to occur, is convincing voters to switch from one candidate to another.[88] A quite small percentage of voters—usually in the low single digits—in any election campaign end up doing this, and this proportion is typically too negligible to calculate. We need to keep in mind, however, that although the number of voters influenced by the campaign to change candidates is low, such vote switching may be decisive in close races. Many major elections are decided by a fraction of a percentage point, and relatively few voters shifting here or there can make all the difference, as the 2000 presidential election clearly illustrated. (Social scientists doing studies of campaigns sometimes rightfully dismiss very small differences in voting behavior as "statistically insignificant"; yet candidates can and do win or lose elections by handfuls of votes.)

A more persuasive influence that election campaigns are likely to have is to keep already decided supporters of a candidate on track, reinforcing their decisions and motivating them to go to the polls. As long as "my" candidates keep feeding me reasons why I should vote for them, it is unlikely, short of a major blunder or scandal on the candidate's part, that I would be attracted by the arguments of other contestants. But faced with a rash of messages from opposing politicians and little or no communication from my initial choices, I could begin to at least waver in my support. Although I might not switch sides, I could simply not bother to vote. A second persuasive influence involves pulling in the undecided voters, who form an increasingly large pool in our more volatile electoral environment. A more difficult task is to reach out to uncommitted and less involved citizens—another increasing cohort—most of whom will end up not bothering to vote at all.

The relative persuasive influences of controlled versus uncontrolled campaign media on the public are unclear. The problem is in separating the possible influences of commercials from those of speeches or debates and those of news coverage and other avenues. Recalling where we heard overlapping bits of information is difficult enough for most of us, let alone recalling who out of a heady mix of sources may have affected or influenced us. News events, commercials, key speeches, debates, and other stimuli likely reach different voters in different ways at different times.

The increased volatility exhibited by the voting public from 1975 through the 1990s has focused more attention on both the kinds of citizens and the kinds of election situations that may lead to greater or lesser campaign effects. People are clearly less consistent in voting by party labels and more apt to choose a candidate later in the campaign or to opt out of voting altogether. Voters who pick a candidate closer to election day are more likely to be influenced by the campaign and to base their choice on issues or candidate characteristics emphasized in the campaign.[89]

An individual's level of involvement in a particular election is likely an important indicator of how the person's decision will be reached and of the kinds of information that will be more influential in that choice. Recall the discussion in Chapter 4 on level of involvement in terms of its impact on how people process information and how much of an impact that information is likely to have. Studies have found that people with higher involvement in a problem or issue—or an election—will make decisions more "logically," carefully processing information and looking for cues more central to the problem at hand.[90] In choosing a candidate, for example, the more involved voter may make a close inspection of contenders' issue positions, voting records, administrative abilities, and the like, comparing and contrasting them.

People with lower involvement, however, make decisions less logically and systematically and base them on more peripheral cues or on ones more available but less central to the decision per se. Not being interested enough in the election, such voters are less willing to go through the difficulty of actively processing information about issues or character. They take the easier way, settling for a set of cues that will justify their decision to themselves. In election decisions, these people might be more swayed by perhaps the looks of a candidate, the offhand advice of a friend, a celebrity endorsement, or the cleverness of a political ad.

Citizens vary a great deal in how willing they are to be involved in election decisions—if at all. Some of us may spend weeks agonizing over a presidential or Senate race choice but may cast a ballot on the same election day for a city councilperson based on whose name is first on the ballot. Involvement is in part a personal attribute, in that some people are less politically interested overall, and a situational one, in that some elections simply generate low attention levels. Campaigners recognize this, particularly in their efforts to reach the less concerned citizens who may be marginally likely to vote. Television commercials that may seem senseless and repetitive to a politically astute voter could conceivably be the only salient message that happens to cross the mind of a far less interested person on election day. Ansolabehere and Iyengar, in their previously mentioned 1992 California studies, found that television ads were far more effective in reinforcing existing partisan sentiments among voters than in manipulating or causing changes in candidate predispositions.[91] Party-unaffiliated citizens appeared the least persuaded—perhaps because they paid less attention to the ads. As for attack ads, for whatever reasons, the California study found Republican attack ads more reinforcing for Republicans, whereas Democrats were more reinforced by positive ads.

Building Citizen Interest

Campaigns build citizen interest in the election, in a sense alerting potential voters that an event of consequence is coming up. Even the most politically disenfranchised and disinterested people find major campaigns hard to avoid, especially given their play on television. Skipping the news is easy, but commercials on popular programs are difficult to avoid, even when they are spiritedly disliked. In presidential campaigns, television appears to heighten early interest among citizens during the primaries, with subsequent spikes of attentiveness during the nominating conventions and candidate debates (see Table 10.3).[92]

Newspapers may stimulate interest more gradually over the campaign period, being less intrusive: Newspaper readers can choose what to read, following their own interests; television may be more able to spark new interest among the initially less motivated because of the "unavoidability" of political content slipped into unrelated programming. Television's pen-

TABLE 10.3   Election Interest at Various Times During the Campaign, 1976 (in percent)

Level of Interest and Location	February	April	June	August	October
Erie					
Strong interest	22	28	26	33	32
Some interest	28	30	34	33	34
No interest	50	42	40	34	34
Total	100	100	100	100	100
Los Angeles					
Strong interest	19	27	32	37	29
Some interest	26	28	33	32	33
No interest	55	45	35	31	38
Total	100	100	100	100	100

SOURCE: Thomas E. Patterson, *The Mass Media Election: How Americans Choose Their President* (New York: Praeger, 1980), table 7.1, p. 68.

chant for the more visually dramatic probably contributes here as well. The visual spectacles of the conventions and debates can draw in more of the less curious, of course giving candidates an opportunity to impress themselves upon those who are only marginally politically interested.

Campaigns also can build the morale of committed campaign workers. Rallies, stump speeches, and blitzes of attractive media ads can add luster and meaning to the otherwise drab and hard work of preparing mailings and canvassing by phone, keeping energy levels and work quality high. Election campaigns can also contribute to the public-spiritedness of the citizenry overall, perhaps reinforcing the legitimacy of the political system.

However, if citizens are exposed to heavy doses of negative advertising across campaigns, one risk is that people will believe all candidates to have salient weaknesses, resulting in less enthusiasm for supporting any of them. Negative advertising may also increase political cynicism and decrease willingness to vote or participate in other ways.[93] Ansolabehere and Iyengar found citizen exposure to attack ads partially related to lower voter turnout in their 1992 California study, especially among independent, less-partisan potential voters.[94] And the authors make the case that these ads appear to have stimulated greater partisanship and polarization among those who did vote.

This is not unlike the argument made for the "videomalaise" syndrome purportedly brought on by negative television news. Although some interesting evidence supports such ill effects of attack ads on the public under some circumstances, it is hardly clear how widespread the influence may be or in what kinds of campaign contexts it might operate. Should "attack" ads that accurately portray genuinely negative characteristics of an arguably poor, or even dangerous, candidate be disallowed?

Preelection polling results have also recently gotten something of a drubbing from some observers. Although there is little evidence that such poll results sway voters from one candidate to another, poll findings may dull interest in a contest in which one candidate or the other appears impossibly ahead, and this might possibly lessen voter turnout.[95] National election-day outcome predictions based upon such techniques as exit polls and sophisticated computer modeling also came under heavy fire for initially miscalling the outcome of the exceptionally close Bush–Gore race in 2000.[96]

WHAT WE DO NOT KNOW ABOUT ELECTION CAMPAIGN INFLUENCES

We do not know that much about how political campaigns *as campaigns*—in the sense of the term defined at the beginning of this chapter—affect voting decisions. One reason for this is that we have not done a very good job of studying how political campaigns work. That may sound strange, given the wealth of curiosity about presidential races, especially, and the seemingly endless outpouring of articles, books, and documentaries analyzing election outcomes. Although such analyses may offer reasoned and sometimes accurate speculation about voting behavior, they lack an adequate view of the multitude of factors that impinge on why citizens vote as they do.

Much of the problem lies in separating the impact of the candidate per se and dramatic events beyond the candidate's control from the campaign operation itself. Many have acclaimed Richard Nixon's 1968 television-based campaign tactics over Hubert Humphrey as pioneering and masterful, yet many polls showed Humphrey gaining significantly on Nixon over the final weeks of the contest. The point is that it is exceptionally difficult to separate out either the campaign plan overall or specific elements of it and point to any one factor as decisive in winning an election. And perhaps fortunately, much of what happens during and around election campaign periods is out of the hands of the planners and strategists. "Real life" goes on, with war, scandal, economic ups and downs, disasters, and similar events being quite out of the control of the candidates, yet often dramatically affecting how voters respond to them. The emotional impact of the terrorist attacks of September 11, 2001, is difficult to gauge, yet by all accounts it at least initially united and solidified U.S. public opinion in favor of a more aggressive foreign policy, a more restrictive homeland policy, and generally more in alignment with the conservative leanings of President George W. Bush.[97]

To get a more complete picture of what kinds of campaign strategies and tactics have what kinds of impact on which voters, we need a far more holistic view of the contest than past analyses have provided. We need to examine carefully the approaches of competing campaigns, the central message themes, the media strategies. We then need to tie those to extensive observations on voters—through surveys and other methods—before, during, and after the campaign. Finally, we need to have some way of in effect "controlling" for the type of candidate in each campaign, the issues raised, and the events unrelated to the campaign that took place during it. This is a tall order and is impractical for many, if not most, campaign research situations. Perhaps the best we can realistically aim for is to tease out which factors are more apt to be important in what kinds of campaigns to what kinds of voters and focus on those.

To return to key points raised earlier: If the candidate (or "product") is a dud, even the most technically perfect campaign operation is unlikely to save that person if the opponent has more going politically.

Also, most previous analyses have dealt with presidential races—the most significant in some ways but also the most closely attended to by the public. We know far less about the role of campaign operations and media use in more localized races, where they could have a greater impact. Media in particular have much more of a chance of establishing a persona for candidates who are normally less in the public eye, about whom voters may know very little, if anything.

As already noted, candidates have turned more to "alternative" media, such as televised talk shows, MTV, and cable offerings more generally. These give candidates more leeway in presenting their own views in an extended format, at least as compared to traditional news programming. Although such audiences are smaller, they tend to be more segmented and may include individuals less involved in politics—or attuned to traditional media formats. There is little evidence so far that viewers who watch them learn much from these appearances, but as they grow in frequency with greater channel diversification, that could change.[98]

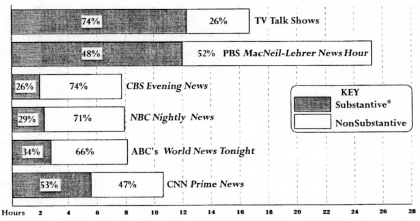

74%	26%	TV Talk Shows
48%	52%	PBS *MacNeil-Lehrer News Hour*
26%	74%	*CBS Evening News*
29%	71%	*NBC Nightly News*
34%	66%	ABC's *World News Tonight*
53%	47%	CNN *Prime News*

KEY
Substantive[a]
NonSubstantive

Hours   2   4   6   8   10   12   14   16   18   20   22   24   26   28

[a]Substance category includes stories primarily about the candidates' qualifications and policy issues.

FIGURE 10.10   Substantive and Nonsubstantive Coverage of the 1992 Presidential Campaign. SOURCE: S. R. Lichter and R. E. Noyes, *Good Intentions Make Bad News: Why Americans Hate Campaign Journalism* (Lanham, MD: Rowman and Littlefield, 1995), p. 247.

HOW WELL IS THE PUBLIC SERVED BY CAMPAIGN PRESS COVERAGE?

Criticism of such campaign techniques as attack messages is as old as democracy and the arts of persuasion and propaganda. A very thin line separates trying to put the best possible perspective or spin on a person or event and outright misrepresentation. Equally open to criticism—at least over the past two centuries—has been the way the press reports campaigns. As we saw early in this chapter, very seldom are journalists seen as objective or disinterested observers of political events, and the coverage of campaigns is certainly no exception.

In recent years, more criticism of press campaign coverage has focused on a charge that newspapers and television news show more concern with the "horse race" aspects of campaigns and with negative depictions of candidates' personal attributes. Critics argue that the news media report more on the campaign as a phenomenon, as opposed to reporting on the substance of the issues of the day, how candidates respond to those, and the candidates' competence to hold office (see Figure 10.10).[99]

Such coverage includes the "horse race" or "hoopla" issues of campaign strategy and tactics, who is ahead and who is behind in the polls, fallout from attack ads and other negative techniques, and making the most of candidate idiosyncracies and blunders. Competitive aspects of the campaign can make for easier and more exciting day-to-day deadline coverage reporting, whereas reporting the deeper aspects of issue positions requires more difficult and skillful explanation to make it appealing to citizens-at-large. The emphasis on reporting who is ahead in the early polls of presidential and other primaries can also have substantial consequences for candidate fund-raising: Donors are obviously attracted much more easily and quickly to candidates whom they think can win, and donors pegged as early supporters of a successful candidate gain in luster and perceived influence. Critics charge that candidate performance on the stump may not translate into effective coalition building, thoughtful policy planning, or leadership in time of crisis. Journalists often respond to these charges by saying that public interest in such matters runs high and that how well candidates manage their run for office can be a telling indicator of administrative ability and style.

The press has also been accused of capitalizing on and magnifying the personal flaws of candidates, and indeed of public persons overall, to the point where some otherwise viable public servants may shy away from the fray because they do not want so much of their personal background and that of their families open to scrutiny. The response of the press is typically the argument that citizens need to be made aware of the character of officeholders and that one relinquishes the private persona by becoming a public person. Critics retort that much of such coverage is simply titillating *National Enquirer*-type reporting to attract a bigger audience and that it is often blown out of proportion.

More recent, and perhaps less important, controversies have grown over such issues as the amount of live television coverage given the national party nominating conventions and that accorded to debates between presidential candidates. Many journalists would argue that these are simply news judgments: If something of public interest is expected to happen at such an event, it will be covered. The political viewpoint is that there is an obligation of the press to cover major national events, even if the outcomes are easily predictable and nothing "new" is anticipated to happen. As political scientist Thomas Patterson notes, the press is "fundamentally ill-suited to fulfilling its inherited role as an election mediator. . . . The problem is that the press is not a political institution. Its business is news, and the values of news are not those of politics."[100]

Resolution of these conflicts is highly unlikely, but much can be gained by greater public awareness of the contrasts among (1) the realities of the political environment, (2) the image of the environment that campaigns present, and (3) the image of that environment that the press presents. In sum, we need more public awareness that the media in their varied shapes and forms provide varied "pictures in our heads" of an environment we do not directly experience, as Lippmann put it so well.[101]

NOTES

1. Harold Lasswell, "The Structure and Function of Communication in Society," in Lyman Bryson, ed., *The Communication of Ideas* (New York: Harper, 1948), pp. 32–51.

2. Charles Wright, "Functional Analysis and Mass Communication," *Public Opinion Quarterly* 24 (1960):606–620.

3. For example, see Herbert Blumer, "The Mass, the Public and Public Opinion," in Bernard Berelson and Morris Janowitz, eds., *Reader in Public Opinion and Communication* (New York: Free Press, 1960), pp. 43–50.

4. Walter Lippmann, *Public Opinion* (New York: Macmillan Co., 1922).

5. Maxwell E. McCombs and Donald L. Shaw, "The Agenda-Setting Function of the Press," *Public Opinion Quarterly* 36 (1972):176–187.

6. Oscar Gandy, *Beyond Agenda Setting* (Norwood, NJ: Ablex, 1982).

7. Michael B. Grossman and Martha J. Kumar, *Portraying the President: The White House and the News Media* (Baltimore: Johns Hopkins University Press, 1981).

8. Benjamin I. Page, Robert Y. Shapiro, and Gregory R. Dempsey, "What Moves Public Opinion?" *American Political Science Review* 81 (1987):23–43.

9. John R. Zaller, *The Nature and Origins of Mass Opinion* (Cambridge: Cambridge University Press, 1992); Robert M. Entman, "Framing: Toward Clarification of a Fractured Paradigm," *Journal of Communication* 43 (1993):293–300.

10. Clarice N. Olien, George A. Donohue, and Phillip J. Tichenor, "Conflict, Consensus and Public Opinion," in Theodore L. Glasser and Charles T. Salmon, eds., *Public Opinion and the Communication of Consent* (New York: Guilford Press, 1995), pp. 301–323.

11. Ibid.

12. Edward Herman and Noam Chomsky, *Manufacturing Consent: The Political Economy of Mass Media* (New York: Pantheon, 1988).

13. Lasswell, "Structure and Function of Communication in Society."

14. Bernard Cohen, *The Press and Foreign Policy* (Princeton: Princeton University Press, 1963), p. 13.

15. McCombs and Shaw, "Agenda-Setting Function of the Press."

16. Shanto Iyengar and Donald R. Kinder, *News That Matters: Television and American Opinion* (Chicago: University of Chicago Press, 1987).

17. David L. Protess et al., *The Journalism of Outrage: Investigative Reporting and Agenda Building in America* (New York: Guilford Press, 1991).

18. Klaus Schoenbach and Lee B. Becker, "Origins and Consequences of Mediated Public Opinion," in Glasser and Salmon, eds., *Public Opinion and the Communication of Consent*, pp. 301–323.

19. Iyengar and Kinder, *News That Matters.*

20. Jon A. Krosnick, "The Media and the Foundations of Presidential Support: George Bush and the Persian Gulf Conflict," *Journal of Social Issues* 49, 4 (1993):167–182.

21. Iyengar and Kinder, *News That Matters.*

22. Maxwell McCombs and Tamara Bell, "The Agenda-Setting Role of Mass Communication," in Michael B. Salwen and Don W. Stacks, eds., *An Integrated Approach to Communication Theory and Research* (Mahwah, NJ: Lawrence Erlbaum, 1996), pp. 93–110.

23. Lutz Erbring, Edith Goldenberg, and Arthur H. Miller, "Front-Page News and Real World Cues: A New Look at Agenda-Setting by the Media," *American Journal of Political Science* 24 (1980):16–49.

24. Iyengar and Kinder, *News That Matters.*

25. John P. Robinson and Mark R. Levy, *The Main Source: Learning from Television News* (Beverly Hills, CA: Sage Publications, 1986).

26. Leo Bogart, *Strategy in Advertising,* 3rd ed. (Lincolnwood, IL: NTC Business Books, 1996).

27. John P. Robinson and Mark R. Levy, "News Media Use and the Informed Public: A 1990s Update," *Journal of Communication* 46 (1996):129–135.

28. Michael X. Delli Carpini and Scott Keeter, "Measuring Political Knowledge: Putting First Things First," *American Journal of Political Science* 37 (1993):1179–1206.

29. Jack M. McLeod, Gerald M. Kosicki, and Douglas M. McLeod, "The Expanding Boundaries of Political Communication Effects," in Jennings Bryant and Dolf Zillman, eds., *Media Effects: Advances in Theory and Research* (Hillsdale, NJ: Lawrence Erlbaum, 1994), pp. 123–162.

30. Phillip J. Tichenor, George A. Donohue, and Clarice N. Olien, "Mass Media and the Differential Growth in Knowledge," *Public Opinion Quarterly* 54 (1970):158–170.

31. K. Viswanath and John R. Finnegan, Jr., "The Knowledge Gap: Twenty-Five Years Later," in Bryant R. Burelson, ed., *Communication Yearbook 19* (Thousand Oaks, CA: Sage Publications, 1996), pp. 187–228.

32. Vincent Price and John Zaller, "Who Gets the News: Alternative Measures of News Reception and Their Implications for Research," *Public Opinion Quarterly* 57 (1993):133–164.

33. Shanto Iyengar, *Is Anyone Responsible: How Television Frames Political Issues* (Chicago: University of Chicago Press, 1993).

34. McLeod, Kosicki, and McLeod, "Expanding Boundaries of Political Communication Effects."

35. Hadley Cantril, Hazel Gaudet, and Herta Hertzog, *The Invasion from Mars* (Princeton: Princeton University Press, 1940); Carl I. Hovland, Arthur A. Lumsdaine, and Fred D. Sheffield, *Experiments in Mass Communication* (Princeton: Princeton University Press, 1949).

36. Paul F. Lazarsfeld, Bernard Berelson, and Hazel Gaudet, *The People's Choice* (New York: Duell, Sloan and Pearce, 1944); Bernard Berelson, Paul. F. Lazarsfeld, and William N. McPhee, *Voting: A Study of Opinion Formation in a Presidential Campaign* (Chicago: University of Chicago Press, 1954).

37. Joseph Klapper, *The Effects of Mass Communication* (New York: Free Press, 1960).

38. Michael J. Robinson, "Public Affairs Television and the Growth of Political Malaise: The Case of 'The Selling of the Pentagon,'" *American Political Science Review* 70 (1976):409–431.

39. Garrett J. O'Keefe, "Political Malaise and Reliance on Media," *Journalism Quarterly* 57 (1980):122–128.

40. See, for example, George Gerbner, Larry Gross, Michael Morgan, and Nancy Signorelli, "Living with Television: The Dynamics of the Cultivation Process," in Jennings Bryant and Dolf Zillman, eds., *Perspectives on Media Effects* (Hillsdale, NJ: Lawrence Erlbaum, 1986), pp. 17–40.

41. Paul M. Hirsch, "The 'Scary World' of the Non-viewer and Other Anomalies—A Reanalysis of Gerbner et al.'s Findings in Cultivation Analysis, Part 1," *Communication Research* 7 (1980):403–456; Anthony Doob and Glenn E. MacDonald, "Television Viewing and the Fear of Victimization: Is the Relationship Causal?" *Journal of Personality and Social Psychology* 37 (1979):170–179; Garrett J. O'Keefe, "Television Exposure, Credibility and Public Views on Crime," in Robert Bostrum, ed., *Communication Yearbook 8* (Newbury Park, CA: Sage Publications, 1984), pp. 513–536.

42. See W. James Potter, "Cultivation Theory and Research: A Conceptual Perspective," *Human Communication Research* 19 (1993):564–601.

43. Wilbur Schramm, Jack Lyle, and Edwin Parker, *Television in the Lives of Our Children* (Palo Alto, CA: Stanford University Press, 1961).

44. Elihu Katz, Jay G. Blumer, and Michael Gurevitch, "Utilization of Mass Media by the Individual," in Jay G. Blumer and Elihu Katz, eds., *The Uses of Mass Communication* (Beverly Hills, CA: Sage Publications, 1974), pp. 9–32.

45. Alan M. Rubin, "The Effect of Locus of Control on Communication Motivation, Anxiety and Satisfaction," *Communication Quarterly* 41 (1993):161–172.

46. Jack M. McLeod and Lee B. Becker, "Testing the Validity of Gratification Measures Through Political Effects Analysis," in Blumer and Katz, eds., *The Uses of Mass Communication*, pp. 137–164.

47. Robert Huckfeldt and John Sprague, *Citizens, Politics, and Social Communication* (New York: Cambridge University Press, 1995), p. 292.

48. Karl E. Rosengren and Sven Windahl, "Mass Media Consumption as a Functional Alternative," in Dennis McQuail, ed., *Sociology of Mass Communication* (Hammondsworth, England: Penguin Books, 1972), pp. 166–194.

49. Sandra J. Ball-Rokeach and Melvin DeFleur, "A Dependency Model of Mass Media Effects," *Communication Research* 3 (1976):3–21.

50. Carl A. Sheingold, "Social Networks and Voting: The Resurrection of a Research Agenda," *American Sociological Review* 38 (1973):712–720.

51. John P. Robinson, "Interpersonal Influence in Election Campaigns: Two-Step Flow Hypotheses," *Public Opinion Quarterly* 40 (1976):304–319.

52. Gabriel Weimann, *The Influentials: People Who Influence People* (Albany: State University of New York Press, 1994).

53. Jeffrey J. Mondak, "Media Exposure and Political Discussion in U.S. Elections," *Journal of Politics* 57 (1995):62–85.

54. Huckfeldt and Sprague, *Citizens, Politics, and Social Communication*.

55. Joshua Meyrowitz, *No Sense of Place* (New York: Oxford University Press, 1985).

56. Robert D. Putnam, "Bowling Alone: America's Declining Social Capital," *Journal of Democracy* 6 (1995):65–78.

57. James W. Carey, "The Press, Public Opinion and Public Discourse," in Glasser and Salmon, eds., *Public Opinion and the Communication of Consent*, pp. 373–402.

58. Everett M. Rogers and J. Douglas Storey, "Communication Campaigns," in Charles R. Berger and Steven H. Chaffee, eds., *Handbook of Communication Science* (Newbury Park, CA: Sage Publications, 1987), p. 821.

59. Philip Kotler and Eduardo L. Roberto, *Social Marketing: Strategies for Changing Public Behavior* (New York: Free Press, 1989).

60. June A. Flora, Nathan Maccoby, and John W. Farquhar, "Communication Campaigns to Prevent Cardiovascular Disease: The Stanford Community Studies," in Ronald Rice and Charles Atkin, eds., *Public Communication Campaigns*, 2nd ed. (Newbury Park, CA: Sage Publications, 1989), pp. 233–252.

61. Rogers and Storey, "Communication Campaigns"; Garrett J. O'Keefe and Kathaleen Reid, "The Uses and Effects of Public Service Advertising," in James Grunig and Larissa Grunig, eds., *Public Relations Research Annual*, Vol. 2 (Hillsdale, NJ: Lawrence Erlbaum, 1990), pp. 67–94.

62. Jean Baudrillard, "Consumer Society," in Jean Baudrillard, *Selected Writings* (Stanford, CA: Stanford University Press, 1988), pp. 29–56.

63. Leo Bogart, *Commercial Culture: The Media System and the Public Interest* (New York: Oxford University Press, 1995).

64. Charles T. Salmon, "Campaigns and Social 'Improvement': An Overview of Values, Rationales, and Impacts," in Charles T. Salmon, ed., *Information Campaigns: Balancing Social Values and Social Change* (Newbury Park, CA: Sage Publications, 1989), pp. 19–53.

65. David Paletz, Roberta Pearson, and David Willis, *Politics in Public Service Advertising on Television* (New York: Springer, 1977).

66. Lana F. Rakow, "Information and Power: Toward a Critical Theory of Information Campaigns," in Salmon, ed., *Information Campaigns*, pp. 164–184.

67. Shirley A. White, with K. Sadanandan Nair and Joseph Ascroft, eds., *Participatory Communication* (Thousand Oaks, CA: Sage Publications, 1994).

68. Richard W. Pollay, "Campaigns, Change and Culture: On the Polluting Potential of Persuasion," in Salmon, ed., *Information Campaigns*, pp. 185–198.

69. Stephen J. Salmore and Barbara G. Salmore, *Candidates, Parties, and Campaigns: Electoral Politics in America* (Washington, DC: CQ Press, 1985).

70. Lawrence R. Jacobs and Robert Y. Shapiro, "The Rise of Presidential Polling: The Nixon White House in Historical Perspective," *Public Opinion Quarterly* 59 (1995): 163–195.

71. Larry J. Sabato, *The Rise of Political Consultants: New Ways of Winning Elections* (New York: Basic Books, 1981).

72. Salmore and Salmore, *Candidates, Parties, and Campaigns*.

73. Margaret M. Conway, "ACs, the New Politics, and Congressional Campaigns," in Alan J. Cigler and Burdett A. Loomis, eds., *Interest Group Politics* (Washington, DC: CQ Press, 1983), pp. 126–144.

74. For an extensive historical overview, see Edward Diamond and Steven Bates, *The Spot: The Rise of Political Advertising on Television* (Cambridge, MA: MIT Press, 1984).

75. June Woong Rhee, "Strategy and Issue Frames in Election Campaign Coverage: A Social Cognitive Account of Framing Effects," *Journal of Communication* 47, 3 (Summer, 1997):26–48.

76. Kim Fridkin Kahn, *The Political Consequences of Being a Woman* (New York: Columbia University Press, 1996).

77. Steven H. Chaffee, Xinsho Zhao, and Glenn Leshner, "Political Knowledge and the Campaign Media of 1992," *Communication Research* 21 (1994):305–324.

78. John P. Robinson and Dennis K. Davis, "Television News and the Informed Public: An Information-Processing Approach," *Journal of Communication* 40 (1990):106–119.

79. Craig Leonard Brians and Martin P. Wattenberg, "Campaign Issue Knowledge and Salience: Comparing Reception from TV Commercials, TV News, and Newspapers," *American Journal of Political Science* 40 (1996):172–193.

80. Thomas E. Patterson, *The Mass Media Election: How Americans Choose Their President* (New York: Praeger, 1980).

81. C. Richard Hofsteter, Cliff Zukin, and Terry F. Buss, "Political Imagery and Information in an Age of Television," *Journalism Quarterly* 55 (1978):562–569.

82. Patterson, *Mass Media Election.*

83. Stanley Kraus, *The Great Debates: Carter vs. Ford* (Bloomington: Indiana University Press, 1979).

84. Kathleen Hall Jamieson and David S. Birdsell, *Presidential Debates: The Challenge of Creating an Informed Electorate* (New York: Oxford University Press, 1988).

85. Thomas E. Patterson and Robert D. McClure, *The Unseeing Eye: The Myth of Television Power in National Politics* (New York: G. P. Putnam's Sons, 1976).

86. Steven Ansolabehere and Shanto Iyengar, *Going Negative: How Attack Ads Shrink and Polarize the Electorate* (New York: Free Press, 1995).

87. Xinshu Zhao and Steven H. Chaffee, "Campaign Advertisements Versus Television News as Sources of Political Information," *Public Opinion Quarterly* 59 (1995):41–65.

88. See, for example, Diana C. Mutz, Paul Sniderman, and Richard Brody, eds., *Political Persuasion and Attitude Change* (Ann Arbor: University of Michigan Press, 1996).

89. Steven H. Chaffee and Sun Yuel Choe, "Time of Decision and Media Use During the Ford–Carter Campaign," *Public Opinion Quarterly* 44 (1980):53–69.

90. Richard E. Petty and John T. Cacioppo, *Communication and Persuasion: Central and Peripheral Routes to Attitude Change* (New York: Springer, 1986).

91. Ansolabehere and Iyengar, *Going Negative.*

92. Patterson, *Mass Media Election.*

93. Kathleen Hall Jamieson, *Dirty Politics: Deception, Distraction, and Democracy* (New York: Oxford University Press, 1992); Ansolabehere and Iyengar, *Going Negative.*

94. Ansolabehere and Iyengar, *Going Negative.*

95. Everett C. Ladd, "The Election Polls: An American Waterloo," *Chronicle of Higher Education,* November 22, 1996, p. A52.

96. Monika L. McDermott and Kathleen A. Frankovic, "Horserace Polling and Survey Method Effects: An Analysis of the 2000 Campaign," *Public Opinion Quarterly* 67 (2003):244–264.

97. Leonie Huddy, Nadia Khatib, and Thersa Capelos, "The Polls—Trends: Reactions to the Terrorist Attacks of September 11, 2001," *Public Opinion Quarterly* 66 (2002):418–450.

98. David Weaver and Dan Drew, "Voter Learning in the 1992 Presidential Election: Did the 'Nontraditional' Media and Debates Matter?" *Journalism Quarterly* 72 (1995):7–17.

99. Larry Sabato, *Feeding Frenzy: How Attack Journalism Has Transformed American Politics* (New York: Free Press, 1993); Twentieth Century Fund, *The Report of the Twentieth Century Fund Task Force on Television and the Campaign of 1992: 1–800-PRESIDENT* (New York: Twentieth Century Fund Press, 1993); S. Robert Lichter and Richard E. Noyes, *Good Intentions Make Bad News: Why Americans Hate Campaign Journalism* (Lanham, MD: Rowman and Littlefield, 1995).

100. Thomas E. Patterson, *Out of Order* (New York: Knopf, 1993), p. 25.

101. Walter Lippmann, *Public Opinion* (New York: Macmillan Co., 1922).

11

Looking Ahead

This text has covered enormous ground because public opinion is such an interesting and complex phenomenon. This complexity makes the field of public opinion research very broad and multidisciplinary. Since there is so much varied research in the area, it is difficult to wrap things up, to come to a clean and decisive halt in our analysis of public opinion. Early on in this book, we argued that the meaning of "public opinion" is always shifting: How we think about the concept depends upon historical circumstance as well as upon our research hypotheses and the technologies we have on hand to assess public opinion. At this point in American politics, it seems as though our techniques for opinion expression and measurement are very sophisticated, but there will always be new developments because candidates for office, elected officials, interest group spokesmen, journalists, party leaders, and citizens will always have an interest in the effective evaluation of the popular mood. We must remember, too, that market researchers have contributed greatly to the development of public opinion measurement techniques and that political actors will continue to look to the commercial world for ideas about persuasion and assessment of public opinion.

From a scholarly perspective, one thing about public opinion is clear: It must be studied from an interdisciplinary viewpoint. As you saw in this book, public opinion is a psychological, sociological, and political phenomenon all at the same time. Public opinion formation takes place constantly as people react to the world around them. We are bombarded with persuasive communications daily, from the mass media, from local political leaders, from our friends and our families. This flood of incoming information—often symbolic in nature—has a tremendous effect on the way we think about particular political events, actors, and policy. We have studied the way individuals' opinions are shaped, but we have also looked at those who do the shaping, the mass media in particular. And we have spent some time on the relationship between public opinion and the nature of American government and social policy. All of these linkages—between people and media, among people, and between people and their leaders—are critical to understanding the role of public opinion in American democracy. It is a challenge to think about the nature of public opinion and how it changes, but it is also one of the most exciting phenomena in democratic theory. We can only improve our democracy by paying attention to public opinion, since the voice of the people is the foundation for self-rule.

It may be clear where scholarship is headed, and we can detect that an increasingly large community of researchers across fields and across academic and commercial lines are interested in studying public opinion. Yet what about public opinion itself? How will citizen expression change in the future? This is an impossible question to address with any confidence, since it involves looking into a crystal ball and speculating on the future. What public opinion becomes, what the channels for expression will be, and how much attention will be paid to it are all highly dependent upon general social trends and the development of our political institutions. For example, if the American political parties decline in strength, will interest groups become more central to the articulation of public opinion? Or will the parties experience a resurgence as strong players on the political scene, becoming more ideological and different from each other? If this were to happen, parties might develop different means of understanding and articulating public opinion.

As shown in this book, technologies for public opinion expression matter very much in any historical period. For the last thirty years, television has dominated the scene as the shaper of public attitudes. Before television, there was radio, and before that, the heyday of newspapers. But what next? The Internet is undoubtedly becoming a crucial site for discussion of political affairs, a site for persuasion, and a source for a tremendous amount of news and information. We are just beginning to look to the Internet as a place to express opinions and collect the opinions of our fellow citizens. And politicians are still exploring ways to keep in touch with constituents and persuade them through this new medium. Possibilities for public opinion expression and evaluation over the Internet are astounding at this early stage, so we can only imagine how diffusion of Internet access will affect citizens. But it is important to keep in mind that technology is ultimately controlled by people: Political culture will always determine how and when the Internet is used for the expression or manipulation of public opinion since technologies do not act—people do.

It is likely that many of the theories and research findings in this book that deal with public opinion change may be replicated in computer-mediated environments. A persuasive speech may be persuasive in the same ways whether it is received in person at a town meeting, in one's living room via television, or over the Internet. Some theories will receive support across media environments, but we will also have to develop new ideas about public opinion that are tied specifically to new technologies like the Internet. Perhaps interpersonal communication looks very different over the Internet than it does in face-to-face interactions, as so many communication scholars have argued. If this is the case, an entirely new sort of political conversation style has developed and we must figure out how best to study such dialogue among citizens and their leaders.

When we think about the future, we must always think about the past. A historical perspective is crucial if we are to consider the shape of public opinion—and indeed democracy—in the next few decades. Our older theories and ideas are of enormous value since they give us guidance, telling us what to look for and what might be important as we describe and analyze the political world. It is a certainty that as long as we live in democracy, public opinion will be the focus of great efforts. People will always want to express their opinions and politicians will always want to hear those opinions, whether to serve citizens better, to manipulate them more effectively, or perhaps just to stay in office.

Perhaps it is best not to end on a cynical note, but on a hopeful and historical one. Abraham Lincoln, one of the most impressive democratic leaders of all time, was also—not surprisingly—very attentive to public opinion. He was attentive to it and thoughtful about it. In many ways, Lincoln anticipated the problems of mass democracy and how difficult it would be for American presidents to hear all the citizens all the time. But Lincoln did his best, creating forums for public expression and listening as hard as he could, given the pressures of his office. Lincoln's writings on public opinion and his thoughtfulness about the concept are inspiring for us. A look back to the nineteenth century, to the words of one of our greatest presidents, should give us all pause as we think about the often troubled but crucial relationship between the public and its leaders. As the Civil War raged in 1863, Lincoln explained to a journalist why he had common citizens visit him at the White House:

> I feel—though the tax on my time is heavy—that no hours of my day are better employed than those which thus bring me again within the direct contact and atmosphere of the average of our whole people. Men moving only in an official circle are apt to become merely official—not to say arbitrary—in their ideas, and are apter and apter, with each passing day, to forget that they only hold power in a representative capacity. Now this is all wrong. I go into these promiscuous receptions of all who claim to have business with me twice a week, and every applicant for audience has to take his turn, as if waiting to be shaved in a barber's shop. Many of the matters brought to my notice are utterly frivolous, but others are of more or less importance, and all serve to renew in me a clearer and more vivid image of that great popular assemblage out of which I sprung, and to which at the end of two years I must return. I tell you . . . that I call these receptions my "*public opinion baths*," for I have but little time to read the papers and gather public opinion that way; and though they may not be pleasant in all their particulars, the effect, as a whole, is renovating and invigorating to my perceptions of responsibility and duty.[1] [emphasis in original]

Do our own leaders do as well as Lincoln in taking public opinion so seriously? No matter how times change, we can only hope that our highest elected officials listen to the voice of the people.

NOTES

1. Abraham Lincoln, Introduction to "My 'Public Opinion Baths,'" in Mario Cuomo and Harold Holzer, eds., *Lincoln and Democracy* (New York: HarperCollins, 1990), pp. 284–285.

INDEX